AF505876

Gender and Global Politics in the Asia-Pacific

Gender and Global Politics in the Asia-Pacific

Edited by Bina D'Costa and Katrina Lee-Koo

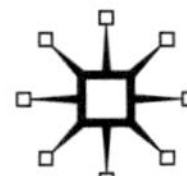

First published in 2009 by PALGRAVE MACMILLAN® in the United States—a division of St. Martin's Press LLC, 175 Fifth Avenue, New York, NY 10010.

Where this book is distributed in the UK, Europe and the rest of the world, this is by Palgrave Macmillan, a division of Macmillan Publishers Limited, registered in England, company number 785998, of Houndmills, Basingstoke, Hampshire RG21 6XS.

Palgrave Macmillan is the global academic imprint of the above companies and has companies and representatives throughout the world.

Palgrave® and Macmillan® are registered trademarks in the United States, the United Kingdom, Europe and other countries.

ISBN-13: 978-0-230-61160-3
ISBN-10: 0-230-61160-5

Library of Congress Cataloging-in-Publication Data is available from the Library of Congress.

A catalogue record of the book is available from the British Library.

Design by Scribe Inc.

First edition: January 2009

10 9 8 7 6 5 4 3 2 1

Printed in the United States of America.

This book is written in honor of Jindy Pettman,
a great scholar and our mentor

It is dedicated to our mothers,
Sabita D'Costa and Valmai Lee-Koo

Contents

Preface: How Jindy Pettman Redrew My Mental Map ix
Cynthia Enloe

List of Contributors xi

Acknowledgments xv

List of Acronyms xvii

Part I: 'Living in the Margins': Gendering the Global 1

1 Critical Feminist International Relations in the Asia-Pacific 3
Bina D'Costa and Katrina Lee-Koo

2 'Worlding Women' in International Law 19
Hilary Charlesworth

3 Gendered Economies in the Asia-Pacific 39
V. Spike Peterson

Part II: Gendering Global Politics in the Asia-Pacific 57

4 The 'Kitsch' of War: Misappropriating Sun Tzu for an American Imperial Hypermasculinity 59
Ching-Chane Hwang and L. H. M. Ling

5 When the UN 'Succeeds': The Case of Cambodia 77
Sandra Whitworth

6 Feminizing Global Governance 95
Shirin M. Rai

Part III: 'Worlding Women': Confronting Gendered Politics in Asia **113**

7 Confessions of a Failed Feminist IR Scholar: Feminist Methodologies in Practice in Peshawar 115
Anne McNevin

8 One Woman's Everyday Resistance: An Empowering Yet Cautionary Tale from Vietnam 129
Kim Huynh

9 Women's Engagement with Islam in South and Southeast Asia 143
Shakira Hussein

Part IV: Linking Local with Global: Feminist Activism in the Pacific **157**

10 Gender Mainstreaming in a Post–conflict State: Toward Democratic Peace in Timor-Leste? 159
Nina Hall and Jacqui True

11 Shifting Terrains of Transnational Engagement: Women's Organizing in Fiji 175
Nicole George

12 Reclaiming Pacific Island Regionalism: Does Neoliberalism Have to Reign? 195
Claire Slatter and Yvonne Underhill-Sem

13 A Feminist Politics of Region?: Reflecting and Revisioning IR from Asia and the Pacific 211
Jindy Pettman

Afterword 233
J. Ann Tickner

Bibliography 237

Index 261

PREFACE

How Jindy Pettman Redrew My Mental Map

Cynthia Enloe

I was trained at Berkeley in the sixties to be an Asian specialist, but I had never been to the Pacific. True, thanks to the British imperialists' manipulations of militarized ethnicities, I had given some passing thought to Fiji. Yet I would have been hard-pressed to find it on a globe. Jindy Pettman changed all this.

It was the winter of 1990 in the southern hemisphere when I took up a short-term visiting post at Australian National University's Pacific Peace Research Centre. From our nice, small apartment on campus, we could see a dusting of July snow on the distant hills outside Canberra. Everyone at the Centre was very welcoming. Many of the senior staff was working on concepts and practices of the relationships that shape security among states in the Pacific. Listening to them in conversation and in seminars, I began to get my first sense of the Pacific as the newly imagined 'back yard' of Australia—the way the Caribbean for two centuries has been the so-called back yard of the United States (at least in the minds of many expansionist Americans).

At the time, Jindy Pettman was doing work and teaching courses at a skeptical arm's length from this core institutional inquiry. As she and I began to have conversations–and walks and meals–I realized that there was quite a different way to become Pacific-conscious. Jindy was energetically asking two fresh questions. First, how were women from Australia's newer immigrant communities, that is, women from backgrounds other than white British or Aborigine—experiencing Australian sociopolitical life and making their diverse marks upon it? Second, how were women from the many small island nations of the Pacific experiencing their relationships to Australia as it was newly flexing its regional muscles? All of this was new to me. I had never before thought about the politics of Italian, Lebanese, or Filipino Australian women as political actors in any efforts to make sense of the dynamic relationships between racism(s), the state, men, and international politics. On top of this, until these lively conversations with Jindy that July, I had never wondered how Papua New Guinean, Fijian,

New Calendonian or Cook Island women could—if only I would pay close attention—help me make better sense of the post–cold war international order.

Jindy Pettman was doing two things simultaneously: first, she was urging us to lift the ungendered curtain on Australia as an interstate actor, so we would be far more realistic about the ways conventional analyses of foreign policy and regional politics mask masculinized privilege. At the same time, she was revealing that women from marginalized local communities and vulnerable island nations could be political actors in their own right, activist thinkers from whom the rest of us could learn.

The Asian Studies Association of the United States—a major academic institution—still does not include Pacific nations' histories, economies, politics, or gendered dynamics in their purview. As a result, for instance, almost no feminist researchers in the northern hemisphere (outside of Hawaii's lively feminist circles) are asking how Fijian women are responding to global, private military contractors recruiting ethnic Fijian men into their ranks for service in Iraq and other war zones. If it weren't for Jindy's initial personal tutoring back in 1990, her subsequent out-pouring of influential writings, her work reshaping the discipline within the International Studies Association, and her role as a founding editor of *The International Feminist Journal of Politics*, perhaps I would still be satisfied to let my feminist curiosity taper off somewhere in the vicinity of Indonesia and the Philippines. But having had my mental map redrawn by Jindy Pettman's feminist curiosity, that intellectual laziness is, thankfully, no longer possible.

Each of the provocative contributions that follow here reflects the impact Jindy Pettman's widely read writings, organizing skills, and dedicated teaching have had on the questions we now ask, and where in the world we go to seek answers to those questions.

Thanks, Jindy.

Contributors

Hilary Charlesworth is a Professor of International Law and Human Rights and Director of the Centre for International Governance and Justice (CIGJ) at the Australian National University. Her research interests include the relevance of feminist theory to understanding international law, the structure of the international human rights system, and the protection of human rights in Australia. She has worked with various non-governmental human rights organizations on ways to implement international human rights standards. She is Patron of the ACT Women's Legal Service. In 2005, she was awarded a Federation Fellowship by the Australian Research Council.

Bina D'Costa is a Research Fellow at the Center for International Governance and Justice (CIGJ) at the Australian National University (ANU). Most of the work for this book was completed while she was the Convener of the Security Analysis program at the Faculty of Asian Studies, the ANU. Bina is currently working on a project titled "Elusive Justice: Reconciliation Processes and Peacebuilding in Asia" and two other smaller research projects titled "Disappeared Generation: Children Conceived through Violent Conflict and National Identity in South Asia" and "Peacekeeping Forces from South Asia." Bina has worked on historical injustices, truth, and memory in relation to the strategies of civil society in demanding justice when there is a hostile government in power. This action-oriented research informs her book manuscript titled "'Burden' of the State: Engendering War Crimes and National Identity Politics in Postcolonial South Asia."

Cynthia Enloe is Research Professor at Clark University in Massachusetts. Among her recent books are *The Curious Feminist: Women in a New Age of Empire* and *Globalization and Militarism: Feminists Make the Link.*

Nicole George holds the position of John Vincent Post-Doctoral Fellow in the Department of International Relations at the Research School of Pacific and Asian Studies, Australian National University. She lectures in the areas of gender, globalization, and development. She is currently preparing a book manuscript from her doctoral research, which examines women's political agency and women's organizing in the Pacific region. Her other research interests include gender and civil society, gender and peacebuilding, women's regionalism, and Pacific masculinities.

Nina Hall is a Masters student in Political Studies at the University of Auckland. Her thesis examines post–conflict reconstruction and democratization in Timor-Leste from a gendered perspective. Her fields of expertise include gender and development, identity politics, and regime transitions. On completion of her Masters, she plans to complete a Ph.D. in political studies. Nina is also involved with the environmental and social justice movement in New Zealand.

Kim Huynh is a lecturer in politics and international relations at the Australian National University. He has published articles in *Alternatives* and *Frontiers: A Journal of Women Studies*. His memoir, *Where the Sea Takes Us*, published by HarperCollins in 2007, tells the story of his parents' lives during and after the Vietnam War. He has co-edited *The Culture Wars: Australian and American Perspectives* published by Pan MacMillan in 2008, and has contributed articles to *ABC Radio National, The Canberra Times, The Daily Telegraph*, and *The Adelaide Advertiser*.

Shakira Hussein is completing her Ph.D. on encounters between Western and Muslim women at the Australian National University. Her publications include "The War on Terror and the Rescue of Muslim Women" in *Islam in World Politics*, edited by Nelly Lahoud and Anthony Johns (Routledge, 2005) as well as many online and newspaper editorials relating to questions of Muslim identities in Australia.

Ching-Chane Hwang is Associate Professor at the Graduate Institute of Political Science, National Sun Yat-sen University, Taiwan. She is interested in feminist political theories and international relations theories.

Katrina Lee-Koo is a Lecturer in International Relations at the Australian National University. Her research interests include critical security studies and feminist international relations. She has recently contributed chapters to: Anthony Burke and Matt McDonald, eds, *Critical Security in the Asia-Pacific* (Manchester University Press, 2007); Alex Bellamy, *et al.*, ed., *Security and the War on Terror* (Routledge, 2008) and Richard Devetak, *et al.*, ed., *An Introduction to International Relations: Australian Perspectives*.

L. H. M. Ling is an Associate Professor in the Graduate Program in International Affairs at The New School in New York City. Ling's research interests include democracy in international relations, critical security studies, transcultural politics and postcolonial discourses, and her geocultural area of interest centers on East, South-East, and South Asia and its relations with the West. Her books include *Postcolonial International Relations: Conquest and Desire between Asia and the West* (London: Palgrave Macmillan, 2002) and *Transforming World*

Politics: From Empire to Multiple Worlds (London: Routledge, forthcoming), co-authored with Anna M. Agathangelou of York University. Ling's publications have appeared in *International Feminist Journal of Politics, International Studies Quarterly, International Studies Review, Journal of Peace Research, Millennium, Positions, Review of International Political Economy*, and *Review of Politics*.

Anne McNevin is a Research Fellow in the Globalism Research Centre, RMIT University, Melbourne. Her work engages issues of citizenship, political belonging, irregular migration, and neoliberal globalization. She has published on these themes in *Citizenship Studies, Review of International Studies* and *The Australian Journal of Political Science*. She is currently undertaking research on the dynamics of citizenship and irregular migration in Kuala Lumpur, Melbourne, and Los Angeles.

V. Spike Peterson is Professor in the Department of Political Science at the University of Arizona, with courtesy appointments in Women's Studies, Institute for LGBT Studies, Center for Latin American Studies, and International Studies. She has published extensively on the topics of feminist international relations theory, global political economy, nationalism, heterosexism, and critical poststructuralist feminist theory. Her most recent book, *A Critical Rewriting of Global Political Economy: Integrating Reproductive, Productive and Virtual Economies*, examines intersections of ethnicity and race, class, sex and gender, and national hierarchies in the context of neoliberal globalization. Her current research investigates informalization and 'coping, combat and criminal economies' in conflict zones.

Jindy Pettman is an Emeritus Professor of the Australian National University. She is the author of *Worlding Women: A Feminist International Politics* (Allen & Unwin, Routledge, 1996); *Living in the Margins: Racism, Sexism and Feminism in Australia* (1996), and numerous book chapters and journal articles. She is the founding editor of the *International Feminist Journal of Politics* (Routledge) and in 2003 was named Eminent Scholar by the International Studies Association.

Shirin M. Rai is Professor in the Department of Politics and International Studies at the University of Warwick. She is Director of the Taught Masters (MA) Programme in Globalization and Development and of a Leverhulme Trust Programme on Gendered Ceremony and Ritual in Parliament. Her research interests lie in the area of feminist politics, democratization, globalization, and development studies. She has consulted with the United Nations' Division for the Advancement of Women and UNDP. She is a founding member of the South Asia Research Network on Gender, Law, and Governance and is on the editorial board of *International Feminist Journal of Politics, Global Ethics and Indian Journal of Gender Studies*. She is the co-editor (with Wyn Grant) of *Perspectives on Democratic Practice*.

Claire Slatter is a Fiji national and a graduate of the University of the South Pacific, Australian National University, and Massey University. She has a background in the women's anti-nuclear and trade union movements and is a founding member (and former General Coordinator) of the Third World feminist network, Development Alternatives with Women for a New Era (DAWN), the Citizens' Constitutional Forum in Fiji and the Pacific Network on Globalisation (PANG). She taught in the Department of History and Politics for seventeen years and now works as a freelance economic and social policy researcher and analyst.

J. Ann Tickner is Professor, School of International Relations at the University of Southern California. She is the author of *Gender in International Relations: Feminist Perspectives on Achieving Global Security* (1992) and *Gendering World Politics: Issues and Approaches in the post-Cold War Era* (2001).

Jacqui True (Ph.D, York University, Canada) is a senior lecturer in international relations at the University of Auckland. Her research interests include gender and international relations, global governance and gender mainstreaming, and feminist methodologies. Her publications include *Gender, Globalization and Postsocialism* (Columbia University Press, 2003), and with Brooke Ackerly and Maria Stern, *Feminist Methodologies for International Relations* (Cambridge University Press, 2006). She is currently working on regional organizations and their efforts to promote gender equity within trade policymaking and trade agreements.

Yvonne Underhill-Sem is currently Director of the Centre for Development Studies at the University of Auckland, New Zealand. Since 1999, she has been Pacific Regional Co-ordinator for DAWN (Development Alternatives with Women for a New Era). She is a feminist development geographer who has ongoing research interests in Papua New Guinea, the Cook Islands (her country of heritage), and the Pacific in general. She has lived and worked in NZ, the Cook Islands, Hawaii, Papua New Guinea, Samoa, Germany, Brussels, and Australia where she has taught and undertaken research and advocacy as an academic, an advocate, and a development practitioner.

Sandra Whitworth is Professor of Political Science at York University in Toronto, Canada. Her first book, *Feminism and International Relations* (Palgrave Macmillan) was published in 1994, translated into Japanese, and published by Fujiwara Shoten Press in 2000. Her most recent book, from which the chapter in this collection is drawn, was published in 2004 (Lynne Rienner) and is entitled *Men, Militarism and UN Peacekeeping: A Gendered Analysis.* She is currently serving as the Graduate Program Director in Political Science at York, and as the home base editor for *International Feminist Journal of Politics.*

Acknowledgments

Nearly two years ago, we decided to write this book as a tribute to Jindy Pettman. Jindy's guidance continues to be invaluable on our respective intellectual journeys. Thank you Jindy, for your generosity, your vision, your kindness, and your heart.

Each contributing author has a special connection to Jindy—as a former student, colleague, or fellow pioneer in feminist scholarship. All authors enthusiastically responded to our call to produce this tribute. This demonstrates that the enduring links among feminists are based not only on intellectual practices but forged through personal friendships, alliances, and mutual respect. We would like to thank all our contributors for their hard work on this book.

This book has greatly benefited from the comments and suggestions made by several people who read earlier drafts and who gave us valuable advice. In particular, we are grateful to Greg Fry, who encouraged us to embark on this project. We also thank our colleagues at the Australian National University for their support. We would further like to thank our many Palgrave partners for their support, encouragement and hard work on this project.

Finally, thanks to David Kilham and Andrew Watts for their commitment to us and assistance to this project.

Acronyms

ADB	Asian Development Bank
ASEAN	Association of Southeast Asian Nations
CEDAW	Convention on the Elimination of All Forms of Discrimination against Women
CPP	The Cambodian People's Party
CNRT	National Council of East Timorese Resistance
CROP	Council of Regional Organizations in the Pacific
DAWN	Development Alternatives for Women in a New Era
ECOSOC	The Economic and Social Council
EPA	Economic Partnership Agreement
FUNCINPEC	National United Front for an Independent, Neutral, Peaceful and Co-operative Cambodia
FWCC	Fiji Women's Crisis Centre
FWRM	Fiji Women's Rights Movement
GAU	Timor-Leste's Gender Affairs Unit
ICRC	International Committee of the Red Cross
IMF	International Monetary Fund
INTERFET	International Force East Timor
KPNLF	Khmer People's National Liberation Front
OPMT	Popular Women's Organization of Timor-Leste
PACER	Pacific Agreement on Closer Economic Relations
PDK	Khmer Rouge (Party of Democratic Kampuchea
PFA	Beijing Platform for Action
PIFS	Pacific Islands Forum Secretariat
RAWA	Revolutionary Association of the Women of Afghanistan
SEPI	Timor-Leste's Secretary of State for Promotion of Equality
SGBV	Sexual and Gender-based Violence
SPC	South Pacific Community
TRIPS	Trade-Related Aspects of Intellectual Property Rights
UNAMIC	United Nations Advance Mission in Cambodia
UNBRO	United Nations Border Relief Operation

UNHCR	Office of the United Nations High Commissioner for Refugees
UNICEF	United Nations Children's Fund
UNIFEM	United Nations Development Fund for Women
UNTAC	United Nations Transitional Authority in Cambodia
UNTAET	United Nations Transitional Authority in East Timor
WDP	Women's Development Project
WTO	World Trade Organization
YWCA	Young Women's Christian Association

PART I

'Living in the Margins'

Gendering the Global

CHAPTER 1

Critical Feminist International Relations in the Asia-Pacific

Bina D'Costa and Katrina Lee-Koo

In a review appearing on the back cover of Jindy Pettman's 1996 book *Worlding Women*, Cynthia Enloe suggests that the value of the work is its brazen courage to ask simple questions about international relations. *Worlding Women* poses questions like, "What can a Filipina mail-order bride living in Sydney, Australia tell us about lofty theorizing in international politics?" The answer, Enloe replies, is "a lot." Through *Worlding Women*, Jindy Pettman is one of the pioneers of the project "to make visible places and ways that women are in the world."[1] Like Enloe's own work, and the work of many since, the straightforward, yet extraordinary value of critical feminist investigations into international relations demonstrates a curiosity regarding how international relations affects and is affected by gendered identities. To those outside the discipline of international relations (IR) this may seem a simple task, yet feminists working inside the discipline know that that is exactly what it is not. It is a testament to the foundationally unsettling nature of critical feminist IR that feminists have faced decades of difficulties in having questions of gender taken seriously. This is because such an enquiry encourages us to challenge the boundaries of the discipline of 'international relations' by exploring the totality of 'global politics.' While the discipline of international relations reserves its reference for the 'high politics' of statecraft in the international system, critical feminist IR scholars concern themselves with the breadth of global politics. Here feminists find that politics pervades the everyday lives of ordinary, gendered identities the world over in ways that are both welcome and pernicious, empowering, and oppressive. The primary goals of this book are to map feminist accounts of global politics in the Asia-Pacific region and situate these accounts in the field of critical feminist international relations.

When considering the approach of *critical* feminist international relations, it is worthwhile to reiterate there are many *feminisms*[2] that comprise the field of feminist international relations. With this in mind, Jill Steans argues all feminist approaches to international relations have four goals: to highlight the exclusions and biases of mainstream IR; to make women visible in international politics; to understand the causes of gender inequalities in the disciplinary study and practice of IR; and finally, "to empower women as subjects of knowledge by building theoretical understandings of IR from the position of women and their lived, embodied experiences."[3] Yet while it may be possible to say that all feminisms share recognition of women's general subordination to men and a commitment to equality between men and women in public and private life, it is difficult to generalize beyond that.[4] Debates within feminism are immediately generated by questioning, for instance, what constitutes subordination and equality between gendered identities and how equality and indeed, emancipation, might be achieved. Decades of feminist politics have demonstrated that universalist claims by scholars on the behalf of all women are not so easy to make and are highly problematic. Recognition of the difficulty associated with thinking through the multiple sources of insecurity and opportunity that confront women in specific political contexts leads us to a critical feminist reading of the Asia-Pacific and its relations with the rest of the world.

Consequently, this collection foregrounds one of the most dynamic, changing, and, some strategic theorists surmise, potentially threatening regions of the world. IR scholars often identify the Asia-Pacific as incorporating the economically and politically volatile Southeast and Northeast Asia; the politically and militarily de-stabilized South and Central Asia; and the politically unstable Pacific Islands. In so doing, political analysts suggest this region includes everything from the 'hotbed of terrorism' to the 'arc of instability' to 'the recruiting ground for Islamic extremism,' to hosting a raft of fragile, failed or failing states. Yet behind this curtain of political volatility, this collection reveals that there are embedded and resistant feminist projects. These projects, reflecting a more inclusive analysis, highlight the diversity of a region that draws upon and reflects a complex interweaving of gendered identities, institutions, knowledge, discourses, and power relationships at the local, state, regional and international levels. In bringing these issues to the fore, feminist projects identify and address sources of gendered oppression. At the same time, they demonstrate the value of critical feminist theorizing, methodology, and activism. This collection reveals the particular positioning of critical feminist scholarship and activism in the Asia-Pacific and places it within a feminist disciplinary context that is often dominated by North America and Europe. As such, this collection demonstrates the symbiosis between the Asia-Pacific, and feminist scholarship from North America and Europe. Unsurprisingly, this collection demonstrates how each one mirrors and informs the other.

Yet there is no guarantee that the feminist scholars contributing to this collection will agree on the gendered challenges facing the Asia-Pacific and the feminist paths that need to be trodden; dissent and debate continue in feminist theorizing. Nonetheless, this collection demonstrates steadfastness to particular feminist positions. Each chapter argues that uncovering knowledge in ways that render visible gender inequity is the primary purpose of feminist research. Each chapter demonstrates that the process of critically engaging alternative methods of re-examining existing knowledge is a worthy pursuit, and each chapter illustrates a commitment to a feminist ethic. In short, the contributions to this collection demonstrate the value of feminist frames for critiquing and developing knowledge regarding the nature, boundaries, and possibilities of global politics. While the contributions reflect a variety of styles, a diversity of scope, and a myriad of topics, the primary goal of this collection is to contribute to forging feminist futures in the Asia-Pacific.

Outlining the Book

With this goal in mind, the collection is divided into four sections. Each section coincides with four significant contributions to international relations made by emeritus professor Jan Jindy Pettman: the initial section, 'Living in the Margins' examines the contributions of feminist theorizing on key issues in mainstream international relations. In particular, it utilizes critical feminist methodologies (outlined later in this chapter) to challenge conventional IR's acceptance of 'home grown truths' regarding the way the business of global politics affects the lives of those living under its supposed protection. It contextualizes this within the Asia-Pacific by highlighting the value of feminist work in the region and arguing for its continuation. In the second chapter, 'Worlding Women in International Law,' Hilary Charlesworth examines feminist intervention in international law concerning issues of state-building, human rights, and security as they apply to Timor-Leste, and compares it with the recent case of Iraq. Charlesworth argues that state-building in Timor-Leste and Iraq is severely affected by women's restricted access to decision-making processes. While women's groups are frustrated by their inability to affect post–conflict settlements, their advocacy does contribute to the attention afforded to women's rights. In chapter three, V. Spike Peterson adopts a poststructural and postcolonial feminist perspective to explore what she refers to as 'reproductive, productive, and virtual (RPV)' economies of the Asia-Pacific. She argues that the current relationship between culture and economy perpetuates the economic inequalities that occur at the intersection of ethnicity, race, gender, class, and national hierarchies.

Section Two, 'Gendered International Relations in the Asia-Pacific,' offers feminist insight into the relationship between the Asia-Pacific region and the wider world. Relations between George W Bush's White House and China, as outlined in chapter four, demonstrate the imperialistic and hypermasculine logic in the division between East and West. Ching-Chane Hwang and L. H. M Ling show how the use of a feminist framework to deconstruct knowledge claims reveals a masculinist misappropriation of the work of Sun Tzu. The authors demonstrate how this misappropriation is used as a template for U.S.

neoimperialism in world politics. They argue that the narrow conceptualization of *The Art of War* by policymakers with its ultimately peaceful message, for the purpose of national self-interest ignores the normative and ontological commitments embedded in Sun Tzu's work. In chapters five and six, Sandra Whitworth and Shirin M. Rai similarly use feminist frameworks to reveal the gendered effects of peace interventions, the political economy, and governance structures throughout Asia. Whitworth draws on the questions raised in Charlesworth's analysis of state-building in her examination of peacekeeping, militaries, and masculinities in Cambodia. Often referred to as an outstanding success, Whitworth argues that the success of the United Nation's Transitional Authority in Cambodia (UNTAC) is questionable in light of feminist goals. Like Peterson, Shirin M. Rai demonstrates the value of a feminist framework for revealing naturalized forms of gendered oppression in global governance. Rai focuses on competing notions of governance developed in the literature and in practice at the local and global level. She explores the experiences of a women's development project in Rajasthan, India and their complex and, at times, confounding interactions with a multilevel governance structure. In doing so, she touches on the themes of the third section in this collection.

The third section, 'Worlding Women: Confronting Gendered Politics in Asia' examines feminist methodologies and feminist practice in the Asia-Pacific. By including some of the region's exciting new feminist scholars, this section reflects on what it means to conduct feminist research, employ feminist methodologies, and pursue a feminist ethic in the Asia-Pacific. Chapter seven documents Anne McNevin's methodological journey: in 'Two Weeks in Peshawar,' McNevin reflects on her troubled engagement with questions of how best to pursue feminist ethics and methodologies while engaging in personalized research. Her concerns in conducting ethical field research in Pakistan and her awareness of deeply embedded power imbalances between the researcher and the research subject demonstrate the self-reflexivity required for feminist research. Such self-reflexivity comes to the fore in the next chapter. In chapter eight, Kim Huynh looks at the individual activism of everyday resistance in his account of his own aunt's struggle to survive and flourish in a Vietnam dominated by imperial forces. Huynh's chapter critically engages some of the assumptions made in global politics: he questions IR's assumption of the vulnerability and political powerlessness of peasant women in war; yet he also reminds critical feminists not to assume an automatic feminist ethic in different women's processes of empowerment. Here, Huynh reminds readers that we should not imagine that all women define or pursue emancipation with an ingrained, critically inspired feminist ethic. Consequently, he promotes an inclusive approach to critical feminist scholarship that reflects upon the lived experiences of *all* 'ordinary' women involved in extraordinary political situations. This, he argues, enriches our understanding of the diversity of women's political agency. In chapter nine, Shakira Hussein similarly examines the relationship between women's activism and feminism in 'Women's Engagement with Islam in South and South-East Asia.' In order to examine Muslim women's political agency, Hussein considers the activism of women in reformist and secular as well as feminist and non-feminist movements, in Afghanistan, Indonesia, and Pakistan. Her analysis demonstrates the diversity of Islamic feminists and their ambitions for transnational cooperation with the West.

The final section, 'Linking Local with the Global: Feminist Action and Activism in the Pacific,' moves from Asia to the Pacific with a more concerted focus on the questions of activism and feminist strategies in politics. In chapter ten, Nina Hall and Jacqui True interrogate the UN-devised policy of gender mainstreaming. Against the backdrop of its institution in the newly independent Timor-Leste, they question the extent to which this strategy is a top-down bureaucratic process imposed upon developing countries or a participatory process infused with a locally envisioned feminist ethic and emancipatory ideal. Like Charlesworth, Hall and True observe that gender equality is a necessary prerequisite for political equality in post–conflict democratization processes. Furthermore, they recognize the value of individual women and women's organizations in promoting change toward gender equity. In chapter eleven, Nicole George also examines the work of individual women and women's groups. George analyzes the linkage between local women's movements and transnational feminist activism in Fiji. George traces the history of women's political engagement in that country to map the path in which women's activism has traveled. She highlights the strategies adopted to pursue feminist ends amidst politically, culturally, economically, and socially complex political landscapes. Following this rich tapestry of women's organizing in chapter twelve, Claire Slatter and Yvonne Underhill-Sem ask where feminist activism should move in the future. They examine questions about the future of regional political solidarity in the Pacific where powers of negotiation and resistance lie against the backdrop of neoliberal-inspired economic restructuring of the entire Pacific region. This chapter argues that there has been a shift in regionalism (recently announced in the *Pacific Plan*) from grassroots political solidarity to neoliberal market integration. Consequently, social movement networks of Pacific women have been marginalized.

Against the backdrop of elucidation and reinterpretation of key themes in her work, in chapter thirteen Jindy Pettman reflects on her more than four decades of feminist activism and scholarship in the Asia-Pacific. This profound yet humble reflection retraces the key accomplishments of feminist activity in recent decades and the promising possibilities of the future. Pettman not only provides her own powerful and personal insight into this field, but also draws together the ambitions of this collection in a discussion of what it means to conduct critical feminist research in the Asia-Pacific; a project to which she has dedicated much of her work and career. For many critical feminist IR scholars, we see the landscape she has bequeathed us as full of passion and rich with opportunity. The remainder of this chapter will be dedicated to illuminating the broader brushstrokes of that landscape, while each subsequent chapter will provide further detail toward developing a critical feminist picture of the Asia-Pacific.

To begin this collection, the remainder of this introductory chapter examines the field of critical feminist international relations scholarship with particular reference to its development within the Asia-Pacific. We argue that scholarship undertaken by researchers loosely identifying themselves with this school offers remarkable and groundbreaking ways of thinking about international relations and global politics. This, in turn, reaches out to the lives of men and women confronted with sometimes violent, constantly changing, and often hidden, practices of politics. By sketching the commitments of critical feminist international relations and identifying its contributions to the Asia-Pacific context, this chapter provides the foundations from which each subsequent chapter works to illustrate the necessity of critical feminist scholarship in and about the Asia-Pacific.

What is Critical Feminist International Relations?

From the moment Cynthia Enloe asked, 'Where are the women?'[5] feminists have sought not just to penetrate the boundaries of international relations but to expand them. The commitment by many feminists to a critical approach to thinking about IR emerged largely out of an inadequacy of the mainstream to account in a self-reflective manner for the experiences of gendered identities in global politics. The curiosity and determination of feminists to address this deficiency brought to the surface of international relations a raft of issues previously unconsidered within IR's rubric but nonetheless clearly connected to its practices. Yet the discipline had no means by which to identify gender based oppression, let alone analyze or accept that its own practices may be causing or contributing to it. For Tickner, this culminated in a recognition that feminists working in IR were dealing with an "ontology based on unitary states, operating in the asocial, anarchical world" and as such it "provided few entry points for feminist theories, since these were grounded in an epistemology that took social relations as its central category of analysis."[6]

This deficiency in mainstream IR led to an exploration of how critical theories in the social sciences and humanities could be utilized to develop critical feminist IR scholarship. In particular, feminists used techniques learned and developed in their own and others' work in critical theory, poststructuralism, postcolonial studies, gender studies, queer theory, and post–positivist approaches to cultural studies and anthropology. They deployed these methods to account for the links between individual men and women, social identities and knowledge, and the practices of global politics. This approach sought to embrace not just the experiences of gendered identities in global politics but also to explore new ways of researching, analyzing, and describing these experiences and their relationships to, and within, the study and practice of IR. In short, the analysis returned to the point of the creation of knowledge about IR and sought to reveal gender and gendered politics.

Armed with critical ideals, feminists seek to 'feminize' international relations, which first involves the application of critical feminist methods through 'gender lenses' to deconstruct and reconstruct knowledge. Second, it seeks to embed feminist ethics into that reconstructed knowledge. Feminist scholars adopt 'gender lenses,' which use gender as both a focus for, and means of analysis. In this sense, gendered identities and structured social relations are revealed as worthy of investigation while attention to the role gender plays in constructing IR is also examined. This is in contrast to mainstream IR, which rarely recognizes the complexity (or sometimes simplicity) with which institutions or identities are politically gendered. As Peterson notes, feminists conceive of gender as being "a historically contingent *social construction* that dichotomizes identities, behaviors, and expectations as masculine–feminine." Furthermore, for Peterson "gender is not simply an empirical category that refers to embodied men and women and their material activities but also a systematically *analytical category* that refers to constructions of (privileged) masculinity and (devalorized) femininity and their ideological effects."[7] Consequently, a gendered analysis reveals not only the production and presence of masculine and feminine identities but also the relationships of power that exist between those identities.

Yet 'gendered analysis' and 'feminist ethics' are not synonymous. While they are closely related, a distinction must be made between the two. The latter, moving beyond the production of reconstructed knowledge, is normative politics driven toward emancipatory ends for the wellbeing of people currently oppressed because of their identities by socially and politically constructed gendered notions. For Tickner, "this means that research must be designed to provide a vision of the future as well as a structural picture of the past."[8] In this sense, a feminist ethic applies a gendered analysis to achieve its goals. The chapters in this collection do not simply present research for the purposes of revealing gendered politics. Rather, the research here reveals gendered politics for the purposes of detailing feminist emancipatory possibilities. Consequently, both the research and the methodologies are deeply embedded with the researcher's own politics. For instance, Huynh reflects on his family background to investigate his aunt's ambition for freedom. Similarly, McNevin demonstrates why it is not possible to detach the researcher from her research, while both George and Slatter and Sem illustrate the insights available when activists become researchers. This collection demonstrates that a critical feminist approach to IR requires feminists to imbue the 'gender lens' method with broader feminist ambitions.

Because of these important interventions into IR, the nineties and early twenty-first century generated essential feminist scholarship. These include, among others, work by Rebecca Grant and Kathleen Newland, Jindy Pettman,

Ann Tickner, Christine Sylvester, V. Spike Peterson, Anne Sisson Runyan, Marysia Zalewski, and Jane Parpart.[9] The contribution of this work has been significant in two ways. First, themes traditionally considered in mainstream IR such as security, peace and conflict, global governance, and the international political economy are revealed as masculinist constructions and generally dismissive of gender politics.[10] Second, drawing upon their disciplinary specializations, feminist scholars develop restructured and expanded discourses of IR. This discourse is a product of the inclusion of, among other things, postcolonial experiences,[11] women's struggles,[12] nationalism,[13] gender politics in education and activism,[14] the political role of women,[15] developmental issues,[16] and human rights and international law.[17] Finally, through its strong bond with both feminist activism and advocacy, feminist scholarship generates transformative shifts in global politics.[18] Networks and global connections among feminist scholars, practitioners, and activists contribute to gender sensitive framing of diverse global agendas.[19]

Feminist scholarship reveals that the effects of global politics on the lives of ordinary people remain underanalyzed in IR. For example, the possibility that policies designed for the state's good, be they for economic prosperity or national security, constitute the source of insecurity for people living inside that state, is a contradiction rarely embraced by mainstream IR. Yet for feminists, the occasion of such situations is not simply coincidental, random, or rare but rather, systemic, widespread, and invisible to the discipline. This is where an indispensable engagement between feminist IR and feminist scholarship from the Asia-Pacific region becomes evident. For example, it seems only feminists working on the Asia-Pacific recognize that the Asian economic boom was purchased by inequitable and shameful working conditions for women. Similarly, feminists working on the region recorded the costs to women of 'security' projects like nuclear weapons testing in the Pacific.[20] The insights of feminist analysis led to recognition of the feminization of Asian migration and its violation of women's rights;[21] the gendered nature of Asian development and human rights discourses;[22] the inadequate understanding by the mainstream of social change from below;[23] the necessity of cultural understandings of gender, sexuality, and reproduction for HIV/AIDS awareness and prevention;[24] and the adverse effects of war and military regimes, and industrialization and urbanization on the personal choices of women.[25]

At the risk of oversimplifying then, it is possible to identify three crucial insights that have materialized from feminists working on or in the Asia-Pacific.[26] First, feminists identify the powerful politics at play in the construction and representation of gendered identities by those inside and out of the region. The explicit attention paid by feminists to historical analyses and postcolonial experiences in the construction of identity[27] has revealed the gendered nature of both colonial and indigenous patriarchal power structures. As a justification to colonize, colonial authorities portrayed local cultures as barbaric and oppressive to women[28] and simultaneously associated 'body politics' and sexual violence with control over land and resources.[29] Indigenous elites, on the other hand, sought women's participation and leadership at the height of the nationalist movements that arose throughout the region,[30] but also exercised power over women's bodies to communicate languages of hatred.[31] Feminist scholarship in the region articulated both the symbolic and material politics of the construction of nation and the gendered nature of the state.

Second, feminist scholarship actively seeks women's voices from Asia and the Pacific. The purpose here is to reveal the endemic gendered exclusions evident in state policies, practices, and institutions. Feminist publishing houses and Web-sustained networks play important roles by identifying work produced by authors from the region and by publicizing systematic blindness to local women's perspectives.[32] Many of these works, published in local languages, have found their way to academic feminism through INGO and NGO reports, policy briefs, academic journals, and feminist Web sites. By undertaking primary field research carried out in the region,[33] vital archival research,[34] and designing and utilizing oral history projects,[35] feminists apply multidisciplinary methodologies to represent identities marginalized by the practices of international relations.[36] Finally, feminist interventions in highlighting and analyzing women's experiences in IR unlock the door to the identification of emancipatory projects for women and other gendered minorities.

'Living in the Margins': Why the Asia-Pacific Region?

In probing both the ontological and methodological boundaries of international relations, critical feminist IR scholars find themselves located (or exiled) on the margins of the discipline. An innovative shift in this collection, however, exists in the recognition that feminist IR sits on the margins of international relations *by choice*. We argue that the margins of IR have not only produced exciting and challenging academic work, but also offer a productive and provocative location. It is these 'borderlands' that provide a fresh perspective and provoke the critical distance that is necessary for feminist IR scholars to engage both the tradition of IR and the global politics extending beyond its boundaries. It is within the margins of IR that these innovative explorations of the boundaries of the global take place. Here feminist IR scholars investigate new methodologies[37] and issues not considered within the confines of traditional approaches to the discipline. These new paths are illuminated through transgressions into different ways of thinking and seeing the world. Moreover, the margins are perhaps the most useful location for this collection as it seeks to probe two issues marginalized by IR: gender and the Asia-Pacific. The Asia-Pacific region reveals the familiar features of forced marginalization. Traditional IR's focus on the Asia-Pacific, in scholarship produced in North America, Europe, and Australia, has primarily offered state-based perspectives and promoted or analyzed each state's geopolitical, strategic, and economic ambitions in the region.[38] In her analysis of this dynamic, Jindy Pettman points out how the politics of difference plays a large role in shaping the West's, particularly Australia's, relations with Asia.[39] These exclusionary approaches by traditional IR contribute to the conceptualization of 'East and West' that simultaneously tells the story of 'who we are' and 'who is not us.' This, in turn, serves to marginalize the Asia-Pacific within IR and stifles emancipatory possibilities for those who call this region home.

While a number of critical IR scholars are attentive to this bias,[40] the gendered political discourse marginalizes minorities, particularly women (but also 'colonized and therefore feminized' men)[41] for a second time. As such, critical scholarship of the region is attentive to the marginality of poverty-stricken communities, refugees, internally displaced populations, and religious and ethnic minorities.[42] These groups are marginal because of their location on the boundaries of marginalized states, and are often silenced because of power inequality. A critical feminist investigation of this space further reveals that gender intersects with all of these marginalized identities. The dual marginalization of women (as members of marginalized communities and as members of the disadvantaged gender) makes the struggle for emancipatory and empowered 'feminist futures' even more complex.[43]

Consequently, the Asia-Pacific region, which has produced the greatest number of female governmental leaders in the world,[44] is still a long way from achieving gender equality and empowerment.[45] Despite the fact that through projects of empowerment women's choices for action have multiplied,[46] gender discrimination in the form of restrictive access to resources, asset ownership, and male-dominated professions such as medicine and engineering, creates vast gender gaps. For example, the United Nations Economic and Social Commission for Asia and the Pacific (UNESCAP) suggests that the gender gap not only creates human rights crises but also causes significant economic loss. Whereas employment restrictions cause the region an estimated \$42 to \$47 billion a year, a further \$16 to \$30 billion is lost due to lack of women's access to education.[47] While the economic rationale should convince IR scholars and policymakers to consider women's issues, human rights concerns must not mask strategic engagements by states. Jude Howell argues that in countries such as China 'state feminism' coupled with the state's political ideology constrains, rather than advances, women's emancipation.[48] Through the Chinese Women's Federation, the state monopolizes definitions of women's oppression as well.[49] While states and international institutions such as the World Bank and the IMF co-opt the language of feminism, they selectively use it to promote their own agenda irrespective of the consequences for women's lives. Similarly, an analysis of conflicts in Asia and the Pacific exposes the reality that the rhetoric of women's rights is used by protagonist states to advance state security. For example, gendered imagery regarding the plight of Afghan women under the Taliban justified the region's commitment to the so-called global War on Terror by suggesting that military intervention was motivated by a desire to *save* the women of Afghanistan.[50]

Jindy Pettman identifies the appropriation of Afghan women's identity to justify militarily belligerent politics by asking, "Why not [an intervention] in other states hostile to women's rights, for example in Saudi Arabia?"[51] Recognition by feminists, however, of state-based oppression of women's rights and identities is simply the beginning of this project.[52]

An in-depth exploration of the Asia-Pacific reveals that voice and silence, choice and coercion, agency and powerlessness coexist in the everyday lives of women. With an awareness of these binary realities, women throughout the region actively participate in feminist networks, and strategically engage with both feminist scholars and practitioners.[53] An excellent example of this activism is the 'Women's International War Crimes Tribunal on Japan's Military Sexual Slavery,' popularly known as the Comfort Women's Tribunal, held in December 2000. Regional and international feminist activism behind the scenes resulted in bringing together sixty-four survivors of Japan's WW II comfort women system from nine countries together with a host of witnesses, Asian women's and human rights organizations, prosecutors, and NGOs.[54] It was a major success in achieving a symbolic and moral victory, and persuading the gendered state to listen to women. In the Pacific, women's advocacy, informed by critical feminist thinking, made it possible to include women as peacemakers and in mediating roles.[55] Women's groups such as Women for Peace in the Solomon Islands, media networks such as fem'Linkpacific, and coordinating bodies such as the National Council of Women Fiji (NCWF) constructively and meaningfully contribute to peacemaking throughout the Pacific Islands.

Inspired by Jindy Pettman's scholarship in IR and activism in the Asia-Pacific, this collection demonstrates that feminist IR scholars and regional feminist activists successfully use the margins to generate a praxis that extends beyond contributing to academic literature by presenting positive possibilities for the lives of both women and men. As this collection demonstrates, feminist scholarship in the margins contributes to actions and strategies for governments, NGOs, civil society groups, and transnational networks. Furthermore, feminist scholarship, in its turn, is informed by these same links. Consequently, this collection explores not only the issues that currently confront feminists in the region, but also, and perhaps most significantly, the cornucopia of opportunities created by critical feminists to negotiate, subvert, manipulate, and astonish standard political practices in order to forge feminist futures in the region.

Notes

1. Jan Jindy Pettman, *Worlding Women* (Sydney: Allen and Unwin, 1996), xi.
2. For an excellent discussion see, Mary E. Hawkesworth, *Globalization and Feminist Activism* (Lanham, MD: Rowman & Littlefield, Inc. 2006), 25–28.
3. Jill Steans, "Engaging from the Margins: Feminist Encounters with the 'Mainstream' of International Relations," *The British Journal of Politics and International Relations* 5, no. 3 (August 2003): 435.

4. Katrina Lee-Koo, "Feminism," in *An Introduction to International Relations: Australian Perspectives*, ed. Richard Devetak, Anthony Burke, and Jim George (Cambridge: Cambridge University Press, 2008), 75–77.
5. Cynthia Enloe, *Bananas, Beaches and Bases: Making Feminist Sense of International Politics* (London: Pandora, 1989).
6. J. Ann Tickner, "You Just Don't Understand: Troubled Engagements Between Feminists and IR Theorists," *International Studies Quarterly* 41, no. 4 (December 1997): 616.
7. V. Spike Peterson, "Feminist Theories Within, Invisible to, and Beyond IR," *Brown Journal of World Affairs* X, no. 2 (Winter/Spring 2004): 39.
8. J. Ann Tickner, "Feminism Meets International Relations: Some Methodological Issues," in *Feminist Methodologies for International Relations*, ed. Brooke A Ackerly, Maria Stern, and Jacqui True (Cambridge: Cambridge University Press, 2006), 25.
9. Rebecca Grant and Kathleen Newland, *Gender and International Relations* (Buckingham: Open University Press, 1991); J. Ann Tickner, *Gender in International Relations: A Feminist Perspective on Achieving Global Security* (New York: Columbia University Press, 1992); V. Spike Peterson, *Gendered States: Feminist (Re)Visions of International Relations Theory* (Boulder, CO: Lynne Reinner, 1992); V. Spike Peterson and Anne Sisson Runyan, ed., *Global Gender Issues* (Boulder, CO: Westview, 1993); Christine Sylvester, *Feminist Theory and International Relations in a Postmodern Era* (Cambridge: Cambridge University Press, 1994); Pettman, *Worlding Women*; Marysia Zalewski and Jane Parpart, ed., *The "Man Question" in International Relations* (Boulder, CO: Westview, 1998); J. Ann Tickner, *Gendering World Politics: Issues and Approaches in the Post-Cold War Era* (New York: Columbia University Press, 2001); Christine Sylvester, *Feminist International Relations: An Unfinished Journey* (Cambridge: Cambridge University Press, 2002).
10. For a review of feminist scholarship in IR see Jill Steans, *Gender and International Relations* (London: Polity Press, 2006), chapters 1 and 2. For thematic contributions see, for example, Carole Pateman, *The Sexual Contract* (Cambridge: Polity Press, 1988); Tickner, *Gender in International Relations*; Zillah Eisenstein, *The Color of Gender: Reimaging Democracy* (Berkeley: University of California Press, 1994); Mary K. Meyer and Elisabeth Prügl, *Gender Politics in Global Governance* (Lanham, MD: Rowman & Littlefield, 1999); Zillah Eisenstein, *Against Empire: Feminisms, Race and the West* (New York: Palgrave Macmillan, 2004).
11. Amrita Basu, ed., *The Challenge of Local Feminisms: Women's Movements in Global Perspective* (Boulder, CO: Westview, 1995); Kumari Jayawardena and Malathi de Alwis, ed., *Embodied Violence: Communalising Women's Sexuality in South Asia* (Delhi: Kali for Women, 1996). Lois Lorentzen and Jennifer Turpin, ed., *The Women and War Reader* (New York: New York University Press, 1998); Ritu Menon and Kamla Bhasin, *Borders and Boundaries: Women in India's Partition* (Delhi: Kali for Women, 1998); Caroline Moser and Fiona Clark, ed., *Victims, Perpetrators or Actors: Gender, Armed Conflict and Political Violence* (London: Zed Books, 2001); Geeta Chowdhury and Sheila Nair. ed., *Power in a Postcolonial World: Race, Gender and Class in International Relations* (New York: Routledge, 2002).

12. Georgina Waylen, *Gender in Third World Politics* (Boulder, CO: Lynne Rienner, 1996); Georgina Waylen, "You Still Don't Understand: Why Troubled Engagements Continue between Feminists and (Critical) IPE," *Review of International Studies* 32, no. 1 (2006): 145–64; Sonia Alvarez, *Engendering Democracy in Brazil: Women's Movements in Transition Politics* (Princeton: Princeton University Press, 1990); Margaret Keck and Kathryn Sikkink, *Activists Beyond Borders: Transnational Advocacy Networks in International Politics* (Ithaca, NY: Cornell University Press, 1998).
13. Nira Yuval-Davis and Floia Anthias, ed., *Woman, Nation, State* (Hampshire: Macmillan, 1989); Nira Yuval-Davis, *Gender and Nation* (London: Sage, 1997); Rita Manchanda, ed., *Women, War and Peace in South Asia: Beyond Victimhood to Agency* (New Delhi: Sage Publishers, 2001); Deniz Kandiyoti, ed., *Women, Islam and the State* (Basingstoke: Macmillan, 1991); Haleh Afshar, ed., *Women and Politics in the Third World* (London: Routledge, 1996).
14. Catherine M. Cole, Takyiwaa Manuh, and Stephan F. Miescher, ed., Africa *After Gender*? (Bloomington: Indiana University Press, 2007); Dong-Sook S. Gills and Nicola Piper, ed., *Women and Work in Globalising Asia (*London: Routledge, 2002); Myra Marx Ferree and Aili Mari Tripp, ed., *Global Feminism: Transnational Women's Activism, Organizing, and Human Rights* (New York: New York University Press, 2006).
15. Anne-Marie Goetz, *Women Development Workers: Implementing Rural Credit Programmes in Bangladesh* (New Delhi: Sage, 2001).
16. Naila Kabeer, *Mainstreaming Gender in Social Protection for the Informal Economy*, Gender Mainstreaming in Development Series (London: Commonwealth Secretariat, 2008); Shirin M. Rai, *Gender and the Political Economy of Development: From Nationalism to Globalization* (Cambridge: Polity, 2002).
17. Rebecca Cook, ed., *Human Rights of Women: National and International Perspectives* (Philadelphia: University of Pennsylvania Press, 1994); Kelly D. Askin and Dorean M. Koenig, ed., *Women and International Human Rights Law: Introduction to Women's Human Rights Issues* (Ardsley, NY: Transnational Publishers, 1999); Hilary Charlesworth and Christine Chinkin, *Boundaries of International Law: A Feminist Analysis* (Manchester: Manchester University Press, 2000).
18. Hawkesworth, *Globalization and Feminist Activism*, 2006; Jutta Joachim, *Agenda Setting, the UN, and NGOs: Gender Violence and Reproductive Rights* (Washington, DC: Georgetown University Press, 2007); Ferree and Tripp, ed., *Global Feminism.*
19. While they have their limitations, some examples are the activism for women's rights, the UNSC 1325, gender-mainstreaming, seeking justice for war crimes, and gender budgeting strategies. For various analyses see, Charlotte Bunch and Niamh Reilly, *Demanding Accountability: The Global Campaign and Vienna Tribunal for Women's Human Rights* (New Brunswick, NJ: Center for Women's Global Leadership, and New York: UN Development Fund for Women, UNIFEM, 1994); Jacqui True and Michael Mintrom, "Transnational Networks and Policy Diffusion: The Case of Gender Mainstreaming," *International Studies Quarterly* 45, no. 1 (March 2001): 27–57; Brooke Ackerly, "Women's Human Rights Activists as Cross-Cultural Theorists," *International Journal of Feminist Politics* 3, no. 3 (2001): 1–36; Jacqui True, "Mainstreaming Gender in Global Public Policy," *International*

Feminist Journal of Politics 5, no. 3 (November 2003): 368–96; Rhonda Sharp and Ray Broomhill, "*Budgeting for Equality: The Australian Experience*," *Feminist Economics* 8, no.1 (2002): 25–47; Bina D'Costa, "Coming to Terms with the Past: Forming Feminist Alliance across Borders," in *Women, Power and Justice: Global Feminist Perspectives, Volume I: Politics and Activism: Ensuring the Protection of Women's Fundamental Human Rights*, ed. Luciana Ricciutelli, Angela Miles, and Margaret McFadden (London: Zed Books, 2005), 227–47.

20. See Nicole George in this volume; see also Lynn Wilson, *Speaking to Power: Gender and Politics in the Western Pacific (*New York: Routledge, 1995); Teresia K. Teaiwa, "Globalizing and Gendered Forces: The Contemporary Militarization of Pacific/Oceania," in *Gender and Globalization in Asia and the Pacific*, ed. Kathy E. Ferguson and Monique Mironescu (Honolulu: University of Hawai'i Press, forthcoming). A group of women organized anti-nuclear activism under the banner of Otil a Beluad, nominated for the Nobel Peace Prize in late eighties.
21. Nicola Piper, "Feminization of Labor Migration as Violence Against Women: International, Regional, and Local Nongovernmental Organization Responses in Asia," *Violence Against Women* 9, no. 6 (2003): 723–45.
22. See, for example, Barbara Earth, "Globalization and Human Rights as Gendered Ideologies: A Case Study from Northeast Thailand," *Gender, Technology and Development* 9, no.1 (2005): 104–22.
23. Naila Kabeer, "Resources, Agency, Achievements: Reflections on the Measurement of Women's Empowerment," in *Gendered Poverty and Well-Being*, ed. Shahra Razavi (Oxford: Blackwell, 2000), 27–56.
24. Katherine Lepani, "Everything Has Come up to the Open Space: Talking about Sex in an Epidemic," *Working paper No. 15* (Canberra: Gender Relations Center, ANU, 2005).
25. Andrea Whittaker, ed., *Women's Health in Mainland Southeast Asia* (Binghamton, NY: Haworth, 2002).
26. This scholarship drew upon critical feminist voices rising in the West. Both Black and Indian feminists in the United States provided a vibrant and critical contribution focused on race and gender. Whereas, bell hooks, *Ain't I A Woman: Black Women and Feminism* (Boston: South End Press, 1981) discussed race and class; Chandra Talpade Mohanty, "Under Western Eyes, Feminist Scholarship and Colonial Discourses," *Boundary 2—An International Journal of Literature and Culture* 13, no. 1 (1984): 333–58, pointed out the connections between nonwestern feminism and race.
27. It is important to note that African feminists have also focused on this, see, for example, Joyce M. Chadya, "Mother Politics: Anti-Colonial Nationalism and the Woman Question in Africa," *Journal of Women's History* 15, no. 3 (2003): 153–57.
28. For example, sati (widow-burning) practices in India and the British rationalization.
29. Patty O'Brien, *The Pacific Muse: Exotic Femininity and the Colonial Pacific* (Washington: University of Washington Press, 2006).
30. Numerous examples from Indonesia, Malaysia, India; see also Pyong Gap Min, "Korean 'Comfort Women': The Intersection of Colonial Power, Gender and

Class," *Gender and* Society 17, no. 6 (December 2003): 938–57; Caroline Kennedy-Pipe, "Whose Security? State-Building and the 'Emancipation' of Women in Central Asia," *International Relations* 18, no. 1 (2004): 91–107; Brenda S. A. Yeoh and Katie Willis, ed., *State/Nation/Transnation: Perspectives on Transnationalism in the Asia-Pacific* (London: Routledge, 2004); Barbara Earth, "Globalization and Human Rights as Gendered Ideologies: A Case Study from Northeast Thailand," *Gender, Technology and Development* 9, no. 1 (2005): 104–23.

31. For example, in South Asia during the partition of India and the creation of Pakistan. Veena Das, *Critical Events: An Anthropological Perspective on Contemporary India* (Delhi: Oxford India, 1996).
32. Examples are Kali for Women (India), Gender Press (Thailand), Blackstone Publishing (Vanuatu), and Narigrantha Prabartana (Bangladesh).
33. See also McNevin, Hussein, and George's work in this volume. All three scholars have made their own feminist journeys in the region.
34. Menon and Bhasin, *Borders and Boundaries.*
35. Urvashi Butalia, *Other Side of Silence* (Delhi: Kali for Women, 1998).
36. Bina D'Costa, "Marginalized Identities: New Frontiers of Research for IR?" in *Feminist Methodologies for International Relations,* ed. Brooke A Ackerly, Maria Stern, and Jacqui True (Cambridge: Cambridge University Press, 2006), 129–52.
37. For a discussion on feminist methodologies in IR, see Ackerly, Stern, and True, *Feminist Methodologies for International Relations.*
38. See, for example, Muthiah Alagappa, ed., *Asian Security Practice: Material and Ideational Influences* (Stanford: Stanford University Press, 1998); Ken Booth and Russell Trood, ed., *Strategic Cultures in the Asia-Pacific Region* (London: Palgrave McMillan, 1999); William T. Tow, Ramesh Thakur, and In-Taek Hyun, ed., *Asia's Emerging Regional Order: Reconciling Traditional and Human Security* (New York: United Nations University Press, 2000).
William T. Tow, *Asia-Pacific Strategic Relations: Seeking Convergent Security* (Cambridge: Cambridge University Press, 2001); security sector reform in post-conflict states or recent police trainings in the Solomon Islands (RAMSI).
39. Jindy Pettman, "Questions of Identity: Australia and Asia," in *Critical Security Studies and World Politics,* ed. Ken Booth (Boulder, CO: Lynne Rienner, 2005), 159–77.
40. See Stephen Chan, Peter G. Mandaville, and Roland Bleiker, ed., *The Zen of International Relations: IR Theory from East to West* (New York: Palgrave Macmillan, 2001); Anthony Burke and Matt McDonald, ed., *Critical Security in the Asia-Pacific* (Manchester: Manchester University Press, 2007); Roland Bleiker, *Divided Korea: Toward A Culture of Reconciliation* (Minneapolis: University of Minnesota Press, 2008).
41. See Pettman, "Questions of Identity."
42. Some examples are refugees on the Thai-Burma border; internally displaced people in Sri Lanka and Afghanistan, "poorest of the poor" in Papua New Guinea; Ainu people in Japan; Falun Gong in China.
43. See V. Spike Peterson in this volume.
44. In India, Sri Lanka, Bangladesh, Pakistan, Indonesia, the Philippines, and New Zealand; see also Mark R. Thompson, "Female Leadership of Democratic Transitions in Asia," *Pacific Affairs* 75, no. 4 (Winter 2002/2003): 535–55. The lowest

representation of women in Parliament is in PNG, Bangladesh (which had two female heads) and Vanuatu. Thalif Deen, New York: Global Information Network, April 23, 2007.

45. Popularized by the feminist discourse of development and women's networks such as DAWN; see also Jane Parpart, Shirin M. Rai, and Kathleen Staudt, ed., *Rethinking Empowerment: Gender and Development in a Global/Local World* (London: Routledge, 2002).
46. Karen Women's Organization in Burma/Myanmar, and Shakti Foundation in Bangladesh.
47. Kim Hak-Su, *China Daily*, April 27, 2007.
48. Bernadette Resurrecion, "Women's Politics in Asia—Conference Report," *Gender, Technology and Development* 7, no. 3, 2003: 441–42.
49. Ibid.
50. See Shakira Hussein, "The War on Terror and the Rescue of Muslim Women," in *Islam in World Politics*, ed. Nelly Lahoud and Anthony Johns (London: Routledge, 2005), 93–103.
51. Jindy Pettman, "Feminist International Relations After 9/11," *Brown Journal of World Affairs* X, no. 2 (2004): 89.
52. Katrina Lee-Koo, "Security as Enslavement/Security as Emancipation: Gendered Legacies and Feminist Futures in the Asia-Pacific," in *Critical Security in the Asia-Pacific*, ed. Anthony Burke and Matt McDonald (Manchester: Manchester University Press, 2007), 231–46.
53. See also Charlesworth, McNevin, Huynh, and George in this volume.
54. For details see "Violence against Women in War, Network, Japan," http://www1.jca.apc.org/vaww-net-japan/english/womenstribunal2000/whatstribunal.html (accessed January 29, 2008); Katharina R. Mendoza, "Freeing the 'Slaves of Destiny': The Lolas of the Filipino Comfort Women Movement," *Cultural Dynamics* 15, no. 3 (2003): 247–66.
55. For example, the Leitana Nehan Women's Development Agency came into existence as part of the Leitana Peace Plan. Based in Bougainville, it works with women affected by the armed conflict in Bougainville. Helen Hakena, "Strengthening Communities for Peace in Bougainville," in *Conflict and Peacemaking in the Pacific: Social and Gender Perspectives*, Development Bulletin, special issue, no. 53: 17–19.

CHAPTER 2

'Worlding Women' in International Law

Hilary Charlesworth

Jindy Pettman's book, *Worlding Women*, sets out to "take women's experiences of the international seriously, while not assuming that any experiences are transparent or politically innocent."[1] In this celebration of Jindy's work, I discuss the challenges of 'worlding' women in the context of international law, a discipline that has an ambivalent relationship to international relations. International lawyers both embrace and reject the relevance of international relations theory to their work, according to their views on the autonomy of legal thinking.[2] International relations scholars, for their part, sometimes regard international law as quaintly utopian and sometimes as an authoritative source of international norms.[3] Stephen Krasner describes a stark 'methodological divide' separating politics and international law, "The task of political science is primarily to explain what is and hereby to hint at what might be. The task of lawyers is more often to elucidate not what is, but what might be."[4] Feminist scholarship in the two disciplines unsettles Krasner's characterizations: both feminist international lawyers and feminist international relations scholars combine an interest in the empirical description of events affecting women with a normative commitment to women's equality.

Feminism and International Law

Questions of sex and gender came late to international law. This reflects the power of the traditional account of law: in contrast to politics, the law offers an impartial system of reasoning about problems, distinct from the actual biases of human decision-makers. Ronald Dworkin summarized this tradition by observing that while law deals with principles, politics deals with policies.[5] Of course the principles and policies dichotomy is always harder to maintain in the area of international law compared to national legal systems. The resilience of the notion of state sovereignty in the international community has led to an understanding of international law as essentially a voluntary system of regulation. The Permanent Court of International Justice gave a pithy account of this approach in the case of the *SS Lotus* saying,

> International Law governs relations between independent states. The rules of law binding upon states therefore emanate from their own free will. . . . Restrictions upon the independence of states cannot therefore be presumed.[6]

The consensual basis of international law gives it a negotiable, political image, when compared to the apparent impartiality of domestic legal systems. Indeed, international lawyers constantly face the question of whether international law is really law at all. Nevertheless, within the world of international law, it is claimed that legal principles are quite distinct from political assertions. While international politics are governed by the rule of military or economic might, international law presents a moral discourse about justice and fairness, which have universal application. This is most obvious in the field of international human rights law, although the discourse on justice informs other areas of international law, such as international law on the environment, and international law on the use of force.

Feminist voices began to emerge in international law in the early 1990s. Inspired by a broad range of feminist scholarship, these voices were primarily influenced by feminist international relations specialists. Scholars such as Cynthia Enloe, Spike Petersen, and Ann Tickner provided perspectives that helped international lawyers unpack the building blocks of international law: the state, sovereignty, conflict, and peace. Jindy Pettman's work was particularly significant for international lawyers because of her emphasis on the relationship of gender to other forms of power like race, nationality, and class. Jindy's writings drew attention to the differences *among* women and the way their power relations are constructed. Those of us lucky enough to know Jindy personally find that she is an inspiring and generous source of ideas, support, and humor. Her warmth, infectious laughter, and fly-away hair symbolize the pleasure of feminist collaboration.

Feminist international relations (IR) scholarship offered international lawyers the tools, and the courage, to challenge the claim that international law supplies a rational, detached, and universal form of justice. It allowed us to argue that international law is both sexed and gendered and that this has skewed the apparently impartial discipline. For example, Marysia Zalewski's questions of international relations, Where are the women? What work is gender doing?[7] can usefully be translated into international law.

Where are the women in international law? There is a disproportionate representation of men in the institutions of international law. The International Court of Justice, the premier judicial body of the international legal system, for example, has one woman among the fifteen elected judges, Dame Roslyn Higgins. She is currently president of the Court. The International Law Commission, established under the United Nations (UN) Charter, a prestigious body of forty-five jurists, has three women members. The UN Secretariat is dominated by men, as are the committees monitoring the human rights treaties of the UN. One important exception to the rule is the International Criminal Court, which has seven women judges among its eighteen members. Few women are involved in the formal international legal system; furthermore, the concepts of international law do not accommodate the realities of most women's lives.[8]

What work is gender doing in international law? The language and imagery of the law draw on gendered categories. International law lays claim to rationality, objectivity, and abstraction, characteristics traditionally associated with western masculinity; it is defined in contrast to emotion, subjectivity, and contextualized thinking. The power of international legal discourse rests on a series of binary oppositions: order and chaos, logic and emotion, legal and political, and binding and nonbinding. Feminist scholars point to the gendered coding of these dichotomies, with the stronger term associated with masculinity and the less preferable one with femininity. The vocabulary of objectivity, logic, and order positions a person as being manly, which immediately gives their words a higher value. The use of subjective, emotional or 'disordered' discourse is coded as feminine and thus devalues a statement or argument.[9]

Feminist analysis points to the gendered categories of analysis of international law. For example, why are highly migratory species of sea life regulated by treaty when the use of breast milk substitutes, which is a major health issue for women in Africa, subject to voluntary World Health Organization codes? Why is extra-territorial jurisdiction, traditionally invoked against violations of monopoly and competition law, rarely used in trafficking of women and children cases?

Critical work on feminism in international law is concerned with questions about the location of women in its structures and investigating the role that gender plays in its formation. At the same time, international law is invoked in feminist struggles as a source of transformation and empowerment. This creates tension within feminist international legal scholarship, and sometimes a deeply fractured politics.[10]

Because of the significant scholarly literature in this area over the last two decades, some feminist ideas have been absorbed into the rhetoric of international law and its institutions. International women's groups have taken up feminist critiques of the international legal order. In many areas, however, progress is limited. Feminist issues are confined to the margins or rendered bland so that they have no transformative bite. The case of women's experiences in the processes of statebuilding illustrates some of the problems involved.

Women's Experiences of State-building

The human rights of women in state-building have become increasingly prominent over the last decade. The United Nations regularly emphasizes human rights in ameliorating the position of women in 'post–conflict' societies. For example, UNIFEM's strategies for women in the reconstruction of Afghanistan and Iraq are couched in terms of rights[11] and the mandate of the UN Peacebuilding Commission recognizes the importance of women's involvement in post–conflict settlements.[12] The protection of women's rights has been endorsed by the U. S. President, George W. Bush, as one major benefit of the invasions of and subsequent state-building exercises in Afghanistan and Iraq.[13]

The translation of the vocabulary of women's rights into two recent state-building exercises, East Timor and Iraq, however, shows that women's rights are often sidelined in the process of state-building and that the 'rebuilt' state both creates and reinforces the inequality of women. Australia is a critical player in East Timor, leading international military forces during the rebuilding period. Australia is also in Iraq, a member of the 'Coalition of the Willing' that invaded Iraq in 2003.

East Timor

The international project to rebuild East Timor began in 1999 after the East Timorese voted for independence following twenty-four years of Indonesian occupation. The vote against integration with Indonesia prompted the destruction of the infrastructure of East Timorese society. After creating a peacekeeping force, International Force East Timor (INTERFET), the UN Security Council established the United Nations Transitional Administration in East Timor (UNTAET) to oversee the transition to statehood.[14] East Timor finally became a new state in May 2002. At first sight, UNTAET appears to be an example of women's rights-sensitive nation-building. In establishing UNTAET, the Security Council emphasized the "importance of including in UNTAET personnel with appropriate training in international humanitarian, human rights, and refugee law, including child and gender related provisions."[15] This is the first such reference in the mandate of an international peacekeeping body and is regarded as implementing the UN's commitment to 'mainstreaming' gender perspectives in peace operations.[16]

Women in East Timor were deeply involved in the independence struggle against Indonesia and suffered all types of violence, such as rape, forced sterilization, and sexual slavery.[17] After the 1999 referendum, the Indonesian military and local militias abducted women and many individual and mass rapes occurred.[18] Women related to pro-independence activists were targeted for sexual violence.[19] Furthermore, the UNTAET era was marked by considerable domestic violence. Estimates of violence against women by male family members constitute 40 percent of all offences committed in East Timor during the year 2000.[20]

One explanation for the increase in family violence is the 80 percent unemployment rate in urban areas. Violence within the family became a way for men to reassert their domestic power.[21]

East Timorese women's groups regularly invoked the language of human rights during the state-building process to make claims about the employment of women, the representation of women in public life, the high rate of female illiteracy, and the issue of violence against women. Another concern raised by the women of East Timor was that of accountability for the crimes committed against them during the Indonesian occupation and its aftermath.

Few East Timorese women played formal roles in the state-building process. The original structure proposed for UNTAET in November 1999 included an administrative unit devoted exclusively to gender issues, but it was not implemented because of competing budget priorities.[22] The intervention of two senior women UN officials, Angela King, Assistant Secretary-General and Special Adviser on Gender Issues and the Advancement of Women, and Mary Robinson, United Nations High Commissioner for Human Rights, finally ensured the creation of a Gender Affairs Unit (GAU) in April 2000. The GAU was eventually responsible for some significant initiatives in East Timor, but the delay in establishing it seriously affected its operations. Funding initially allocated to the payment of gender affairs officers was redistributed, and no program or operational budget was created even when the GAU was reinstated. Thus, preliminary tasks that underlie the functions of the GAU, such as assessing the impact of post–referendum violence and identifying the different needs of men and women, were delayed.

UNTAET established a Special Panel for Serious Crimes to try acts of international criminality occurring after the 1999 referendum. The Panel's decisions with respect to crimes against women were criticized, however,[23] and women's groups called, so far unsuccessfully, for an international criminal tribunal to provide greater accountability for crimes.

There is implicit recognition in various public statements made by the Transitional Administrator, Sergio Viera de Mello, that East Timorese men and women had very different experiences under the Indonesian regime; their sex significantly affected their opportunities in the transitional and independence eras. This was not, however, reflected in UNTAET's actions. In particular, the employment of women in UNTAET is an issue. East Timorese women's groups looked for assurance that one-third of the East Timorese people employed by the UN are women. A directive issued by the Transitional Administrator, after intense lobbying by the major women's organization, REDE stated, "a minimum of all national and district hiring shall comprise 30 percent women within every classification/level of employment."[24] In the end, however, this commitment was not realized: 33 percent of the international civilian officials working for UNTAET were women but women comprised only 11 percent of the UNTAET East Timorese staff. Women are represented in even lower numbers in the civilian police and peacekeeping force in East Timor, which are 4 percent and 2.4 percent women, respectively.[25]

The reaction of local groups to assertions of women's human rights was significant in East Timor. It is evident that traditional law practices that disadvantage women are reinforced by religious conservatism and forms of patriotism.[26] This phenomenon was evident in East Timor; it was mixed with ambivalence about the UN presence. Thus, in his 2001 New Year's speech to the nation, the resistance leader Xanana Gusmao criticized what he called the "obsessive acculturation to standards that hundreds of international experts try to convey to the East Timorese, who are hungry for values."[27] Gusmao went on to acknowledge that some of the "standards" that UNTAET aspired to entrench in East Timor law are universal in the sense that they are recognized as such in international law. However, he implied that the standards relating to the rights of women, particularly the right of women to determine their own lives did not find natural affinity or reflection in East Timorese culture. These standards were regarded by Gusmao as difficult to absorb locally. Gusmao suggested that the values, especially with respect to women's human rights, being introduced into East Timorese society were beset by colonial attitudes amongst the international workers, and unthinking receptiveness by some East Timorese.

Milena Pires, Deputy Speaker of the National Council, responded to Gusmao. She spoke of problems caused by a combination of traditional culture with religiously-based social conservatism. Pires observed,

> cultural discourse is invoked frequently to quash attempts to introduce discussions on women's rights into the East Timorese political equation. The incompatibility between East Timorese culture and what is popularly cited as a western feminist imposition is used to dismiss even the notion that Timorese women's rights may need to be nurtured and defended so as to become a reality. Undermining the importance of women's human rights because it only considers half of the East Timorese population is another argument put forward to prevent its elaboration.[28]

These arguments were invoked against proposals to boost the political representation of women in East Timor, not only by the East Timorese but also by UN officials. For example, a public debate about quotas for women was ignited by a proposal to entrench in law a requirement for political parties to field women in at least 30 percent of their nominated representative positions for election to the Constituent Assembly, which was responsible for drafting the constitution. Some influential UNTAET officers were opposed to the proposal, arguing that quotas infringed the concept of free and fair elections.[29] The proposal was ultimately defeated in the National Council in March 2001, although in the end 27 percent of the seats in the Constituent Assembly are held by women.

After broad community consultation, a Gender and Constitutional Working Group prepared a Charter for Women's Rights.[30] The charter sought the prohibition of all forms of discrimination and the adoption of positive measures to promote equality. It demanded the protection of women's right to live free from any form of violence, both public and private, and regulation of the dowry system to prevent violence against women. The charter also sought to guarantee women's participation in traditional decision-making processes. The constitution, however, contains only a few traces of the charter's provisions, for example, its reference to nondiscrimination based on gender for access to political positions.[31]

State-building in East Timor under international auspices did not give adequate attention to the involvement of East Timorese women and has produced limited gains for them. Women are poorly represented in public life and in governmental positions, domestic violence remains at extremely high levels, and women have little hope of economic freedom. The waves of unrest and violence in East Timor between 2006 and 2007 have led women's groups once again to appeal to the international community for support in ensuring women's involvement in decision-making, equality of access to employment, reform of the police and public service, and ending impunity for human rights violations against women.[32]

Iraq

State-building in Iraq is a response to the political and physical chaos caused by the 2003 invasion by the United States and its partners in the so-called Coalition of the Willing. David Frum, a former speech writer in the Bush White House, reported that he was asked in 2002 to sum up in a sentence or two the best case for invading Iraq.[33] One proposal he devised as a rationale for military action was for President Bush to promote the appeal of democracy and women's rights to Muslim world. This plan was abandoned because the White House was concerned that the call for women's rights would destabilize some of Washington's most important allies in the Middle East.

Yet women increasingly are featured in the official White House material on state- building in Iraq and officials state that "women's rights are at the core of building a civil, law-abiding society, a pre-requisite for true democracies."[34] This commitment is haphazardly observed. The Iraqi government in exile, created by the United States before the invasion, had three women out of sixty-five members. Only three of twenty-five members of the Iraqi Governing Council, established by the U. S.-led Coalition Provisional Authority (CPA)after the invasion, were women and there was only one woman in the Cabinet. No women served on the twenty-four member constitutional drafting committee that produced the interim constitution. The Iraq Interim Government, appointed July 1, 2004, had six women out of thirty members.

The pressures against the participation of women in state-building are a product of the ambivalence of the United States toward women's rights. For example, the CPA was reluctant to support Iraqi women's groups call for a 50 percent quota for women's seats in the National Assembly responsible for drafting an interim constitution in 2004[35] because it was regarded as inconsistent with U. S. anti-affirmative action policies. A far greater problem for women, however, is the local hostility to their involvement in public life, particularly from religious groups.[36] Coalition officials tend to postpone overt support for women until the time that proper security is established, which will make it harder to involve women after conservative religious and community leaders are entrenched in power.[37]

In the end, the interim Constitution prescribed a *goal*, not a quota, of 25 percent of the seats be held by women; the election regulations, however, mandate that one-third of the candidates on electoral lists be women. This is an important step, although it is considerably less than the percentage sought by Iraqi women's groups. Most women candidates refused to campaign in public in the lead-up to the January 2005 elections because of fears of violence. Of course men are concerned about violence too, but the violence against women has religious support. In the end, women won 31 percent of the seats in the legislature. The fifty-five-member committee established to draft the constitution, however, included only eight women; five were members of the main Shiite party, and two came from the Kurdish Alliance. There was a single independent woman member.

The 2005 Iraqi Constitution includes specific reference to women's rights to vote and to stand for election[38] and prohibits gender discrimination.[39] It includes an aspiration, rather than a requirement, that voting laws enable 25 percent of the Council of Representatives to be women for a transitional period.[40] The constitution's commitment to equality before the law[41] is potentially undermined by the declaration that Islam is "a fundamental source of legislation"[42] and that "no law that contradicts the established provisions of Islam may be established."[43] Depending on the interpretation of *Sharia* law that is adopted, the constitution could invalidate civil laws similar to those adopted by Iraq in 1959, which accorded women equal rights in relation to marriage, divorce, and inheritance.[44] Another troubling provision of the constitution gives individuals a choice of personal status law.[45] For example, it is not clear what will happen if there is a conflict between spouses over the law to apply for a divorce. The constitution provides for an independent judiciary,[46] but it also mandates the appointment of clerics and religious judges to the Federal Supreme Court.[47] The appointment of religious judges will affect the interpretation of the constitution.

The invasion of Iraq replaced a secular regime with a government of strong religious affiliation. Rebel groups are characterized by a commitment to fundamentalist religion. The major protagonists in the chaotic process of state-building are at best ambivalent and at worst hostile to the involvement of women. Moreover, the continuing violence in Iraq has destroyed daily domestic security, leaving little space for women's lives.

Women's Rights in State-Building

State-building is often regarded as process that has the capacity to deliver a new dispensation for women. Simona Sharoni observes, "while in some instances, political conflict may complicate women's lives and set back their struggles for gender equality, in a different context and under different circumstances, a heightened political conflict may become a springboard for gender equality."[48] She notes, for example, that in Ireland "far from being mutually exclusive or irreconcilable, feminism and nationalism are presented as two complementary movements wh[ich] seek to radically transform existing social and political relationships and structures as a stepping stone for the future envisioned nation."[49]

Over the last decade, the international state-building industry has embraced the language of women's human rights, supporting women's capacity "to take their rightful and equal place at the decision-making table in questions of peace and security."[50] However, the cases of state-building of East Timor and Iraq illustrate the complexity of the translation of the worthy public statements about the equality of women in modern state-building. Cynthia Enloe suggests a series of questions for feminist inquiries in international relations that are useful in the context of women and state-building, Where are the women in state-building and what women are there? How did these women get there and what do they think about their position?[51] Unlike some state-building ventures,[52] women in East Timor and Iraq have little representation in the peacemaking and state-building process after conflict and they have been unable to alter the asymmetry of power relations. In both East Timor and Iraq, attention to women's human rights is largely the product of women's groups, with the support of individuals within UNTAET and the CPA, respectively. With limited spheres of influence in respect to official policy, these groups use international and local networks to pressure state-building institutions to take women's concerns seriously. They contend with official attitudes of skepticism or resentment toward what is seen as subversive distractions. Most women's groups in East Timor and Iraq express great frustration with their inability to affect the post–conflict settlement. The examples of East Timor and Iraq suggest three major issues for women in the state-rebuilding process.

Women's Rights vs. Local Cultures

A significant issue in both countries is the association of women's rights with imposed, international standards, which inevitably leads to tension with local cultures. In East Timor, gender roles that assign men to the public world of politics and employment and women to the private world of home and family pervade social and economic relations. They are supported by religious doctrine, low levels of education, and traditional practices. The situation in Iraq is more complex. Despite the oppressive nature of Saddam Hussein's regime,

Iraqi women generally benefited from its secular approach to personal status laws.[53] The UN Arab Development Report noted in 2002 that Iraqi women rated highest among Arab women on UN measures of 'gender empowerment' because of their significant political participation.[54] The 2003 invasion of Iraq, among other things, allowed Iraqi men to assert masculine traditionalism to reclaim authenticity and authority.

Noah Feldman, an American constitutional lawyer who worked with the CPA, concludes from his experience in Iraq that international standards should not be imposed on or even influence new democracies.[55] New constitutions, he argues, should "get off the ground through a process of adoption by localized self-interest, not out of episodic external pressure that will soon be lifted."[56] Feldman's deference to 'localized self-interest' in the context of women's rights, however, allows particular local male elites to define the substance of state-building. Women's rights are unlikely to appeal to the self-interest of such elites. Feldman's argument also assumes that there is one set of local views that should be respected while ignoring the aspirations of 'internal reformers' within state-building societies.[57]

The respect ascribed to culture from the international community is based on a monolithic view of culture, as though it had no internal diversity. We often see a similar assumption made about religious culture.[58] But it is important to be aware of the politics of the culture being invoked as part of state-building. For example, whose culture is being invoked? What is the status of the interpreter of culture? In whose name is the argument advanced? And, who are the primary beneficiaries of the claim?[59] The cultures of the international communities involved in state-building also require scrutiny. Few women hold senior positions in state-building agencies, an absence that sends a strong message to post–conflict societies. Evidence from the last decade of state-building shows an institutional forgetfulness about the position of women, with mistakes being repeated in subsequent missions.[60]

Limited Definitions of Human Rights

A second concern for women in state-building is the way that relevant international human rights standards are defined. The representation of women is a major concern, albeit inadequately, by the international community, with intense debate about the legitimacy of quotas for women. Other problems women face in particular contexts are obscured. For example, Sumie Nakaya points to the lack of attention paid to the gendered impact of the ethnic partition models used in state-building in Bosnia-Herzegovina and Kosovo.[61] Moreover, the right to equality in international law invoked in state-building remains tethered to a limited, procedural account of nondiscrimination. A more useful analysis of inequality is in terms of oppression and domination, rather than in terms of discrimination in the distribution of social goods. Iris Marion Young notes, "while discriminatory policies sometimes cause or reinforce oppression,

oppression involves many actions, practices, and structures that have little to do with preferring or excluding members of groups in the awarding of benefits."[62] This suggests an understanding of equality and inequality that attends to structures of oppression and domination. Linking the idea of equality with nondomination allows for a consideration of the context of inequality and relative distributions of power.

A related problem is the tendency of state-building to emphasize civil and political rights over economic, social, and cultural rights.[63] Of course, this is an issue for men as well as women. If the empowerment of women is understood to depend on the inclusion of women in various spheres of public life, there will be inadequate attention to the gendered nature of the rules of the game that women are required to play. We need to rethink traditional structures of public and private life, such as ideas of economic activity, to accommodate women's lives. We must consider the effects of the unequal balance of domestic labor, which limits the capacity of women to operate in the public sphere.

State-building relies on the human rights concept of self-determination. In international law, self-determination accords a people the right to autonomy, freedom from alien oppression, and the right to choose an economic, political, and social system "free from outside intervention, subversion, coercion, or constraint of any kind whatsoever."[64] Once external self-determination is achieved and internal self-determination is guaranteed, it is assumed that all members of the group will equally benefit, in other words, the terms 'self' and 'peoples' are homogenous. Individual and group aspirations, both before and after the achievement of self-determination, are subsumed within those of the self-determining unit.

This assumption of group identity and commonality is open to challenge. The notion of a self-determining unit collapses many forms of diversity, but most particularly that of sex. The consequences of this limited definition are evident in the fact that apparently successful claims to self-determination typically fail to deliver the same level of personal freedom and autonomy for women as for men, despite many cases of the historical association between nationalist and feminist movements and a high degree of participation in the decolonization process. Indeed, in many cases the achievement of national self-determination has led to deterioration in the position of women.

Narrow Conceptions of Gender

A third problem for the protection of women's human rights in state-building is its relationship to the flawed gender mainstreaming enterprise endorsed by international institutions. There are important analyses of the failure to implement gender mainstreaming projects in state-building.[65] But more significant is the inadequacy of the concept itself.[66] In the international arena the notion of gender mainstreaming is both too broad and too narrow. In one sense, it has become an almost meaningless term. Most commitments to gender mainstreaming draw on the definition adopted by ECOSOC in 1997:

> Mainstreaming a gender perspective is the process of assessing the implications for women and men of any planned action, including legislation, policies or programmes, in all areas and at all levels. It is a strategy for making women's as well as men's concerns and experiences an integral dimension of the design, implementation, monitoring and evaluation of policies and programmes in all political, economic and societal spheres so that women and men benefit equally and inequality is not perpetuated. The ultimate goal is to achieve gender equality.[67]

This definition is so broad that it is difficult to see how it can work. If gender mainstreaming is "the process of assessing the implications for women and men of any planned action," how can we assess what it means in any context and how is it different from a standard policy consideration of impact?

On the other hand, the ECOSOC definition is also a very narrow one: it reads as if animated by an idea of equality as equal treatment of women and men, assuming symmetry of position between women and men. It does not address the complex way that gender is created and sustained by social and power relations.[68] Treating women and men as though they face similar obstacles will perpetuate existing disparities between them. In some accounts of gender mainstreaming, the strategy has become simply a head count of women in particular positions, a modest variation on the 'equal opportunity' agenda.[69] While increasing women's participation in institutions is important, it does not itself change institutional agendas.

Moreover, the definition of gender mainstreaming in international institutions contemplates a limited sphere for its operation. It is regarded as primarily relevant to policy development in particular areas, such as development, human rights, and some aspects of labor markets. Other fields appear immune to gendered scrutiny. For example, the European Union has not extended gender mainstreaming to competition policy.[70] Within the United Nations, most areas of law have been treated as if they were impervious to concerns of gender: gender mainstreaming mandates are not given to either the International Law Commission or the International Court of Justice. The Statute of the International Criminal Court refers to gender in the definition of crimes within the Court's jurisdiction, but defines it in a curiously restrictive way as "the two sexes, male and female, within the context of society."[71]

Perhaps the most fundamental problem with the strategy of gender mainstreaming is that it rests on a bland concept of gender that has little bite. In some contexts, the UN follows the second wave of feminist thought in drawing a clear distinction between the concepts of 'sex' and 'gender.'[72] It defines sex as a matter of biology and gender as the constructed meaning of sex, the designation of social roles. This distinction has come under scrutiny from feminist scholars, who question whether the category of 'sex' can be regarded as natural and uncontentious.[73]

In the case of gender mainstreaming, however, the sex and gender distinction has been elided. UN gender mainstreaming policies assume that gender is a synonym for women. This is evident in the influential ECOSOC definition, previously quoted. The elision causes a number of problems. First, it links gender with biology, implying that gender is a fixed, objective fact about a person. It does not capture the ways that gender is constructed in society to make some actions seem natural and others controversial. It reaffirms the 'naturalness' of female and male identities and bypasses the performative aspects of gender. Understanding gender as essentially about women does not capture the relational nature of gender, the role of power relations, and the way that structures of subordination are reproduced.[74] It allows problems facing women to be understood as the product of particular cultures, lack of participation in public arenas, or lack of information and skills, and obscures the way that gender shapes our understanding of the world. It requires women to change, but not men. Most significantly, the association of the term 'gender' primarily with women leaves both the roles of men and male gender identities unexamined, as though they were somehow natural and immutable.

An example of the depoliticization of the notion of gender is Security Council resolution 1325 adopted on October 31, 2000. This resolution contributes to a growing body of UN-sponsored declarations linking the attainment of peace and security with the achievement of equality between women and men and advocating a "gender perspective" to permeate all peace missions.[75] Many feminists have hailed Resolution 1325 as a significant success story for gender mainstreaming.[76] The commitment to gender mainstreaming as an integral aspect of all UN peace operations has indeed met no formal opposition from states. But what is a 'gender perspective' in peace negotiations? Security Council Resolution 1325 defines it as giving attention to the special needs of women and girls during repatriation, supporting local women's peace initiatives, and protecting the human rights of women and girls in any new legal order. In this sense, Resolution 1325 presents gender as all about women and unconnected with masculine identities in times of conflict and violent patterns of conduct accepted because they are coded as male. Ideas about gender are central to the way that international conflicts are identified and resolved,[77] but these assumptions are left untouched in the resolution. The UN Secretary-General's 2004 report on the implementation of Resolution 1325 similarly understands gender as essentially about women, or, the even narrower meaning of 'women-and-children.'[78] 'Gender perspectives' become, in the bureaucratese of the UN, "the need to prioritize the proactive role women can play in peace-building"[79] or "to take into consideration the special needs of women and girls"[80] or increasing the number of women in national and international military forces.[81] Unless state-building addresses the gendered structures of power and domination in a society, it will always fail women.

Conclusion

In the early years of this century many see international law as a fragile institution. The antagonism of the United States toward the institutions of the international legal order prompts fears that we live in a lawless world. In this context feminist challenges to the impartiality of international law are suspect. Martti Koskenniemi, for example, criticizes the feminist project of reconceiving international law, "We can reconceive international law every now and then, but not all the time." He argues,

> Our immediate fears and hopes do not necessarily match to produce the good society. . . . At some point, we need distance from those fears and hopes—if not objective distance, then at least a partial, consensual, formal distance. That the law makes this distance possible (if always only for a moment) is not a defect of law, but its most immediate benefit.[82]

International law does not provide, however, even a momentary distance from subjectivity because it is intertwined with a sexed and gendered subjectivity, but this does not mean that it will inevitably reinforce male domination. Worlding women in international law requires chronicling women's experiences of the international, and investigating their politics. It disrupts international law by telling stories that shatter the categories of the discipline. While this may not always, or even often, lead to transformation and change, the vocabulary of justice and international law nevertheless contains radical potential. International human rights law in particular, as Sally Engle Merry observes, "is always in danger of escaping its bounds and working in a genuinely emancipatory way."[83] Worlding women is one way to make that escape more likely.

Notes

1. Jan Jindy Pettman, *Worlding Women: A Feminist International Politics* (Sydney: Allen and Unwin, 1996).
2. Kenneth W. Abbott, "International Relations Theory, International Law and the Regime Governing Atrocities in Internal Conflicts," in *The Methods of International Law*, American Society of International Law Studies in Transnational Legal Policy, no. 36, ed. Steven R. Ratner and Anne-Marie Slaughter (Washington: ASIL, 2004), 127.
3. For a comprehensive analysis of this relationship, see Robert J. Beck, "International Law and International Relations: The Prospects for Interdisciplinary Collaboration," in *International Rules: Approaches from International Law and International Relations*, ed. Robert J. Beck, Anthony Clark Arend, and Robert D. Vander Lugt, 3 (New York: Oxford University Press, 1996).

4. Stephen Krasner, "International Law and International Relations: Together, Apart, Together," *Chicago Journal of International Law* 1 (2000):93, 98. Although Krasner advocates closer links between the normative project of international law and the empirical project of international relations, he is pessimistic about the likelihood of this occurring.
5. Ronald Dworkin, *A Matter of Principle* (Cambridge: Harvard University Press, 1985).
6. *The S.S. Lotus Case* (France *v.* Turkey) PCIJ Rep. Ser. A, No 10, 4, 18 (1927).
7. Marysia Zalewski, "Well, What is the Feminist Perspective on Bosnia?" *International Affairs* 71, no. 2 (1995): 339.
8. Hilary Charlesworth and Christine Chinkin, *The Boundaries of International Law: A Feminist Analysis* (Manchester: Manchester University Press, 2000); Christine Chinkin, Shelley Wright, and Hilary Charlesworth, "Feminist Approaches to International Law: Reflections from Another Century," in *International Law: Modern Feminist Approaches*, ed. Doris Buss and Ambreena Manji (Portland: Hart Publishing, 2006), 17.
9. Carol Cohn, "War, Wimps, and Women: Talking Gender and Thinking War," in *Gendering War Talk*, ed. Miriam Cooke and Angela Woollacott, 227–46 (Princeton: Princeton University Press, 1993), 397.
10. The differences between Catharine MacKinnon, *Are Women Human? And Other International Dialogues* (Cambridge: Harvard University Press, 2006), and Janet Halley, *Split Decisions: How and Why to Take a Break from Feminism* (Princeton: Princeton University Press, 2006), are an example of this. See also Karen Engle, "'Calling in the Troops': The Uneasy Relationship Among Women's Rights, Human Rights, and Humanitarian Intervention," *Harvard Human Rights Journal* 20 (2007): 189;. Marysia Zalewski, "Do We Understand each Other Yet? Troubling Feminist Encounters With(in) International Relations," *British Journal of Politics and International Relations* 9, no. 2 (2007): 302, describes a parallel debate within feminist IR.
11. United Nations Development Fund for Women (UNIFEM), "Afghanistan," http://www.unifem.undp.org/afghanistan (accessed March 12, 2008) and, "Iraq," Women War Peace, http://www.womenwarpeace.org/iraq/iraq.htm (accessed March 12, 2008).
12. United Nations, *Security Council Resolution 1645* UN Doc S/Res/1645(2005), December 20, 2005.
13. Karen Engle, "Liberal Internationalism, Feminism, and the Suppression of Critique: Contemporary Approaches to Global Order in the United States," *Harvard International Law Journal* 46, no. 2 (2005): 427; Vasuki Nesiah, "From Berlin to Bonn to Baghdad: A Space for Infinite Justice," *Harvard Human Rights Journal* 17 (2004): 75.
14. United Nations, *SC Res 1272* (1999) on the Situation in East Timor. An interim United Nations presence had been provided for earlier in 1999 in the May agreements between Indonesia, Portugal, and the United Nations about the conduct of the elections. See "Agreement between the Republic of Indonesia and the Portuguese Republic on the Question of East Timor," May 5, 1999, http://www.un.org/peace/etimor99/agreement/agreeFrame_Eng01.html, Art. 6 (accessed March 12, 2008).

15. United Nations, SC Res 1272, para. 15.
16. United Nations, "Windhoek Declaration and the Namibia Plan of Action," (presented to Mainstreaming a Gender Perspective in Multidimensional Peace Support Operations Seminar, Windhoek, Namibia, May, 29–2000), http://www.un.org/womenwatch/osagi/wps/windhoek_declaration.pdf (accessed March 12, 2008).
17. Commission for Reception, Truth and Reconciliation (CAVR), *Chega! Report on East Timor*, 2006, http://www.ictj.org/en/news/features/846.html, provides significant evidence of sexual violence during the occupation (see in particular Chapter 7.7). See also UNIFEM Timor Leste Country Report, http://www.womenwarpeace.org/timor_leste/timor_leste.htm (accessed March 12, 2008).
18. United Nations, *Report of the Independent Commission of Inquiry on East Timor to the Secretary-General*, UN Doc. A/54/726 (2000); Seth Mydans, "Sexual Violence as a Tool of War: Pattern Emerging in East Timor," *New York Times*, March 1, 2001.
19. Susan Harris Rimmer, "East Timorese Women and Transitional Justice," in *Global Issues: Women and Justice*, ed. Sharon Pickering and Caroline Lambert (Sydney: Institute of Criminology, 2004), 335, 339.
20. Maggie O'Kane, "Return of the Revolutionaries," *Guardian Weekly*, January 15, 2001.
21. Tracy Fitzsimmons, "Engendering Justice and Security After War," in *Constructing Justice and Security After War*, ed. Charles T. Call (Washington, DC: U. S. Institute of Peace Press, 2007), 351, 353.
22. Sherrill Whittington, "Gender and Peacekeeping: The United Nations Transitional Administration in East Timor," *Signs: Journal of Women in Culture and Society* 28, no. 4 (2003): 1283.
23. Harris Rimmer, "East Timorese Women," 16.
24. UNTAET internal memo, September 7, 2000.
25. Hilary Charlesworth and Mary Wood, "Women and Human Rights in the Rebuilding of East Timor," *Nordic Journal of International Law* 71 (2002): 325.
26. Heather Wallace, "Gender and the Reform Process in Vanuatu and Solomon Islands," *Development Bulletin* 51 (March 2000): 23; Suzette Mitchell, "Women in Leadership in Vietnam," *Development Bulletin* 51 (March 2000): 30; Anne Hellum, "Human Rights and Gender Relations in Postcolonial Africa: Options and Limits for the Subjects of Legal Pluralism," *Law and Social Inquiry* 25 (2000): 635.
27. Kay Rala Xanana Gusmão, *New Year's Message*, December 31, 2000, http://www.pcug.org.au/~wildwood/JanNewYear.htm (accessed March 12, 2008).
28. Milena Pires, "Strategic Development Plan for East Timor," (paper presented at Conselho Nacional de Resistencia Timorese Conference, Dili, August 2000).
29. Jonathan Morrow and Rachel White, "The United Nations in Transitional East Timor: International Standards and the Reality of Governance," *Australian Yearbook of International Law* 22 (2002): 1–46.
30. "Campaign to Support Women's Rights in the Commission," *La'O Hamutuk Bulletin* 5, no. 2, August 2001, http://www.laohamutuk.org/Bulletin/2001/Aug/bulletinv2n5.html#Campaign%20to%20Support% 20Women'20Rights%20in%20Constitution (accessed March 12, 2008).

31. Ibid., section 63.
32. Rede Feto (Women's Network) Timor Leste, *Letter to Ian Martin, Special Envoy of the UN Secretary-General for Timor Leste,* July 7, 2006, http://www.etan.org/et2006/july/22/21letter.html (accessed March 12, 2008).
33. David Frum, *The Right Man: The Surprise Presidency of George W. Bush* (New York: Random House, 2003).
34. Paula Dobriansky, *Women and the Transition to Democracy: Iraq, Afghanistan, and Beyond,* Heritage Foundation Lecture to the Conservative Women's Network, June 2003, http://www.heritage.org/Research/MiddleEast/HL793.cfm (accessed March 12, 2008).
35. Basma Fakri, *Letter to Ambassador Lakhdar Brahimi, Chief Representative, Special Envoy to Iraq,* May 12, 2004, http://i.b5z.net/i/u/2003095/i/pdf/Election_commission_1_.pdf (accessed March 12, 2008).
36. Swanee Hunt and Cristina Posa, "Iraq's Excluded Women," *Foreign Policy* 143 (July/August 2004): 40.
37. Hunt and Posa, "Iraq's Excluded Women," 40; Isobel Coleman, "Women, Islam, and the New Iraq," *Foreign Affairs* 85, no. 1 (January/Feb ruary 2006): 24, 35.
38. Iraqi Constitution, 2005, Article 20. http://www.uniraq.org/documents/iraqi_constitution.pdf
39. Ibid., Article 14.
40. Ibid., Article 47.
41. Ibid., Article 14.
42. Ibid., Article 2. The religious parties argued strongly that Islam be recognized as *the* source of legislation, while the Kurds and secular groups supported a reference to Islam as *a* source. The indefinite article was finally used after pressure from the United States. Coleman, "Women, Islam," 37, 30.
43. Iraqi Constitution, 2005, Article 2.
44. An attempt was made by the Iraq Governing Council in 2003 to overturn the 1959 personal status law and replace it with *Sharia* law. A resolution adopted by the Council to this effect was eventually vetoed by Paul Bremer, head of the Coalition Provisional Authority after intensive lobbying by Iraqi women's groups.
45. Iraqi Constitution, 2005, Article 39.
46. Ibid., Article 19
47. Ibid., Article 89.
48. Simona Sharoni, "The Empowering and Disempowering Effects of Conflict and Violence," (paper presented to the Gender, Armed Conflict, and Political Violence Conference, World Bank, Washington DC, June 10–11, 1999), 1.
49. Ibid., 7.
50. United Nations. *Press Release from the Secretariat on the Secretary-General's Address to the Special Meeting of the Security Council Meeting on Women and Peace and Security.* UN Doc. SG/SM/7598, October 24, 2000.
51. Cynthia Enloe, *Maneuvers: The International Politics of Militarizing Women's Lives* (Berkeley: University of California Press, 2000), 294.
52. Sumie Nakaya, "Women and Gender Equality in Peacebuilding: Somalia and Mozambique," in *Building Sustainable Peace,* ed. Tom Keating and W. Andy Knight (Tokyo: UNUP, 2004), 143.

53. Gihane Tabet, "Women in Personal Status Laws: Iraq, Jordan, Lebanon, Palestine, Syria," *SHS Papers in Women's Studies/Gender Research*, 4 (Paris: UNESCO, July 2005), 11–12.
54. United Nations Development Program, *Arab Human Development Report: Creating Opportunities for future Generations* (New York: United Nations Publications, 2002). In 2002, women held almost 20 percent of the parliamentary seats in Iraq compared to the 3.5 percent average for Arab states.
55. Noah Feldman, *After Jihad: American and the Struggle for Islamic Democracy* (New York: Farrar, Straus and Giroux, 2003), 29–33.
56. Ibid., 29–30.
57. Madhavi Sunder, "Enlightened Constitutionalism," *Connecticut Law Review* 37, no. 4 (2005): 891, 892.
58. Ibid., 895.
59. Arati Rao, "The Politics of Gender and Culture in International Human Rights Discourse," in *Women's Rights Human Rights: International Feminist Perspectives*, ed. Julie Peters and Andrea Wolper (New York: Routledge, 1995), 167.
60. Hilary Charlesworth and Christine Chinkin, "Regulatory Frameworks in International Law," in *Regulating Law*, ed. Christine Parker et al. (Melbourne: Oxford University Press, 2004), 246; Tammy Smith, "Post-War Bosnia and Herzegovina: The Erosion of Women's Rights under International Governance," *Critical Half* 38(2005): 2, 3.
61. Nayaka, "Women and Gender," 146.
62. Iris Marion Young, *Justice and the Politics of Difference* (Princeton: Princeton University Press, 1990), 195.
63. Christine Chinkin and Hilary Charlesworth, "Building Women into Peace: The International Legal Framework," *Third World Quarterly* 27 no. 5 (2006): 937.
64. The wording is taken from a General Assembly Resolution on Afghanistan after the Soviet invasion in 1979. GA Res. ES-6 2, January 14, 1980.
65. Lori Handrahan, "Rhetoric and Reality: Post-Conflict Recovery and Development—the UN and Gender Reform," in *The UN, Human Rights and Post-Conflict Situations*, ed. Nigel D. White and Dirk Klaasen (Huntington, NY: Juris Publishing, 2005), 404, 414–18.
66. Hilary Charlesworth, "Not Waving but Drowning: Gender Mainstreaming and Human Rights," *Harvard Human Rights Journal* 18 (2005): 1.
67. United Nations, *Platform for Action, ECOSOC Agreed Conclusions* 1997/2 (1997) http://www.un.org/womenwatch/osagi/pdf/ECOSOCAC1997.2.PDF (accessed March 12, 2008).
68. Elizabeth Reid, "Transformational Development and the Wellbeing of Women," *Development Bulletin* 64 (2004): 19.
69. Alison Woodward, "Gender Mainstreaming in European Policy: Innovation or Deception?" Wissenschaftzentrum Berlin fur Sozialforschung Discussion Paper FS I (2001), 22.
70. See Mark Pollack and Emilie Hafner-Burton, "Mainstreaming Gender in Global Governance," *European Journal of International Relations* 8 (2002), 339–73.

71. United Nations, *Rome Statute of the International Criminal Court*, ICC-ASP/2/Res.3, September 12, 2003. Article 7 (3). http://www.icc- cpi.int/library/about/officialjournal/Rome_Statute_120704-EN.pdf (accessed March 12, 2008).
72. Nicola Lacey, "Feminist Legal Theory and the Rights of Women," in *Gender and Human Rights*, ed. Karen Knop (Oxford: Oxford University Press, 2004), 13.
73. Margaret Davies, "Taking the Inside Out: Sex and Gender in the Legal Subject," in *Sexing the Subject of Law*, ed. Ngaire Naffine and Rosemary Owens (Sydney: Law Book Company, 1997), 27.
74. Sally Baden and Anne Marie Goetz, "Who Needs [Sex] When You Can Have [Gender]?" *Feminist Review* 56 (1997): 3, 7.
75. United Nations, "Windhoek Declaration."
76. Jacqui True, "Mainstreaming Gender in Global Public Policy," *International Feminist Journal of Politics* 5, no. 3 (2003): 368, 373.
77. Carol Cohn, "War, Wimps and Women," 227; Hilary Charlesworth and Christine Chinkin, "Sex, Gender, and September 11," *American Journal of International Law* 96 (2002): 600–605.
78. United Nations, *Women and Peace and Security: Report of the Secretary-General*, UN Doc. S/2004/814, 1, October 13, 2004; See also United Nations, *Report of the Secretary-General on Women, Peace and Security* UN Doc S/2006/770, September 27, 2006.
79. Ibid.
80. Ibid., paragraph 13.
81. Ibid., paragraph 48.
82. Ibid., paragraph 90.
83. Martti Koskenniemi, "Book review of Dallmeyer, Dorinda ed. Reconceiving Reality: Women and International Law," *American Journal of International Law* 89 (1995): 227, 230.

CHAPTER 3

Gendered Economies in the Asia-Pacific

V. Spike Peterson

This chapter provides a view of how economies in the Asia-Pacific are gendered by pursuing three questions. First, What macrotrends can we identify as effects of neoliberal globalization policies? Second and more specifically, How are these trends reconstituting identities, ideologies, and practices associated with socially necessary labor, informalization, migration, and financial flows in the Asia-Pacific? And third, What are the gendered and economic implications of these developments?

To develop the argument I draw on analytical framing from my recent book, *A Critical Rewriting of Global Political Economy: Integrating Reproductive, Productive and Virtual Economies*,[1] which attempts to demonstrate the interdependence of these—reproductive, productive, and virtual (RPV)—economies, and to advance critical theory by illuminating the intersection of race, gender, and economic inequalities (within and among states) as structural features of globalization. I note here that this framing refers not to conventional but Foucauldian economies: mutually constituted (and therefore interactive) systemic sites through and across which power operates. These sites involve familiar exchanges but also include sociocultural processes of subject formation and cultural socialization that underpin identities and shape interactive practices. The conceptual and cultural dimensions of these sites are inextricable from material effects, social practices, and institutional structures. The primary objective of this work is to illumine the co-constitution of culture and economy, the interaction of identification processes and their politics, and the importance of a feminist, postcolonial, and poststructuralist orientation for exposing the operating codes of neoliberal capitalism.

I first situate the book and introduce alternative analytics. I then use the RPV framing and empirical data to address the questions posed above and illuminate gendered economies in the Asia-Pacific. This abbreviated presentation necessarily favors major trends and patterns over the complexity of lived processes, especially for a region as diverse as the Asia-Pacific. I hope, nonetheless, that identifying macropatterns can productively inform a regional analysis, and begin to illumine developments at the microlevel of individuals and families.

Rewriting Global Political Economy

With other critical scholars I argue that dominant accounts of global political economy (GPE) perpetuate economistic, modernist/positivist, and masculinist commitments that preclude adequate analyses of restructuring at regional or global levels.[2] On one hand, I argue that a more expansive 'RPV framing' is necessary to address two central *trends*: explosive growth in financialization,[3] which shapes business decision-making and public policymaking; and dramatic growth in informalization,[4] which shapes income-generation and family well-being. While these developments are widely recognized, they are rarely analyzed *in relation*. In contrast, RPV framing provides a way to see household reproduction, informal activities, migration flows, remittances and capital mobility as interacting dimensions of regional and global processes.

On the other hand, I argue that two central *features* of globalization expose the inadequacy of conventional orientations. First, today's globalization is distinguished by its dependence on information and communication technologies (ICT) specific to the late twentieth century. Due to the inherently conceptual/cultural nature of information, not only empirical but also analytical challenges are posed by the unprecedented fusion of culture and economy—of virtual and material dimensions—afforded by ICTs. In brief, the symbolic/virtual aspects of today's GPE expose—to a unique extent and in new developments—how conventional (positivist) separation of culture from economy are (more than ever) problematized and how interpretive/poststructural/postmodern[5] lenses are essential for adequately analyzing today's GPE. Second, globalization and its effects are extremely uneven; this is starkly manifest in global intersecting stratifications of ethnicity/race, class, gender, and nation. Advocates of globalization avoid theorizing about the nature and role of oppression in relation to neoliberal policies. Critics tend to focus on one aspect of these hierarchies or at best 'add' one aspect to another. The point here is that theoretical attention to hierarchies as a *structural* feature of globalization, especially their *intersections*, remains underdeveloped;[6] in this sense, not only a poststructuralist but also a critical feminist, postcolonial orientation is essential.

Specifically, to investigate the interconnections among structural hierarchies I deploy gender analytically, arguing that denigration of the feminine (coded into masculinist/modernist dichotomies as hierarchical) pervades language and culture, with systemic effects on how we 'take for granted,' that is, normalize and depoliticize, the devalorization of feminized bodies, identities, and activities.[7] This has particular relevance for gendered economies, in which assessments of value are key. *I argue that feminization of identities and practices effectively devalues them in cultural as well as economic terms.* In short, under neoliberal globalization the taken-for-granted devalorization of so-called women's work is generalized from women to include feminized 'others': migrants, marginalized populations, 'unskilled' workers, the urban underclass, and developing countries. Women and feminized others constitute the vast majority of the world's population, as well as the vast majority of poor, less skilled, insecure, informalized, and flexibilized workers; and the global economy absolutely depends on the work that they do. Yet their work is variously unpaid, underpaid, trivialized, denigrated, obscured and uncounted: it is devalorized. This economic devalorization is either hardly noticed or deemed 'acceptable' because it is consistent with cultural devalorization of that which is feminized. The key point here is that feminization devalorizes not only women but also racially, culturally, and economically marginalized men and work that is deemed unskilled, menial, and 'merely' reproductive.

In summary, RPV framing brings the conceptual and material dimensions of 'social reproduction,' non-wage labor, and informalization *into relation with* the increasingly global, flexibilized, information-based, and service-oriented 'productive economy,' as well as with the increasingly consequential 'virtual economy' of financial markets, commodified knowledge, and the exchange of cultural codes/signs. Including the reproductive economy invites attention to otherwise marginalized agents and activities, and acknowledges especially the importance of gender-sensitive research and analysis. Including the virtual economy addresses developments in 'symbolic money,' informationalism, and the commodification of intangibles and aesthetics. It acknowledges the importance of poststructuralist approaches for analyzing how symbols and expectations mediate our constructions of 'value.'

While RPV framing is more specific to rewriting global political economy, I also deploy a second analytical innovation, 'triad analytics,' which is applicable to social relations more generally. To facilitate a shift from the binary tendencies of conventional framing, triad analytics posits identities (subjectivity, self-formation, desires), meaning systems (symbols, discourse, ideologies), and social practices/institutions (actions, social structures) as *co-constituting* dimensions of social reality. Stated simply, the triad insists on fully *integrating* who we are, how we think, and what we do.[8] It is particularly useful for illuminating how identities involve emotional and normative investments that 'matter.'

Briefly, in this chapter globalization refers to large-scale transnational processes occurring today at an accelerated pace (due to ICTs) with extremely uneven effects (due to continuing and new inequalities). The uneven effects are exacerbated by neoliberal policies—deregulation, liberalization, privatization—that constitute global capitalism as market fundamentalism. Neoliberalism is advocated primarily by geopolitical elites in the interest of powerful states and the inter- and trans-national institutions they effectively control. Deregulation permits the hypermobility of ('foot-loose') capital, induces phenomenal growth in financialization, and increases the power of private capital interests. Liberalization is selectively implemented: powerful states engage in protectionism while developing countries have limited control over protecting domestic industries and the jobs they provide. Privatization entails the loss of nationalized industries in developing economies, decrease in public sector employment, and a worldwide decrease of social services. The results of restructuring are complex, uneven, and controversial. While economic growth is the objective and has been realized in some areas amd sectors, evidence increasingly suggests growing inequalities, indeed a polarization, of resources within and between countries.[9]

RPV Economies, Major Trends, and the Asia-Pacific Region

I now turn to macrotrends of neoliberal globalization as rendered by RPV framing, with particular attention to gendered economies in the Asia-Pacific. It is crucial to note at the outset that this region is marked by stark contrasts and extraordinary diversity. The Asia-Pacific includes very small and very large national economies; very small and very large populations and land masses; advanced industrialized countries with leading ICT sectors, newly industrialized countries (NIC) with a variety of manufacturing and technological sectors, and developing countries with minimal infrastructure; democratic, authoritarian, militarized, and socialist regimes; former imperial nations, former settler colonies, and numerous neocolonial arrangements. The region is additionally marked by offshore banking facilities and global giants of finance; extensive emigration, immigration, and foreign remittance flows; thriving drug industries and trafficking rings, entrenched organized crime networks, and the world's 'worst record on forced labor.'[10] And it is diverse in sociocultural terms: ancient civilizations and relative newcomers; longstanding and emerging diasporas; disparate linguistic, aesthetic, ideological, and spiritual traditions; large and complex Islamic, Confucian, and Christian communities; and a dizzying array of family forms, generational dynamics, and household structures.

Given this heterogeneity, no simple generalizations regarding the region or its articulation into global capitalism can be sustained. Rather, various countries within the region, and various groups within those countries, experience, mirror, and may contradict the identified macrotrends in ways that are always conditioned by local context.[11] Gender shapes, and is shaped by, the patterns as well as the exceptions. In the Asia-Pacific, gender and its effects are particularly visible and significant in relation to processes of socially necessary labor, informalization, migration, and financial flows. I therefore foreground these in the elaboration of RPV trends and in the concluding discussion.

Productive Economy (PrE)

Because it is the focus of conventional economic analysis, the productive economy is most familiar. These economic accounts are concerned with prominent shifts in formalized work and market-based exchanges. First, declining world prices and demand for (non-oil) primary products have devastated economies where primary production dominates. Typical effects include decreased ability to attract foreign investment, increased debt dependency, and deteriorating conditions of employment such that governments may encourage emigration in search of work. Many countries in the Asia-Pacific exemplify these trends and especially the emigration of temporary migrants in search of economic opportunities in other countries within and outside of the region. As Pettman notes, "The 'export of women' from states such as the Philippines, Indonesia, and Sri Lanka is part of the international politics of debt, and of poorer states' search for hard currency in the form of remittances, as well as reflecting lack of employment opportunities at home."[12]

Second, de-industrialization in advanced economies involves downsizing, relocation of production to lower wage areas, loss of skilled and unionized positions, and a dramatic shift from jobs in manufacturing to services. The latter fuels income polarization between an elite tier of skilled (high technology and information-based) professionals and a larger bottom tier of informal, low-wage, and semi- and unskilled (feminized) workers. Differential access to education, training, and career opportunities structures who does what work and for the most part tends to reinforce historical inequalities of gender, race, class, and national location.[13] But there are unexpected outcomes as well. Consider, for example, how geopolitical histories favorably positioned Indians and Filipinos as educated and English-speaking workers in global labor markets.

Third, job security is eroded for all but elite workers through 'flexibilization': more temporary, part-time, and non-unionized jobs with fewer benefits, and more subcontracted production processes. Increasing un- and under-employment (especially of men), flexibilization, and erosion or prohibition of union power translate into a decline in real incomes and household resources for the majority. Flexibilization may be attractive to those with highly valued skills but worldwide it is feminized—with reference to both degraded conditions of employment and women being sought as employees.[14] It is also racialized and geopolitically differentiated with reference to concentrations of flexibilized jobs (among the urban lower class, migrants, and semi-peripheral countries). Trade liberalization and structural adjustment policies (SAP) illustrate, and also complicate, these patterns.[15]

Fourth, globalization increases flows of people to urban areas, export-processing zones, high wage areas, and tourist destinations. Migrations are shaped by colonial histories, geopolitics, immigration policies, capital flows, labor markets, cultural stereotypes, skill attributions, kinship networks, and identity markers. The temporary migration of service workers is associated with enormous growth in foreign remittances, which improves both household and national economies 'at home.' Given the nature of 'unskilled' jobs most frequently available (cleaning, harvesting, domestic service, care labor, and sex work), migrant worker populations are especially marked by gender, race, and ethnicity. Being on the move—for work or recreation or escape—affects personal and collective identities and cultural reproduction. Not least, traditional family forms and divisions of labor are disrupted, destabilizing men's and women's identities and gender relations more generally. Shifting identities have complex effects at numerous levels, whether expressed in anti-immigrant racism, nationalist state-building, ethno-cultural diasporas or patriarchal religious fundamentalisms.

In the Asia-Pacific, these trends take a variety of forms. They are often encouraged by governmental policies and regional development plans; countries experiencing high un- and under-employment 'export' seasonal agricultural laborers and service workers (Pacific Islands and East Timor) to areas where labor is in demand (New Zealand and Australia).[16] The flow of remittances in the region, as well as the growth of a commercial industry in support of trade-related remittance channels, link the PrE and VE and are important aspects of economic activity. Migration for work is both internal—rural to urban—and international; most migration occurs through personal and kinship networks. Today "half of all the world's migrants are women."[17] In the Asia-Pacific region, women 'often' outnumber men, making up "over half of Filipino migrants to all countries and 84 percent of Sri Lankan migrants to the Middle East."[18] Regional migration and work arrangements are more likely to be formal and legal when skilled labor is involved, which is particularly evident in the migration of nurses. Illicit informal networks also operate, exemplified by trafficking in drugs, humans, body organs, expropriated natural resources, and small arms. These in turn depend on and produce money laundering and other financial practices that evade regulatory authorities. While only recently addressed in conventional accounts, the economic, political, and sociocultural impact of illicit economies is staggering and, unfortunately, growing.[19]

Reproductive Economy (RE)

The reproductive economy is typically neglected in conventional accounts, which are preoccupied with masculinized waged labor, formal markets, and public sphere activities. The RE involves essential social reproduction and informal economic activities (the latter merge with flexibilization in the PrE), and the productive and virtual economies depend on it in non-trivial ways (e.g., to produce appropriately socialized workers and desiring consumers; to provide socially necessary but not socialized welfare and caretaking). Shifting public-private boundaries reveal both the significance of social reproduction for political-economic analysis, and the impact of global restructuring on social reproduction, especially gender relations.[20] Not least, women who voluntarily and otherwise assume a 'breadwinner' role profoundly disrupt traditional divisions of labor, patriarchal norms, and identity investments.

Social reproduction involves learning the codes of a particular cultural environment; family life is where this learning and subject formation begins and the 'ordering' (language, cultural rules, and ideologies) we acritically imbibe in childhood is especially influential. This is the primary site of gender acculturation and is inextricable from beliefs about sexuality, race/ethnicity, class, religion, nationalism, and other axes of 'difference.' Subject formation matters structurally for neoliberalism. It produces individuals who are then able to 'work' and this unpaid reproductive labor saves capital the costs of producing labor inputs. Socialization and the caring labor required to sustain family relations are stereotyped as 'women's work' worldwide. Yet in spite of romanticized motherhood and pro-family rhetoric, neoliberal globalization reduces the emotional, cultural, and material resources necessary for the well-being of most women and families. Indeed, there is increasing evidence that women work a triple shift, of 'formal, informal, and family or subsistence activities.'[21]

As PrE trends indicate, conditions of employment, real incomes, job security, and labor power are deteriorating for the majority worldwide. Deregulation and privatization undercut welfare provisioning, state employment, and collective supports for family well-being. As families confront shrinking economic resources, gender stereotypes assign women disproportionate responsibility for family survival—they are expected to absorb the costs of restructuring and often do so through informal or flexibilized work. Consider the state's promotion of Confucian ideology in Taiwan and 'ibuism' in Indonesia to reinforce traditional gender obligations and roles.[22] As a result, many women are pushed to engage in informal activities as a household survival strategy. At the same time, a pull factor emerges as women who enjoy formal, well-paid jobs increasingly rely on domestic and caring labor provided by others, that is, feminized workers who are often migrants. As Ehrenreich and Hochschild put it: "The lifestyles of the First World are made possible by a global transfer of the services associated with a wife's traditional role—child care, home-making, and sex—from poor countries to rich ones."[23]

The transfer of all three of these 'wifely services' is notable in the Asia-Pacific, where migration is extensive. Tracking women's migration patterns, Piper observes that female foreign workers are "channeled into gender-specific jobs or female-dominated sectors. . . . [For skilled women] nursing is the most female-dominated sector. . . . As unskilled migrants, most women migrate as domestic or care workers, or as 'entertainers.'"[24] Domestic work has indeed become a global industry, and the maid trade is "a multimillion-dollar transnational business which is closely related to other agencies that facilitate the migration process, such as banks, money-lenders, hotels, airlines, illegal money-changers, translation services, medical clinics, and training institutions."[25] Domestic work also constitutes an important source of foreign remittances. In the Asia-Pacific, women from various countries seek work as maids or domestics, traveling within and outside of the region: from Bangladesh, Sri Lanka, Indonesia, Philippines to Hong Kong, Malaysia and Singapore as well as to Kuwait, Saudi Arabia, and Europe.[26]

But in spite of providing socially necessary labor, domestic workers—especially migrants—typically reap modest benefits and face multiple hardships. In general, they are poorly paid, work long and arduous hours, are separated from their own families and communities, lack control over resources sent back home, face pressures to 'behave' while away, and have few protections against abusive employers. Domestic work is also problematic socioculturally and politically, especially for feminists. First, it is work done in the 'private sphere' where 'outsiders' are conventionally neither expected nor welcome. Second, commercializing labor that is presumably done for love is uncomfortable. Moreover, while paying 'other'—often non-citizen—women for these services avoids disrupting gendered divisions of labor within the household, it exacerbates class (and often racial and national) divisions among women, as well as relieving pressure on states to support social reproduction. These dynamics are further complicated by the fact that many domestic workers are themselves married women with children.[27] Drawing global linkages, Pettman argues that domestic workers' "support of social reproduction and of particular families in the rich states is at the expense of their own families at home, and a drain of resources, skills and energy from their poorer states."[28] Third, who hires and who serves may reflect colonial histories (black maids of white madams in South Africa) or new geopolitical hierarchies of international debt and employment opportunities (Filipino maids in Saudi Arabia). As Anderson observes, "racist stereotypes intersect with issues of citizenship, and result in a racist hierarchy which uses skin color, religion, and nationality to construct some women as being more suitable for domestic work than others."[29]

If domestic workers provide the wifely services of childcare and homemaking, many other women in the Asia-Pacific provide feminized services associated with 'entertainment' and sex. Women may undertake sexual and sex work on a part-time basis, as a full-time 'job' or in the case of Japanese schoolgirls, as occasional 'prostitution' in the form of 'telephone clubs.'[30] These women share some of the hardships identified for domestic workers, but in addition are frequently trafficked, more vulnerable to health problems and physical harm, and more subject to cultural devalorization both in their 'home' and 'host' countries. A now extensive literature reveals the increasing volume of sex work, its dependence on racial and heterosexist stereotypes, its relationship to labor markets and migration flows, and its costs in health and, especially, in vulnerable women's and children's lives.[31] The sex trade is gendered and raced, and also nationalized insofar as particular countries promote sex tourism and hence, provide significant 'employment' opportunities and accrue substantial foreign earnings.

What is less interrogated is the demand side, primarily shaped by men's expectations regarding sexual services—from hospitality hostesses and erotic entertainment to temporary or permanent rights over a woman's body—and the economic resources to acquire such services. Supply and demand thus mirror familiar economic hierarchies, with richer men and states as buyers and poorer women and states as sellers. The profits generated return primarily to rich states, organized crime, and transnational corporations associated with the tourist industry.[32]

In addition to 'unskilled' domestic and sexual workers, the Asia-Pacific is marked by extensive migration of skilled workers, most notably women who are healthcare providers. The demand for childcare, home-making, and sexual services is part of a larger 'care deficit,' which is emerging globally. Even as economic conditions push and pull more women into full-time employment, and the size of dependent populations increases (due to environmental, epidemiological, and demographic trends), public services in support of childcare, healthcare, eldercare, and family well-being are declining. In particular, "for the ill and elderly, care of the body has created a global market for nurses and healthcare paraprofessionals, recruited from . . . India, South Korea, and China, in response to the growing demand for health care services in wealthy nations."[33] At the same time, there is a 'care drain' as "women who normally care for the young, the old, and the sick in their own poor countries move to care for the young, the old, and the sick in rich countries."[34]

Migration of healthcare professionals serves some at the expense of others. Receiving countries improve healthcare delivery and at minimal expense: they are not paying the costs of training (which are borne by sending states) and insofar as migrant workers have less bargaining power than citizens they will accept lower wages. Sending countries gain when remittances are significant, and nurses are especially 'good remitters,'[35] but they also lose costly, often scarce, and extremely valuable healthcare providers in their own countries, which can have catastrophic consequences in the face of pandemic threats.[36] While individuals and families in receiving countries are able to access much-needed and valued care of the ill and elderly, this represents a loss of access and care for others. In the Asia-Pacific, Aiken et al. observe that English-speaking countries, including Australia and New Zealand, "predict needing more nurses than they are producing and retaining; their predicted nurse requirements are large enough to deplete the supply of qualified nurses throughout the developing world";[37] that "host countries have at least twice as many nurses for the populations as the source countries";[38] and that "an estimated 85 percent of employed Filipino nurses . . . are working internationally."[39]

It is not simply that healthcare provision is depleted where it is comparatively most needed—in poor source countries. It is also that "the quality of family life progressively declines as care is passed down the international division of care work"[40] and migrant women and their children pay a steep personal price through isolation and alienation. Finally, there is a systemic cost when (feminized) caring labor is devalued: "the low market value of care keeps the status of women who do it—and ultimately, all women—low."[41]

The RE involves socially necessary, intimate, caring, and informal labor. The latter is heterogeneous and controversial, not least because it *blurs* conventional boundaries separating public and private, licit and illicit, production and reproduction, national and international. The key issue here is explosive growth in informal activities and its implications for global hierarchies. While estimates vary, several measures indicate that informal activities constitute more than one-half of all economic output and 75 percent of the gross domestic product of some countries.[42] Given this scale, there can be little doubt that informalization *matters*. For example, avoidance of taxes decreases public revenues and affects distribution of resources; unregulated work practices pose safety, health, and environmental risks; criminal activities thwart collective interests in law and order; and critics argue that informalization decreases the structural power of workers, reaps higher profits for capital, depresses formal wages, disciplines all workers, and through the isolation of informalized labor, impedes collective resistance.

Women, the poor, migrants, and recent immigrants are the prototypical (feminized) workers of the RE, and informalization mirrors and reproduces intersections of ethnicity, race, gender, class, and national hierarchies.[43] Yet, and especially in the Asia-Pacific, states often tolerate various expressions of informalization and even cultivate particular entrepreneurial activities.

Virtual Economy (VE)

This economy is least familiar to noneconomists yet crucial to analyzing globalization; it is characterized by flows of symbols, information, and communication through electronic and wireless transmissions that defy territorial constraints. The scale and velocity of these transmissions as well as the symbolic, virtual nature of these processes expose the inadequacy of conventional orientations. Intangible symbols contravene familiar notions of time and space as well as conventional analyses of material goods. In short, the virtual economy effectively forces analysts to adopt a poststructuralist lens, which takes symbols seriously. Hence, we need an interpretive, poststructuralist approach to address the vastly expanded role of symbolic goods like money, information, and signs in today's global political economy.

There are three modes of the virtual economy: global finance (with reference to the history, operation, and implications of transnational capital movements), the informational economy (with reference to the informational component of commodities and knowledge itself as a commodity), and the aestheticized consumerism of signs (with reference to the production and consumption of ephemeral, ever changing tastes, desires, fashion, and style). For the purposes of this chapter, I focus on the first mode, financial transactions, especially foreign remittances, to explore its links to social reproduction and informalization.[44]

Briefly, since the 1970s floating exchange rates, reduced capital controls, offshore transactions, desegmentation, new financial instruments, securitization, and the rise of institutional investors have interacted to amplify the speed and complexity of transnational capital flows. The effects of financialization are many.

The allure of financial trading exacerbates the devalorization of manufacturing, and encourages short-term over long-term investments in industry and infrastructure. The opportunity to profit from transnational trade in workers and associated financial flows spawns institutional and commercial infrastructures. The foreign remittances of temporary and permanent migrants increase in volume and in their implications for local, national, and transnational development.

The value of remittances has grown sharply in recent decades; in developing countries the official flow of remittances has doubled in the past five years.[45] When both official and informal channels are included, the World Bank estimates remittances to developing countries in 2005 may have exceeded US $250 billion.[46] In the Asia-Pacific, four South Asian countries—Bangladesh, India, Pakistan, and Sri Lanka—are among the world's top twenty receivers of remittances,[47] with India reporting "a spectacular increase in remittance inflows—from $13 billion in 2001 to more than $20 billion in 2003."[48] It is widely recognized that the Philippines' economic development policies explicitly depend on remittances for foreign currency earnings. Maclellan observes that Fiji's economy increasingly depends on remittances from overseas workers; these currently 'run to more than F$200 million a year,' hence earning more than hard-hit traditional sectors of sugar production and garment manufacturing.[49]

The value of remittances in the Asia-Pacific is quite substantial, and of course there are multiple, and controversial, effects. Orthodox economists tend to view remittances favorably, not least because migrants "can earn salaries that reflect industrial-country prices and spend the money in developing countries where prices are lower."[50] As noted concerning healthcare workers, destination countries benefit from migrant workers because of the increased availability of labor and reduced costs of production. Sending countries benefit by the reduction of unemployment pressures, the increased availability of foreign currency, and poverty reduction. In addition, "migration helps households diversify their sources of income (and thus reduce their vulnerability to risks) while providing a much needed source of savings and capital for investment."[51] Finally, remittances are important in terms of making households as well as receiving countries more creditworthy. In short, remittances are particularly significant in the gendered economies of the Asia-Pacific, and gender is especially visible insofar as women constitute the majority of migrant workers generating these payments.

Globally, the deregulation, expansion, and nontransparency of global financial transactions enables "foot-loose" capital and makes money laundering easier, which enhances opportunities for illicit financial trading as well as organized crime. Increasing urgency in regard to 'managing money' and investment strategies shifts status and decision-making power within households, businesses, governments, and global institutions. These changes disrupt conventional identities, functions, and sites of authority. Of particular relevance is the increasing authority and power of financial agents, practices and institutions—including women who are primary earners and who determine how household income is distributed. Also important are the risks of financial crises, as the Asia-Pacific knows very well, and the ominous power of organized criminal networks. The illicit international political economy is a growing phenomenon that not only affects those subject to drug addiction and human trafficking, but all who are subject to conflicts and terrorism that are increasingly financed by illicit informalization.

Concluding Discussion

The gendered economies of the Asia-Pacific shape, and are shaped by, neoliberal globalization. Macrotrends as well as exceptions and variations are visible through an analytical framing that integrates RPV economies. In this chapter I have emphasized socially necessary labor, informalization, migration, and financial flows to illuminate the gendered economies of the Asia-Pacific. I conclude with points that link the RPV economies in this context.

First, socially necessary and informal labor in the reproductive economy is a condition of—and not coincidental to—the so-called productive economy. To adequately understand either economy, we must analyze their interaction and take 'feminized' work seriously, whether done by women or marginalized men. The point is not simply that feminized labor is un- and underpaid but that the larger crisis in social reproduction is powerfully shaped by gender identities. Key here is the significance of masculine identities that prevent men from undertaking a larger, and urgently needed, role in domestic labor.

Second, reproductive and productive economies overlap because the ideologies of gendered and racialized divisions of labor are deployed throughout both to structure and depoliticize hierarchical arrangements. While this tends to reproduce structural inequalities, it is always subject to disruption (for example, when women become primary wage earners or when they are empowered by new opportunities). Racialized geopolitical hierarchies may also be reproduced, as informalization and temporary migration tend to favor rich country accumulation without significantly advancing poor country development.

Third, these gendered, racialized linkages are particularly visible in relation to reduced public welfare in the context of global restructuring and the dynamics of the virtual economy. The 'leaner and meaner' practices of neoliberalism have devastating (though not homogeneous) effects on women as a structurally vulnerable population, as the care-takers of society's dependent members, and as the 'buffers' when economic conditions deteriorate. Although these conditions typically exacerbate the feminization of poverty, they may also promote social change by politicizing gendered and racialized linkages among households, states, and global dynamics.

Fourth, reproductive and informal labor enables the productive economy *and* the accumulation of wealth that underpins the virtual economy. This is especially evident when we consider VE remittances and their multiplier effects in both countries of origin and destination. While reproduction, informalization, and production constitute the basis of accumulation, the virtual economy structurally shapes the work undertaken—and the value it is accorded—in the reproductive and productive economies; all these economies are interdependent.

Finally, because global restructuring is social and cultural, ideologies and identities are also being restructured. In particular, the heteronormative patriarchal family and the gender division of labor upon which constructions of masculine and feminine depend are being transformed by women's increasing labor—the feminization of flexibilization and informalization—and the relative loss of men's traditional breadwinner role. The effects of this transformation are far-reaching, exceedingly complex, and difficult to characterize. Most obvious and most substantiated in the literature are worldwide changes in marriage patterns, family forms, and gender relations. A concluding point is that these are not personal or private issues, but *structurally* significant for specifying and analyzing the gendered economies of the Asia-Pacific.

Notes

1. V. Spike Peterson, *A Critical Rewriting of Global Political Economy: Integrating Reproductive, Productive, and Virtual Economies* (London: Routledge, 2003). See for argumentation, empirical evidence, and citations supporting the claims made throughout this chapter.
2. Shirin M. Rai, *Gender and the Political Economy of Development* (Cambridge: Polity, 2002); Drucilla K. Barker and Susan F. Feiner, *Liberating Economics: Feminist Perspectives on Families, Work, and Globalization* (Ann Arbor: University of Michigan Press, 2004); V. Spike Peterson, "How (the Meaning of) Gender Matters in Political Economy," *New Political Economy* 10, no. 4 (2005): 499–521; Georgina Waylen, "You Still Don't Understand: Why Troubled Engagements Continue Between Feminists and (Critical) IPE," *Review of International Studies* 32 (2006): 145–64.
3. Financialization refers here to expansion—facilitated by deregulation and ICTs—of financial transactions in support of accumulation, consumption, and/or investment.
4. Informalization refers here to expansion of activities outside of 'formal' markets and exchanges. These activities range from domestic/socially necessary and voluntary 'work,' where cash is rarely exchanged and 'regulatory authorities' are absent (e.g., childrearing, housekeeping, neighborhood projects) to secondary, 'shadow' and 'irregular' activities where some form of enterprise and payment is expected but regulation is either difficult to enforce or intentionally avoided/evaded (e.g., baby sitting, housecleaning, home-based production, street vending, seasonal harvesting, sex work, drug dealing).
5. Setting aside the contentious issue of distinguishing among these approaches, I focus instead on what is common to them and which differentiates them 'definitively' from positivist/empiricist and 'rationalist' commitments that dominate in economics and IR. In brief, positivist dichotomies differentiate concepts both

oppositionally (as mutually exclusive and essentialized—that is, prediscursive, presocial—categories) and hierarchically (privileging the first term over the second); they fuel knowledge claims that are problematically reductionist, ahistorical, and noncritical. 'Posties' reject this binary logic and its corollary view of language as a neutral tool or medium in which symbols/signs simply refer to 'objective' phenomena. Rather, they view language, knowledge, and power as mutually constituting such that objective and subjective are necessarily inextricable. Similarly, they argue that the meaning of all words, 'things' and subjectivities is produced through/by discursive practices that are embedded in relations of power; that language produces power by constituting the codes of meaning that govern how we think, communicate, and generate knowledge claims–indeed, how we understand 'reality' and act 'accordingly.' Operations of power are not extricable from the power coded into our meaning systems; therefore, the latter are not coincidental to but constitute power manifested 'materially.' Moreover, positivist binaries are inherently masculinist insofar as the privileged terms in foundational dichotomies—reason, mind, objectivity, culture—are associated with valorized masculinity and the devalued terms—affect, body, subjectivity, nature—with denigrated femininity. Also see Drucilla K. Barker, "Beyond women and economics: rereading 'women's work,'" *Signs* 30, no. 4 (2005): 2189–209; J. K. Gibson-Graham, *The End of Capitalism (as we knew it): A Feminist Critique of Political Economy* (Cambridge, MA: Blackwell, 1996); Gillian J. Hewitson, *Feminist Economics: Interrogating the Masculinity of Rational Economic Man* (Cheltenham: Edward Elgar, 1999); Drucilla K. Barker and Edith Kuiper, ed, *Toward a Feminist Philosophy of Economics* (London and New York: Routledge, 2003); Marieke De Goede, "Beyond Economism in International Political Economy," *Review of International Studies* 29, no. 1 (2003): 79–97; Drucilla K. Barker and Susan F. Feiner, *Liberating Economics: Feminist Perspectives on Families, Work, and Globalization* (Ann Arbor: University of Michigan Press, 2004); V. Spike Peterson, *A Critical Rewriting of Global Political Economy: Integrating Reproductive, Productive, and Virtual Economies*. London: Routledge, 2003; V. Spike Peterson, "How (the Meaning of) Gender Matters in Political Economy." *New Political Economy* 10, no. 4 (2005): 499–521; V. Spike Peterson, "Getting Real: The Necessity of Poststructuralism in Global Political Economy," in *International Political Economy and Poststructural Politics*, ed. Marieke de Goede (London: Palgrave, 2006), 119–38; Georgina Waylen, "You still don't understand: Why troubled engagements continue between feminists and (critical) IPE," *Review of International Studies* 32 (2006): 145–64.

6. On diversity, identities/subjectivities, and intersections of structural hierarchies see, for example, Kimberle Crenshaw, "Mapping the Margins: Intersectionality, Identity Politics, and Violence Against Women of Color," *Stanford Law Review* 43 (1991): 1241–99; Chandra Talpade Mohanty, *Feminism Without Borders: Decolonizing Theory, Practicing Solidarity* (Durham: Duke University Press, 2003); Geeta Chowdhry and Sheila Nair, ed., *Power, Postcolonialism and International Relations: Reading Race, Gender and Class* (New York: Routledge, 2003).
7. The implications of analytical gender are far-reaching, but continue to be missed by mainstream and even many critical approaches, which retain an exclusively empirical understanding of gender—the 'add women and stir' approach. The transformative

potential of the feminist orientation invoked here resides in subverting *all* hierarchies that rely on denigration of 'the feminine' to naturalize domination. To forestall misunderstanding, I am not arguing for the primacy of 'women's oppression,' but rather insisting that gender is an historically contingent *structural* feature of social relations, that the subordination of women is not reducible to other structural oppressions (or vice versa), and that the dichotomy of gender underpins—as the denigration of the feminine naturalizes—hierarchies of gender, sexuality, class, race, and geopolitical 'differences.'

8. This framing invokes familiar categories (concrete practices/institutions, and conceptual symbols/language/ideology) but complicates their juxtaposition in two crucial, even transformative, ways. First, it rejects oppositional framing in favor of understanding the material and symbolic relationally, that is, as *interactive* and co-constituting dimensions of social reality. Second, it insists that social practices and conceptual habits are equally inextricable from emotional/affective/psychological/psychoanalytical dimensions, processes of sexual-, identity-, subject-formation, and the complex politics these entail.
9. United Nations Development Program, *Human Development Report 2002* (New York: Oxford University Press, 2002); Robert H. Wade, "Is Globalization Reducing Poverty and Inequality?" *World Development* 32, no. 4 (2004): 567–89.
10. "Asia Has World's Worst Record on Forced Labor: ILO," *Agence France Presse*, May 11, 2005.
11. As Stivens aptly observes, "there are many 'Asias' and as many modernities" (10). She also notes the particular location of Australian scholarship on Asia: "it is of the West and yet on its margins, reading across varying positions from within an Asian-Pacific context, while being located within a national project" (23). Maila Stivens, "Theorizing Gender, Power and Modernity in Affluent Asia," in *Gender and Power in Affluent Asia*, ed. Krishna Sen and Maila Stivens (London: Routledge, 1998), 1–34.
12. Jan Jindy Pettman, *Worlding Women: A Feminist International Politics* (Sydney: Allen and Unwin, 1996), 191.
13. Pettman notes migration "from poorer South and South-East Asian states to comparatively richer neighbors . . . [and] trans-Pacific migration and remittance networks enclosing Pacific ministates and larger, richer Pacific-rim cities" (Pettman, *Worlding Women*, 66); and from poorer states within the region to, for example, oil-rich Middle Eastern states and to Europe and the United States (Pettman, *Worlding Women*, 188).
14. Women continue to earn 30 to 40 percent less than men worldwide and in spite of heading almost one-third of the world's households, their lower wages are ideologically/culturally 'justified' by casting them as secondary earners. A corollary stereotype and sometimes reality, is that flexible work arrangements are therefore attractive to some women. Women's employment also reflects changes in life cycles and demographic patterns: women are staying in the labor force longer, delaying maternity, and decreasing the number of children they have, working throughout their reproductive years, and increasingly subsidizing family/household income.
15. Insofar as SAPs reduce public spending, they have the following gendered effects: women are disproportionately affected because they are more likely to depend on

secure government jobs and on public resources in support of reproductive labor, and women are expected to fill the gap of reduced welfare, in spite of fewer available resources and more demands on their time. The poor are also disproportionately affected by reduced public spending because they have the fewest (private) resources, and hence are most in need of public services and the support they provide. Because poverty is marked by race and gender, the effects of privatization—especially of cutbacks in public welfare—evidence systematic patterns that fuel the reproduction of intersecting structural hierarchies (Peterson, *A Critical Rewriting*, 73). On SAPs see also Isabella Bakker and Stephen Gill, ed., *Power, Production and Social Reproduction: Human In/security in the Global Political Economy* (Hampshire: Palgrave Macmillan, 2003); Rai, *Gender and the Political Economy*; Lourdes Benería, *Gender, Development and Globalization: Economics as if All People Mattered* (New York: Routledge, 2003).

16. For example, Peter Mares, "Workers for All Seasons: Can Pacific Islanders Fill Seasonal Jobs in Australia? Canada Has Had Such a Scheme for 40 years," *The Diplomat*, July/August 2006, http://www.sisr.net/publications/0607mares.pdf (accessed November 13, 2006).
17. Arlie R. Hochschild, "Love and Gold," in *Global Woman: Nannies, Maids, and Sex Workers in the New Economy*, ed. Barbara Ehrenreich and Arlie R. Hochschild (New York: Henry Holt, 2002), 19.
18. Ehrenreich and Hochschild, "Introduction," in *Global Woman*, 6.
19. Richard Friman and Peter Andreas, ed., *The Illicit Global Economy and State Power* (Lanham, MD: Rowman & Littlefield, 1999); R. T. Naylor, *Wages of Crime: Black Markets, Illegal Finance, and the Underground Economy* (Ithaca: Cornell University Press, 2002); Peter Andreas, "Illicit International Political Economy: The Clandestine Side of Globalization," *Review of International Political Economy* 11, no. 3 (2004): 631–52.
20. Feminist economists have produced a wealth of literature on social reproduction, some of which is cited in this chapter and more extensively in Peterson, 2003; Bakker and Gill offer perhaps the most comprehensive account of social reproduction in crisis as an effect of neoliberal globalization.
21. Brigette Young, "Globalization and Gender: A European Perspective," in *Gender, Globalization, & Democratization*, ed. Rita Mae Kelly, et al. (Lanham, MD: Rowman & Littlefield Publishers, 2001), 39.
22. Brenda S. A. Yeoh, Peggy Teo, and Shirlena Huang, "Introduction," in *Gender Politics in the Asia-Pacific Region*, ed. Brenda S. A. Yeoh, Peggy Teo, and Shirlena Huang (London: Routledge, 2002).
23. Ehrenreich and Hochschild, "Introduction," in Ehrenreich and Hochschild, *Global Woman*, 4.
24. Nicola Piper, "Gendering the Politics of Migration," *International Migration Review* 40, no. 1 (2006): 143.
25. Geertje Lycklama à Nijeholt, "Women in International Migration," in *A Commitment to the World's Women*, ed. Noleen Heyzer (New York: UNIFEM, 1995), 61.
26. Lindio-McGovern observes that the bulk of Philippine export labor is domestic workers. Ligaya Lindio-McGovern, "Alienation and Labor Export in the Context of Globalization: Filipino Migrant Domestic Workers in Taiwan and Hong Kong"

Critical Asian Studies 36, no. 2 (2004): 217; she also discusses how domestic workers resist the forms of alienation that they experience. On women's agency and activism in the Asia-Pacific, see Yeoh, Teo, and Huang, "Introduction," in *Gender Politics in the Asia-Pacific*; on domestic workers in the context of modernizing projects, see Christine B. Chin, *In Service and Servitude: Foreign Female Domestic Workers and the Malaysian "Modernity" Project* (New York: Columbia University Press, 1998); on gendering "Asia and the West," see L. H. M. Ling, *Postcolonial International Relations: Conquest and Desire between Asia and the West* (London: Palgrave, 2002).

27. Brigette Young, "Globalization and Gender," 57.
28. Pettman, *Worlding Women*, 190.
29. Bridget Anderson, *Doing the Dirty Work? The Global Politics of Domestic Labour* (London: Zed Books, 2000), 2.
30. Hanochi notes this activity. Seiko Hanochi, "Japan and the Global Sex Industry," in *Gender, Globalization, and Democratization*, 144; Greimel notes that Kadokura estimates, "US $522 million in 'pocket money' part-time schoolgirl prostitutes get." Hans Greimel, "Japan's Other Economy," review of Takashi Kadokura, *Japan "Underground Economy" White Paper*," *San Francisco Chronicle* (July 23, 2002): B1.
31. See, for example, Thanh-Dam Truong, *Sex, Money and Morality: Prostitution and Tourism in Southeast Asia* (London: Zed Books, 1990); Pettman, *Worlding Women*; Jan Jindy Pettman, "Body Politics: International Sex Tourism," *Third World Quarterly* 18, no.1 (1997): 93–108; Kamala Kempadoo and Jo Doezema, ed., *Global Sex Workers* (New York: Routledge, 1998); Lin Lean Lim, ed., *The Sex Sector: The Economic and Social Bases of Prostitution in Southeast Asia* (Geneva: International Labor Office, 1998); Hanochi, "Japan and the Global Sex Industry"; Kinhide Mushakoji, "Engendering the Japanese 'Double Standard' Patriarchal Democracy," in *Gender, Globalization, & Democratization*; Navarro Alys Willman, "Making it at the Margins: The Criminalization of Nicaraguan Women's Labor under Structural Reform," *International Feminist Journal of Politics* 8, 2 (2006): 243–66. Although important, I do not here address the complex, gendered dynamics of homosexual activities, child prostitution, female tourists seeking sex, or militarization.
32. Pettman, "Body Politics," 96.
33. Mary E. Hawkesworth, *Globalization and Feminist Activism* (Lanham, MD: Rowman & Littlefield, 2006), 2.
34. Hochschild, "Love and Gold," 17.
35. Richard Brown and John Connell, "Occupation-Specific Analysis of Migration and Remittance Behaviour: Pacific Island Nurses in Australia and New Zealand," Asia *Pacific Viewpoint* 47, no. 1 (2006): 135–50.
36. Linda H. Aiken, et al., "Trends in International Nurse Migration," *Health Affairs* 23, no. 3 (2004): 69–77; "Nurses," *Guardian*, May 18, 2005.
37. Aiken, et al., "Trends," 70.
38. Ibid., 71.
39. Ibid., 75.
40. Rhacel Salazar Parreñas, "The International Division of Reproductive Labor: Paid Domestic Work and Globalization," in *Critical Globalization Studies*, ed. Richard P. Appelbaum and William I. Robinson (New York: Routledge, 2005), 239. She

describes the three-tier transfer of care among women: "class-privileged women pass down the care of their families to migrant domestic workers as migrant domestic workers simultaneously pass down the care of their own families—most of whom are left behind in the country of origin—to their relatives or sometimes to even poorer women whom they hire as their own domestic workers' (238).

41. Hochschild, "Love and Gold," 29.
42. Debates regarding how to theorize, define, measure, and evaluate informalization are addressed in Peterson, *A Critical Rewriting*. The underground economy has been estimated to be $9 trillion, "Black Hole," *The Economist* (August 28, 1999): 59; the value of 'housework' to be $10 to $15 trillion, Mary Ann Tetreault and Ronnie D. Lipschutz, *Global Politics as if People Mattered* (Boulder, CO: Rowman & Littlefield, 2005): 25.
43. For example, the stereotypes of the Asian woman as quintessentially 'feminine' that fuel sex tourism and the desirability of Asian 'mail order brides'; the racial hierarchy exhibited by Jordanians preferring lighter-skinned Filipinas over maids from Sri Lanka (Pettman, *Worlding Women*, 191); and hierarchies of sex workers such that (white) Australian sex workers have greater power to demand condom-use by clients than migrant Asian sex workers in brothels that advertise 'condom-free' pleasures (Pettman,"Body Politics,"103).
44. On the gender of financial arrangements, see also Aslanbeigui and Summerfield, "The Asian Crisis, Gender, and the International Financial Architecture"; Aslanbeigui and Summerfield, "Risk, Gender and the International Financial Architecture"; van Staveren, "Global Finance and Gender"; De Goede, "Mastering Lady Credit."
45. World Bank, *Global Economic Prospects: Economic Implications of Remittances and Migration* (Washington, DC: World Bank, 2006), xiii.
46. Ibid., 85.
47. Samuel M. Maimbo, et al., ed., *Migrant Labour Remittances in South Asia* (Directions in Development, 2005).
48. World Bank, *Global Economic Prospects*, 89.
49. Nic Maclellan, "Fiji, the War in Iraq, and the Privatisation of Pacific Island Security," *Australia Policy Forum* 06-11A, April 6, 2006, http://www.nautilus.org/~rmit/forum-reports/0611a-maclellan.html (accessed November 9, 2006).
50. World Bank, *Global Economic Prospects*, xii.
51. Ibid., xiii.

PART II

Gendering Global Politics in the Asia-Pacific

CHAPTER 4

The 'Kitsch' of War

Misappropriating Sun Tzu for an American Imperial Hypermasculinity

Ching-Chane Hwang and L. H. M. Ling

U.S. interest in *The Art of War* (*sunzi bingfa*, 512 BCE) has risen dramatically since 9/11.[1] Both former Secretary of Defense Donald Rumsfeld and General Tommy Franks, masterminds of the Iraq campaign, regularly quote Sun Tzu.[2] The *New York Times* notes that insurgents in Iraq and Afghanistan may also be learning from *The Art of War*.[3]

For its part, the U.S. Defense Department utilizes strategies such as 'shock and awe' and 'decapitation.' Typically attributed to *The Art of War*, shock and awe calls for an extreme show of force to cower the enemy so the war will be shortened; decapitation is cutting off the head or leader of enemy forces to enable easier capture of the enemy forces. Some scholars compare Sun Tzu's teachings with former U.S. Defense Secretary Caspar Weinberger's doctrine of war.[4] Others ask whether Sun Tzu's war theory necessitates a certain cultural environment that other societies cannot match.[5] Still others note Sun Tzu's relevance to the military professionalism of the People's Liberation Army (PLA) in Chinese foreign policy decision-making.[6] One pair of scholars applied a game-theortic model to *The Art of War*.[7] This interest builds upon longstanding attention to *The Art of War* in the U.S. military and its foreign policy thinking, especially since the Vietnam War.[8]

The Art of War has entered mainstream American culture. Some cite Sun Tzu's principles to critique the Bush Administration's conduct of the war in Iraq.[9] Others use the same to blame the Clinton administration for weak leadership that, they claim, jeopardized U.S. national security interests.[10] Pundits and commentators evaluate leaders from George W. Bush to Saddam Hussein to Osama bin Laden through the filter of Sun Tzu's principles.[11] Executives also see value in *The Art of War*.[12] Even Tony Soprano, a fictional character in the HBO series "The Sopranos" reads Sun Tzu, sparking interest in the sixth century BCE Chinese general and philosopher for another generation of Americans.

This treatment of Sun Tzu, however, is disturbing on three, interrelated levels. It (1) reinforces an imperial hypermasculinity in U.S. foreign policy that (2) projects the same onto all others, thereby rationalizing its own, and (3) provokes rather than co-opts the enemy. To lock the world into irreconcilable opposites that unceasingly battle each other, we argue, contradicts Sun Tzu's purpose. *The Art of War* seeks to transform not annihilate the enemy. In misappropriating Sun Tzu, the Bush Administration and any other perpetrator of such willful ignorance, turns *The Art of War* into mere *kitsch*.

This paper begins with shock and awe, and decapitation. After demonstrating their absence in *The Art of War*, we show how they reinforce an American imperial hypermasculinity in world politics. We juxtapose this modernization of Sun Tzu with the ontological and epistemological principles that governed Sun Tzu's world order and for which he wrote *The Art of War*. We conclude with the implications of American imperial hypermasculinity for world politics.

Shocking, Awing, and Decapitating

The Pentagon used the so-called shock and awe strategy in its second war against Iraq in March 2003. Then U.S. Defense Secretary Donald Rumsfeld supplemented this strategy with 'decapitating' the enemy, especially Saddam Hussein. Accordingly, the United States dropped three thousand bombs and missiles on Baghdad within the first forty-eight hours. Civilian casualties mushroomed, Saddam fled, and Iraq collapsed in April 2003. Shock and awe, followed by decapitation, won the war in Iraq for the United States in less than a month.

These strategies were attributed to Sun Tzu. Ullman and Wade describe shock and awe as an explicit policy to overwhelm the enemy, rendering it 'totally impotent and vulnerable' with no will to resist.[13] Justification for this strategy is found in Tolan.[14] He refers to photographs of survivors from World War I, their 'comatose and glazed expressions' affirm that shock and awe in war "transcend race, culture, and history. . . . [This strategy vaporizes] the public will of the adversary to resist and, ideally or theoretically, would instantly or quickly incapacitate that will over the space of a few hours or days."[15]

Utter devastation of the enemy reflects a classical, realist approach to warfare. Realists traditionally hail the Melian Dialogue in Thucydides' *Peloponnesian War* as the epitome of power politics in international relations: the Athenian generals would not consider neutrality for the Melians, as requested by them, for it would signal weakness to others. Accordingly, the Athenians killed all the men and enslaved all the women and children. George W. Bush voiced a similar fear when Al Qaeda's suicide bombers flew the planes into New York's World Trade Center. 'They'll think we're soft,' he said,[16] if the U.S. did not show immediate and unequivocal retaliation against the terrorists. Since then, Bush often resorts to this imagery. Note this comment when signing the Defense Appropriations Bill on January 10, 2002: "Today, more than ever, we also owe those in uniform the resources they need to maintain a very high state of readiness. Our enemies rely upon surprise and deception. They used to rely upon the fact that they thought we were soft. I don't think they think that way anymore." [17]

Nowhere, however, does *The Art of War* advocate shock and awe or decapitation. Especially nonexistent is a warning against appearing soft in contrast to being hard. If such notions were to appear in *The Art of War*, Sun Tzu's dialectical method, as we will demonstrate, required him to consider their complementarities and contradictions. That is, Sun Tzu would have discussed softness in the context of hardness and vice versa, showing that one condition is neither exclusive nor a negation of the other. Furthermore, Sun Tzu would have pointed to the potential of one condition to disrupt or subsume and thereby transform the other.

Instead, shock and awe, and decapitation come from an anecdote first recorded in the *Shiji* or *Records of the Grand Historian* (109–191 BCE) by Sima Qian. One version popularized in the West goes something like this:[18] Sun Tzu was conducting a military drill for a group of concubines. Two of the ladies laughed at him, so he decapitated them, shocking and awing the other concubines into compliance. This is why, according to the tale, decapitation typically accompanies shock and awe. Lo elaborates upon this story, interpreting it as a morality play about military authority.[19] That is, when a general has been given the authority to lead his army, he takes this responsibility so seriously that even the king cannot order him to desist.

According to Lo, the tale unfolds in this way: [20] After reading *The Art of War*, Ho Lu, the king of Wu, summoned Sun Tzu to court to train the king's concubines. He wanted them to learn about weapons and war.[21] Sun Tzu divided one hundred and eighty concubines into two companies and put Ho Lu's two favorite concubines in command. He taught them how to hold halberds and asked them to follow his orders. He gave the orders three times and explained the orders five times, but the women only tittered and tattled. Sun Tzu reasoned, "If regulations are not clear and orders not thoroughly explained, it is the commander's fault." He repeated the orders three times and explained them again five times. This time, the women burst into full, outright laughter. Sun Tzu responded, "If instructions are not clear and commands not explicit, it is the commander's fault. However, when they have been made clear, and are not carried out in accordance with military law, it is a crime on the part of the officers." He ordered the two chief concubines be beheaded. Ho Lu was astounded. The king feared losing his two favorite concubines and asked for mercy on their behalf.

> "I cannot live without these two women!" he impressed upon Sun Tzu. "Please pardon them."

> "Your servant received your appointment as Commander," Sun Tzu replied, "and when the commander is at the head of the army he need not accept all the sovereign's orders"[22]

Sun Tzu continued with both the execution and the drill. The other concubines dared not make a peep. Ho Lu fumed but knew thereafter that Sun Tzu proved himself a capable leader.

Even if we take this story at face value, we note that Sun Tzu did not shock, awe, or decapitate the enemy. Rather, these tactics were directed at his own troops, aiming to discipline them, and violence came only when reason failed. This re-reading of the story underscores that for Sun Tzu such tactics were not a 'must' but a last resort.

A feminist inquiry is warranted here. It asks, What does this story say about a man, vested with all the authority of a king's commander, to decapitate two, defenseless women, awing and shocking their counterparts into . . . what, more submission than they must endure already? In Sun Tzu's era, kings held concubines in conditions similar to a lifetime of house arrest at best, and slavery at worst: each was restricted to her own small courtyard, subject to constant gossip and slander in competition against *hundreds* of other concubines,[23] waiting for that one night when the master might visit, praying for the honor of bearing him a son but usually disgraced forever for failing to do so. The concubines at Sun Tzu's command, moreover, were not operating in a real war with explicit stakes involved but participating in a drill![24]

Given such horrific abuse for a triviality, what does it mean to take this tale unquestioningly? One must conclude that such willing ignorance covers a shameful perversion of power. Mainstream readings of this tale completely ignore the asymmetries that skew power relations between the concubines and the king. Similarly, contemporary strategists use shock and awe, and decapitation without considering the social and power differentials between perpetrators and victims. Note Secretary Rumsfeld's response to the number of civilian casualties caused by the U.S. bombing of Iraq: totally ignoring the U.S. role, Rumsfeld thundered against the Iraqi government's inhumanity to its own people by using them as human shields. Whether or not the Iraqi government did or not is not examined. Meanwhile, such 'crimes' affirm America's virtue as a beacon of democracy, liberty, and human rights: "[Using human shields] is murder, a violation of the laws of armed conflict, and a crime against humanity, and it will be treated as such."[25]

What the act, and the strategy behind it, reveals is the hollowness of military might directed against a population that cannot defend itself in kind. Thus the U.S. military, like the power of Sun Tzu and the king in the spurious story, punishes the punished, subjugates the subjugated, and exploits the exploited. In short, this is bullying at its worst.

The previous inquiry motivates another, more general one. *Should* commanders, albeit sanctioned by the king, wield such authority that the king himself cannot retract or check it? For example, Harry Truman demonstrated in 1951 that a working democracy cannot allow military authority to disregard the state's constitutional authority when he fired General Douglas MacArthur, Supreme Commander for the Allied Powers in the Pacific. Granted, Sun Tzu neither lived in nor wrote about military and political relations in a democracy. Nonetheless, the principle still stands. Why would any leader–whether king, president, or chief executive officer–permit his lieutenants the ideological *legitimacy* of disobeying a direct order? Sun Tzu himself stated in Chapter VII ("Maneuvering," *junzheng*) that "in war, the general receives his commands from the sovereign" (*fan yung bin zhi fa, jiang shou ming yu jun*).[26]

Even where Sun Tzu's text is followed more precisely, we see that its meaning is understood selectively at best. For instance, Sun Tzu is frequently quoted as saying, "all warfare is based on deception." The Bush Administration, however, has taken this strategy to include deceiving one's own population, not just the enemy. Campbell shows how the Pentagon and the military used sophisticated tools of cultural governance to prevent the public from distinguishing "the original and the new, the real, from the reproduced."[27] Yet Sun Tzu advocated deception of the enemy only, never one's own people. To Sun Tzu, the word 'deception' included the notion of flexibility. To appear flexible through diplomacy and other means before a war starts is also a kind of deception, according to Sun Tzu.[28]

Misappropriating *The Art of War* would seem trivial were not for its consequences. It rationalizes, we argue, an imperial hypermasculinity for U.S. foreign policy. To understand how, we must begin with neoliberalism's logic for so-called self and other relations, which is conversion or discipline.

Neoliberal Self/Other Relations: Conversion or Discipline

Neoliberal self and other relations stem from classical liberal theory, which assigns to the self the right to convert the other through education, religion, civilization or some other means of salvation. The other *must* oblige or else suffer the consequences of discipline from the self. This imperative, liberals believe, ensures enduring peace for peace can come about only when all others resemble the self.[29]

These injunctions reflect liberalism's historical commitment to Christianity *and* capitalism, later transmitted to colonialism and imperialism. Locke, for example, integrated Hobbesian authoritarianism with Protestant acquisitiveness to ultimately condone a "rapacious capitalism."[30] He inherited Hobbes' patriarchal designation of 'women, children, and chattel,' as property for men to bring into civil society.[31] For Mehta, classical liberalism is devoted to containing the bourgeois order.[32] From internal others like women and children, classical liberalism easily moves to subordinating and exploiting external others like India, now labeled "inscrutable."[33] In each case, liberals use strategies of exclusion not just to marginalize women, children, and others but also to educate them into the so-called adult, civilized world of the hardworking, penny-pinching bourgeois. Colonialism, in short, reframes the Hobbesian-Lockean tradition from educating the child to training the colonial other.

Rudyard Kipling's ode to empire, "The White Man's Burden," exemplifies classical liberal self and other relations. Published in February 1899 in *McClure's Magazine*, Kipling exhorted the United States to take over where Spain could no longer rule, that is, the Philippines. (Often, the poem's subtitle is overlooked: "The United States and the Philippine Islands.") The poem demarcates clear boundaries between the American Self and its Filipino Other. The American Self, the poem argues, has an obligation to colonize, civilize, and enlighten its Filipino Other. After all, the American Self, like its British counterpart, gains its privileges through a naturally endowed superiority. The Filipinos, in turn, have no role other than to emulate, as best as possible, the Anglo-American Self. Accordingly, the relationship between Self and Other can only be unilateral, hierarchical, authoritative (if not authoritarian), and predictable. In a word: imperial.[34]

Neoliberalism recasts this bourgeois order as multicultural and fun even hip. When the Soviet Union disbanded, for instance, neoliberals in the West celebrated with a series of television commercials that showed the former Communist bloc's dull, grey, uptight command economies finally freed to pursue western-style capitalism.[35] By implication, everyone not only should, but also *want* to become like the western, Christian neoliberal self. Fukuyama coined it "the end of history."[36] Note these advertising slogans from one of corporate capitalism's enduring icons, the Coca-Cola Company. A sample from the end of the cold war in 1989 to the present conveys the easy, everyday allure promised by a bottle of Coke:

1990: "You Can't Beat the Real Thing."
2001: "Life is Good/Life Tastes Good."
2005: "Make it Real."
2006: "Welcome to the Coke side of Life."[37]

Updating Kipling, neoliberalism turns his world-weary White Man into an unstoppably cheerful Cosmo Man who dispenses economic *and* sociopolitical good wherever the gig takes him. *The Economist*, that tony mouthpiece of the neoliberal world order, serves as an apt example. It devoted a special report in its August 14, 2003 issue to the topic: 'America and Empire.' Is America, it asked, as the world's only military and economic superpower now also an empire? The magazine concluded with a resounding 'no' for two reasons: (1) the natives (in Iraq and Afghanistan) do not like it ("Please leave us to get on with our own affairs") and (2) neither do Americans ("Freedom is in their blood; it is integral to their sense of themselves").

The Economist understands U.S. history selectively at best. When do natives ever welcome an occupying power? Since when does local resentment, even constant insurgency, ever stop colonization? The magazine acknowledged that white settlers in America's thirteen colonies rebelled against British rule ("Americans know that empires lack democratic legitimacy. They once had a tea party to prove it"), but the magazine conveniently omitted the fact that those same settlers did the same to natives of the land they depopulated, arrogantly called the New World, through genocide and other forms of mass killing. As Hunt demonstrates, American state-building was historically based on the annihilation, domination, and enslavement of the racialized, sexualized other.[38] Untold millions of native peoples died through a combination of wars, reneged treaties, dislocations, relocations, and most unexpectedly, germs.[39] To erase this history, as the *Economist* did, with a facile gesture toward the rhetoric of American democracy, claiming that it is in the blood, constitutes irony of the highest and most grotesque order.

These are familiar tactics. As Hooper shows, the *Economist* has long participated in a neocolonial narrative of the all-conquering, globe-straddling (western) capitalist ready to take (Third World) 'virgin' economies and resources at will making them 'productive' in the image of the self.[40] Even in this special report, *The Economist* revealed its racist, sexist, and imperialist stripes by claiming that "a surprising number have welcomed the new role" of America as an imperial power. It named Max Boot, an Englishman transplanted to New York initially as editorial features editor of *The Wall Street Journal* and now Olin Senior Fellow in National Security Studies with the Council on Foreign Relations, a conservative think tank. The title of Boot's book, *The Savage Wars of Peace*, is a line taken from "The White Man's Burden," to underscore his support of this nineteenth century approach to world affairs.[41] The book received the Best Book Award of 2002 from the *Washington Post*, *Christian Science Monitor*, and the *Los Angeles Times* and won the 2003 General Wallace M. Greene, Jr. Award for the best nonfiction book pertaining to Marine Corps history. They lauded the book for presenting "the U.S. imperial role in the Philippines . . . as a model for the kind of imperial role that Boot and other neoconservatives are now urging on the United States."[42]

Hypermasculinity accompanies such arrogance and willful ignorance. Just as the magazine infantilized whole societies and peoples in this manner, so too did it sexualize power, especially for the United States. "In short, the empire now proclaimed in America's name is at best a dull duck, at worst a dead duck, unless it is to be a big strong drake that intends to throw its weight around for quite a while." Such thinking is pervasive. Note this cautionary note from a senior advisor to the draft constitution in Iraq. "Elections," he declares, "can seduce with the promise of release."[43] His explanation merits quoting at length:

> Elections hold out the hope of successful consummation, the seed of democracy implanted and the door opened for subsequent withdrawal. In this troubling

> vision, the occupied people grip the occupier in an embrace both pleasurable and terrifying. In the imagined "successful" scenario, the occupier builds and leaves. When things go wrong, he [*sic*] cannot get out but is sucked into what American vernacular calls "the quagmire"—a situation from which he cannot extract himself, but in which he cannot remain without suffering unmanning damage.[44]

However, for the occupied democracy may be a disturbing wet dream. The occupied could wake up in sweaty disillusion to find no love there after all, just more anxieties about one's own uncontrollable urges.

> From the perspective of the nation under occupation, elections seduce in a different sort of way. On one hand, they promise to give voice to the voiceless. . . . In that same moment of self-creation . . . the nation being built can throw off the yoke of its occupier and declare its independence, thus breaking free of the humiliating status of being subordinated. . . . On the other hand, people under nation building fear elections for the danger of what they may reveal. Fragmented results may show that there is no nation there at all, just a collection of divergent interest groups who lack the common vision to make a government that will endure. The election of undemocratic forces is also to be feared.[45]

Such fantasizing in rhetoric plays out all too gruesomely in reality. A small article in the *New York Times* reported on the conviction of a U.S. soldier of a March 2006 rape and murder of a fourteen-year-old Iraqi girl, including the murders of her parents and younger sister.[46] After raping the girl, the soldier (one of five conspirators) "poured kerosene on her body and set it on fire in an attempt to hide evidence of the crime."[47] Given the history of U.S. military atrocities, especially rape, in locales like Okinawa, South Korea, the Philippines, and other parts of East and South-East Asia during the cold war,[48] it is not hard to imagine why both men and women in Iraq and Afghanistan, not to mention the rest of the Muslim world, hypermasculinize in reaction.[49]

Assassinations and bomb attacks in Iraq have only increased, endangering U.S. security forces in the country.[50] The insurgency in Afghanistan has not abated. "In the spring of 2006," the *New York Times* reported, "the Taliban carried out their [*sic*] largest offensive since 2001," resulting in a quintupling of suicide bombings and doubling of roadside bombings.[51] "All told," the report continued, "191 American and NATO troops died in 2006, a 20 percent increase over the 2005 toll."[52] As Osama bin Laden declared on October 7, 2001: "what the United States tastes today is a very small thing compared to what we have tasted for tens of years."[53]

Mutual war seems inevitable for all. "By now," an article in the February 24, 2008 issue of *The New York Times Magazine* reported, "seven years of air strikes and civilian casualties, humiliating house searches, and arbitrary detentions have pushed many families and tribes to revenge. The Americans then see every Afghan in those pockets of recalcitrance as an enemy."[54]

Locked in unending, mindless hostility, the occupiers suffer as much as the occupied. The same article continues,

> "I hate this country!" [the young sergeant] shouted. Then he smiled and walked back into the hut. "He's on medication," Kearney said quietly to me. Then another soldier walked by and shouted, "Hey, I'm with you, sir!" and Kearney said to me, "Prozac. Serious P.T.S.D. from last tour." Another one popped out of the HQ cursing and muttering. "Medicated," Kearney said. "Last tour, if you didn't give him information, he'd burn down your house. He killed so many people. He's checked out."[55]

Imperial hypermasculinity, we contend, contradicts the very purpose of *The Art of War*. Let us reconsider Sun Tzu in his own time and on his terms.

Sun Tzu: In His Time, On His Terms

The Art of War is not just a manual on war. It is also a book of philosophy and peace. For Sun Tzu, diplomacy, negotiations, and even deception were preferable to war. Sun Tzu's perfect scenario was to win war without sacrificing blood or treasure.

Chapter 1 ("Laying Plans," *ji*), for example, cites five considerations when planning a war. These are: (1) the moral law (*dao*), (2) heaven (*tian*),[56] (3) earth (*di*),[57] (4) the commander (*jiang*),[58] and (5) method and discipline (*fa*).[59] The first and most important consideration, moral law, is that which "causes the people to be in complete accord with their ruler, so that they will follow him regardless of their lives, undismayed by any danger." Moral law determines whether the people are willing to die for their sovereign and their way of life. Before waging war, then, the first question should be: "Which of the two [contending] sovereigns is imbued with the moral law?" (*ju shu you dao*?)

Sun Tzu advised that only when the attacking sovereign has the superior moral law should the campaign proceed. Put in contemporary terms, waging a war cannot be based on technicalities like the number of weapons, soldiers or amount of monies. Such considerations cannot outweigh the 'hearts and minds' of the people for it is only the latter that will determine the war's outcome. This maxim pertains to both invaders and those being invaded.

Chapter 3 ("Attack by Stratagem," *mou gong*) prioritizes submission over destruction. Whether the enemy's or one's own, costs should be minimized.

> In the practical art of war, the best thing of all is to take the enemy's country whole and intact (*quan guo wei shang*); to shatter and destroy it is not so good (*puo guo ci zhi*). So, too, it is better to recapture an army (*jun*) entire than to destroy (*puo*) it, to capture a regiment (*lu*), a detachment (*zu*) or a company (*wu*) entire than to destroy them. Hence to fight and conquer in all your battles is not supreme excellence (*shi gu bai zhan bai sheng, fei shan zhi shan ye*); supreme excellence consists in breaking the enemy's resistance without fighting (*bu zhan er qu ren zhi bin, shan zhi shan zhe ye*).[60]

Most especially, war should be a last resort only. Once it is inevitable, then the prince and general should pursue war cautiously (*shen zhan*) by minimizing its costs. One way is to battle in sequence. First, apply strategy; if that fails, then offer diplomacy; if that fails, then attack, if that fails, as a last resort, "storm cities and seize territory." Again, from chapter 3:

> Thus the highest form of generalship is to balk the enemy's plans (*fa mou*); the next best is to prevent the junction of the enemy's forces (*fa jiao*); the next in order is to attack the enemy's army in the field (*fa bin*); and the worst policy of all is to besiege walled cities (*gong cheng*).[61]

Sun Tzu aimed to transform (*zhuanhua*) the enemy not simply to defeat him.[62] Rulers and generals, he emphasized, must have a sense of moral obligation (*dao yi*) toward those who pay the highest price on the battlefield: soldiers. "Regard your soldiers as if they were your children" (*shi zu ru ying er*), he wrote. "Regard your soldiers like beloved sons" (*shi zu ru ai zi*).[63] This principle extended to enemy soldiers as well. Prisoners of war, Sun Tzu instructed, should be treated with kindness and nurtured (*zu shan er yang zhi*) just as *all* people should be protected and allowed to live in security and prosperity.[64] Hence, caution in war includes preserving the lives of friend and foe alike, not to enslave or oppress them to serve the new regime, but to transform them into new allies and supporters.

Sun Tzu drew on dialectics to warrant such caution. The prince and general should never undertake war from a position of anger or indignation, he wrote, for it blinds one to a situation's *inherent* possibilities for change. Every assumption, Sun Tzu stressed, has the potential of being overthrown by the dialectical forces operating within it. Such instability stems from the interaction of opposites, which range from physical conditions[65] to social roles[66] to point of action[67] to type of action[68] to time constraints,[69] and many more.[70] Each element must be evaluated with its complementary opposite in mind. Only in this way, can the prudent ruler and general anticipate and manage crises. As Yang notes,

> Sun Tzu found contradictions everywhere in the world. Everywhere, everything was in mutual contradiction yet also in mutual reliance, leading to the possibility of transformation. Because everything in the world was undergoing a thousand changes, he advocated using different methods to deal with different situations. One could never be fixed, rigid, or doctrinaire (*qian pian yi lu*).[71]

Here, Sun Tzu was not just advocating a prudent, humane approach to war. He was also drawing from a larger worldview, which sees opposites as complements rather than in competition with one another.

Tianxia: Ren, Xianghua, Huairou

A relational ontology, *tianxia*, governed Sun Tzu's time. Known as all-under-heaven, it has three meanings: (1) "the universe" or "the world," (2) the "hearts of all peoples" (*minxin*) or the "general will of the people," and (3) "a world institution, or a universal system for the world, a utopia of the world-as-one-family."[72] This latter signifies not an empire in the usual sense but a universal state of world-ness, that is, a world composed of many worlds. Only from the interaction of these many worlds can mankind realize *tianxia*.

Put differently, *tianxia* reflects systemic fluidity and dynamism. It accepts instability as the norm, which is not only due to shifts in geopolitical circumstance but also to the provisional and contingent nature of the *social relations* that constitute constructed borders, territories, nations, identities, and roles. Ling notes, for instance, how Chinese elites felt Japan had transgressed the Confucian world order in the nineteenth century when the Meiji Restoration embarked on full-scale westernization.[73] No borders physically changed but Japan was no longer China's cultural cousin based on "speaking through brush-strokes" (*bi tan*).

Historically, the Emperor used rituals (*li*) and tributes (*gong*) to 'center' (*shi-zhong*) social relations,[74] applying the mean of ritual and tribute precisely balanced social relations because social relations are in constant flux. Even the emperor, to whom all perform the *koutou*, prostrated himself on hands and knees before his parents and the Temple of Heaven. *Tianxia* as empire, though, "could only be an exemplar passively *in situ*, rather than positively become missionary" because of its foundational concept in *ren*.[75]

Ren accounts for *tianxia* both structurally and ethically. Identified as Confucian practical humanism, *ren* operated as a normative standard even during Sun Tzu's time. (Sun Tzu and Confucius were contemporaries.) Variously translated 'universal virtue,' 'benevolence,' 'golden rule,' 'love' or 'compassion,' *ren* conveys a fundamental sense of "sociality or reciprocity in the everyday action of man [that produces] an all-encompassing network of social relationships."[76] A compound of two ideograms—'person' (also pronounced *ren*) and the number 'two'—*ren* underscores that "man [*sic*] is involved in mankind and lives his everyday life in relation to others, i.e., in the family, in the community, and in the nation."[77] Zhao notes the oldest rendition of *ren* defines it as 'thousands of hearts.' "Reciprocity understood in the Chinese way has less to do with the reciprocal utilitarianism or balance in commercial exchange and much more to do with the *reciprocity of hearts*."[78] Literally and figuratively, *ren* cannot allow or even concede that an individual entity (whether person, group, society, or state) be alienated from another. One is *necessarily* enmeshed with others. As "the primary index of man's existence," writes Jung, *ren*'s sociality "entail[s] morality and [is] regarded as the highest moral norm attainable by man."[79]

Ren's radical sociality stipulates a multiple understanding of subjectivity. An event or character, for example, can be described "from different perspectives in different parts of the narrative" or be recognized in "the plurality of human existence, which rise above immediate considerations of success and failure" or reflect the notion that "truth is apprehended through plurality."[80] Sima Qian, the Grand Historian, utilized this principle of 'mutual illumination' (*hujian fa*) when recording, for example, an assassin as a 'romantic avenger' in one passage, and a 'bandit' in another.[81]

In *ren*, there is no self vs. other, only many kinds of 'other-ness.' As Zhao describes,

> The Bible's golden rule, "Do unto others as you would have them do to you" sounds promising, but it would encounter challenges and difficulties when other hearts are taken into account. The other-ness of the other heart [as understood in *ren*] is something absolute and transcendent, so the other heart might reasonably want a different life. In terms of other-ness, the Chinese ethical principle thus runs: "Let others reach their goals if you reach yours."[82]

With its fluidity and flux, other-ness allowed for 'transformation' or *xianghua*. Such transformation usually takes hold unidimensionally, that is, from the periphery to the center, the barbarian to the 'way,' and in Sun Tzu's case, foe to friend. Transformation never involved both parties simultaneously turning toward each other. In this sense, *xianghua* is not unlike classical liberalism's penchant for "education" or neoliberalism's for 'conversion.' However, unlike these Western counterparts, *xianghua* does not advocate discipline or other forms of punishment should transformation fail.

One policy, for example, is to 'cherish men from afar' or *huairou yuanren*.[83] It usually came in the form of bribery with gifts in goods or people, the latter through the emperor ceding a concubine or sister in marriage to a tribal chief. With co-optation by greed or blood or both, *huairou* aims to integrate other-ness into a familial relationship. In this way, *huairou* policies helped to approximate *tianxia*'s ideal of the world-as-one-family. This strategy lasted from Sun Tzu's time until well into the eighteenth century as demonstrated by the Qing court's reception of England's first embassy to China. Note this instruction from the Qianlong emperor to his officials, written in 1793, on how to receive Lord Macartney and his mission:

> The way of cherishing men from afar is also lost when not enough is done. . . . When foreigners turn toward transformation, We simply consider their intentions in coming. If they are reverent, obedient, humble and respectful, then we increase Our grace. If they do not understand aspects of the rite, then We guide them by means of ritual practices.[84]

From this passage, we detect the social relations behind *huairou*. The Qianlong emperor clearly represents 'the center' to the Englishmen's 'periphery' and all the attributes associated with such hierarchy, for example, 'high grandeur' to their 'lowly supplicant status,' 'didactic teacher' to their 'naive student,' and 'wise parent' to their 'callow youth.' Nonetheless, the Qianlong emperor sought greater education, not punishment, should the transformation fail to take place.

Granted, *huairou* draws on patriarchal relations to solidify alliances that treat women as only a means to realizing transformation. For example, the Chinese emperor related to the King of Siam as a 'younger uncle' to his 'nephew.'[85] Clearly, *huairou* was a gentlemen's agreement. Still, these patriarchal relations did not feminize other-ness into sexual prey for the center's hypermasculine adventures. Parental governance under *tianxia* was explicitly a family affair, supervised by both parents. Their title 'father-mother officials' (*fumu guan*) reminded representatives of the state that their moral obligation to society was analogous to that of parents to children, that is, they should govern with firmness combined with kindness, authority balanced with love.[86]

Conclusion

To summarize, Sun Tzu instructed on war but taught peace. *Tianxia*'s relational ontology compelled a radical sociality in *ren* so that Sun Tzu's first consideration is moral law, that is, whether war can be justified. Should war be justified *and* unavoidable, rendering war a last resort, Sun Tzu's dialectics calls for transformation (*xianghua*), not annihilation, of the enemy. Not simply a Lockean frugality to save on resources, Sun Tzu believed that rulers and generals had a moral obligation to protect and care for life in general, and their soldiers in particular. This accounted for *huairou* and other policies of co-optation whether through bribery or marriage. Though patriarchal in content, *huairou* policies instilled a sociality of family relations that had no role for hypermasculinity.

The Art of War in neoliberal hands, however, strays far from the source. In plucking Sun Tzu's maxims out of context and inserting them into a dichotomy of self vs. other, neoliberals repudiate both the relational ontology of *tianxia* and its dialectical epistemology. Indeed, Sun Tzu would have strongly objected to the damage done to soldiers in Iraq, both local and U.S. troops. He might have applauded the ability of neoliberal commercial hip to co-opt others into the U.S. hegemonic fold, but he would have advised against fixing on discipline as the only alternative to conversion. The conversion and discipline dichotomy tends to turn Others into reactionary versions of the hypermasculine self, reducing the world to Hobbes' scary state of nature where a perpetual state of "warre of all against all" prevails. Sun Tzu would blanch.

Ironically, many think this misappropriation of Sun Tzu clever. They rationalize it as using the Other to defeat the Other. Explanations range from the speculative to the libelous, as evidenced by two random yet representative sources:

> Although there is no evidence to suggest that al Qaeda's top leaders base their battlefield strategies directly on this ancient Chinese text, there are some clear parallels between their "art of terrorism" and the principles of Sun Tzu's *Art of War*:[87]
>
> Both Sun Tzu and his ancient Chinese commentators say success in battle sometimes depends on placing soldiers in positions where they must fight or die. This is not part of the American way of war. Nonetheless, we should recognize that for other cultures this is standard procedure, and it will affect the tactics of U.S. units facing such enemies.[88]

Some in China are beginning to react with an imperial hypermasculinity of their own. Yes, they affirm, Sun Tzu was a realist[89] who saw power as key[90]; therefore, his strategies are more applicable than ever to contemporary international relations.[91] Ho argues that Sun Tzu *would* deceive his own soldiers by rallying or brainwashing them, for example, so they would be willing to die for the cause.[92] Thus, neoliberal self-and-other relations have been globalized.

Notes

1. For interest in Sun Tzu, see Sonshi, a Web site devoted to Sun Tzu and his principles for U.S. foreign and military policy, http://www.sonshi.com/sun-tzu-terrorism .htm (accessed March 11, 2008). There are many inaccuracies regarding Sun Tzu in U.S. literature, e.g., he is sometimes confused with Machiavelli, his era is cited as the Warring States (475–221 BCE) period when Sun Tzu identified himself with the Spring and Autumn period (722–481 B.CE), and he is dated as from the fifth century BCE when he lived during the sixth century BCE (544–496).
2. See Marwaan Macan-Markar, "Sun Tzu: The Real Father of 'Shock and Awe,'" *Asia Times On-Line*, April 2, 2003, http://www.freerepublic.com/focus/f-news/8830662/posts (accessed March 11, 2008); http://www.sonshi.com/holmes.htmlpal-dcosta-04.doc (accessed March 11, 2008). Sun Tzu is the Wade-Giles transliteration of the Chinese characters that mean, "Master Sun" (Sunzi, the pinyin). We retain the Wade-Giles version here given its familiarity in the West.
3. Milt T. Bearden, "Perspective/Inside the CIA: Iraqi Insurgents Take a Page from the Afghan 'Freedom Fighters,'" November 9, 2003, http://query.nytimes.comgst/fullpage .html?res=9E00EFDB1339F93AA35752C1A9659C8B63 (accessed March 11, 2008).
4. Bruce Bueno de Mesquita, James D. Morrow, Randolph M. Siverson, and Alastair Smith, "Testing Novel Implications from the Selectorate Theory of War," *World Politics* 56 (April 2004): 363–88.
5. Stephen Peter Rosen, "Military Effectiveness: Why Society Matters," *International Security* 19, no. 4 (1995): 5–31.
6. Gerald Segal, "The PLA and Chinese Foreign Policy Decision-Making," *International Affairs* 57, no. 3 (1981): 449–66.
7. Emerson M. Niou and Peter C. Ordershook, "A Game-theoretic Interpretation of Sun Tzu's *The Art of War*," *Journal of Peace Research* 31, no. 2 (1994): 161–74.

8. See Douglas M Mecready, "Learning from Sun Tzu," *Military Review* (May/June 2003): 85–88. The first English translation of *The Art of War* appeared in 1910. De-shun Lo, ed. *Sun tzu bing fa* (Taipei: Li-ming Wen Hua, 1991), 21–22.
9. John Walsh, "Flunking the Art of War: Master Sun-Tzu, President Hu and Bush," *Counterpunch*, June 7, 2006, http://www.counterpunch.org/walsh06072006.html (accessed March 11, 2008); Tom Bevan, "Bush's Sun Tzu 'Strategery,'" *RealClearPolitics*, March 22, 2006, http://www.realclearpolitics.com/articles/2006/03/bushs_suntsu_strategery.html (accessed March 11, 2008).
10. James Henry, "China's Military and Sun Tzu: What Every American Should Know," 2004, http://www.brookesnews.com/04190/china.html (accessed March 11, 2008).
11. Tom Adkins, "Sun Tzu Visits the Middle East," 2002 http://www.freerepublic.com/focus/f-news/928498/posts (accessed March 11, 2008).
12. See also Chow-hou Wee, *Sun Zi Bingfa: Selected Insights and Applications* (Singapore: Pearson, 2005).
13. Harlan Ullman and James P. Wade, Shock *and Awe: Achieving Rapid Dominance*, ebook, 2005, http://www.gutenberg.org/etext/7259 (accessed March 11, 2008).
14. Sandy Tolan, "Incomprehensible Destruction," *Al-Ahram Weekly Online* No. 630, 2003, http://weekly.ahram.org.eg/2003/630/op13.html (accessed March 11, 2008).
15. Ibid.
16. In Mark Crispin Miller, *The Bush Dyslexicon: Observations on a National Disorder* (New York: Norton, 2003).
17. See http://www.whitehouse.gov/news/releases/2002/01/20020110-5.html (accessed March 11, 2008).
18. Ullman and Wade, *Shock and Awe*; Tolan, "Incomprehensible Destruction"; Macan-Marker, "Sun Tzu."
19. De-shun, Lo, ed., *Sun tzu bing fa* (Taipei: Li-ming Wen Hua Publishing House, 1991).
20. Ibid., 19–21.
21. Ho Lu wanted to test the caliber of Sun Tzu's military strategies by having him train those believed to know least about warfare: women.
22. Lo, *Sun Tzu Bing Fa*, 29–30.
23. The Emperor usually presided over a court of three thousand concubines.
24. Lo, *Sun Tzu Bing Fa*, 27–30.
25. Rumsfeld quoted in Tolan, "Incomprehensible Destruction," 2.
26. All quotes of Sun Tzu's in English and Chinese are from Lionel Giles, translated in 1910, http://www.chinapage.com/sunzi-e.html (accessed March 11, 2008).
27. David Campbell, "Cultural Governance and Pictorial Resistance: Reflections on the Imaging of War," *Review of International Studies* 29 (2003): 57–73.
28. Xian Zhong Niu, *Sun tzu san lun: cong gu bing fa dao xin zhan lue* (Taipei: Mai Tian Publishing House, 1996) 47–49.
29. Note, for example, the argument about a democratic peace. This school of thought proposes that warfare will cease when all states convert to liberal democracy; see also Erik Gartzke, "The Capitalist Peace," *American Journal of Political Science* 51, no. 1 (2007): 166–91.

30. Joshua Foa Dienstag, "Serving God and Mammon: The Lockean Sympathy in Early American Political Thought," *American Political Science Review* 90, no. 3 (1996): 499.
31. Carole Pateman, *The Sexual Contract* (Stanford: Stanford University Press, 1988). Also, according to Lloyd, western intellectual thought never considered women capable of reason—the necessary criterion for entering into the social contract. Only men could transcend the banal shackles of the Body to soar into the heavenly realm of Reason. Genevieve Lloyd, *Man of Reason* (Minneapolis: University of Minnesota Press, 1993).
32. Uday S. Mehta, "Liberal Strategies of Exclusion," in *Tensions of Empire: Colonial Cultures in a Bourgeois World*, ed. Frederick Cooper and Ann Laura Stoler (Berkeley: University of California Press, 1997), 59–86.
33. Ibid.
34. See Roxanne L. Doty, *Imperial Encounters: The Politics of Representation in North–South Relations* (Minneapolis: University of Minnesota Press, 1996).
35. See, for example, the commercial for "Nestles Crunch" made and shown in the 1990s: http://youtube.com/watch?v=o8T2JQizPaM (accessed March 11, 2008).
36. Francis Fukuyama, "The End of History?" *The National Interest* (Summer 1989): 3–18.
37. See http://www.2collectcola.com/page/ACC/slogan (accessed March 11, 2008).
38. Michael Hunt, *Ideology and US Foreign Policy* (New Haven: Yale University Press, 1987).
39. Ward Churchill, *A Little Matter of Genocide: Holocaust and Denial in the Americas from 1492 to the Present* (San Francisco: City Lights Books, 1998).
40. Charlotte Hooper, *Manly States: Masculinities, International Relations, and Gender Politics* (New York: Columbia University Press, 2001).
41. Max Boot, *The Savage Wars of Peace: Small Wars and the Rise of American Power* (New York: Basic Books, 2002).
42. *Monthly Review*, "Kipling, the White Man's Burden, and US Imperialism," November 2003, http://www.findarticles.com/p/articles/mi_m1132/is_6_55/ai_111269066 (accessed March 11, 2008).
43. Noah Feldman, *What We Owe Iraq: War and the Ethics of Nation Building* (Princeton: Princeton University Press, 2004), 95.
44. Ibid.
45. Ibid.
46. *New York Times*, August 5, 2007.
47. Ibid., 14.
48. See L. H. M. Ling, *Postcolonial International Relations: Conquest and Desire between Asia and the West* (London: Palgrave Macmillan, 2002).
49. L. H. M. Ling, "Borderlands: A Postcolonial-Feminist Alternative to Neoliberal Self/Other Relations," in ed. Susanne Zwingel, Heike Brandt, and Bettina Bross, *Mehrheit am Rand? Geschlechterverhaeltnisse, globale Ungleichheit und transnationale Loesungsansaetze*, 105–24 (Berlin: VS Verlag, 2008).
50. Solomon Moore and Richard A. Oppel, Jr., "Attacks Imperil U.S.-Backed Militias in Iraq," *International Herald Tribune*, January 24, 2008, http://www.iht.com/articles/2008/01/24/africa/24sunni.php.

51. David Rohde and David E. Sanger, "How the 'Good War' in Afghanistan Went Bad," *New York Times*. August 12, 2007, 1, 12–13.
52. Ibid., 13.
53. See http://users.skynet.be/terrorism/html/laden_statement.htm (accessed March 11, 2008).
54. Elizabeth Rubin, "Battle Company is Out There," *The New York Times Magazine*, February 24, 2008, 41.
55. Ibid., 42.
56. This refers to "night and day, cold and heat, times and seasons."
57. This refers to "distances, great and small; danger and security; open ground and narrow passes; the chances of life and death."
58. "The Commander stands for the virtues of wisdom, sincerely, benevolence, courage and strictness."
59. "By method and discipline are to be understood the marshaling of the army in its proper subdivisions, the graduations of rank among the officers, the maintenance of roads by which supplies may reach the army, and the control of military expenditure."
60. Lo, *Sun Tzu Bng Fa.*, 67.
61. Ibid.
62. Ping-ti Ho, *Youguan sunzi laozi de sanpian kaocheng* (Three Studies on Sun Tzu and Lao Tzu) (Taipei: Institute of Modern History, Academica Sinica, 2002).
63. In Ju Lu, *Sunzi bingfa gongliguan bianxi* (An Analysis of Sunzi's Utilitarianism), Chongqing youdianxueyuan xuebao shehuikexue ban 5 (2006): 741.
64. Ibid., 742.
65. For example: soft/hard (*ying yang*), hot/cold (*han shou*).
66. For example: big/small (*da xiao*), brave/cowardly (*yung qie*), host/guest (*zhu ke*), foe/friend (*di wuo*).
67. For example: up/down (*shang xia*), left/right (*zuo you*), horizontal/vertical (*zung heng*).
68. For example: smooth/difficult (*shun ni*), dead/live or fixed/mobile (*si sheng*), victory/defeat (*sheng bai*)
69. For example: past/present (*wang lai*).
70. See Ho, *Youguan sunzi laozi de sanpian kaocheng*, 3–4.
71. Shan-ch'un Yang, *Sun Tzu* (Taipei: Zhishufang Publishers, 1999), 227. Translation by the authors.
72. Tingyang Zhao, "Rethinking Empire from a Chinese Concept 'All-under-Heaven' (*Tian-xia*)," *Social Identities* 12, no. 1 (January 2006): 30.
73. L. H. M. Ling, "Borders of Our Minds: Territories, Boundaries, and Power in the Confucian Tradition," in *States, Nations, and Borders: The Ethics of Making Boundaries*, ed. Margaret Moore and Allen Buchanan (Cambridge: Cambridge University Press, 2003).
74. James L. Hevia, *Cherishing Men from Afar: Qing Guest Ritual and the Macartney Embassy of 1793* (Durham: Duke University Press, 1995).
75. Zhao, "Rethinking Empire,"36.

76. Hwa Yol Jung, "Confucianism and Existentialism: Intersubjectivity as the Way of Man," *Philosophy and the Phenomenological Research* 30, no. 2 (December 1969): 193–94.
77. Jung, "Confucianism and Existentialism," 193–94.
78. Zhao, "Rethinking Empire," 35.
79. Jung, "Confucianism and Existentialism," 195.
80. Wai-Yee Li, "The Idea of Authority in the Shih chi (Records of the Historian)," *Harvard Journal of Asiatic Studies* 54, no. 2 (December 1994): 395, 399, 400.
81. Li, "The Idea of Authority," 400.
82. Zhao, "Rethinking Empire," 35.
83. Hevia, *Cherishing Men from Afar*; Xu 2003. Xu, Jie Ling (2003) "Chunqiu bangjiao sixiang shulun." Qiushi xuekan (Seeking Truth) 30(1) January: 106–10.
84. Qianlong Emperor cited in Hevia, *Cherishing Men from Afar*, 186.
85. Ling, "Borders of Our Minds."
86. L. H. M. Ling, "Rationalizations for State Violence in Chinese Politics: The Hegemony of Parental Governance," *Journal of Peace Research* 31, no. 4 (November 1994): 393–405.
87. Bartley, Caleb M. (2005) "The Art of Terrorism: What Sun Tzu Can Teach Us about International Terrorism." *Comparative Strategy* 24: 237–51.
88. McCready, "Learning from Sun Tzu," 87–88.
89. Dongpuo Li, "Sunzi zhanzhengguan xinlun" (A New Approach to Sun Tzu's View of War), *Zhexue baijia* 6 (2007): 190–92.
90. Zhanwu Wei and Zhongxiang Jing, "Lun 'Sunzi bingfa' zhong de zhexue tixi yu zheli tedian (On the Philosophical System and Philosophical Distinguishing Characteristics of Sun-tzu's *Art of War*)," *Journal of Jilin National University*, Humanities and Social Science Edition 1 (February 2007): 9–12.
91. Liou Yang, "Guanzi de guojia guanxi sixiang ganwei" (A Brief Probe into Guanzi's Inter-State Theory), *Guanzi xuekan* 4 (2006): 9–11.
92. Ho, *Youguan sunzi laozi de sanpian kaocheng*, 30–31, 40.

CHAPTER 5

When the UN 'Succeeds'

The Case of Cambodia

Sandra Whitworth

> Cambodia demonstrates what the international community can accomplish when the collective will of the major powers acts in concert for the larger good.
>
> —Stephen J. Randall

Chea Veth[1] returned to her home country after more than two decades away when the United Nations launched a peacekeeping mission in 1991, known as the United Nations Transitional Authority in Cambodia (UNTAC). Chea was a member of Cambodia's former elite and had left Cambodia long before the American bombings of the 1970s and the subsequent Khmer Rouge atrocities that would leave her homeland with the infamous moniker 'the killing fields.' But when the UN went to Cambodia in the early 1990s to broker a peace agreement, Chea decided it was time to return to Cambodia to lend a hand. In her Phnom Penh neighborhood she carried not only the privilege of her background, but was known to be well-connected with the UN mission, and her facility with a variety of languages meant that she was sometimes called upon by neighbors who needed assistance in dealing with UNTAC personnel. When a local woman whose daughter had been employed as a cook and cleaner by a number of men working as part of UNTAC asked for help in finding out why her daughter had suddenly quit her job and was not acting like herself, Chea probably already had a good idea about what might be causing the unusual behavior. Likely, so too did the mother.

The neighbor's daughter eventually revealed to Chea that her employers had demanded she have sex with them, and that when she resisted, they raped her. The young woman was unable to tell anyone of her ordeal: the men who assaulted her ensured her silence—and compounded her sense of shame—by telling her repeatedly that she should have known from the beginning what was expected of her, that they had hired her to prostitute herself. A job that she had felt fortunate to get, and through which she had proudly contributed to her family's income, had turned into a nightmare. As Chea describes,

> I was not entirely surprised, we had all heard the stories by that point. I went with her to the UNTAC authorities, but the things that had happened to her had happened weeks before. UNTAC said there was no evidence, to go home, that we had waited too long to make our complaint. By the end of the mission, I knew directly of at least three other such complaints and heard of many more. We were so busy, we were trying to make the election happen. Maybe we should have tried to follow up on issues like this more than we did, but there were so many things happening and it was such a busy time.[2]

One of the first multilevel peacekeeping missions conducted by the United Nations in the post–cold war period, the eighteen-month mission to Cambodia was considered something of a test case for the UN, insofar as its success or failure would have important implications for future, large-scale missions.[3] Most observers cite a series of lessons learned that emerged from the mission, but by and large it is regarded as a success story for the UN.[4] From a feminist or critical perspective, one of the tests of UNTAC was to discover whether the thousands of young men deployed as soldiers on this mission would act any differently than soldiers deployed in more traditional forms of combat. Would wearing a blue helmet make a difference? The accounts of the mission given by the UN and mainstream observers seldom reported the enormous social dislocation that resulted from the deployment of twenty-three thousand foreign personnel—some seventeen thousand of whom were soldiers—into a fragile, conflict-weary society. That dislocation included skyrocketing inflation, the eruption of prostitution to service UNTAC personnel, the exponential increase of HIV/AIDS in Cambodia, as well as charges of assault and harassment directed at UNTAC by both expatriate and local citizens.[5] Even as early supporters of the mission began to question UNTAC's effectiveness—especially after the 1997 coup mounted by Second Prime Minister Hun Sen—that questioning rarely included a consideration of the impact the mission had on local people's own sense of security, and particularly on women's sense of security.

This chapter briefly explores the background to UNTAC and the mission itself. The argument here is that, far from 'setting a new standard' for peacekeeping operations as Boutros-Ghali so enthusiastically proclaimed, soldiers deployed on this mission—along with their military and political leaders—were operating on the same assumptions about women and, "about the roles women must play if a male soldier is to be able to do his job,"[6] as soldiers deployed on more traditional military missions have operated throughout history. Those assumptions include the expectation that prostitutes will be available to sexually service male soldiers, that it is appropriate to pursue local women, whether prostitutes or not, and that a certain level of violence directed toward the local population, both physical and sexual, is part and parcel of any military operation. As will be discussed throughout this chapter, those assumptions seriously undermine any real sense of security and lay bare the optimistic conclusions drawn by the UN and its supporters about this mission. Alternatively, as Cynthia Enloe notes, "Everyone who sends troops needs to rethink what kind of soldiering works to keep the peace. Because a peace that involves sexual exploitation and sexual violence is no peace at all."[7]

Background to the UNTAC Mission

Prior to the UN mission, Cambodia's complex history had involved in 1970 a military coup, which ousted from power the popular but erratic, Prince Norodom Sihanouk. His successor, General Lon Nol, was supported by the United States and Lon Nol who, in turn, directly supported the United States by engaging with Vietnamese troops both inside and outside Cambodian borders. Along with the overwhelming and largely covert bombing of Cambodian targets by the United States, an estimated half million Cambodians, mostly noncombatants, lost their lives between 1970 and 1975 and many more were turned into internal refugees.[8] The mayhem caused by the United States' undeclared war in Cambodia set the stage for the Angkor Revolution—the overthrow of the Cambodian state, and indeed of all Cambodian society, by the Khmer Rouge beginning in 1975. The Khmer Rouge left an estimated one and a half to two million Cambodians dead out of a total population of only six or seven million.[9]

When the Vietnamese government invaded Cambodia in 1978 to topple the Khmer Rouge, it may have ended the genocide, but it did not bring an end to conflict in Cambodia. For the next decade, four factions engaged in a civil war within Cambodia: the Vietnamese-backed Heng Samrin-Hun Sen regime, or the Cambodian People's Party (the CPP, which because it held power, would later also be called the State of Cambodia, or SOC), the royalist party, FUNCINPEC (National United Front for an Independent, Neutral, Peaceful and Co-operative Cambodia, led by the former king of Cambodia, Prince Norodom Sihanouk), the Khmer People's National Liberation Front (KPNLF) and the Khmer Rouge (Party of Democratic Kampuchea, or PDK). The Hun Sen regime, which served as the government within Cambodia throughout the 1980s, was supported by both Vietnam and the Soviet Union. The other three factions waged a largely guerilla war and received support from the West, China, and ASEAN (the Association of Southeast Asian Nations).[10] Cambodians continued to be displaced during the 1980s because of the civil war, and most suffered extreme poverty that resulted, at least in part, from an international aid embargo mounted against Cambodia by the United Nations in an effort to force an end to Vietnam's occupation.[11]

Throughout the Khmer Rouge period and subsequent civil war, a half million Cambodians fled the country to live in exile in Thailand and other parts of the world. Some 362,000 refugees were still in the refugee camps along the Thai border when the Peace Agreements were signed in 1991, many of whom had lived in "the violent limbo [of] the border camps"[12] for as long as thirteen years. The camps were supervised by the United Nations' High Commissioner for Refugees (UNHCR), the International Committee of the Red Cross (ICRC) and the United Nations Border Relief Operation (UNBRO), but were also separately administered by each of the three ousted warring Cambodian factions.[13]

Diplomatic efforts in the early 1980s failed to resolve the civil war, but by the end of the decade, the economic, military, and political price to Vietnam of directly maintaining its regime in Cambodia became increasingly costly at the same time that support from the Soviet Union began to diminish. Rising Western and ASEAN interests in the investment potential of Cambodia, diplomatic efforts on the part of Indonesia and France, and the withdrawal of China's support for the Khmer Rouge all pushed the various factions into a series of informal meetings and negotiations.[14] In October of 1991, after several years of intense bargaining and international pressure, the four factions signed the peace agreements, and committed themselves to a framework for achieving peace in Cambodia and an unprecedented role for the UN in implementing that peace.

The UNTAC Mission

The lengthy and detailed Paris Peace Agreements established both UNTAC and the Supreme National Council (SNC), a body composed of the four main Cambodian factions under the chairmanship of Prince Norodom Sihanouk. The SNC was intended to serve as the sovereign authority of Cambodia during the transition to a democratically elected government.[15] Almost immediately upon signing, in November of 1991, the United Nations Advance Mission in Cambodia (UNAMIC) was deployed, but involved initially only fifty military liaison officers and a twenty-person mine awareness unit. UNAMIC was viewed as being largely ineffective, and by December of 1991, the advance mission was expanded to involve an additional 1,100 personnel and to include a more extensive mine clearance operation, road and bridge repair, and in conjunction with the UNHCR, the preparation of repatriation routes, reception centers, and resettlement areas.[16] UNTAC the largest UN peacekeeping operation ever, requiring over fifteen thousand troops and seven thousand civilian personnel and costing over an estimated US$2.8 billion during the span of eighteen months.[17] In addition to the UN personnel involved, the mission to Cambodia also recruited some sixty thousand local Cambodian staff, most involved in election-related activities. UNTAC, in short, was the first of a growing post–cold war trend for the UN: enormously complex missions involving the vast expenditure of both resources and personnel.

The scale of the mission may have been unprecedented, but its composition, worked out at UN Headquarters in New York, reflected a fairly traditional, highly militarized, and male-dominated venture. Of the nearly twenty-three thousand international military and civilian personnel, there were no women appointed to Director-level posts within the mission, very few women in the military contingents, and little presence of women in high-level posts among international civil servants assigned from UN Headquarters or UN specialized agencies. There were so few women appointed to UNTAC, in fact, that a UN Division for the Advancement of Women study on women's involvement in peacekeeping missions registers their presence, in statistical terms, as 'zero.' As the UN study notes, one woman serving on the mission noted that more women in either the military or the police components of the mission might have dispelled the local impression that the United Nations was 'an army of occupation.'[18]

Luckily for the UN, most mainstream observers were happy to focus on UNTAC's various successes. Over eighteen months, the UNTAC mission contributed to some reduction of the violence that prevailed in Cambodia, it successfully repatriated the almost 370,000 Cambodian refugees who had been living along the Thai border and perhaps most important, conducted a relatively free and fair election in which some four million people, or 85 percent of Cambodia's registered voters participated.[19] The UN claimed as well that the mission "boosted Cambodia's economy by raising funds internationally for economic rehabilitation and expansion throughout the country."[20]

There are also some discussions within mainstream accounts of problems associated with the mission. For example, the UN failed to achieve a situation of political neutrality, as pledged in the 1991 Paris Peace Agreement, in part, because the Khmer Rouge withdrew from the demobilization and cantonment process and threatened throughout the mission to disrupt the election campaign.[21] The Khmer Rouge blamed the UN for not adequately monitoring the withdrawal process of Vietnamese troops and accused the UN mission of recolonizing Cambodia. Likewise, the presence of UNTAC may have diminished, but it did not stop political violence, which was aimed at both political party members and ethnic Vietnamese.[22]

In addition to the critiques revealed in official accounts of the mission, a series of other concerns about the mission were raised by local Cambodian individuals and agencies and a few outside observers. One damning set of criticisms focuses on the repatriation efforts, one of the elements of the mission usually touted as a success. While the UN did manage to repatriate the 362,000 refugees living along the Thai border back to Cambodia in time for the election, it was widely reported that the speed of the repatriation resulted in many people remaining unsettled long after their return to Cambodia and few received sufficient support to re-enter Cambodian society easily. The Cambodia to which the refugees returned was also one that was experiencing the economic dislocation of the UNTAC mission. As Court Robinson notes, "the signing of the Paris Agreements had unleashed what some observers called '*capitalism sauvage*.'"[23] The influx of nearly twenty-three thousand people into Cambodia, many of whom were making more in a single day than the average Cambodian made in an entire year, drove up the price of food, housing, and basic goods.[24]

Cambodia, UNTAC, and Women

The picture of the UN peacekeeping mission to Cambodia becomes even more complicated if we ask the question, what was the impact on women? It is easy to 'read' the peacekeeping mission in Cambodia without any consideration of gender: as the previous few sections illustrate, the history of the conflict is sufficiently complex, and the mission itself so enormous that it is a daunting task just to convey the official accounts. So, it is perhaps not too surprising that those accounts are not only silent about the impact of the mission on local people generally, but that they are particularly silent about the impact of the mission on women. Ironically, those accounts remain silent even when that impact is not entirely negative. Many women within Cambodia report that in addition to the formal proclamations of success, the UNTAC effort also achieved some notable successes with regard to women.

One of Cambodia's most striking demographic characteristics has long been its preponderance of women and children: at the time the Paris Peace Agreements were being negotiated, it was estimated that 65 percent of the population was female, women headed 35 percent of all households, and more than half of the population was under the age of fifteen.[25] These characteristics were a direct result of Cambodia's violent past. As Judy Ledgerwood notes, "More women than men survived the traumas of [the Khmer Rouge] period. Women are better able to survive conditions of severe malnutrition, fewer women were targeted for execution because of connections to the old regime, and fewer women were killed in battles."[26] Even after the Khmer Rouge fled to the northeastern part of the country, men continued to be 'drained off' from society in order to serve as soldiers during Cambodia's long civil war.[27]

Despite the fact that women significantly outnumbered men in Cambodia, the position of women within Cambodian society was at best mixed, reflecting both their revered status as wives and mothers coupled with a set of expectations about appropriate feminine behavior that was far more constraining than anything faced by men. The revered status of women is described well by one Cambodian proverb: "One father is worth one thousand friends; one mother is worth one thousand fathers."[28] Women in Cambodia often managed the household economy as well as the family itself, and women were legally entitled to inherit property from either spouses or parents.

At the same time, however, the virtuous Cambodian woman was expected to be shy, to act in a reserved manner and to walk quietly, making as little noise as possible. Many young women in Cambodia do not continue in school after puberty, are expected instead to help their mother within the home, and, ideally, will be married to a man chosen by their family by the time they are eighteen years old. Reflecting the assumption that Cambodian women are more properly involved within the household than outside of it, work and political activity outside of the home is not always available to Cambodian women. While of course many women did end up participating in agricultural production and the paid labor force out of economic necessity (in some industries and in agricultural production generally, in fact, women outnumbered men),[29] they usually earned far less than their male counterparts did.[30] Likewise, women in Cambodia were not well represented in positions of political decision-making authority. Grant Curtis wrote that in the Cambodian government of the 1980s, there was only a single woman member of the Politburo and five women in the thirty-member Party Central Committee. The total number of women within the governing party membership as a whole was only some 5 percent.[31]

One of UNTAC's most notable successes with regard to women resulted from the freedom of association that prevailed in many respects during the peacekeeping mission and in particular, the efforts of the United Nations Development Fund for Women (UNIFEM) to incorporate women's issues into the general election. UNIFEM engaged in public education and information campaigns in the printed media and on radio and television as well as a four-day National Women's Summit. The aim was to get women out to vote, to get them involved politically (whether within formal political structures of government, social movements or non-governmental organizations) and to get them talking with one another. UNTAC Radio, for example, offered a regular segment on some of the particular difficulties faced by women in Cambodia generally, and in particular, how this might affect their ability to vote in the upcoming general elections. Similarly, the Women's Summit brought together Cambodian women from all sectors of society to identify and prioritize women's issues in order to lobby political parties contesting the election and then later the government itself.[32]

These efforts were not only successful in getting a large proportion of the female electorate to participate in the May 1993 elections, but were also credited with encouraging the emergence of an indigenous women's movement within Cambodia and as well saw specific material support directed to existing indigenous women's NGOs and for the creation of some new women's NGOs. These NGOs, in turn, mounted a very effective lobby of the Cambodian government such that important equality rights provisions eventually made it into the new Cambodian constitution. Even more important, perhaps, they started to set the tone that women's participation in politics, broadly defined, was both legitimate and useful. In addition to lobbying the new Cambodian government around equality rights, Cambodian women's NGOs have also through the kinds of preliminary discussions that were made possible at the Women's Summit, organized around some of the priorities that were identified in those meetings, such as literacy for women, economic independence, health, and so on.[33]

Another way in which UNTAC is cited as having contributed in a positive way to women's lives concerned domestic violence. The Project Against Domestic Violence in Phnom Penh reported that in a context where few cases of domestic violence are ever brought to the authorities and fewer still are prosecuted, one provincial judge described the only criminal case of domestic violence she had ever presided over as one in which UNTAC officers brought in a man caught beating his wife in a marketplace.[34] Violence against women was politicized through the discussions at the Women's Summit, with a demand from participants that the new Cambodian state protect women against domestic violence, along with calls for measures to promote women's equality in the workforce, in politics, and to provide more equitable divorce laws, among other things.

UNTAC and Women: The Critique

Just as neither the positive consequences for women that resulted from the UNTAC mission merit much specific discussion within official sources, nor did a whole series of more negative consequences. The already difficult adjustment that local people made to the arrival of the UN into Cambodia was more difficult still for many women. For those coming from the refugee camps, repatriation often meant being dropped into a situation of greater, rather than less, insecurity. Eight months into the repatriation effort, UNHCR designated Female Heads of Household an 'at risk' group. Groups at risk were intended to receive extra support and extra counseling before the repatriation to help prepare them; but even after they were designated an at risk group, many female heads of households received no extra support and often only a few minutes of counseling to know what they might face upon their return.[35] Cambodian women's groups and human rights workers were concerned that many of the women who returned from the camps faced a life of homelessness in which their options were limited to becoming beggars or prostitutes.[36]

Indeed, with the arrival of UNTAC prostitution became a booming business within Cambodia and certainly one to which many women turned in order to survive. The Cambodian Women's Development Association estimated that the number of prostitutes in Cambodia grew from about six thousand in 1992 to more than twenty-five thousand at the height of the mission.[37] While the presence of prostitutes was not new (according to numerous accounts, frequenting prostitutes is a regular feature of many Cambodian men's behavior), many Cambodians were nonetheless alarmed by the dramatic increase in prostitution and its far more open nature. Prostitution spread to the provincial villages of Cambodia, where previously it had been concentrated in the capital, and many observers report a rise in child prostitution with the arrival of UNTAC.[38]

Early reports indicate that the vast majority, if not all, of the prostitutes were young Vietnamese women who emigrated into Cambodia to take advantage of the growing prostitution business. These estimates result more from the prevailing anti-Vietnamese sentiment than any reflection of reality.[39] As the 'ethnic other' in Cambodia, Vietnamese women represent all prostitutes, on the assumption that virtuous Cambodian women and girls would not partake of such an activity. The perception that prostitutes were all Vietnamese and the widespread use of prostitutes by UNTAC personnel, played nicely into hands of the Khmer Rouge in their efforts to undermine the peace process. They accused peacekeepers of being too busy with prostitutes to check on the presence of Vietnamese soldiers and as Judy Ledgerwood writes, "Some Cambodians were more inclined to believe Khmer Rouge propaganda that UNTAC was collaborating with the Vietnamese to colonize Cambodia when they saw UNTAC personnel taking Vietnamese 'wives.'"[40] In fact, of course, Cambodian women and girls did work as prostitutes, and as Cambodians began to realize that 'even' good Cambodian women were being drawn into prostitution to service UNTAC personnel, their anger toward the UN flared even further. As one man described it, "Everybody started to wonder what they had come here for, to implement a peace accord or to turn our women into prostitutes."[41]

The influx of nearly twenty-three thousand UN personnel and the dramatic rise in prostitution also appears to have resulted in a dramatic rise in cases of HIV and AIDS, with the WHO reporting that 75 percent of people giving blood in Phnom Penh were infected with HIV (though this is considered inflated by some observers) and another report indicating that 20 percent of the soldiers in one French battalion tested positive when they finished their six month tour of duty.[42] Most observers noted that while UNTAC was not responsible for bringing HIV and AIDS to Cambodia, it did contribute to its spread. Nonetheless, one of the pejoratives sometimes directed at UNTAC by citizens was to re-name the acronym UNTAC to "the United Nations Transmission of AIDS to Cambodia." UNTAC's chief medical officer predicted that as many as seven times more UN personnel would eventually die of AIDS contracted in Cambodia than had died because of hostile action.[43] A United Nations training document published by the Department of Peacekeeping Operations and the Joint UN Programme on HIV/AIDS several years after the UNTAC mission confirms that "over 100 peacekeeping troops were infected with HIV—and may have infected others—during the UNTAC Mission in Cambodia."[44]

As criticism toward UN personnel within Cambodia grew, a number of what Judy Ledgerwood describes as 'telling' actions were announced. As the 'Observer of Business and Politics in Bombay' noted, "Peacekeeping chiefs have warned their men to be more discrete, for example, by not parking their distinctive white vehicles outside massage parlors and in red light areas."[45] Eva Arnvig also reports that in the same directive UN personnel were asked not to frequent brothels in uniform.[46] A second response was to ship an additional 800,000 condoms to Cambodia.[47]

The association of peacekeeping with prostitution in Cambodia remains a strong sentiment to this day. In the Cambodian Cultural Village, opened in 2003 in the city of Siem Reap, a wax museum displays different scenes from Cambodia's history and culture. Its representation of the UNTAC era depicts a male UN peacekeeper with arms draped around a prostitute. The display was not, apparently, intended as a critique of the mission, simply as a presentation of typical scenes from different moments in Cambodia's past.

In addition to prostitution, charges emerged also of sexual abuse and violence. Raoul Jennar reports that in 1993, "in the Preah Vihear hospital, there was for a time a majority of injured people who were young kids, the victims of sexual abuse by UN soldiers."[48] There were frequent claims of rape and sexual assault brought to women's NGOs during the UNTAC period, but (as in the story with which this chapter opened), often days or weeks after the rapes were alleged to have taken place such that the usual expectations surrounding evidence collection could not be carried out and claims could not be substantiated to the satisfaction of UN officials.[49] As one women's group organizer describes, "I remember one nineteen-year-old girl who had bathed and didn't tell anyone about what had happened to her for two days. The UN said we had no evidence. We learned from that."[50]

It is also a widely shared view among many Cambodian women and men that the phenomenon of 'fake marriages' was widespread during the UNTAC mission. Simply put, a UN soldier would marry a Cambodian woman, but only for the duration of his posting to Cambodia, at which point he would abandon her. Some women are reported to have been abandoned as far away as Bangkok, and left to their own devices to make their ways home. In addition to the emotional trauma of fake marriages, they were enormously shameful for women in a society with very strict norms about what is appropriate behavior in good women. For the same reason, they could also have deadly consequences for the men involved: some Cambodians and expatriates allege that at least one of the UN's casualties in Phnom Penh was a retribution killing in which family members murdered a soldier who had just informed his 'wife' that he had no intention of bringing her with him once he was re-deployed home.[51]

Women also reported being sexually harassed by UNTAC soldiers and personnel. As one expatriate woman describes, "I thought, if this happens to me, think what Khmer[52] women have to face. . . . After 13 years of war, people feel afraid. There's no place for them to go, no support if they want to say no. And now they have another form of harassment: UNTAC."[53] A UN Report confirmed the harassment, and rather belatedly, suggests some guidelines:

> Perhaps because many UNTAC personnel only have contact with Khmer (and Vietnamese) women through prostitution, there is a tendency on the part of some personnel to treat all women as though they were prostitutes. This includes

> grabbing at women on the street, making inappropriate gestures and remarks and physically following or chasing women travelling in public. UNTAC personnel should be briefed on the fact that gender conceptions in Khmer culture are different from their own. Physical contact between the sexes in public is NEVER acceptable. If a woman laughs when she is touched, this laughter is probably a sign of embarrassment or fear and not encouragement. The problem is not exclusively one between Khmer women and male UNTAC staff, but is a generalized problem. Female UNTAC staff have similarly expressed problems with sexual harassment. The problem is not a small problem.[54]

When concerns about the drunken behavior and sexual misconduct that prevailed during UNTAC were brought to the attention of the UN Secretary-General's Special Representative to Cambodia at a meeting for nongovernmental organizations, Mr. Yasushi Akashi stunned those in attendance by saying that it was natural for hot-blooded young soldiers who had endured the rigors of the field to want to have a few beers and to chase "young beautiful beings of the opposite sex."[55] Akashi's 'boys will be boys' attitude galvanized those at the meeting, who then delivered an open letter of protest signed by 165 Cambodian and expatriate women and men accusing some UNTAC personnel of sexual harassment and assault, violence against women and prostitutes, and of being responsible for the dramatic rise of prostitution and HIV/AIDS. The letter described how women felt restricted in their movements and powerless as a result of UNTAC's presence in Cambodia.[56] Having recovered from his earlier faux pas, Akashi pledged to assign a Community Relations officer to hear the complaints of the Cambodian community.[57]

One commonly held observation was that many of the problems associated with UNTAC were exacerbated by the fact that there were very few women involved in the mission. The UN may have had good ideas about women's participation in politics, but it did not really practice what it preached. Many Cambodian women noted, for example, that although UNIFEM tried to highlight women's issues in the electoral process, because UNTAC itself had very few women involved at any level within the mission, and none at all in positions of decision-making authority, it undermined their own message about women's political participation. As one woman says,

> We are trying to incorporate women at all levels of government, and we face opposition from men in Cambodia for trying to do that. We point to the UN to support our arguments about women's participation in politics. But there were no women in high positions in UNTAC. Why should men here give up positions of authority to women when the UN came here and didn't even do it themselves?[58]

Too Few Women or Too Many Soldiers?

The problem, however, may not have been simply the result of a lack of women, but rather a preponderance of soldiers. UNTAC not only deployed some seventeen thousand soldiers, but many contributing countries sent some of their elite units on this mission. Yeshua Moser-Puangsuwan notes that Malaysia sent its Rangers, because, as a Malaysian Major reported, "they had the 'highest kill ratio' of any Malaysian military units against internal insurgents."[59] Other units, such as those from India and Bangladesh received commando training before their departure for Cambodia, but little in the way of specific training for peacekeeping or Cambodia. The Indian unit had conducted counter-insurgency operations in Kashmir, Sri Lanka, and Assam prior to its deployment to Cambodia and the Bangladeshi unit was trained in counter-insurgency warfare and is regularly "sent on rotation to the Chittagong Hill Tracts in Bangladesh to wage war against non-Bengali indigenous groups."[60] Only the Indonesian military had provided extensive cultural and language training, information about the Paris Peace Accords, handling land mines and the command structure of UNTAC, but had put its training program together on its own initiative, having received no formal instructions from the UN about how to train military troops for peacekeeping missions.[61]

Instead of human relationship skills, however, some members of the foreign militaries deployed to Cambodia were quick to dehumanize local citizens, seeing them and their country as hopelessly irrational and backward. The view of some soldiers was that the UN mission was in Cambodia to save it from itself.[62] As postcolonial theorists have long argued, those who 'need to be saved' are often depicted as less than fully human. One Bangladeshi sergeant's comments are illustrative here: "[Cambodians] think nothing of laying mines. . . . They scatter them about like popped rice. Often they mine their own doorstep before going to bed. . . . They don't care who gets killed; life really has no value here."[63]

However, it was when they received assistance toward what Amitav Ghosh describes as 'the tiny, cumulative efforts' by which people reclaim their lives, that local people report UNTAC contributed most to enhancing their real sense of security—it was when peacekeepers rebuilt homes, schools and parks, opened hospitals or rebuilt—that UNTAC is best remembered by Cambodians.[64] However, the tiny, cumulative ways in which people rebuild their lives do not provide the rationale for enormously complex, multidimensional peacekeeping missions. The kinds of missions, in the words of Anne Orford, that depend upon the 'heroic narratives' of intervention—those that tell us who needs to be saved and how (and by whom) they are to be saved.[65] They do not provide the legitimations for a militarized presence. Building schools and hospitals, parks and bridges, or providing medical services in the end do not depend on the specific skills associated with soldiering. They are skills possessed by carpenters or engineers or doctors. The argument of this chapter is that in deploying a highly militarized, and highly masculinized, peacekeeping mission to Cambodia, increasing, rather than alleviating, the insecurities of many local people was almost ensured.

Conclusions

Mainstream accounts of the kinds of issues raised here about the UNTAC mission are often attributed, as Janet Heininger writes, to the problems of establishing a 'common standard of behavior' among contributing countries.[66] Or in Alan James' even more dismissive comments: "In Cambodia the libidinal proclivities of one contingent apparently led to a great deal of local embarrassment for the United Nations."[67] In other words, the problem is explained by the fact that some contributing countries, usually those with less experience in peacekeeping missions—or perhaps more libidinous proclivities—send troops not well-suited to the expectations associated with peacekeeping. In the Cambodian case, the Bulgarians are cited as the chief offenders.

While not denying that particular contributing country soldiers may have caused specific sets of problems, it is important to note also that this kind of argument deflects attention away from critical concerns and turns soaring rates of prostitution and HIV/AIDS, sexual harassment and exploitation into a set of 'technical problems.' Thus, rather than ask questions about the value of relying chiefly on soldiers as peacekeepers,[68] ethnic arguments are deployed instead, and so the primary concern becomes 'problems of co-ordination.' Rethinking how peacekeeping is conducted or how soldiers are constituted remains unasked.

Notes

1. All the names of interviewees have been changed to protect their identity, except in cases where their interviews corresponded to material they have published or otherwise made public; respondents in discussion with the author, Phnom Penh, Cambodia, March and April 1996.
2. Interviews, Phnom Penh, Cambodia, March and April 1996.
3. Janet E. Heininger, *Peacekeeping in Transition: The United Nations in Cambodia* (New York: The Twentieth Century Fund, 1994), 7.
4. See, for example, Paul F. Diehl, *International Peacekeeping* (Baltimore: Johns Hopkins University Press, 1994), 198–99.
5. An important exception here is the collection by Peter Utting, ed., *Between Hope and Insecurity: The Social Consequences of the Cambodian Peace Process* (Geneva: UN Research Institute for Social Development, 1994).
6. Cynthia Enloe, *The Morning After: Sexual Politics at the End of the Cold War* (Berkeley: University of Southern California Press, 1993), 35.
7. Cited from Gayle Kirshenbaum, "Who's Watching the Peacekeepers?" *Ms.* (May/June 1994): 15.
8. David P. Chandler, *The Tragedy of Cambodian History: Politics, War and Revolution Since 1945* (New Haven: Yale University Press, 1991), 215.

9. Much of the information in this section draws on this work and Aihwa Ong, "Mother's Milk in War and Diaspora," *Cultural Survival Quarterly* (Spring 1995): 61–64.
10. Michael W. Doyle, *UN Peacekeeping in Cambodia: UNTAC's Civil Mandate* (Boulder, CO: Lynne Rienner, 1995), 16.
11. See Eva Mysliwiec, *Punishing the Poor: The International Isolation of Kampuchea* (Oxford: Oxfam, 1988); and Eva L. Mysliwiec, "Cambodia: NGOs in Transition," in Utting, *Between Hope and Insecurity*, 104.
12. May M. Ebihara, Carol A. Mortland, and Judy Ledgerwood, "Introduction" in *Cambodian Culture since 1975: Homeland and Exile* (Ithaca: Cornell University Press, 1994), 20; quoting Al Santoli, "Voices from the Refugee Camps," in *First International Scholars Conference on Cambodia, Selected Papers*, ed. R.A. Judkins (Geneso, NY: SUNY Department of Anthropology and the Geneso Foundation, 1988), 9–12.
13. Aungkana Kamonpetch, "The Progress of Preliminary Phase of Khmer Repatriation," *Occasional Paper Series No. 6* (Bangkok: Indochinese Refugee Information Center, Institute of Asian Studies, Chulalongkorn University, May 1993), 28–29.
14. Doyle, *UN Peacekeeping in Cambodia*, 21–24.
15. Michael W. Doyle and Nishkala Suntharalignam, "The UN in Cambodia: Lessons for Complex Peacekeeping," *International Peacekeeping* 1, no. 2 (Summer 1994): 120.
16. Boutros-Ghali, Boutros, "Introduction," in *The United Nations and Cambodia 1991–1995*, The UN Blue Book Series, vol. 2 (New York: UN Department of Public Information, 1995), 10–11; Jarat Chopra, "United Nations Authority in Cambodia," Occasional Paper 15 (Providence: Thomas J. Watson, Jr. Institute for International Studies, 1994), 1.
17. Doyle and Suntharalignam, "The UN in Cambodia," 121.
18. Ibid.
19. Ker Munthit, "Akashi: Election 'Free and Fair,'" *Phnom Penh Post* (June 6–12, 1993): 3.
20. Boutros-Ghali, *The United Nations and Cambodia*, 54.
21. Ramses Amer, "The United Nations' Peacekeeping Operation in Cambodia: Overview and Assessment," *Contemporary Southeast Asia* 15, no. 2 (September 1993): 211–31.
22. Nate Thayer, "Sihanouk Slams Political Violence," *Phnom Penh Post* 2, no. 2 (January 15–28, 1993): 1; Tom McCarthy, "Slaughter of Vietnamese in Phum Taches Was Cold and Calculated," *Phnom Penh Post* 2, no. 2 (January 15–28, 1993): 3; Nate Thayer, "UNTAC Fails to Stem Political Violence," *Phnom Penh Post* 2, no. 4 (February 12–25, 1993): 3; Andrea Hamilton, "Murders of Party Officials Continue," *Phnom Penh Post* 2, no. 14 (July 2–15, 1993): 1.
23. Court Robinson, "Rupture and Return: Repatriation, Displacement and Reintegration in Battambang Province Cambodia," *Occasional Paper Series No. 7* (Indochinese Refugee Information Center, Institute of Asian Studies, Chulllongkorn University, November 1994), 10.
24. William Shawcross, *Deliver Us From Evil: Peacekeepers, Warlords and a World of Endless Conflict* (New York: Simon and Schuster, 2000), 71–73; Judy Ledgerwood,

"UN Peacekeeping Missions: The Lessons from Cambodia," in *Analysis from the East-West Center No. 11* (Honolulu: East-West Center, March 1994), 6–7.

25. See Judy Ledgerwood, *Analysis of the Situation of Women in Cambodia* (Phnom Penh: UNICEF, February–June, 1992), 7.
26. Ibid.
27. Ibid.
28. The proverb was used by the UN Development Fund for Women as part of its efforts to advertise the National Women's Summit, see UNIFEM, "Report from the National Women's Summit," (Phnom Penh: UNIFEM, March 5–8, 1993), n.p.
29. Secretariat of State for Women's Affairs, Kingdom of Cambodia, *Cambodia's Country Report: Women in Development* (Phnom Penh: July 1994), 10.
30. Eva Arnvig, "Women, Children and Returnees," in ed. Peter Utting, *Between Hope and Insecurity*, 147.
31. Grant Curtis, *Cambodia: A Country Profile* (Stockholm: The Swedish International Development Agency, 1980), 160.
32. "Report from the National Women's Summit," Phnom Penh, March 5–8, 1993; see also Interviews, March and April 1996; Mang Channo, "Women's Day Highlights Gender Inequalities," *Phnom Penh Post* (March 12–25, 1993).
33. Interviews, March and April 1996; "Report from the National Women's Summit," *Phnom Penh*, March 5–8, 1993, n.p.
34. Cathy Zimmerman, Sar Samen, and Men Savorn, "Plates in a Basket Will Rattle: Domestic Violence in Cambodia," (Phnom Penh: Asia Foundation, 1994), 141 and 137–42 passim.
35. Interviews, Phnom Penh, March and April 1995; Women's Commission for Refugee Women and Children, "Cambodia Can't Wait," 5–6.
36. Interviews, Phnom Penh, March and April 1995.
37. Mang Channo, "Sex Trade Flourishing in Capital," *Phnom Penh Post* (February 12–25, 1993): 6; "The Problem of Prostitution," *Phnom Penh Post* (February 12–25, 1993): 6; Andrew Nettie, "Cambodia: UN Mission Cited as Sex Slavery Spreads," *Sunday Age* (Melbourne), June 25, 1995; Eva Arnvig, "Women, Children and Returnees," 166–69; Kien Serey Phal, "The Lessons of the UNTAC Experience and the Ongoing Responsibilities of the International Community for Peacebuilding and Development in Cambodia," 129–33; Kirshenbaum, "Who's Watching the Peacekeepers?," 13. Interviews conducted in Phnom Penh from March to April 1996 as well as numerous reports by NGOs within Phnom Penh that confirm these observations; see, for example, Mona Mehta, "Gender Dimensions of Poverty in Cambodia: A Survey Report," (Phnom Penh: Oxfam, 1993), 7.
38. Interviews, Phnom Penh, March and April 1996.
39. Jon Swain, "UN Losing Battle for Cambodia in the Brothels of Phnom Penh," *Sunday Times*, December 27, 1992; Annuska Derks, "Vietnamese Prostitutes in Cambodia," 6; *Asian Recorder* (May 21–27, 1993): 23144.
40. Ledgerwood, "The Lessons from Cambodia," 7; Swain, "UN Losing Battle for Cambodia in the Brothels of Phnom Penh."
41. The Cambodian Women's Development Association indicated in 1994 that the majority of prostitutes working in the Toul Kork area of Phnom Penh were likely

Cambodian, and others have indicated that the ethnic origin of prostitutes in Cambodia has always varied, depending on the location of the brothels, Cambodian Women's Development Association, "Prostitution Survey Results," 1994; Interviews, Phnom Penh, March and April 1996.

42. Swain, "UN losing Battle for Cambodia in the Brothels of Phnom Penh," and *Asian Recorder*, February 5–11, 1993, 22903.
43. Twenty-one UNTAC personnel lost their lives as a result of hostile action, but UNTAC's chief medical officer, Col. Dr. Peter Fraps estimated that as many as 150 would eventually die of AIDS. Katrina Peach, "HIV threatens to claim UNTAC's highest casualties," *Phnom Penh Post*, October 22–November 4, 1993, 4.
44. UN Department of Peacekeeping Operations and the Joint UN Programme on HIV/AIDS, "Protect Yourself, and Those you Care About, Against HIV/AIDS," (New York: United Nations, April 1998), 6.
45. Noted in *Asian Recorder*, April 16–22, 1993, 23060; Ledgerwood, "The Lessons from Cambodia," 8.
46. Arnvig, "Women, Children and Returnees," 165.
47. The Reuters Library Report, November 18, 1992.
48. Jennar,"International Triumph in Cambodia?" 154.
49. Interviews, March and April 1996; see also Kirshenbaum, "Who's Watching the Peacekeepers?" 13.
50. Interviews, March and April 1996.
51. Ibid.
52. Though Khmer denotes a distinct ethnic group within Cambodia, some people use the term synonymously with Cambodian.
53. Sara Colm, "U.N. Agrees to Address Sexual Harassment Issue," *Phnom Penh Post* 1, no. 7 (October 11, 1992): 1.
54. UNTAC, September 18, 1992, Information/Education Division, Analysis Report, "Report on Public Perceptions of UNTAC in the City of Phnom Penh," appendix 1 in Arnvig, "Women, Children and Returnees," 177.
55. Sara Colm, "U.N. Agrees to Address Sexual Harassment Issue"; Swain, "UN Losing Battle for Cambodia in the Brothels of Phnom Penh."
56. "An Open Letter to Yasushi Akashi," *Phnom Penh Post* 1, no. 7, October 11, 1992, 2; "Allegations of Sexual Harassment hit U.N. Peacekeeping Forces in Cambodia," Business Wire, January 11, 1993.
57. Colm, "U.N. Agrees to Address Sexual Harassment Issue," and "Akashi Responds to Community Concerns," *Phnom Penh Post* 1, no. 10 (November 20–December 3, 1992): 2.
58. Interviews, March and April 1996; "An Open Letter to Yasushi Akashi."
59. Yeshua Moser-Puangsuwan, "U.N. Peacekeeping in Cambodia: Whose Needs Were Met?" *Pacifica Review* 7, no. 2 (1995): 106.
60. Ibid., 106–7.
61. Ibid., 107.
62. Amitav Ghosh, "The Global Reservation: Notes Toward an Ethnography of International Peacekeeping," *Cultural Anthropology* 9, no. 3 (1994): 415.
63. Ibid.

64. Interviews, March and April 1996; Michael Hayes, "Indibatt Gets High Marks for Civic Work," *Phnom Penh Post* 2, no. 20 (September 24–October 7, 1993): 8; Moeun Chhean Nariddh, "German Doctors Prepare to Pack Up," *Phnom Penh Post* 2, no. 20 (September 24–October 7, 1993): 9; Michael Hayes, "With a Little Help From the Troops," *Phnom Penh Post* 2, no. 9 (April 23–May 6, 1993): 16.
65. Anne Orford, *Reading Humanitarian Intervention: Human Rights and the Use of Force in International Law* (Cambridge: Cambridge University Press, 2003), 160 and chapter 5 *passim*.
66. Heininger, *Peacekeeping in Transition: The United Nations in Cambodia*, 75–76, 129.
67. Alan James, "Peacekeeping in the Post-Cold War Era," *International Journal*, L2 (Spring 1995): 246.
68. A.B. Fetherston makes a similar argument in "UN Peacekeepers and Cultures of Violence," *Cultural Survival Quarterly* 19, no. 1 (1995): 19–23.

CHAPTER 6

Feminizing Global Governance

Shirin M. Rai

This chapter begins with a story of a women's development project (WDP) in Rajasthan, India through which we can not only learn about women's oppression, their struggles to overcome it, and the resulting highs and lows, and successes and failures, but also reflect upon the gendered nature of multilevel governance and how it is operationalized.

The WDP was launched in 1984 in six districts of Rajasthan with the assistance of UNICEF. The aims of this project included creating "a new sense of worth among poor rural women and facilitating their awareness to develop strategies regarding social and development issues."[1] This was to be done through mechanisms that were both flexible and diverse. These mechanisms focused on improving women's participation in development schemes, "especially [of women] from disadvantaged communities."[2] The agents of change in this scheme were the *sathin* (the feminine form of the word friend) at the village level, and the *pracheta* (secular preacher) at the district level. The following agencies participated in the training, communication, and monitoring required by the program: the District Level Women's Development Agency headed by the District Collector representing the governmental authority; the State Information Development Agency (a voluntary organization), the Institute of Development Studies, an autonomous research institute in Jaipur, Rajasthan, and UNICEF, which provided funding for the training of *sathins*. The "structure was an attempt to balance power between the government and nongovernmental segments" of the program, and reflected the concern of a wide range of women's groups that had been consulted in the process of setting up WDP. While most women's groups supported the program, many were skeptical "about the possibility of a fruitful collaboration between the state and the women's movement in any form"[3]: "The *sathin* was envisaged as a worker with a difference: a catalyst of women's empowerment at the grassroots. She was to be instrumental in the growth of women's collective strength, to increase women's bargaining capacity, and help them to articulate collective interests. . . . But the effectiveness of the *sathin* was predicated upon a transformation within the *sathin* herself so that she could become, through this process, a woman leader."[4] Training the *sathin* was thus an important element of the program. At the heart of their work was a commitment to "collective processes, working upward through first evolving village level platforms for articulating women's points of view and then moving outward to other groups of women engaged in similar processes."[5] Both practical and strategic interests were identified through this process: from famine relief measures to combating gross forms of patriarchal and social oppressions, minimum wages, recovery of land from encroachers, issues of widows' claim to land, employment opportunities for women to safe drinking water and healthcare. The articulation of these interests and mobilizations resulting from these inevitably brought the *sathin* into conflict with village social and political hierarchies. As long as the *sathins* received support from the district agencies, the voluntary organizations, and through them, the government authorities, the *sathins* were not alone in their activities. The support of the district agencies was a crucial element in women's confrontations with caste and class oppressions within rural society.[6] This edifice, however, which was based on cooperation between multilevel agencies and actors, revealed tremendous strains as the government moved to prioritize the family planning program at a time of drought and crop failure in Rajasthan between 1985 and 1988.

On the one hand, government-run famine relief programs were the major means of survival for the rural poor, on the other, these programs were used by local government officials to fulfill their quotas for the sterilization of women as part of the family planning program. Women were caught between these twin pressures. The *sathins* mobilized opposition to this double oppression with the support of the nongovernmental organizations involved in WDP. The district governmental sector, however, refused to discuss the issue.[7] In a parallel move, *sathins* from villages and districts met in 1986 and identified land and health as the two areas that most needed to be addressed by WDP. As Chakravarti comments, "The only aspect of women's health the state was interested in was that they should stop 'breeding.' The women who participated in the health camps held in Ajmer District, on the other hand, were concerned with a whole host of issues around their bodies."[8] As this dispute on the question of linking family planning and famine relief shows, the alliance between various sectors of governance is a fragile one when competing interests clash. The state institutions had a powerful position in this dispute.

This clash of interests became even more pronounced when the *sathins* tried to mobilize their resources by organizing themselves into a union, and by demanding the 'regularizing' of their status within the state structure as government employees enjoying security of employment and an adequate wage for their work. In 1990, *sathins* went on strike on this issue. The government agencies refused their demands stating that the *sathins* were volunteers, not employees; that they were uneducated and illiterate and therefore could not *be* government employees. The fact that the WDP envisioned the participation of poor, low caste women as central to the success of the program, and that these women could not be educated and literate did not enter into their consciousness. The local government officials, such as Block Development Officers, even sent letters to the husbands of the *sathins* instructing them to 'bring their wives to their senses' or accept the consequences. Chakravarti comments, "From the movement of the *sathin* around wages and other related issues it is clear that while the *sathins* had been transformed from being 'passive recipients' of development policies the 'upper' levels of the WDP had remained class [and caste] bound and instrumentalist in their approach to the program."[9]

The tensions resulting from this fracturing of the WDP came to a head with the gruesome gang rape of one *sathin*, Bhanwari Devi, in 1992. Bhanwari Devi was paraded naked through the streets of the village and her husband was beaten for not being able to keep his wife under control. The Magistrates' Court acquitted the men involved because "an upper caste man would not disregard caste . . . differences to rape a low caste woman."[10] In the last few years, the *sathin* program has been bureaucratized and starved of funds. Chakravarti concludes from this that "the government wants empowerment without breaking into the power of those including themselves, who have power over the disempowered . . . while the *sathins* struggle . . . for the statutory minimum wage of workers and the survival and expansion of the scheme, the government claims credit for the 'success' of the *sathin* program in Beijing, Vienna and Geneva."[11] This story raises many questions. For the women's movements, there is the danger of providing legitimacy to programs that are not under their control. For international organizations such as UNICEF there is the question regarding the nature and focus of training provision—by focusing on the training of *sathins* and not at the upper echelons of the government hierarchy and the village level political actors, the clash of political cultures was inevitable. For the nongovernmental organizations and academic institutes there is the question of providing legitimacy to state programs, but also of delivering appropriate levels of support for the *sathins* when and where these were needed. And for *sathins* there is the real question of levels of risk involved in doing their work without adequate support, as well as of how to translate conscientization into practical results when the structures of power are supported by political hierarchies at every level.

Governance of Polities and Governance of Communities

In the context of this story, I suggest that governance be examined in two different ways. The one that most political scientists focus on is the *governance of polities*. It is about regulating political life at different levels—local government, the nation-state, international institutions—and is also about the role that different actors play in this regulation, state and non-state actors, epistemic communities, and social movements at the local, national, and global levels. The second, which does not get much attention but is equally important for daily lived lives of women such as Bhanwari Devi is the *governance of communities*. There are processes and rituals as well as discourses and spectacles of violence that are deployed in order to police community boundaries and punish transgression. The parallel sovereignties thus created both challenge and work within the state. The boundaries of communities are defined, policed, and defended through education, through popular mobilization, through rituals, festivals, and in many parts of the world, through arranged marriages. Through all these, modes of thinking are given shape—of the 'Self' and of the 'Other.' In the name of culture the languages of hatred—racism, sexism, and homophobia, for example—are aired and those of alternative visions of community contained. The community governance is aligned with the perpetuation of gendered traditions.

The regulation of this realm of the community takes place through both formal and informal institutions, systems, and discourses—caste, religious, ethnic local governing councils, modes of communications and excommunication—and through spectacles of violence to subdue the rebels within communities. Governance of communities is carried out through powerful nonstate parallel systems of 'justice.' These include not only resolving disputes between members of the community but also passing judgments on matters deemed relevant to the honor of the caste and ensuring the execution of such judgments. Whether this involves regulating sexualities at the local level, or it involves constructed civilizational clashes between Muslim and Christian worlds, these nonstate governance institutions, mechanisms, and discourses play a critical role in disciplining the way we live our lives. The state is mobilized in defense of the dominant familial norms through constitutional, legal, and policy frameworks as well as through modes of policy implementation—police personnel, for example, are often implicated in religious riots as participants in the ritual humiliation of the transgressors of community norms.

These boundaries are also defended and policed through demonstrations of violence, although not legitimated by all state factions, are tolerated and even participated in by others. The magistrate in the case of Bhanwari Devi, for example, invoked caste prejudice as a defense for the accusers; caste trumps evidence here. In addition, such violence is seen as a 'legitimate' means of regulating communities, securing borders and insuring against transgression of its norms.

These traditions bleed over time—diasporic communities everywhere take with them the burdens and the markers of community norms, rituals, and diasporic legalities that regulate their life away from home. Whether migrants within national borders or diasporic international communities, these traditions help define them in new contexts and provide them with internal resources of solidarity to cope in situations of social exclusion. They help them to make sense of politicized otherness in strange lands. From the local to the global the governance of communities involves disciplinary modes of discursive as well as social power.

As with governance of polities, however, governance of communities is constantly challenged and reshaped by the struggles of individuals and groups who cross boundaries of race, caste, religion, and sexuality. These challenges tap into both internal sources of strength like networks of sympathisers, as well as networks of support from outside. Circulation of political vocabulary allows them access to alternative political languages, visions of society, and of other imagined communities. It is in the interplay of the two levels of governance—of polities and communities—that governance is best understood.

Framing Global Governance Literature

Governance is thus be defined as a system of rules for public life. In this definition we go beyond the concept of government and include both state and nonstate disciplinary modes. Governance includes multiple actors as well as multiple sites. At the heart of the concept there is an assumption of a shift in the spheres of authority from the state to multiple actors and sites.[12] In this context, the state becomes only one of the many institutions that regulate our lives by making rules, ensuring these rules are accepted and implemented, and enforcing the rules. This insight is further reinforced by the inclusion of the concept of governance of communities within the ambit of governance. The fracturing of state forms in the face of other hegemonic discourses and regimes of social power becomes part of the narrative of governance. This needs to be mapped out to analyze the unexpected and most often contingent flows of power in particular moments and spaces. Feminist work in this area needs to be more systematically brought together and further theorized. The mainstream literature discusses the concept of governance in three main arenas: markets, institutions, and ideology.

Markets

Markets include traditional markets in goods and services as well as markets of knowledge—information technology, patents on knowledge-based products, etc. The volume as well as volatility of market interactions drives the need to transcend the bounded regulation of the state. The argument goes that global markets are now too big, the volume of exchange of goods and services too high, and the complexity of interactions, especially in the sphere of finance, too great to be regulated by the state. The linking of local, national, regional, and international markets creates multiple sites of both production and exchange, which per force mean that the state is unable to exercise its authority over market processes.

Institutions

Institutions include the three levels of governance—local, national (sometimes regional and sub-regional), and international. It largely focuses on the way in which the nation-state either has been overtaken by or has had to transform itself in response to globalization. Here the argument is that institutions participating in the regulation of the global economy are increasingly of a wide range—from the national state to private agencies. This reflects the complexity of market interactions on the one hand, and changing patterns of political actors and their behavior on the other. Transnational companies as well as transnational movements operate both on the ground and virtually, making it difficult for states to mediate among them or to exercise its authority over them.

Ideology

Ideology includes analyses of how certain ideas attain the status 'common sense,' that is, how the normativity of particular discourses becomes entrenched as self-evident. This is what Rossenau calls the ontological and the paradigmatical force of the concept.[13] It suggests the hegemonic dominance of certain epistemic communities—experts, policy analysts, policy makers, and intellectuals. The literature takes into account how these ontologies are promoted through the networks of influence and authority of the richer countries as well as how these are embedded institutionally through international policies, conventions, treaties, etc.

I suggest adding another dimension to the understanding of governance here in order to understand the interplay between these three arenas—markets, institutions and ideologies—and to arrive at a more complex picture of governance. This is the arena of political spectacle.

Spectacle

Spectacle here refers to the modes of production of meanings through a display of political power such that transgression and disciplining of the other are seen as the exercise of legitimate power. Some cultural norms then become human rights and other human wrongs. Consent to, and legitimacy of, dominant relations of power are produced for us through performance at international summits, through military success that 'shocks and awes,' and through participatory modes of politics both violent and peaceful at local and global levels. The capturing of these spectacles and their distribution is carried through both traditional and new means of communication, print and electronic media, that circulate images of these spectacles, which supports the ideologies of power.

It is unsurprising that most of the mainstream literature on governance not only ignores governance of communities as an area of research, but also is largely ungendered in its approach to the governance of polities. The eliding of governance with the public sphere ensures that these exclusions take place. Feminist approaches to global governance address this gap by engendering debates on governance. In the next section, I discuss the four arenas of governance previously outlined and examine the shape of the debate within each.

The Governance of Markets

Markets lie at the heart of capitalist social relations. The dominant market actors, in the context of globalization, are those that control transnational capital, through speculation on money markets and capital movements as well as through tax evasion and money laundering. While mainstream critical IPE theorists focus on the unevenness of the market arena in the context of capitalist social relations, feminists argue that markets are socially embedded institutions and roles "within market systems are structured by non-market criteria."[14] These nonmarket, although clearly not noneconomic, criteria lead to gender based distortions in the markets.[15] In the market system, participants come to specific markets with unequal bargaining capacities and resources as a result of gendered state formations, which are characterized by unequal power, class and gender being two bases for unequal power relations. Dominant neoliberal economic theorizing, however, does not question whether individuals can pursue their economic self-interests in ways that have nothing to do with the best price. Neither does it question the "degree to which self-interest places economic goals ahead of friendship, family ties, spiritual considerations or morality."[16] Nor, indeed, how reproductive roles might change in the playing out of market roles.[17] Finally, there is an assumption that instrumentality in decision making goes hand-in- hand with obedience to rules and maximizing interests, rather than with a set of signals that can lead to conflictual economic and social behavior in different groups of populations. The social embeddedness of markets is therefore not considered, other than as a distortion, by neoclassical economists. This brings into question the neutrality of class, gender, and other inequalities in markets in terms of access, competitiveness, and efficiency.

Because of the primacy accorded to markets within the neoliberal frame, their regulation becomes a key issue. The state is assumed to be, together with social embeddedness, a force that undermines and distorts the efficient running of markets. States themselves are seen as suspect economic actors—their regulatory reach needs to be contained in the interest of good governance, which is associated with the qualities deemed by global governance institutions to emphasize the discipline of the market and enhance that discipline through increasing transparency and accountability of the state. While the state is found wanting in its capacity or ability to regulate global markets, 'new constitutionalism'—in contrast to traditional constitutionalism that is associated with the state—is identified, which "can be defined as the political project of attempting to make transnational liberalism, and if possible liberal democratic capitalism the sole model for future development."[18] It is in this project that institutions of global governance—IMF, World Bank, and WTO—become stronger *vis-à-vis* the state, and are presented as neutral players seeking maximum economic efficiency for all through attempting to ensure fair dealing in the markets.

If institutions regulate markets, markets leech into institutions their operative dynamics. Institutions begin to frame policies, to justify these policies, and to seek alternative policies within marketized norms. Governance institutions are themselves marketized. Feminists have assessed the nature of gendered, marketized global institutions as based on market principles, promoting market-based solutions to social and political problems, and stabilizing these solutions with the support of dominant elites.[19]

The privatization of public goods such as health and education and the erosion of our commons are cause for concern. As the *sathins* saw in Rajastan, the marketized institutions of the state did not regard their priorities—access to land and access to health—as primary to a women's development program. Access to land is too sensitive and disruptive of the dominant local social relations, and health is interpreted as simply working toward containing population growth. Thus, in analyzing the constitutive parts of governance, feminist analysis deepens, historicizes, and engenders debates on the governance of markets, the changing role of the state, and the ideologies of governance.

Governance of and through Institutions

Institutional structures—formal as well as informal, their operations, the processes through which these operations are conceived of and put into effect, the outcomes resultant from these processes, and the analysis of these outcomes all form part of governance of and through institutions. The actors involved in these institutional processes and their relationship to others are also a key part of the story of governance—the access to networks, both formal and informal, the political spaces available or not available, and the control over economic resources that service these institutions. Strategies to open access, spaces and control are devised, refined, and operationalized in this context.

In the literature on global governance, a key debate has been on the nature of the state in the context of globalization. It is suggested that the state is no longer capable of addressing the issues arising from the global reach of capitalism whether these are relating to competition in and regulation of the market, or to maintaining rules within its borders in order to resolve the collective problems of its citizens. In the neoliberal literature, the state was presented not only as weak but also as dysfunctional. "Weak institutions—tangled laws, corrupt courts, deeply biased credit systems, and elaborate business registration requirements—hurt poor people and hinder development" according to a recent report.[20] The question then was whether the state could respond to the new pressures of global political economy and if so, what should be the parameters of its functioning?

To these questions, the realists reply with a defense of the state. They emphasize the continued centrality of the state by asserting "the absence of a legitimate authority to which states are subordinate and give allegiance."[21] Upon this rather well rehearsed position, the state and its interests—security and independence—continue to hold supreme and determine national behavior. For the realists, the clearest rejection of the governance discourse comes from asking question of power, "governance for what? What are the social, political, and economic purposes that governance is to serve? Unless these issues can be resolved, proposals for international governance must be greeted with considerable skepticism."[22] This obviously does not attend to questions of process—of an examination of new institutional frameworks that might be worked out, new regimes that might be stabilized with state complicity or that might in the end overtake the state. Neo-Marxists argue that what we are witnessing is not the demise of the nation-state but its 'internationalization'; not its destruction but its transformation. In brief, Cox argues that from being bulwarks against the global intrusions into national economies, today's states are becoming mediators, adapters, and negotiators with the global political economy. The state's role, therefore, becomes one of helping to adjust the domestic economy to the requirements of the world economy.[23]

One of the most important insights that feminists have brought to bear on the state debate is that gendered social relations are constitutive of the state while at the same time, the state is crucial to the continued dominance of patriarchal relations of social production and reproduction. Therefore, the state can become the focus of feminist engagement both as a mediator between communities and the market, and as complicit in marketizing institutions and privatizing social provision. In order to influence the state, feminists have focused on institutional structures and processes at both state and sub-state levels, as well as at the global level "in which women have found or carved out niches for themselves and their interests as women" and therefore "introduce into global governance women-centered ways of framing issues."[24] In order to lobby and hold the state accountable, women's groups have approached governance at a global level through critical gender politics "exploring the purposive, goal-oriented . . . social-movement strategies to influence the United Nations" and Bretton Woods institutions[25] as well as encouraging civil society mobilization.

The problem of the state is evident in the story of the Women's Development Program. The modernizing and liberalizing Indian state is convinced of the need to change not only India's economy but also its gendered social relations—up to a point, so long as such change is not too disruptive or too quick or too deep. International organizations, especially the UN, have been instrumental in providing the framework where such important changes can be discussed safely, and at a distance, with the support of major international actors.

They have also, as with UNICEF, provided resources for programs approved by the UN—women's empowerment being one. The various women's conferences have been catalysts for the Indian state. However, as Bhanwari Devi had to recognize, the state's impulse to change is limited by lack of resources and hierarchical distribution of resources. Asking for land is a revolutionary and disruptive act, which needs to be stopped and to be punished. Like Oliver Twist, the *sathins* need to be taught a lesson such that they do not dare to ask for more again. The governance of polities' axis come into play when the state, through its institutions and actors, refuses the *sathin's* demands, focuses on family planning, and eventually starves the Women's Development Fund of its radical edge. Simultaneously, the governance of communities' axis plays out in the violence made attendant upon disciplining lower caste Bhanwari Devi for daring to raise her voice against domestic violence of upper caste males in her village.

Governance as Ideology

The stabilization of markets and marketized institutions requires this third form of governance. Governance as ideology is produced and circulated through hegemonic discourses, educational institutions, and media (both traditional and digital). Critical scholars point to the ways in which epistemic authority secures neoliberal discourse by evoking images of knowledge based managerialism, which allows access to governance channels and results in efficiency gains based on objective problem solving approaches to the challenges of globalization.[26] The hegemonic dominance of certain professional communities—experts, policy analysts, policy makers, and intellectuals—at multiple levels of governance can be assessed by focusing on the construction of epistemic authority. Such authority then reinforces the ideological message through research and its dissemination through seminars, publications, and policy networks.[27]

Three different strands become visible when we examine the context in which governance emerged as a discourse. First, was the collapse of the Soviet Union and the beginning of the post–cold war period in the international system and building on this, was the convergence of economic policies under globalization within a neoliberal framework. Second, because of the collapse of communism and the rise of the neoliberal framework in the global economy, it was necessary to examine the role of the state in the context of the post–cold war globalization. Third, the emergence of the discourse of democratization as the most appropriate framework for political and economic transitions made democracy the bulwark against totalitarianism or any return to state managed economies. The concept, indeed ideology, of global governance takes account of these three strands.

In the wake of the collapse of the Soviet Union and of the socialist state model of development, macroeconomic thinking converged on the primacy markets. The discourse of neoliberalism emphasizes, indeed, normalizes, the "efficiency, welfare, and the freedom of the market, and self-actualization through the process of consumption"[28] even though the outcomes of these policies are contradictory, hierarchical, and ineffectively protect human life and the world in which we live. This discourse of the market also has another message—if market based competition is the most efficient way of allocating resources in society, then any attempts to interfere in its functioning is per se inimical to the 'greater good.' As we have seen, any attempts by the state to regulate markets came under the scrutiny of economic actors that occupy dominant positions in the market.

In his critique of the work of the Commission on Global Governance, Baxi comments on the discrepancy between the assumptions of globality by the commission and the "central facts of contemporary world disorder."[29] Violence and poverty are growing apace, and both affect women in particular ways. The feminization of poverty and violence against women in creating and policing interstate borders makes this cooperative development a fraught discourse for women. As Baxi rightly comments, "If governance is to be conceived as a process, it is well to recall that process is permeated by structures-in-dominance, both in states and civil societies."[30] The contradictions that arise out of capitalism's march across the globe are embedded in social relations by inequalities based on class, gender, ethnicity, and religion. The assessment of processes and institutions of governance need to be aware of these contradictions and the power relations that frame them.

Finally, feminist scholars have long challenged the recognized processes of knowledge production to show the role that epistemic authority plays in legitimating and stabilizing discourse. Feminist critics focus on epistemological frameworks constituted by binaries of rational and emotional, universal and particular, objective and subjective.

As Harstock points out, "the vision of the ruling class (or gender) structures the material relations in which all parties are forced to participate, and therefore cannot be dismissed as simply false."[31] Feminist work, however, is a more assertive project. As Alison Jaggar points out, this means rethinking the relationship between these binaries so that the historical identification of emotions, particularity, and subjectivity with the subordinate is challenged by suggesting the mutually constitutive nature of these binaries.[32] Regarding the central concerns of regulatory regimes of global capitalism, and the role of global governance institutions in securing these regimes through TRIPs, feminist intervention in knowledge production has a radical impact on our understanding of the roles that institutions play in stabilizing structures-in-dominance. These interventions lead us to ask different and important questions about the nature of privatized knowledge and the application of this framework to global regulatory regimes. Indeed, some argue that these insights should lead us to explore the merits of 'social patents,' thus broadening knowledge creation. Therefore, investigation of gendered dimensions of knowledge production provides insight into the nature of epistemic authority, practical policy shifts, and a critical evaluation of how disciplinary neoliberalism works to entrench dominant social relations through legal provisions, such as TRIPS, regulated by institutions of global governance such as the WTO.

The power of ideology manifests itself in many ways in the story of the *sathins* of Rajasthan. From macrolevel policy on health to microlevel patriarchal satrapies of Block Development Officers, they traverse a hostile terrain. The assumption that women's work is voluntary work meshes neatly with the assumptions of the macroeconomic framework that feminist economists have long critiqued; the denial of appropriate remuneration for their work flows easily from these assumptions. There are assumptions, in addition, about appropriate behavior of women, particularly low caste women—and the price of transgression of these boundaries of appropriateness are high. If ideologies justify the playing out of dominant modes of power then the judgment in the Bhanvari Devi's rape case is governance as ideology par excellence; the power of the law swings behind caste, gender, and class based hierarchies to crush the defiant voice of one woman.

Governance as Spectacle

Power displays through the production of spectacle is an important arena of governance that we need to analyze. This arena was first opened for scholarly scrutiny by Guy Debord who in his *The Society of the Spectacle* (1967) argued that modern spectacle was "the autocratic reign of the market economy which had acceded to an irresponsible sovereignty, and the totality of new techniques of government which accompanied this reign."[33] The spectacular power was, he suggested concentrated (totalitarian state power such as the Soviet Union) as well as diffuse (democratic systems such as the United States). In his 1988 *Comments on the Society of the Spectacle*, he expanded this to include integrated power of the spectacle through which spectacle has gone global: "the globalization of the false was also the falsification of the globe."[34] What we see, therefore, in 24/7 media news disciplines our senses as well as our understanding of this world; it makes our choices for us while at the same time giving the appearance of endless choice to us. Further expanding this discussion of the political economy of the imagery of power, Michel Foucault argued in his book *Discipline and Punish* that the spectacle of corporeal punishment is disciplining not only of the one being punished but also of those who witness the punishment being meted out. Foucault sees the exercise of power as not limited within the boundaries of sovereign states, through the enforcement of law: "We must eschew the model of Leviathan in the study of power. We must escape from the limited field of juridical sovereignty and state institutions, and instead base our analysis of power on the study of the techniques and tactics of domination."[35] The state is then only one of the sites of disciplinary power, which takes many forms of which enacting (together with the exercise) of disciplinary power is an important part. Building on this analysis of power, Judith Butler in her book *Gender Trouble* argued that gendered power is a fiction that needs to be sustained in the domain of political economy through social performitivity.[36] Through the enactment of dominant gender roles we recognize, circulate, and reproduce the meanings of masculinity and femininity and thus perpetuate gendered social hierarchies. Though both these interventions have been challenged, they do open up an important analytical seam for the construction of governance theory. We have seen how the concept of governance has evolved, been embraced and then challenged. The dominance of certain states and ideologies within international relations literature leads to an increasing acceptance of the term despite some unease about its political foundations. I would suggest that this dominance is embedded in the popular imagination about governance through the casting of political spectacles. Therefore on the one hand, we need to understand the importance of these spectacles and dissect these to lay bare their politics. On the other hand, we can understand spectacle *as* politics in contemporary times where it stands for "the colonization of social life by capitalism: it is the submission of ever more facets of human sociality to the 'deadly solicitations' of the market."[37] Such analysis adds another dimension to our understanding of the concept of governance. This dimension is particularly important to understand as increasingly the media—traditional and virtual—becomes a battleground of ideas and spaces where ideologies of governance converge and contend. Thus, as Debord states, "The spectacle is not a collection of images; it is a social relation between people that is mediated by images. . . . Understood in its totality, the spectacle is both the result and the project of the dominant mode of production."[38]

As Butler's work shows, feminist scholarship has ranged widely to understand the exercise of gendered power. It has always incorporated photography, theatre, poetry, and art into mainstream feminist political analysis to 'display' the varied ways in which patriarchy holds sway. If we examine the three arenas of market, institutions, and ideology we find that all three are consolidated through and in the space of the unfolding spectacle of governance; whether the shock and awe of the Iraqi war, the grey-suited men pictured at G-8 summits surrounded by security barriers, the Abu Ghraib prisoners carted in shackles or indeed, the counter-spectacles of the Battle of Seattle, the World Social Forum, and Live 8 concerts. Dominant states such as the United States put up purposefully aggressive displays of military power as well as the spectacle of a siege of civilization through the media's coverage of radical movements—Islamist, but also Cuba or the streets of Seattle and Genoa. These images create a powerful visual medium that capture, reinforce, and circulate the dominant modes of power. Challenges to that power display are mounted through alternative modes of communication, largely on the Web, through blogs presented to new audiences. The co-option of journalists into the military as embedded reporters, for example, show us how the creation of spectacle and its distribution is organized, by congealing markets, institutions, and ideology into a visual manifestation of power. From Lynndie England at Abu Ghraib to Bhanwari Devi in Rajasthan, women have both participated in and been the victims of repressive governance regimes. Feminist scholars and women activists understand that gender discipline is enforced through economic dependence, political exclusion, and cultural markers of the subjugation of women by men.

Conclusion: Challenges by and for Feminist Politics

Feminists build their engagements with governance institutions on key concepts that emerge from women's struggles and scholarship. First, they developed a gendered analysis of the political economy and relations between states and markets; second, a challenge to divisions between the public and the private produced by the state, and finally, a commitment to transformation of gender relations, which is the basis of formal and informal politics. If we take these insights into account when assessing the key areas previously identified—markets, institutions, ideologies, and spectacles—of global governance, we stretch the boundaries of governance debates.

Feminist scholarship and activism, however, face important challenges. While feminists posit a powerful critique of mainstream global governance literature, they also need to present an alternative articulation of what governance means.[39] If they do not like marketized institutions, they need to be able to sketch the outline of governance institutions that they would like to see. Catherine Hoskyns and I argue that "for both strategic as well as practical reasons women have had to organize separately as women. . . . [However, the] feminist challenge is limited by a current lack of focus on the importance of redistributive policies that are rooted in the structural inequalities of capitalist production and exchange."[40] We posed the question, Can gender recover class? Following Spivak, I argue that a recognition of the importance of redistribution allows us "both in the economic area (capitalist) and in the political (world-historical agent) . . . to construct models of a divided and dislocated subject whose parts are not continuous or coherent with each other."[41] In addition, these dislocations and discontinuities are where women seeking transformation within political economy as well as the discursive circuits of power can find agency. This is particularly relevant now when marketization and the retrenchment of welfare provision under globalization are creating tremendous pressures and inequalities across social and spatial boundaries. We see, however, that feminists are engaging with institutions within the convergent ideological framework of neoliberal governance because the space for alternatives has scaled down even as the recognition of gender-based inequalities has increased. This is not to suggest that these engagements are not important. Indeed, the solid ground of liberalism has fractured so much under the neoliberal onslaught that the protection of the welfare state seems a radical project well worth participating in. Yet recognition of the limits of the strategies of engagement with "constitutional neoliberalism" must be taken seriously if we are to be effective in developing political strategies of empowerment for both poor women and men.

Issues of gender have particular salience in the debates on governance. Unless we use the insights that have emerged from feminist theory and practice, we will not be able to encompass the needs of the future in the conversations about the global present. To reiterate, feminist contributions to these conversations lie in ways in which political activism and theoretical insights are methodologically imbricated to develop insights on governance. These methodologies examine the discursive as well as the material power wielded in embedding certain dominant explanations of governance in mainstream literature, which shapes agendas for 'governing.'[42] Specifically, feminist interventions in the areas of knowledge creation, recognition, and institutionalization have particular salience for the processes of embedding neoliberal marketized discourses of globalization and governance. Feminist debates on the state and democracy are relevant to the way in which political activism as well as the relational understanding between the state and global institutions of governance is viewed. Gendered critiques of markets as not only uneven spaces of exchange, but also inefficient and distorted mechanisms that build upon unequal gendered social relations subject the normalization of rationality of the market to rigorous scrutiny.

The global governance debate needs to make a conceptual shift to embed these insights, developed through everyday struggle at local, state and global levels, as well as through engagements with and critiques of mainstream literature if theories of critical governance are fundamentally to challenge the structures-in-dominance in this field. Specifically, we would suggest three areas where feminist deconstructions of the concept provide radical insights into the concept. First, such an analysis becomes an exercise in the recognition of the multiple bases of inequalities that are being stabilized through systems of global governance: class, North–South relations, and gender as the unequal social relations constitutive of global capitalism, which find reflection in marketized institutions. Second, it allows us to reflect on gendered arguments and political strategies that challenge these inequalities—from gender mainstreaming to gender budgets, from gendered codes of conduct to gendering unions, from enhancing the scope of microcredit to the extension of Tobin Tax to Maria Tax.[43] Finally, while these multiple strategies are critical to addressing gendered inequalities, the focus on the study of how global capitalism is embedded in socially unequal regimes of production and social reproduction allows us to view the limits of these strategies. However important to the lives of individual men and women, shifts in specific policies cannot offset the disciplinary dominance of global capitalist relations. To challenge that a broader alliance of feminists is necessary. As I have argued elsewhere, "the next phase of women's struggles needs to take on board more centrally the issue of redistribution of resources if power relations in society are to be refashioned."[44]

Notes

1. Uma Chakravarti, "Rhetoric and Substance of Empowerment, Women, Development and the State," in *Contested Transformations: Changing Economies and Identities in Contemporary India*, ed. Mary E. John, Praveen Kumar Jha, and Surinder S. Jodhka (New Delhi: Tulika Books, 2006).
2. Ibid., 2.
3. Ibid., 3.
4. Ibid., 3–4.
5. Ibid.
6. Ibid., 5.
7. Ibid., 7.
8. Ibid., 8.
9. Ibid., 11.
10. Ibid., 16.
11. Ibid., 18.
12. James Rosenau, "Towards an Ontology for Global Governance," in *Governance without Government: Order and Change in World Politics*, ed. Martin Hewson and Timothy Sinclair (Cambridge: Cambridge University Press, 1999), 287–301.
13. Ibid.
14. Barbara Harriss-White, "Female and Male Grain Marketing Systems, Analytical and Policy issues for West Africa and India," in *Feminist Visions of Development*, ed. Cecile Jackson and Ruth Pearson (London: Routledge, 1998), 201.
15. See Irene Van Staveren, "Global Finance and Gender," in *Civil Society and Global Finance*, ed. Jan Aart Scholte and Albrecht Schnabel (London: Routledge, 2002), 228–46; Shirin M. Rai, *Gender and the Political Economy of Development* (Cambridge, Polity, 2002).
16. Fred Block, *Postindustrial Possibilities, A Critique of Economic Discourse* (Berkeley, University of California Press, 1990), 54.
17. Harriss-White, "Female and Male Grain Marketing Systems."
18. Ibid., 412.
19. Viviene Taylor, "Marketization of Governance: Critical Feminist Perspectives from the South," 2000, DAWN, http://www.DAWN.org/publications.
20. World Bank, *World Development Report 2002: Building Institutions for Markets* (Washington, DC: Oxford University Press, September 2001), http://econ.worldbank.org/wdr/pal-dcosta-06.docWDR2002/text-2394/ (accessed March 20, 2008).
21. Robert Gilpin, *The Challenge of Global Capitalism. The World Economy in the 21st Century* (Princeton: Princeton University Press, 2002), 237.
22. Gilpin, *The Challenge of Global Capitalism*, 246.
23. See Robert Cox and Timothy J. Sinclair, *Approaches to World Order* (Cambridge: Cambridge University Press, 1996).

24. Mary K. Meyer and Elisabeth Prugl, ed., *Gender Politics in Global Governance Gender Politics* (Lanham, MD: Rowman & Littlefield, 1999), 4–5.
25. Ibid., 5; see also Robert O'Brien, et al., *Contesting Globalization* (Cambridge: Cambridge University Press, 2000).
26. Stephen Gill, "Globalization, Market Civilization, and Disciplinary Neoliberalism," *Millennium* 23, no.3 (1995): 399–423; Philip McMichael, *Development and Social Change: A Global Perspective*, 2nd ed. (Thousand Oaks, CA: Pine Force Press, 2000); Upendra Baxi, "Global Justice and the Failure of Deliberative Democracy," in *Democracy Unrealized*, ed. Okwui Enweror, et.al. (Kassel: Hatje Cantz, 2002) 113–32; Shirin M. Rai, *Gender and the Political Economy of Development* (Cambridge: Polity, 2002).
27. Shirin M. Rai, "Gendering Global Governance," *International Feminist Journal of Politics* 6, no. 4: (2004): 579–601.
28. Gill, "Globalization, Market Civilization," 401.
29. Upendra Baxi, "'Global Neighborhood' and the 'Universal Otherhood': Notes on the Report of the Commission on Global Governance," *Alternatives* 21 (1996): 530.
30. Ibid., 532.
31. Hartsock 1997, 153.
32. Alison Jaggar, "Love and Knowledge: Emotion in Feminist Epistemology," in *Feminisms*, ed. Sandra Kemp and Judith Squires (Oxford: Oxford University Press, 1997), 188–93.
33. Guy Debord, *The Society of the Spectacle*, trans. Donald Nicholson-Smith (New York: Zone Books, 1995), 2.
34. Guy Debord, *Comments on the Society of the Spectacle* (London: Verso, 1998), 10.
35. Foucault, Michel. *Discipline and Punish: the birth of the prison*, trans. Alan Sheridan (London: Penguin, 1991), 102.
36. Butler, Judith P., *Gender Trouble: Feminism and the Subversion of Identity* (New York: Routledge, 1990).
37. Julian Stallabrass, "Spectacle and Terror," *New Left Review* 37 (2006): 92–93.
38. Ken Knabb, "The Society of the Spectacle," 2005, http://www.bopsecrets.org/SI/debord/ (accessed March 19, 2008).
39. Ruth Pearson, "The Social is Political: Towards the Reconceptualization of Feminist Analysis of the Global Economy," *International Feminist Journal of Politics* 6, no.4 (2004): 603–22.
40. Catherine Hoskyns and Shirin M. Rai, "Gendering International Political Economy," *CSGR Working Paper* 170/05 (May 2005): 362.
41. Ibid., 276.
42. Jan Kooiman, *Governing as Governance* (London: Sage, 2003).
43. Pearson, "The Social is Political."
44. Hoskyns and Rai, "Gendering International Political Economy," 363.

PART III

'Worlding Women'

Confronting Gendered Politics in Asia

CHAPTER 7

Confessions of a Failed Feminist IR Scholar

Feminist Methodologies in Practice in Peshawar

*Anne McNevin**

In 2001, Sandra Whitworth commented that while critical and feminist theories of International Relations had made an important contribution to the discipline by opening up what counts as the subject matter of international relations (IR), those same theories "have been almost completely silent on theorizing about or thinking through the political implications of conducting research on so-called marginalized communities." Whitworth hoped to contribute to discussion about "what happens" when feminist IR theorists "go out into the world and actually talk to the people they study."[1] Five years earlier and writing from an interdisciplinary feminist perspective, Diane Wolf expressed her own dilemmas about aspects of the research process that she experienced whilst conducting fieldwork in Java.[2] She encouraged others to write about "the secrets of fieldwork, things that people don't talk about"[3] particularly in relation to research that crossed national, cultural, gender, and class boundaries in the dynamic between researcher and research subject. A recent volume devoted to methodological issues attempts to fill the gap in "scholarly work that discusses *how* IR feminist research is conducted"[4] and includes insightful reflections upon fieldwork in particular.[5] Notwithstanding these efforts and the increasing recognition of feminist approaches to IR in general, sustained analysis of feminist methodologies *in practice* remain few in number within the discipline.

* My thanks to the people in Peshawar who generously and patiently shared their time and stories with me. I am grateful to Mary O'Kane, Kim Huynh, Katrina Lee-Koo, and Shakira Hussein for reading earlier drafts of this chapter and for their thoughtful comments and suggestions, and to Bina D'Costa for encouraging me to write about my fieldwork.

This chapter aims, therefore, to continue a discussion about 'what happens' when feminist methodological principles confront a host of unanticipated quandaries on the ground. By methodology *in practice*, I do not mean to imply a false dichotomy between theory and practice as if the undertaking of qualitative research could be logically separated from its subsequent representation in a theoretical text. My intention is to focus upon feminist methodologies at the point of the research process called 'fieldwork' but also to reflect upon how methodologies informing fieldwork necessarily impact upon the entirety of the research process. The discussion draws on my own brief experience of crosscultural IR fieldwork, "that brash, awkward, hit-and-run encounter of one sensibility with others."[6] In 2004, I spent two weeks in Peshawar, Pakistan, conducting meetings and interviews with women's NGOs working with Afghan women refugees. This chapter reflects on that experience in something of a confessional style. It reveals a number of failures to sustain feminist methodological principles in practice. These are failings that sometimes call for greater forethought and consistency. In this respect, they are indicative of a beginner's approach and may offer some insight for others who are contemplating fieldwork for the first time. They are also failings, however, that reflect the imperfections and power dynamics that are, I suggest, an unavoidable part of doing critical feminist research in IR as in any discipline and, as such, will resonate with more experienced researchers.

Feminist methodologies draw heavily upon a framework for feminist research developed by Sandra Harding some twenty years ago.[7] Harding insists that the researcher be located "in the same critical plane as the overt subject matter" thus bringing the entire research process and its unavoidable biases into the field of critical inquiry.[8] Ackerly et al. have subsequently identified this injunction to reflexivity as the distinctive component of feminist methodologies within and beyond IR.[9] It requires clear positioning on several accounts: to make explicit the partial intentions of research (to be in women's interests); to make explicit the personal partiality of the researcher that arises from her/his own unique social positioning; to acknowledge and mitigate the power dynamics between researcher and research subjects; and to acknowledge the necessary limits of research in which some subjects and voices are privileged over others. This chapter focuses specifically on the notion of reflexivity in a transnational and intercultural context. It begins with a brief reflection upon the contribution of feminist IR theorists to my own field of migration and refugee studies, which establishes the theoretical armor and methodological imperatives with which I approached my fieldwork in Peshawar. Descriptions of some of the methodological dilemmas I encountered in that city are interspersed with narrative passages that draw upon my field notes. This format is intended to direct critical scrutiny toward myself and my research methods as objects of inquiry and to convey the awkwardness and uncertainty that characterized my fieldwork experience.

From Canberra to Peshawar: Why Do Feminist IR Fieldwork?

My fieldwork in Peshawar stemmed from research in the interdisciplinary field of migration and refugee studies. My work is concerned with the ways in which identities connected to migration (migrant, refugee, asylum seeker, and citizen) play into those practices of sovereignty that structure our understandings of states, borders, and nations. Specifically, I aim to highlight how particular groups of people constructed in terms of those identities are marginalized and made *in*secure by these processes. This critical approach is heavily influenced by feminist scholars who identify human stories and women's everyday experiences as part of the substance of IR.[10] It is also informed by feminist critiques of dichotomies between public and private, domestic and international, and feminine and masculine that traditionally serve to relegate migration (amongst other issues) to an inferior, 'feminine,' domestic sphere.[11] My approach also draws upon migration-specific feminist scholarship that reveals how gendered experiences of migration are implicated in the sovereign practices of the state and in the workings of a global political economy.[12] These are significant inquiries not only because they document the experiences of marginalized women and migrants but also because the gendered lenses they deploy help to shape new conceptual frameworks for understanding and challenging the power dynamics that infuse contemporary IR.

Reflecting upon the insights of this pioneering body of work, it seemed to me that insofar as the experiences of refugees are related to the contemporary discourses and practices of IR, the experiences of particular women in particular places is marginalized within that story. In contemplating fieldwork, I was conscious that my thoughts on global issues of migration were being shaped from my desk, as a postgraduate student in Canberra, and from my own strong reactions to the Australian government's scandalous treatment of asylum seekers arriving by boat on its shores.[13] While Australia had become a global leader in punitive border policing and was therefore a suitable context for the critical study of migration and IR, it was also confronting significantly lower numbers of refugees and asylum seekers than many other countries. The majority of asylum seekers arriving in Australia were from Afghanistan and Iraq and many had transited through Iran and Pakistan. Clearly, the view from such places would be extremely different, both because of the numbers of refugees (well into the millions) and because of diverse national, cultural, gender, and geopolitical contexts. As a starting point for challenging my limited perspective, I settled on a visit to Peshawar. I chose this destination for a number of reasons including the fact that English is widely spoken. The northern regions of Pakistan are also of particular relevance to the so-called War on Terror, which shaped the politics of asylum in Australia, as elsewhere. Finally, I was aware that as a woman in Peshawar, I might be able to gain access to women's organizations and women refugees in a way that would be unavailable to male researchers in such a highly patriarchal and gender segregated society. Hence, Peshawar offered particular opportunities for me to engage with marginalized perspectives in IR.

Eager to broaden and deepen my research, I was also aware of the very limited perspective I would be able to gain from a short stint of fieldwork. I had never been to South Asia before, spoke neither Pashtu nor Urdu, and had little exposure to the cultural dynamics of the area. I approached my time in Peshawar as a kind of preparatory trip, if not for further fieldwork in that location, then at least for the process of fieldwork elsewhere.

At the same time, I was uncomfortable with the idea of approaching refugees themselves. I felt it would be impossible to do justice to feminist injunctions to develop more than superficial relationships with research participants in such a short period. I was conscious of ethical considerations to do with questions about their experiences as refugees that might prompt traumatic memories. Moreover, being more generally averse to awkward conversations, I was nervous about interactions with refugees, wondering what on earth we would find to say to each other. At the time, I considered my inexperience and limited time in Peshawar as justifiable reasons for avoiding such encounters. I decided, instead, to seek out the English-speaking staff of local organizations working with refugees, imagining that they might offer a less ethically fraught introduction to politics on the ground. I did not intend to conduct formal interviews, but to watch, listen, and learn what I could from both prearranged and informal exchanges. I was determined not to be a bumbling, overzealous, western academic with too much ambition and too little sensitivity. I expected that this would be a cautious and moderate learning experience that would help me gain the expertise for conducting feminist fieldwork in the future without exposing myself to problematic encounters in the present. That the NGO staff might themselves be refugees had not occurred to me.

Tensions, Dilemmas, and Politics in a Globalised City

Sunday, June 20: Arrival in Peshawar

I have no idea what kind of fashion crimes I'm committing. My dupatta (I've only recently learnt it's a dupatta and not a scarf) doesn't seem to match my trousers or the long-sleeved tunic I've borrowed from a friend, but I can't be sure. Unskillfully adjusting what seems, in this heat, to be excessive layers of fabric, I push my trolley through the arrival gate, hoping the billowing folds won't get caught in the wheels. I had watched women wrap themselves with effortless style as we stepped off the plane, and had tried with little success to copy their movements. A young man in chinos, Ray-Bans and a perfectly pressed corporate casual shirt spots me instantly. Oh God, I think, have I overdone it with the get-up? Asif, an economics student from the University of Peshawar, will be my guide to his city for the next two weeks. More chaperone than driver, Asif plays me Crowded House and Celine Dion on his new MP3 player, hooked into the car stereo socket. Our battle of egos is yet to begin in earnest. For now, he arranges a few essential things on my behalf: a local mobile phone connection and breakfast at my guesthouse, simple things that may have taken me hours and days to arrange on my own.

This description of my arrival in Peshawar captures a number of surprises through which I was confronted with my own preconceptions about what the city would be like and what doing research there would entail. Peshawar, I discovered, is a globalised city. Forty miles from the Khyber Pass, it is the capital of Pakistan's North-West Frontier Province. Most of its population, like that of southern Afghanistan, is Pashtun. The border with Afghanistan is porous, open in places and highly regulated in others. The stretch along the Tribal Areas is not policed and people cross back and forth constantly. Amidst this constant traffic, 'Afghan refugee' is a fluid, ubiquitous identity. Cheap, expendable labor flows from Peshawar and all of Pakistan to the Gulf States. Pashto enclaves develop in Bahrain and Dubai while remittances flow back to Peshawar. Wahhabi Islam flows into madrassas throughout the province along with Saudi funding for religious movements. Western aid money flows in and out along with foreign aid workers on their way to Kabul. Drugs, arms, and high-tech consumer goods are traded in markets on the outskirts of the city, which are spoken of in dangerous, exotic terms. Income circulates and concentrates in gaudy new middle class housing developments. Cable TV from India and America feeds aspirations for 'lifestyle.' A younger generation of students pursues their education in foreign, especially American, universities. Tourism has all but ground to a halt since Pakistan has become a front in the War on Terror.[14]

I had not expected a globalised city. Indeed, I quickly realized that my images of Pakistan and the people I expected to find there had been shaped by a number of far from complex stereotypes about the generic poverty and oppression to be found in Third World places. These were precisely the kind of ideas that many years of critical and feminist education had trained me to problematize. I had naively imagined Asif, a student and driver, as someone I would 'help out' with extra pocket money, much as casual work might 'help' a struggling student in Australia. I had imagined someone who had less of the First World advantages that my birthplace provided, and someone who would simply arrange my transport on request. However, Asif arrived with his own cosmopolitan airs and aspirations and his own clear agenda in being of assistance to me. My interactions with Asif were longer, more personal, more meaningful and far more excruciating than any with my designated 'research subjects.' It was through Asif's world, his family and their hospitality, that I became most aware of the universalizing assumptions about Third World people and places I had unconsciously adopted. Upon reflection, I was surprised by the extent to which I had internalized these. I now believe that I would not have confronted these assumptions with anything like the same level of reflexivity without being placed in contexts well outside of my comfort zone. It was somewhat later that I realized how much a part of this process Asif had been.

Monday, June 21

Asif arrives at my guesthouse in the morning. We discuss my plans for the next fortnight. There are a number of organizations I want to visit and we set off for one of them. Asif lets me pay for petrol and food, as arranged, but won't let me out of the car to purchase anything. He raves about the new Subway store that's just opened up. He tells me that my fair skin and blue eyes are considered beautiful here. "And the hair?" (Mine is cropped short.) "Well . . . the hair doesn't matter so much." He seems irritated when I ask him when I should and shouldn't wear my headscarf. "Do what you like—it's OK. People expect you to be different."

Asif, I think, expects me to be better connected than I am. He has his own reasons for driving me around. He explains that he hopes I will introduce him to foreign NGO circles where he might land himself a high paying job and a ticket out of Pakistan. Fair enough. It's not as if he needs the relatively meager sum (for him) we have agreed on as payment. I'm more surprised when he jumps out of the car and strides into the meeting I have arranged with the staff of an Afghan Women's NGO. He is the only man at the table, and presumably in the building, but seems confident enough in being there. I introduce Asif and he launches into Pashtu but our hosts interrupt, asking if it's not more polite to continue in English. Asif's neck pulls back in surprise. Stumped for a moment, and only for a moment, he changes languages. There is lots of tea, lots of smiles and nodding, and a string of pregnant pauses. Back in form, Asif fills the gaps with his own ambitions. I'm not with him, I want to say. I don't even know him, we are separate. Finally, we arrange a visit in the coming days to Marteni Refugee Camp, where the organization runs a health program for nursing mothers and malnourished children. I'm relieved when Bushra, a doctor who works on the program, says she will pick me up and take me herself. Am I not the first to arrive with a chaperone? Or is Asif uniquely annoying? Is a pick up standard practice? The meeting does not come to a natural close, but neither does it continue in comfort. I wind things up feeling impolite and brusque, though I'm not sure why or how else to go about it.

That afternoon, Asif takes me for a drive to a village just outside the city where he is a landowner. He explains that every so often he visits with muscle and guns, just for show. He says if he doesn't make his strength obvious and intimidating to the tenants who work the land and whoever else is hanging about, he might have problems. There is no way he is letting me out of the car around here. I am beginning to understand what two weeks with Asif is going to be like.

If I had misjudged Asif's neediness, he had also misjudged the extent of my connections. Our newfound relationship is not only leading to personal discomfort but has implications for the entire research process. What did it mean, in that context, to arrive at a women's NGO with Asif as my chaperone–a member of a wealthy, high status, and politically connected family? How had that arrival already shaped the interaction I would have with the staff? How might the staff be compelled to counter and contain the patriarchal, hierarchical dynamics in which I was already implicated? Was I drawing undesired attention to them in a place where their work was already controversial? As I blundered through these encounters, I failed to anticipate the extent to which those staff were experienced with foreign researchers (and potentially with the local drivers and assistants they brought along). Indeed *their* assumptions about 'the researcher' were a match for my assumptions about 'refugees.'

Wednesday, June 23: Marteni Camp

In Peshawar, anyone who is Afghan is a refugee, at least that's the way the word is used here. Afghans in Peshawar are rich and poor, well connected and vulnerable, smugglers, traders, mothers, fathers, carpet weavers and dyers, shopkeepers, property developers, doctors and NGO staff. Some are destitute. In the hot June nights the strips of grass in the middle of the road outside the university are crowded with men sleeping outside. Asif points out a group of armed men driving past in a shiny new land cruiser. "Look," he says, "there are some of those refugees you're studying." He drives me to the construction site of the soon-to-be biggest shopping mall in Asia. "Owned by Afghan *refugees*, you know." I cannot explain my relief that Bushra has arranged transport for me today without Asif.

Marteni Refugee Camp is about a forty-minute drive from the center of Peshawar. It is one of two hundred camps sprawling out around the city: permanent or semi-permanent mud and brick housing with narrow dirt streets and a jumble of electricity wiring strung up between dwellings like cobwebs. This place conveys the stereotypical image of refugee camps I had imagined from afar. The dust stirs up and coats us, sticking to our sweat as we enter this mini-city. I cover my nose and eyes with my dupatta until it settles. Bushra introduces me to three maternal health workers and a group of about fifteen women and children. They are sitting in a makeshift courtyard under shade cloth, waiting for a health session to begin. I'm struck by their ages: some look no more than sixteen while others look ancient beyond their years.

"Now, what do you want to ask them?" Bushra begins. I'm shocked. I'm not sure I have any business asking anyone anything. I suppose I had envisaged a tour of some kind, rather than an interview, a series of observations from a distance. Bushra looks at me strangely when I explain this. I wonder how many other researchers have come and gone, whether there is a format to this sort of thing. It's as if I'm in the background of a BBC news report. There are women looking up at me as if a show is about to begin. Are they wondering what I'm doing there? *I* wonder what I'm doing there. Reluctantly, I begin stilted conversations while Bushra interprets.

One woman is keen to talk and waits for me to initiate questions. She looks directly at me: her eyes penetrating from within her nameless body, the body I had wanted to observe, not engage. She brushes her hair from her face and the flies from her daughter's, sighs for want of activity, tells me intimate stories of her life, her income, her prospects, watches me nod, mute in response. Here is 'the refugee' I have flown in to witness from afar, without offence or intimacy, whom I encounter as a human being. Here is a woman unknown, unknowable, whom I will tell stories about. In six to eight days, she will manage to spin one ball of yarn, which will go some way, not very far, toward the monthly cost of her children's schooling. She is determined that they go to school. Finally, I ask if there is anything she wants to ask me. There isn't. I'm presented with a mango. I say thank you, and it sits in my lap all the way home, fragile proof of the lives that have just crossed paths.

My caution in seeking to observe rather than engage with refugees was driven, in part, by my reading of feminist scholarship on the unequal power dynamics between researcher and research subject.[15] Feminists argue that if research is to be in women's (and men's) interest, then the researcher must be careful that the research interaction does not become yet another instance of wresting control from already marginalized people. One way to mitigate this effect is to foster trust-based relationships with research subjects. Yet the sincerity of any extension of friendship or involvement is undermined by the researcher's capacity to leave the site of research and disengage at any time.[16] My strategy was to postpone such dilemmas until I could design more thorough fieldwork methodologies based on the lessons of this preparatory trip. However, the level of distance I had hoped to sustain proved difficult when NGO staff made assumptions about what I wanted to see, who I wanted to talk to, and how. Before I knew what hit me, I was conducting precisely that worst kind of fly-in and fly-out superficial encounter I had intended to avoid.

This awkward encounter arose not least because of my own unconscious absorption of statist constructions of refugees as poor, passive, politically disabled beings.[17] This kind of construction led me to distinguish between NGO staff and those who lived in refugee camps as if the term 'refugee' could only apply to the latter precisely because it implied a lack of agency. A little more forethought might have prompted me to think about whom I might encounter both in my visit to Marteni and to women's NGOs and the likelihood of them being both refugees *and* speaking subjects. My visit to Marteni was always going to be beset by power dynamics: my power to fly in and fly out and some middle class refugee women's power over others. Yet avoiding this encounter because of those dynamics seems neither to confront their reality nor to generate opportunities to witness moments in which 'powerless' identities are disrupted.

This encounter highlights the tensions that arose between my efforts to adhere to feminist methodologies and the critical goal of politically transformative research. I approached this experience with particular assumptions about the relation between researcher and researched as one of power to powerlessness, observer to observed, knowing subject to research object. These inflexible binaries clouded my judgment so that I did not anticipate the possibility of the autonomous input of NGO staff in hosting 'the researcher.' Nor did I expect spontaneous interactions with women at Marteni as people with something to say, regardless of what my own research plan and process dictated about when and how to hear that message. The point, in other words, is that my attempts to avoid any contexts in which power dynamics would play a role in the research, in some ways actually exacerbated the power imbalances at hand. My reluctance to offend prevented what might have been more meaningful and productive exchanges, in the sense of the women at Marteni having greater opportunity to tell their stories to a more receptive listener; in the sense of my being open to seeing how women refugees might be acting as agents in the politics of IR; and in the sense of my being better prepared to incorporate this interaction into a story of IR informed by marginalized perspectives. This is not so much a criticism of the imperative to be conscious of power imbalances, as much as a note of caution against seeking to find a power-neutral way of doing research.

Attempting to negotiate an environment where power is absent cannot prepare the researcher for a world in which power is present in obvious but also in unanticipated forms. Indeed the forms unanticipated by us are likely to reflect precisely those power relations in which we ourselves are most strongly implicated. In this way, uncomfortable fieldwork can provide invaluable insight into aspects of power that otherwise remain invisible to us.

Monday, June 28: Interview with Serina

Back in Peshawar I feign heat exhaustion and food poisoning to give myself some time free from Asif's watchful eye. I decide to make my own way to my next appointment. Unaccompanied and on foot, struggling to keep my headscarf in place, I am quite a spectacle. There are jeers and comments that I'm glad I can't understand. A man walking behind me for a couple of blocks finally plucks up his nerve. He says, "I love you. Sex, sex, sex?" and hurries on ahead, psyches himself up once more, drops back, and tries his luck a second time. I begin to wonder if my solo excursion was a foolish idea. When I look up and mutter, "Go away," the man runs off in what appears to be fright—whether at *my* forwardness or *his* lack of success, I don't know. A worried looking stranger asks with grave concern and limited eye contact if he can be of assistance, after apologizing for approaching me in the first place. I thank him; he helps me hail a taxi and speaks sternly to the driver. I slink in the back seat, covering my face except for my eyes as the path of least resistance, wishing I could climb inside one of those all concealing burqas. I wonder if I will arrive at my preferred destination, but try not to dwell on the probabilities. I begin to think I have been far too harsh with Asif. But back at the organization where Bushra works (and I do arrive safely, if via a very long route) the atmosphere, without Asif there, is markedly more relaxed.

There I meet Serina, a social worker, a human rights activist, and the director of the organization. She has just returned from Kabul visibly distressed by events two days earlier in which a bomb killed two women and a child near Jalalabad. These Afghan women were employed by the UN Assistant Mission for Afghanistan to encourage the enrollment of female voters for the election to be held in September. The bomb was planted inside their minibus, which was taking women to register to vote. The Taliban claimed responsibility shortly afterward.[18] This single event captures for me the dilemmas that Serina faces daily. The empowerment of women's lives is dangerous work.

In Afghanistan Serina runs a literacy and income generation project for rural women, many of whom have returned from Pakistan. She tells me stories: threats to kill women who object to conditions at checkpoints controlled by various warlord groups; village women divide the nighttime into three watches to keep guard against thieves and thugs. I sense I am one of a stream of researchers to whom Serina patiently explains the point. She sees the genuine shock in my sheltered face and wants to make sure I understand: "It is nothing to kill a person in Afghanistan and Pakistan. It happens regularly." This is how control is maintained. These are standard working conditions. This is why, understandably, foreign NGOs sometimes pull out, and why Serina's organization stays functioning as best it can. This is home. There is nowhere to pull out to, and nowhere to go for the women whose livelihoods depend on the organization's projects.

When I mention the upcoming election, Serina rolls her eyes and shakes her head. The tiredness seeps from her body. There are tears welling in her eyes, but she pushes past them. She is angry. With this violence and intimidation what sort of procedure can we expect? What should liberation mean? Liberation from the Taliban? Liberation from warlords now contesting roles in government? Liberation from the burqa? There is no disarmament and no peacekeeping. Money is being diverted from development projects to electioneering while three quarters of Afghan women are illiterate. What sort of liberation is this?

Serina shrugs her shoulders and throws her arms down in frustration. "Sometimes," she reflects, "I don't know if it's the right thing to do, to teach my daughters to believe in change, and to expect something better than what they are offered." She looks at her friends who enjoy their family life, have time for leisure, relaxation, pampering themselves, *who are not always fighting*. She looks at her own life—weighing the moments of joy with those of struggle and setback. Is this what she wants for her children?

This interview with Serina had a profound effect on me. I was moved and impressed by her convictions and her quandaries, her seesaw of hope and despair. Without being cynical, Serina struck me as experienced and focused in generating a message for western intellectual consumption, as did other middle class Afghan (refugee) women I met. They thus had their own agendas to push via the research encounter. Here again, I became aware of my own problematic assumptions about power and agency across the divides between First World and Third World, researcher and research subject.[19] It struck me as patronizing to assume that the First World researcher would always have the upper hand.

My interview with Serina took my awareness of First World and Third World binaries beyond methodological considerations and into a different analytical terrain. I was made aware of the reasons why women refugees returning from Pakistan to Afghanistan might welcome an international peacekeeping force endowed with sufficient resources to effectively maintain physical security. In that context, simply staying alive was a more immediate goal than democratic governance and civil society. I was aware of the tendency for powerful western nations to impose their interests on countries like Afghanistan. However, I now came away with a whole new set of questions about the extent to which an alternative caution *against* cultural and political imposition could generate a dangerous policy paralysis and a perverse justification for (yet another) failure to act in the interests of marginalized people. I came away with a new set of questions about the moral implications of cultural relativism. I was able to see how relativism is often based on false dichotomies between us and them, power and powerlessness, agent and victim, privilege and oppression that permeate ideas about different nations, cultures, and states.

Coming to Terms with Power in Feminist Practice

What can be drawn from this experience of fieldwork to inform a critical feminist methodology in IR? Some feminists advocate the notion of "studying up" in order to avoid the unequal power dynamics that operate when researchers focus upon marginalized research subjects ("studying down").[20] In the context of refugee politics in Peshawar, this implies shifting the research focus from the experiences of refugees to the structures of power that shape those experiences such as the operations of the UNHCR. In terms of IR theory it implies a shift in focus from how the identity of the refugee plays into those practices of sovereignty that structure our understandings of states, borders, and nations, to understanding the role in those same processes of the refugee's privileged corollaries—the citizen and the hypermobile cosmopolitan. While these analytical foci provide important additional insights, an exclusive focus upon them cannot convey the experiences of those very people marginalized in the first place. There are also more fundamental problems with establishing the categories of up and down. It is not obvious to me where certain people I encountered in Peshawar would be placed on this binary—middle class Afghan (refugee) women working in local and international NGOs, or in the UNHCR itself, for example. Such an approach is indicative of the problematic assumptions I have highlighted in which marginalized research subjects are imagined in simplistic terms as passive beings and as consistently less powerful than the researcher.

This is not to deny the very real power imbalances that persist in research encounters but simply to register some important qualifications about that power: (1) that power imbalances will not always be absolute and power may shift in different ways between researcher and research subject; and (2) that power imbalances cannot be avoided. On this latter point, I concur with Jayati Lal who argues that social science research "unavoidably reflects the social world in which it and we are situated. And if the social world that is being investigated is a sexist and hierarchical one, the process of research is sure to become a sexist and hierarchical social interaction."[21] Many feminists would doubtless agree with the impossibility of nonhierarchical research. Such a position reflects the spirit of Sandra Harding's original critique of positivist research practices and her injunction to bring inevitable biases into the field of critical scrutiny. The point here is one of emphasis rather than fundamental critique of feminist methodologies. In my view, there is a need to be *more* explicit about the unavoidable persistence of power within *feminist* research practice as much as any other, and to recognize this power as *dynamic* in nature. The emphasis must remain on minimizing power imbalances where we can, and learning to live with them where we cannot. This means being more honest about the limitations and partiality that will necessarily characterize our research.

Finally, it is important to note, as Lal does, that reflexivity is merely a tool of research and should therefore be kept in perspective alongside the broader purposes of critical feminist scholarship.[22] Losing this perspective allows reflexivity to slip into the rather less productive notion of guilt. This slippage threatens to disengage from power imbalances rather than confront them through the awkward, noninnocent, and invaluable lessons that fieldwork can provide.

Notes

1. Sandra Whitworth, "The Practice, and Praxis, of Feminist Research in International Relations," in *Critical Theory and World Politics*, ed. Richard W. Jones (Boulder: Lynne Rienner Publishers, 2001), 149.
2. Diane L. Wolf, "Preface," in *Feminist Dilemmas in Fieldwork*, ed. Diane L. Wolf (Boulder: Westview Press, 1996), ix–x; idem, "Situating Feminist Dilemmas in Fieldwork," 12.
3. Wolf, "Preface," xi.
4. Brooke A. Ackerly, Maria Stern, and Jacqui True, "Feminist Methodologies for International Relations," in *Feminist Methodologies for International Relations*, ed. Brooke A. Ackerly, et al. (Cambridge: Cambridge University Press, 2006), 2.
5. See in particular Bina D'Costa,"Marginalized Identity: New Frontiers of Research for IR?" in *Feminist Methodologies, ed.* Ackerly, et al., 129–52.
6. Nita Kumar cited in Wolf, "Situating Feminist Dilemmas in Fieldwork," 6.
7. See, for example, Navnita Chadha Behera, "Introduction," in *Gender, Conflict and Migration*, ed. Navnita Chadha Behera (New Delhi: Sage, 2006), 47–50; J. Ann Tickner, "What Is Your Research Program? Some Feminist Answers to International Relations Methodological Questions," *International Studies Quarterly* 49, no. 1 (2005): 4–10.
8. Sandra Harding, "Introduction: Is There a Feminist Method?" in *Feminism and Methodology*, ed. Sandra Harding (Bloomington: Indiana University Press, 1987), 9.
9. Ackerly, Stern, and True, "Feminist Methodologies for International Relations," 4.
10. See in particular Cynthia Enloe, *Bananas, Beaches and Bases: Making Feminist Sense of International Politics* (Berkeley: University of California Press, 1989).

11. J. Ann Tickner, *Gender in International Relations* (New York: Columbia University Press, 1992), especially chapter 1; Anne Sisson Runyan and V. Spike Peterson, "The Radical Future of Realism: Feminist Subversions of IR Theory," *Alternatives* 16 (1991): 68–72; Rebecca Grant, "The Sources of Gender Bias in International Relations Theory," in *Gender and International Relations*, ed. Rebecca Grant and Kathleen Newland (Buckingham: The Millennium Publishing Group, 1991), 11–17.
12. Christine Chin, *In Service and Servitude: Foreign Domestic Workers and the Malaysian "Modernity Project"* (New York: Columbia University Press, 1998); Saskia Sassen, *Globalization and Its Discontents: Essays on the New Mobility of People and Money* (New York: The New Press, 1998), chapters 2 and 3; Saskia Sassen, *Cities in a World Economy*, 2nd ed. (Thousand Oaks, CA: Pine Forge, 2000), chapter 6; V. Spike Peterson, *A Critical Rewriting of Global Political Economy: Integrating Reproductive, Productive and Virtual Economies* (London: Routledge, 2003); Jan Jindy Pettman, *Worlding Women: A Feminist International Politics* (Sydney: Allen and Unwin, 1996), 185–207.
13. For a critical summary of the Australian Government's recent asylum policies see Robert Manne and David Corlett, "Sending Them Home: Refugees and the New Politics of Indifference," *Quarterly Essay*, no. 13 (2004).
14. For these and other impressions of the globalized aspects of life in Peshawar, I am indebted to conversations with Robert Nichols.
15. Wolf, "Situating Feminist Dilemmas in Fieldwork," 2–4.
16. For an insightful discussion of this issue see Gesa E Kirsch, "Friendship, Friendliness, and Feminist Fieldwork," *Signs* 30, no. 4 (2005).
17. On the construction of refugee identity as an instrument of statecraft see Nevzat Soguk, *States and Strangers: Refugees and Displacements of Statecraft* (Minneapolis: University of Minnesota Press, 1999), chapter 1. On political passivity as a central component of statist refugee identity see Peter Nyers, *Rethinking Refugees: Beyond States of Emergency* (New York: Routledge, 2006), chapter 5.
18. "Jalalabad Bomb Attack Toll Rises to Four," *The Frontier Post*, July 2, 2004.
19. On this point see also Shahnaz Khan, "Reconfiguring the Native Informant: Positionality in the Global Age," *Signs* 30, no. 4 (2005): 2026.
20. Sandra Harding and Kathryn Norberg, "New Feminist Approaches to Social Science Methodologies: An Introduction," *Signs* 30, no. 4 (2005): 2011.
21. Jayati Lal, "Situating Locations: The Politics of Self, Identity, And 'Other' In Living and Writing the Text," in *Feminist Dilemmas in Fieldwork*, ed. Diane L. Wolf (Boulder, CO: Westview, 1996), 196.
22. Ibid., 207.

CHAPTER 8

One Woman's Everyday Resistance

An Empowering Yet Cautionary Tale from Vietnam

Kim Huynh

Difference and Emancipation

Jindy Pettman stresses that "differences among women must be part of theorizing women's experiences of states and citizenship, and of power more generally."[1] As the introduction to this collection suggests, this involves understanding how individuals are effected by, and respond to, oppression in varied ways while maintaining a commitment to an overarching feminist ethic. By this account, successful critical theory—feminist or otherwise—demands constant negotiation between induction and deduction, empathy and judgment, difference and emancipation.

There are, of course, many women in the Asia-Pacific who have ambivalent relationships with feminist empowerment. This denies any easy approach to feminist analysis. As First Lady and special envoy for the Philippines, Imelda Marcos conducted diplomatic and trade negotiations around the world but is now commonly associated with the corruption of the Marcos regime and her extravagant collection of shoes. Madame Ngo Dinh Nhu was the de facto first lady of South Vietnam during the Diem era from 1955 to 1963 during which time she championed women's liberation against the prevailing patriarchy of Vietnamese society. At the same time, however, Madame Nhu banned divorce, contraception, and abortion, and when monks committed self-immolation protesting against the Diem regime she infamously proclaimed that she would clap her hands at the next Buddhist barbecue. It is easy to exclude such problematic individuals from our spheres of interest. However, by carefully examining their experiences and motivations, critical feminist scholars can learn much about how gendered oppression, resistance, and emancipation operate in complicated and unfamiliar environments.

My Aunt Huong is a far less prominent figure in international relations than Marcos or Nhu; however, she shares a somewhat vexed relationship with feminism with them. More specifically, Huong confronted oppression throughout her life *without* any commitment to established feminist ethics. Indeed, she is scornful of shared emancipation. In resisting French colonialism, American neoimperialism and Vietnamese communism, she never sought truly to connect to a social movement or comforting ideology; but rather, she was driven by her desire to be wealthy, cherished, and feared. While Aunt Huong's story is not a typical celebration of feminist agency and liberation, understanding it in the context of everyday resistance can help reconcile the demands of difference and emancipation in critical feminist theory. Everyday resistance offers a lens through which we perceive the underlying resilience in acts of submission and the strands of rebellion intertwined with corruption. In a small but significant way, Aunt Huong's story exposes forms of gendered resistance and forges brighter feminist futures in the Asia-Pacific.

Everyday Resistance

Everyday resistance is a conceptual tool that provides a way to better understand women's experiences and navigate the straights between advancing emancipation and celebrating difference. In the foundational text on this topic, *Weapons of the Weak*, James C. Scott observed Malaysian villagers carrying out concealed acts of arson, pilfering, foot dragging, dissimulation, false compliance, feigned ignorance, slander, and sabotage against their employers, overseers, and landlords.[2] Significantly, these surreptitious acts of defiance maintained the impression of compliance in an oppressive system without its substance.[3] They required little coordination, and often represented a form of individual self-help. Typically, the villagers avoided direct symbolic confrontation with the authorities, preferring to maximize their meager benefits under the ruling system rather than risk the ramifications of an uncertain uprising.[4] Most controversially, Scott contends that everyday resistance is often more effective than open and violent revolt when it comes to achieving real socioeconomic gains for subordinate classes.[5]

This message is reaffirmed in Scott's, *Domination and the Arts of Resistance: Hidden Transcripts*, in which he argues that any rigorous investigation of political or economic activity must pay attention not only to the public transcripts that tell the official narrative, but also to the hidden transcripts performed beyond the spotlight of public scrutiny.[6] Within the hidden transcript, the roles of the powerful and powerless are far from clear-cut. While subordinate groups do not dominate power relations within their concealed spheres of action, they exercise *infrapolitics* in ways that increase their practical benefits while decreasing—if not eliminating—retribution from superordinate groups.

In *The Practice of Everyday Life*, Michel de Certeau offers further insights into the nature of everyday resistance. He provides a lively account of how people regularly 'make do' in the face of tyranny.[7] Certeau is an incorrigible optimist who believes that oppression gives birth to insurrection and that even in the most disciplined environment, a flight of escape is always at hand. Certeau's "science of the ordinary" illuminates the way people use tricks of language and culture to subvert hegemonic regimes without leaving or reforming them ("subversion from within"). These covert victories of the weak are achieved using 'tactics' that correlate with "the age-old ruses of fishes and insects that disguise or transform themselves in order to survive."[8] Tactical behavior is characterized by its transience and is predicated upon cunning rather than brute force. This is particularly evident when people 'poach' and re-employ for subversive purposes the cultural and material weapons of the strong. Certeau's tactical ideal is contrasted with his understanding of strategic action, which is based on long-term plans to consolidate capital and actualize abstract ideologies. Unlike fleeting tactics, strategies seek to establish for their constituents a permanent political and physical space in the public sphere.[9]

Everyday Resistance and Feminist International Relations

Appreciating the differences between tactics and strategies in the context of everyday resistance assists us in moving away from disempowering distinctions between victims and perpetrators. Given this potential, it is surprising that scholars of feminism and everyday resistance do not readily turn to one another to elaborate their ideas and substantiate their arguments. Specifically, neither Scott and Certeau ask gender questions nor, to date, does feminist international relations (IR) have any engagement with them.[10] This is despite acknowledgement from key feminist IR scholars like Cynthia Enloe that the, "world has been made with blunt power, but also with sleights of hand."[11]

This disconnect is in part due to a conflict between the emancipatory goals of feminists and the conservative consequences of sustained everyday resistance. Tactical behavior and subversions from within are regularly criticized as modes of false consciousness or a safety valve that prevents 'real' revolutionary change.[12] According to this view, everyday resistance is a hegemonic concession that helps the powerful stay in control.

Yet even if some feminists do not agree with the potential outcomes of everyday resistance, the very fact that women use their gendered identities to resist in an everyday manner suggests that it is worthy of investigation. However, there are stronger reasons for bringing together everyday resistance and feminist IR than empirical necessity. For while tactical behavior has the potential to maintain the status quo, it can just as easily contribute to progressive change. In other words, Scott's assertion that peasants are *often* better off feigning compliance, does not mean that this is *always* the case. He points out that everyday resistance, while internally directed at immediate survival, can provide the foundation for large-scale reform. He illustrates this point using the example of polyps in a coral reef.

> Just as millions of anthozoan polyps create, willy-nilly, a coral reef, so do thousands upon thousands of individual acts of insubordination and evasion create a political or economic barrier reef of their own. There is rarely any dramatic confrontation, any moment that is particularly newsworthy. And whenever, to pursue the simile, the ship of state runs aground on such a reef, attention is typically directed to the shipwreck itself and not to the vast aggregation of petty acts that made it possible.[13]

Feminist international relations has much to offer the analysis of everyday resistance, if only because women around the world are generally worse off than men and therefore more likely to exercise power in tactical ways. In addition, because tactical behavior does not register on the official radar, understanding it requires intensive qualitative research that conflates the private and public spheres and problematizes traditional distinctions between objectivity and subjectivity. This is the very research in which many critical feminist scholars specialize. Thus, feminist IR is well equipped to answer the fundamental questions about everyday resistance: When do everyday practices like moving about and cooking become subversive turns? What are the long-term consequences for individuals who act in tactical ways? Where does the distinction lie between condemnable law-breaking and everyday resistance? How might we ensure that everyday resistance serves socially progressive goals rather than perpetuate oppression?

Aunt Huong's Tactical Victories*

According to an obscure Vietnamese saying from the countryside, "Having an eldest daughter is better than having deep paddy fields and female buffaloes."[14] This was certainly true with respect to my Aunt Huong; however, it was also unfortunate because many of the responsibilities that she had taken on by the age of twelve were imposed upon her by conflict and the death of loved ones. In 1947 she and her family were forced to abandon their home in the central Vietnamese village of Bo Ban not far from Danang. For much of that year, the First Indochina War relentlessly pursued them as they fled burning villages, makeshift tents, and mountain hideouts. During that ordeal, Huong's oldest brother Khiet died from disease and malnutrition. A year later her father, Viet, was assassinated by Viet Minh militia after being falsely accused of collaborating with the French. This left Huong, her mother,Thua, and her three surviving

---

* The following story is a modified extract from my book, *Where the Sea Takes Us: A Vietnamese-Australian Story* (Sydney: HarperCollins, 2007).

siblings, a girl named Truong who suffered from epilepsy, and two small boys (the youngest being my father Thiet). We pick up Thua and Huong's story of wartime survival and women's everyday resistance shortly after Viet's assassination.

* * *

My grandmother Thua had resolved never to remarry becuase she was convinced that a wife's fidelity extends beyond the grave. Nevertheless, she was aware of how difficult it would be without her husband to protect her children from disease, starvation, and war. In the words of the proverb, "A child without a father is like a house without a roof."[15] Neverthe less, this wiry woman in her mid-thirties was well equipped for single parenthood. For while Viet had been the head of the family, the trying nature of peasant life meant that his widow and children were resourceful and accustomed to toil.

In the days after Viet's murder, Thua borrowed money from relatives in order to buy time to decide how they were going to make a living. Her first thought was to farm their small plot of land but Huong quickly convinced her mother that this was a dangerous path because it meant hiring men as farmhands at the market and depending on these strangers for their survival. Even at that early stage in her life, Huong possessed a stridently independent will fed by distrust of others.

Instead, Huong suggested they go into business trading banana palm leaves—used to wrap traditional rice cakes—that littered the countryside after storms. The young girl astutely surmised that banana palm owners would be happy for them to clean up the leaves at no cost. After collecting the leaves, the mother and daughter team washed the leaves, removed the stems, rolled them up to soften the fibers, and took them to the market to sell for a profitable pittance.

After a few months, Thua and Huong saved enough money to branch out into items that brought higher returns like salted fish, areca nuts, rice, peanuts, and textiles. To acquire the goods Huong commuted to the city of Danang every week and in the process both the French colonists and the Viet Minh revolutionaries terrorized her. The French banned all inter-village commerce that was not under their control, suspecting that villagers like Huong were selling goods to the Viet Minh but also disregarding the fact that most of her wares were bought by noncombatants. As the crackdown intensified and French soldiers started blockading roads, Huong had to get off the bus early, tie up her goods and balance them on her head as she crossed a river before walking the rest of the way home. Even then, she was not safe. Pairs of clandestine Viet Minh guerrillas stopped Huong several times to ask what a young girl was doing with so much merchandise. If she responded truthfully that she was going to sell it at the market then she was guilty of supporting the colonial economy. The alternative was to say the merchandise was intended for the Viet Minh. Either way, it is confiscated, and Huong went home empty-handed

Thua and Huong were particularly afraid of the French, Moroccan, and Algerian expeditionary troops who raided towns looking for black market materials to commandeer, women to molest, and men to force into work and war. Displaying remnants of gashes on their cheeks from tribal rituals, the North Africans attracted the pseudonym, "scar faced ghouls." When the troops charged into the village grunting and howling, many women at the market gathered what they could and fled. Thua and Huong, on the other hand, hastened to conceal their goods and rub dirt into their faces in the hope of appearing so unhygienic and unhealthy that even the most licentious soldier would be too repulsed to trouble them.

With each grubby smear, Huong and her mother perpetuated a preconception among the invaders of natives as dirty, diseased, and barbaric. This preconception complemented their colonial air of superiority and helped to justify the French civilizing mission. At the same time, their camouflage served as a short-term survival tactic, which confirmed in their own minds that shrewd maneuvering could fool the mightiest soldier. In this way, Huong and her mother turned the myth of colonial liberation against the French as one would a knife in a struggle to the death. Such was the common necessity of these guileful ruses among women at the markets that songs were composed in which they boasted about having "hair full of small stone flints" (prized by the Viet Minh guerrillas for lighting fires) and being "pregnant with bundles of khaki material" stuffed under their shirts.[16]

Using the savings from the market, Thua and Huong built a hut made of thatch, mud, and buffalo dung to replace the brick house that had been seized by the Viet Minh at the outset of the war and later bombed by the French. Depending on the seasons, they grew cassava, sesame, and rice and they were even able to raise a pig and a few chickens. My father, Thiet, and his brother, Biet, were old enough to look after the small plot of land while their mother and sisters worked at the market. Laboring with the dirt between their toes, sleeping under that grass roof, and inhaling the smells of the earth, Huong's family was not unlike many other Vietnamese peasants in terms of what they had lost and regained during the French war. A folksong from that time sings,

> The enemy razes our tile roof house,
> And we erect a thatch hut.
> The enemy sets our boats ablaze,
> And yet we still go fishing.[17]

This is not to say that the First Indochina War had abated or that life for Huong and her family had become comfortable and secure; only that by the middle of 1949 they were finding and fine-tuning ways to make do. Every afternoon after returning home and eating the evening meal, Thua and Huong made an instinctive life-and-death decision as to where the family would spend the night. If there was a scent of security in the air, then they slept in their thatch hut. But when village gossip or their sharpened instincts suggested that a battle was imminent, they would march back to Huong's grandfather's house where the family either bedded in a small corridor between the main house and the ancestral shrine or were shoved into an adjacent dug-out as flames lit up the night sky.

There are several reasons for why such critical decisions became commonplace for Huong and her family. At a local level, Bo Ban was a village of hard beans and sticky rice; the contrasting texture of these two staple foods represents the difference between villagers who supported Ho Chi Minh's Democratic Republic of Vietnam (supported by the communist bloc) and those who followed Bao Dai's republic (which was backed by the French who were in turn funded by the United States). The divisions in Bo Ban reflected heightened hostilities at a national level. After being driven into the jungle-covered mountains at the outset of the conflict, from the late 1940s onward the Viet Minh had been increasing their activity. Still meager in number and militarily ill-equipped, the revolutionaries in Huong's province of Quang Nam mobilized to enlist troops, consolidate their liberated zones, and harass areas like Bo Ban that the French had pacified. All of this accorded with the cold war divisions of the international sphere.

For Huong's family, the cold war remapping of their lives during the early 1950s was neither neat nor painless. The descending of an iron curtain upon Bo Ban did not provide security from a partitioned enemy, but rather the curtain collapsed upon them instigating fear, suspicion, and malice. The cold war meant that during the day when the village was officially "pacified," Moroccan and Algerian expeditionary troops assaulted and arrested villagers who to them were indistinguishable from Viet Minh guerrillas. The terror continued after sunset when the real revolutionaries crept into the towns to attack French outposts and those who they had identified as *collaborateurs*.

Theft, deception, and double-crossing were common features of Huong's daily interactions. When buying wares from Danang, she had somehow to ensure that her wholesaler was not an undercover agent working for the French on a mission to trap Viet Minh suppliers. Dealings with customers demanded great caution. Many women purchased food and merchandise for their revolutionary husbands and sons. If caught by the French, they would implicate Huong as their supplier and she too would suffer retribution. When the Viet Minh solicited "donations" for the national revolution Huong knew that if she did not pay enough, or did not pay with enough enthusiasm, she would be reported to the French as a member of the anti-colonial movement. Moreover, there was always the prospect that a petty village disagreement would lead to denunciation, imprisonment or murder. The flow chart of threats and enemies was so complex; it would have baffled a crack intelligence agent. Yet this was the everyday environment in which Huong grew up. She had to scan for potential foes, choose her words with the skill and sensitivity of a diplomat, and never come to rest on a particular plan of attack as if she were an insect in a field of Venus flytraps. Huong and Thua often resorted to feigning complete ignorance with everyone. They would recall much later that, "knowing nothing, hearing nothing, and seeing nothing," was the only way to get by. They played up to the popular image of the ignorant woman peasant, which shielded them from a war in which civilians were both soldiers and targets.

These impressive threat perception and business acumen skills served Huong and her family for many years to come. Huong always worked longer and haggled harder than her competitors at the market. She made frequent trips to Danang where she bought entire bolts of material that were difficult to conceal but fetched higher profits. However, Huong did not care for material wealth as an end in itself. Money was a means to a more magnificent end. With money, she gained power. Every time she pulled off a deal, convinced customers that they were profiting from the exchange or even taking advantage of the sweet-mannered youth, Huong's heart soared with victory. When she bettered another, for the first time in her life she felt she was worth something. The teenager could not get her fill of this sensation, but in order to maintain the high, she could not afford to be complacent. Huong thus decided to direct her emancipatory struggle toward decidedly non-feminist goals.

Huong shortly after she arrived in Saigon in 1956. This is the first picture ever taken of her.

* * *

Huong was also wearing areca leaves on the day in 1956 when her entrepreneurial spirit inspired her to leave Central Vietnam and her family to travel to Saigon (see Figure 8.1). Over the next two decades, with typical resolve, she learnt to read and write Vietnamese along with a little French and English. She also learned to drive a car and type, won beauty contests, purchased two bars and a restaurant, got rich speculating in the property market, consorted with the wealthy and powerful, sponsored her family to come and live with her in the city, and bore a son named Tam. Along the way, Huong replaced her country drawl with a Southern city accent that complemented her modern poise and wardrobe bursting with lavish outfits and platform shoes.

Yet in an important sense, the areca leaves never left Huong's feet. That ability to make something out of nothing, which was forged and refined during the First Indochina War, laid the tactical foundation for her to prosper throughout the Second Indochina War. A similar spirit of Vietnamese everyday resistance underpinned efforts by communist revolutionaries to turn old truck tires into sandals and rusty bicycles into all-terrain, stealth, pinpoint attack vehicles. The same spirit was found around the American military bases of South Vietnam in the makeshift cardboard box cities occupied by women who provided foreign soldiers with laundry, food, entertainment, and conjugal services. This whatever-it-takes attitude was so ensconced in Huong that the North Vietnamese victory in 1975 did not represent to her the end of an era and way of life; but rather, the emergence of bountiful opportunities.

Aunt Huong's Strategic Defeats

After the fall of Saigon, almost all of the cars, busses and trucks were requisitioned by the government for official use. This meant that only the most audacious private citizens dared to drive in the open without proper registration plates or a uniformed cadre traveling with them. Huong considered herself to be above such earthly laws. By the end of the 1970s, she was convinced that the Socialist Republic of Vietnam would exonerate her of all her crimes and that heaven would absolve her of all her sins: all of them, that is, except poverty and faint-heartedness.

She stuck on the windscreen of her little white Peugeot a sign that read, "I Have the Right to Drive!" For those lowly cadres who were not satisfied with her self-registration sticker and who failed to recognize her commanding air, Huong kept irrefutable documentation of her eminence and clout in the glove box. This allowed her to stand over the young communists who stopped her in the street and declare in a manner that exploited their fear of offending power, "See here, I have a driver's license from the 1950s. This other certificate proves that I am a movie star and member of the People's Film Council. I am also an important exporter and a prominent figure in society. Consider yourself lucky because I am in a generous mood and realize that, now and then, we are all prone to error. I will not report your insolence, but I must go in haste. Now, move aside. I am very busy." Her demeanor was so full of pomp and her self-belief so complete that Huong was always allowed to continue on her way. In the brutal post–1975 era, in which thousands of people like my parents left Vietnam, my aunt was at home and at times reigned supreme.

Huong was not overly concerned on April 30, 1975 when the communists arrived. She feared a massacre and even tried to escape on a plane to the United States with her boyfriend, but Huong was not running away from communism. Communism, republicanism, and all the other "isms" were indistinguishable and irrelevant to her. Revolution, independence, and even liberty were nothing more than vacuous concepts—words in the wind—and the fact that anyone would bother to die for them was so pathetic as to be amusing. From Huong's perspective, there were only two political camps: her camp (which consisted of her alone); and the enemy camp (into which just about everyone else fell). Naturally, her camp would seek to accumulate as much financial and social capital as possible, and just as naturally, the other camp would try to stop her through various laws, customs, and principles. She despised them for this but to attempt to change the leadership of the day was pure folly. It would make no difference. It was like striving to postpone nightfall. After the blood of the rebellion had dried and the dust of the uprising had settled, nothing would change. The rational thing to do, then, was exist within those structures; to break rules and rituals in such a way that those who were "in control" were left unawares. Using these evasive tactics in the age of French colonialism, the cold war, and into the modern era of Vietnamese socialism, Huong managed to thrive like a glistening fern under the dense canopy of ideology.

The day after the war ended, Huong stepped out into the city. It was May Day and the sun rose for the first time in almost thirty years over a nation free from foreign occupation. A new page turned in Vietnam's proud history. From a contrasting view, this was the first full day of communist oppression and if a new page in Vietnam's history was in fact turning, then the people were like tiny bugs being squashed in the spine of that little red book. Huong did not care for such dramatics. What concerned her was that there was money to be made. She carefully analyzed the market prospects and determined that she could take advantage of the prevailing chaos. Not long afterward, Huong was at the black markets with a suitcase full of gold, U.S. dollars, republican piastres, and the new Uncle Ho money. The middle-aged woman was a sagacious speculator and guileful go-between, buying currency from one desperate soul and selling it to another. A few months after the fall of Saigon, a thief posing as a prospective customer stuck a gun into her chest and took off on a waiting motorcycle with twenty-four taels of gold (almost one kilogram or around 32 ounces). Huong returned home furious but she was not disheartened.

In the years after the Revolution, Huong, her mother, Thua, and sister, Truong, moved house and changed trades many times. They were like insects that fly in jagged paths in order to avoid the beaks of birds or chameleons that blend into their surroundings by changing the color of their skin. They sold electrical goods, sticky rice, blocks of ice, and Hue-style beef soup. At one point Huong sold coffee, green bean pudding, and balloons with such success that during the New Year's festive season her shop opened for six days straight and attracted so much business that the local authorities arrived to direct traffic around the crowd of customers that flowed into the street.

In the 1980s, when the economic climate was more amenable to big business, Huong set up factories that manufactured solder and nails for export to Kampuchea and the USSR. Of course, she never engaged in manual labor herself, leaving such menial work to her relatives and hired help. Huong was no longer willing to dirty her hands, but she was always there in the background, orchestrating the affair, determining when it was time to pull out and move on. She also devoted herself to the big deals, trading in the cut-price properties and bullion that came onto the black market whenever families exiled themselves from Vietnam.

Even so, making money was not everything to Huong. There was the critical matter of accumulating status and fame. From the 1980s onward, Huong decided that she could best achieve this in the nascent Socialist Republic of Vietnam film industry. She paid her way into cameo roles and was soon hobnobbing with famous directors and movie stars. Her glamorous lifestyle and elevation to the highest artistic echelons demanded a name-change. And so those who could be bothered to read the flying credits at the end of her films did not know her as the mundane, Huynh Thi Huong, but rather the more illustrious, Trang Thien Huong (derived from *trang nha*, which means well-bred and refined and *thien huong*, which connotes a pure and natural fragrance). The movies were made in the socialist realist tradition. They praised the Party and the Revolution, depicted the bravery of the peasants in overcoming the evil of the French and American colonizers, and condemned the dastardly puppets of the old republic. Nevertheless, by appearing in these films, Huong had not turned red. On the contrary, her acting career represented the ultimate subversion from within an otherwise totalitarian society.

We can take for example her role in *Old Lady Number Six*, the story of an elderly woman who risked her life during the War of Resistance against the Americans to smuggle letters between guerrillas and their loved ones. The villains of the film are the generals and leaders of the South Vietnamese regime who are depicted as unprincipled, slovenly, and rich beyond all integrity. One memorable scene filmed on site at the Reunification Palace (previously the Independence Palace) shows a small band of treacherous millionaires dancing to lurid Western music. The camera pans across to portray the obscene nature of the defeated republic. In this instant, Huong is dazzling in a pink taffeta dress, which is laden with her most garish jewelry. She cha-cha-chas with an elderly gentleman in an oversized pinstriped suit. Before the eyes of the nation, *Old Lady Number Six* allowed Huong to flaunt everything the communists tried to take away from her and even to be congratulated for it. Prior to the revolution she had never come close to being invited to the Presidential Palace, let alone be permitted to glide through its lofty halls. It was only after 1975 that Huong was free to realize her dreams.

However, Huong's freedom was far from enduring or complete, and her conquests over time, truth, and despair were pyrrhic victories. In another film entitled *The Undisguisable Blemish*, she played a South Vietnamese general's wife. After shooting a raunchy scene in which she wore a lacy ivory-colored negligee, Huong's director-friend praised her acting and beauty before adding that her breasts were a little uneven and saggy. Priding herself on being twice the age of her lacquer-face movie star friends but no less youthful, Huong sought out a plastic surgeon who introduced to her the revolutionary procedure of silicone injection. Months later a thick clear sludge was inserted into Huong's once-proud chest and pumped directly into her drooping arms.

In a psychological and spiritual sense, Huong was contaminated long before this fateful procedure. Decades of existing in the shadows had made her adverse to the light, allowing a malignant tumor to take hold of her soul. Since she was a teenager, Huong had evaded the authorities, brazenly bent the truth, and sacrificed all principle in order to stay alive and flourish. Somewhere along the line, despite her adaptation skills, she became incapable of acting out a public script in which she could be honest, open, earnest, and herself. At crucial points in her life, Huong did not recognize that she could make real choices involving something more than momentary survival and the accumulation of reputation and money. There were also options of virtue, dignity, and compassion, which Huong either never saw or could not take. Perhaps this had something to do with the violent wrongs that had been committed against her in her youth by figures—republican soldiers, Confucian fathers, and communist revolutionaries—who promoted themselves as exemplars of righteousness? No doubt, she was devoid of civic virtue and believed that those who possessed such qualities deserved her scorn. As Huong saw it, the world was bad and could never be made good. She was unable to turn her outward hardship into inner triumph and somehow prove that she was more than worthy of her sufferings.

Conclusion

Feminist IR scholars have been exploring the politics of everyday life for some time. In 1989 Cynthia Enloe argued that everyday goings-on involving women as secretaries, shoppers, prostitutes, factory workers, and mothers were far from benign. In fact, they are intrinsically tied to political activities like the provision of foreign loans, the maintenance of armies, and the morale of nations.[18]

Her work unveils a landscape of underappreciated female political activity and invites us to contemplate not only how to think and do international relations, but also what constitutes it.

This study of my Aunt Huong seeks to build upon this tradition. Specifically, it adopts a conceptual framework of everyday resistance to understand how she confronted oppression over three decades. When she was young and relatively powerless, Huong tenaciously existed and resisted a harrowing political milieu. During the First Indochina War, she made do by selling everything from banana leaves to peanuts to fabric. Moreover, like many Vietnamese she did so in a clandestine manner that did not directly challenge the prevailing ideologies and regimes (Confucian patriarchy, French colonialism, Vietnamese Marxism and American neocolonialism), but which contributed to their erosion. After moving to Saigon and accumulating a significant amount of socioeconomic capital, Huong was capable of not only making do for herself but also making a difference to the lives of others. However, she could not step out of her murky comfort zone and incorporate her self-centered tactics into strategies for greater liberation. Instead, Huong continued, and would continue for the rest of her life, to be locked inside a hidden transcript. She was constantly resisting *against* something without ever being *for* a cause that transcended her own immediate needs and desires.

Huong's story is thus both inspirational and cautionary for feminist IR scholars. It compels us to appreciate how women who are uncommitted to feminist goals and who have ostensibly accepted patriarchal structures can still quietly contribute to a resistance movement. By better understanding their differences and acknowledging the logic behind their everyday acts we can find ways to unite their tactics with grander strategies for social emancipation. While Aunt Huong's story is not communal, ostensibly feminist or ultimately liberating, it reminds us of the enduring value of telling *all* women's stories.

Notes

1. Jan Jindy Pettman, *Worlding Women: A Feminist International Politics* (Sydney: Allen and Unwin, 1996), 22.
2. James C. Scott, *Weapons of the Weak: Everyday Forms of Peasant Resistance* (New Haven: Yale University Press, 1985), 30.
3. Ibid., 26.
4. Ibid., 30.
5. Ibid., xvi.
6. James C. Scott, *Domination and the Arts of Resistance: Hidden Transcripts* (New Haven: Yale University Press, 1990).
7. Michel de Certeau, trans. Steven Rendall, *The Practice of Everyday Life* (Berkeley: University of California Press, 1984).
8. Ibid., xi.
9. Ibid., 34–37.

10. Vietnamese women and everyday resistance are examined in Kim Huynh, "Modernity and My Mum: a Literary Exploration into the (Extra)ordinary Sacrifices and Everyday Resistance of a Vietnamese Woman," *Frontiers: A Journal of Women Studies*, 25:2 (2004), 1–25; see also Stephanie M. H. Camp, *Closer to Freedom: Enslaved Women and Everyday Resistance in the Plantation South* (Chapel Hill: University of North Carolina Press, 2004); Marguerite R. Waller and Jennifer Rycenga, ed, *Frontline Feminisms: Women, War, and Resistance* (New York: Routledge, 2001).
11. Cynthia Enloe, *Bananas, Beaches and Bases: Making Feminist Sense of International Politics* (London: Pandora, 1989), 17.
12. See Matthew Gutmann, "Rituals of Resistance: a Critique of the Theory of Everyday Forms of Resistance," *Latin American Perspectives* 20:2 (Spring 1993), 74–96; James C. Scott and Benedict J. Tria Kerkvliet, *Everyday Forms of Peasant Resistance in South-East Asia* (London: Frank Cass, 1986).
13. Scott, *Weapons of the Weak*, 36.
14. Pham Van Bich, *The Vietnamese Family in Change: The Case of the Red River Delta* (Surrey: Curzon Press, 1999), 188.
15. *Con khong cha nhu nha khong noc*. Recounted by Thua. All translations are by the author.
16. *Dau phong da lua, Co chua Ka Ki. Recounted by Huong.*
17. *Giac dot nha ngoi, ta dung leu tranh, / Giac dot ghe manh, sam thung di cau.* Recounted by Thua.
18. Enloe, *Bananas, Beaches & Bases*, 1989.

CHAPTER 9

Women's Engagement with Islam in South and Southeast Asia

Shakira Hussein

Perhaps the most striking feature of contemporary Muslim women's conversations about gender is the sheer breadth of the territory covered. Such conversations may range from interpretation of disputes among the Prophet's wives in the sixth century CE, to medieval jurisprudence, to CEDAW (Convention on the Elimination of All Forms of Discrimination against Women) conventions, domestic violence, militarism, imperialism, and the alleviation of poverty. In some conversations, the question of what is or is not 'Islamic' may loom large; in others, the issue of religious identity barely features.

Despite the dominance of patriarchy in Muslim communities across Asia, Muslim women play a vital political role, and not only in secular political movements that espouse western models of gender equality. An often-overlooked facet of Islamist politics is that Islamic movements across the ideological spectrum have highly active women's wings, without which they could not function. (The Taliban is a notable exception, and the fact that it attempted to promote absolute gender segregation without having in place a strong women's organization to operate within the female space is one reason why its rule was so seriously dysfunctional.) Islamist movements derive much of their political legitimacy from their extensive welfare and educational programmes that often fill the spaces left by the failure of the state to provide such services. Given that the communities to which these services are delivered practice varying degrees of gender segregation, the work of female members who are permitted access to the home and who can interact freely with women and children is essential.

In considering Muslim women's political agency, then, it is necessary to consider not only the activism of women in reformist Muslim or secular movements, but also those who belong to Islamist movements that promote a highly patriarchal agenda. Muslim women enact political agency through a diverse range of formal and informal networks. These networks are not ideologically compartmentalized—there is a flow of ideas and opinions both among Muslim women's political movements and between those movements and women's movements located outside the Muslim world. However, while all these networks provide some form of agency to their members, not all are committed to the exercise of female agency outside certain narrowly defined circumstances.

This chapter examines the various forms of political agency exercised by contemporary Muslim women and their complex and at times ambivalent relationship to western feminists. Occasionally prevalent amongst some feminisms are Orientalist and neo-Orientalist representations of Muslim women, which usually focus on the image of the Muslim woman as a victim of her religion and culture. However, a growing body of critical scholarship analyzes the role of Muslim women as participants in a range of contemporary social and political movements.[1] I begin by discussing the complex relationship between some western feminists and 'Other' women (particularly Muslim women), before discussing Muslim women's political agency within the framework of the concepts of transnational feminism and Islamic feminism. Case studies of Afghani, Pakistani, and Indonesian women activists illustrate their diverse forms of political participation.

Muslim Women and Feminism: Engagement, Ambivalence, and Rejection

For feminists seeking to understand the role that feminist movements play in Muslim communities, the most obvious initial hurdle is the negative reaction—ranging from discomfort to outright hostility—that the very word 'feminism' elicits from many Muslim women. In the majority of cases, this hostility does not arise from any fondness for patriarchy or sense of comfort with the status quo. Rather, it stems from a perception that feminism is not concerned with their lives or interested in hearing their voices. Muslim women often perceive feminism as a movement for western women, who are thought to be either indifferent to Muslim women, or intent on imposing their own culture and agenda upon them. It is not always recognized as a heterogeneous movement that has generated a strong internal critique regarding engagement with the issues facing 'Other' women.[2]

This concern arises from the fact that many calls for the liberation of Muslim women do not come from feminists at all. Rather, they come from those like the former Australian Prime Minister John Howard or former United States President George Bush that Christina Ho somewhat sarcastically terms "new feminists": "all kinds of conservative male public figures seem to have become feminists"—but only in support of women victimized by Muslim men.[3] This pseudo-feminism serves a variety of political ends, from domestic 'dog- whistle' politics to promoting the War on Terror as a battle for the rights of women in Afghanistan and Iraq.[4] In fact, these pseudo-feminists are quite hostile to feminism, which they accuse of abandoning Muslim women in the name of multicultural tolerance.[5] Many Muslim listeners, however, do not distinguish between discourse emerging from committed critical feminists and the self-serving championing of "oppressed Muslim women" by public figures that otherwise have little time for women's rights.

These pseudo-feminists, however, must be subject to the same critique as some of the other neo-imperialist and overbearing western–based (pseudo) feminisms. Such groups, which include the present-day neo-conservative U.S.-based Independent Women's Forum, have been described as ethnocentric and engaged in a process of 'Othering' not only Muslim women, but also black women, working- class women, and indeed, any woman located outside the 'developed West' or global metropolitan centers.[6] Critiques of these feminists, particularly by critical feminist scholarship, draw upon a well-established literature generated by postcolonial writers seeking to maximize feminism's relevance and emancipatory potential for all women.

Nearly twenty-five years ago Chandra Talpade Mohanty pioneered these critiques in her landmark essay "Under Western Eyes: Feminist Scholarship and Colonial Discourses."[7] She pointed to how, when faced with the reality of difference, what she described as 'western feminism's' universal category of 'woman,' collapsed into a dichotomy between western and Third World women. According to Mohanty, like western Orientalism (with which it shares considerable overlap); what she called 'western feminism' organized its 'Others' into a unified category, 'Third World women.' Like Orientalists, Third World women are portrayed as opposites of their western counterparts. In Mohanty's words, women of the Third World are "ignorant, poor, uneducated, tradition-bound, religious, domesticated, family-oriented, [and] victimized," as opposed to "the (implicit) self-representation of western women as educated, modern, as having control over their own bodies and sexualities, and the 'freedom' to make their own decisions."[8] There is, of course, a paradox here, in that most of Mohanty's 'western feminists' would not describe the position of women in western societies in this way *except* when comparing themselves with 'Other' women.

In this western/Other dichotomy, the privilege of being the subject rather than the object of knowledge is conferred upon western women. This has consequences both at the analytical and normative levels. At the analytical level, the assignment 'Third World women' to a single category erases the highly varied nature of their relationship to power, automatically casting them into the role of victim. The binary nature of the label masks the multiplicity of identities that exist within a single individual, never mind the many identities within societies and communities. Consequently, 'western feminism's' appeal to supposedly universal feminist underpinnings means that it need not engage with 'Otherness' in discussing 'Third World gender issues' like female genital mutilation, veiling, and honor killings, since these are simply manifestations of the problem of patriarchy. Yet not only do these various practices arise from specific contexts, but individual practices do not have a stable meaning across time and space. Mohanty is only one of many analysts to cite veiling as an example—a practice that is both a form of oppression forced *upon* women, and as a form of resistance adopted *by* them.[9]

Analyses like Mohanty's have been read as relativist accounts that reject the possibility of collaboration between 'western' and 'Third World' women. Revisiting her essay in 2003, Mohanty rejects such readings, "I did not write 'Under Western Eyes' as a testament to the impossibility of egalitarian and noncolonizing cross-cultural scholarship, nor did I define 'Western' and 'Third World' feminism in such oppositional ways that there would be no possibility of solidarity between Western and Third World feminists."[10] Rather, Mohanty continues, she wishes to focus on "an anticapitalist transnational feminist practice—and on the possibilities, indeed on the necessities, of cross-national solidarity and organizing against capitalism."[11] In a similar vein, Vron Ware writes that Mohanty's revisiting of her seminal essay "signals the end of the road for a trenchant form of identity politics, hopelessly identified with an imperializing agenda from the north. . . . Mohanty accepts that allocating fixed identities to groups of women along the lines of race, ethnicity, and national origin is no longer sufficient to explain their political location and outlook."[12] This rejection of fixed identities facilitates the building of transcultural feminist alliances. The challenge for feminists—both 'western' and 'Third World'—is to build effective transnational alliances that do not reproduce other forms of inequality.

Particularly in light of a post– 9/11 revival of the universalist application of labels like 'Third World' and 'western' to women in global politics, there are serious risks for Muslim women in allowing feminism to become synonymous with oppressive western-based notions. Feminist organizations in Muslim societies are frequently accused of being a fifth column for the West; of using women's rights as part of an attempt to introduce western sexual norms (in the form of promiscuity and family breakdown) and facilitate western political hegemony. In this climate, feminism is characterized (or caricatured) as an alien and hostile force. In the words of Lila Abu Lughod, "it is . . . strategically dangerous to accept this cultural opposition between Islam and the West, between fundamentalism and feminism, because those many people within Muslim countries who are trying to find alternatives to present injustices, those who might want to refuse the divide and take from different histories and cultures, who do not accept that being feminist means being Western, will be under pressure to choose, just as we are: are you with us or against us?"[13] Muslim women have resisted this pressure to choose both by creating activist networks within their own communities and by building networks that link Muslim and non-Muslim women across transnational boundaries.

Muslim Women as Political Actors: Transnational Feminism and/or Islamic Feminism?

Two major trends are identifiable in current analysis of Muslim female agency: transnational feminism and Islamic feminism. The two are not mutually exclusive. Some versions of Islamic feminism are forms of religious nationalism that explicitly reject the possibility of collaboration with non-Muslim and specifically western women. However, some of those who have been named Islamic feminists are actively engaged in transnational feminist politics and are as well-known in the West as they are in their own societies.

Transnational Feminism

The most basic definition of transnational feminism refers to global networking among individual women and women's groups in order to address gender issues. Transnational feminism is distinguished from international feminism by its grassroots nature, its self-reflexivity, its awareness of the multiple modes of identity among women and the unequal relationships this produces, and the potential for reproducing similar inequalities within feminist movements. Transnational feminism aims to create a space for Muslim and other Third World women to act as participants rather than objects of rescue. For example, while the international campaign against the Taliban has been criticized for its "imperial feminist" elements,[14] it also generated relationships of transnational feminist solidarity.

Feminism that transcends national, religious, and cultural boundaries is not new—international feminism, including feminist efforts that link Muslim and western women, has been a trend from the early twentieth century onward. An iconic moment in Arab women's movements was Huda Shar'awi's public removal of her veil on her return from the International Feminist's Union Congress in Rome in 1923. Val Moghadam points to the 1980s, particularly the Nairobi conference of 1985, as an important time during which increased dialogue between women from the North and South served as the foundation for building formal and informal networks, which was facilitated by the United Nations.[15] Recently, transnational feminism has been further enabled by the growth of global media and communications, especially the Internet, which played a key role in the global feminist resistance to the Taliban.[16]

However, most theorists of transnational feminism define it not only as feminism that traverses geographic space, but also as feminism characterized by an ideological agenda. Like other transnational social movements, it has developed in response to the growth of repressive global social and political forces, such as neoliberal economics. Moghadam further identifies extremist Hindu and Islamic political movements among the forces that helped to generate transnational feminist alliances.[17]

Thus, transnational feminism recognizes that the forces that oppress women are neither simply local in origin nor solely grounded in a particular cultural or religious tradition. For an Afghan woman dispossessed by war, or an Indonesian factory worker surviving on sweatshop wages, geopolitics and neoliberal economics are more relevant than Islam in their discussion of oppression. While recognizing the importance of the local and particular, transnational feminism recognizes that where oppression is transnational, so must be the resistance

Islamic Feminism

The term "Islamic feminism" came into circulation during the 1990s, initially among scholars of Middle Eastern gender studies. As a concept, it holds many attractions, suggesting as it does that feminism is not the sole preserve of western women and that Muslim women, too, have access to a history and a discourse of women's rights. Many Muslim women are uncomfortable with claims made of behalf of feminist universalism, with which feminism as a whole has often come to be associated. As Badran and Cooke write, for many Arabs (as for many Muslims) feminism is seen as "western—the cultural arm of imperialism or neo-imperialism out to destabilize local society and to destroy indigenous cultural identity; anti-Islamic."[18] Modifying the word "feminist" with "Islamic" pre-empts the reflexive hostile response that may otherwise be evoked. However, this creates new questions and problems, and does not fully resolve the old ones.

A growing number of Muslim women's movements attempt to challenge the moral authority of Islamist patriarchy by grounding their discussions of women's rights on a religious foundation. They dispute the basis of discriminatory laws and social practices by questioning the extent to which they truly can be regarded as Islamic. Furthermore, they offer alternative and (they maintain) more authentic interpretations of Islam that are consistent with the principles of gender equity. For example, the Malaysian NGO, Sisters in Islam, describes itself as "believ[ing] in an Islam that upholds the principles of equality, justice, freedom and dignity."[19] The organization acts on this belief by publishing books, lobbying, and running educational and research projects that seek to promote "the rights of women within an Islamic framework."[20] Similar religiously based movements have arisen across the Muslim world, many of them focused on developing women's religious scholarship and breaking the masculinist monopoly on the interpretation of Islamic texts.

Islamic feminism, however, remains highly contested, not least by many of the women who are supposed to be its practitioners. Miriam Cooke defines it in very sweeping terms:"Whenever Muslim women offer a critique of some aspect of Islamic history or hermeneutics, and they do so with, and/or on behalf of all Muslim women and their right to enjoy with men full participation in a just community, I call them Islamic feminists. This label is not rigid. It does not describe an identity, but rather an attitude and intention to seek justice and citizenship for Muslim women."[21] By this definition, she includes as Islamic feminists women from an extremely broad range of ideologies—from the doctor and writer Nawal es-Sadaawi (who as an alleged apostate faced court attempts to dissolve her marriage), to Zaynab al Ghazali (Egypt's most important woman Islamist and a supporter of the Muslim Brotherhood). While women at one end of this ideological spectrum may object to being referred to as Islamic, women at the other end vociferously reject the label feminist.

The term Islamic feminist is often seen as having been imposed upon its subjects by outsiders, that is, non-Muslim feminist scholars (although more and more Muslim women are adopting the term with regard to their own work). The fact that many Islamic feminists do not regard themselves as such, or indeed, are actively hostile to the term, does not in itself invalidate it. However, there are problems with the term that go beyond the rejection it has encountered from some of those it supposedly describes. As defined by Cooke, it encompasses such a broad range of women, united only by their gender and by what is in some cases a tenuous affiliation with Islam, as to make its usefulness seem very doubtful. For example, Abou Bakr questions Cooke's "strange" decision to include Sadaawi under the banner of Islamic feminism due to her only occasional adoption of an Islamic speaking position.[22]

In contrast, Margot Badran's definition of Islamic feminism places much greater emphasis on its theological dimension. She describes it "as a feminist discourse and practice that derives its understanding and mandate from the Qur'an, seeking rights and justice within the framework of gender equality for women and men in the totality of their existence."[23] This definition certainly strengthens the Islamic side of the definition and clarifies the ways it is distinct from other forms of feminism. However, this more narrowly focused definition raises problems of its own, in that by validating the enterprise of Islamic feminism, it risks labeling non-Islamic those Muslim women engaged in non-theological forms of feminism. It is only a small step from being non-Islamic to being unIslamic, a highly dangerous label to carry in contemporary Muslim societies. To date, this risk has been limited because religious conservatives have regarded Islamic feminism as an alien force (since they consider feminism of any description a western concept). However, the term is gaining widespread use among Muslims. In so doing, it is becoming associated with a form of religious authenticity, at the expense of other forms of feminism.

Similar criticisms have been made not only of the term Islamic feminism, but also the practice it describes. As Moghadam summarizes, "Islamic feminists and their expatriate academic supporters, [critics argue], either unconsciously or unwittingly delegitimize secular trends and social forces."[24] Such critics claim that by accepting the basic premise of using theology as the foundation for social norms, Islamic feminists reinforce the patriarchal power structures that they claim to challenge. Female empowerment, they claim, requires the wholesale removal of religion from public life.

However, the distinction between secular and Islamic feminism is often an artificial one. Islamic feminism is generally represented as a practice rather than an identity, and as such, it is not necessarily incompatible with other feminist practices. Some prominent Islamic feminists, like Fatima Mernissi and Afsaneh Najmabadi, have been secular feminists at earlier stages of their careers, and many continue to practice both forms of feminism in recognition of the fact that the problems confronting Muslim women are only partly theological in origin. As Moghadam points out "most Islamic feminists[25] combine their religious reinterpretations with recognition of universal standards, such as the UN's Convention of the Elimination of All Forms of Discrimination against Women (CEDAW)."[26]

With the rise of global Islamist movements, a feminist discourse that challenges the religious legitimacy of gender oppression is a legitimate and arguably a necessary response to them. However, it is vital that such an approach not be exclusive, but continues to work in conjunction with other forms of feminism. Despite the care of its major theorists to name Islamic feminism a strategy rather than an identity, tagging theologically based feminist discourse with the adjective, Islamic, reinforces already-existing perceptions that other forms of feminism are alien to Muslim societies. Although less succinct, it may be less divisive to deploy a more specific description, such as "feminist exegesis," which more clearly describes the particular task to be integrated into the larger strategy, rather than a worldview.

Muslim Women Activists and Diverse Relationships to Islam

The complex nature of Muslim feminist identity, and the limitations inherent to assigning identities like secular or religious to Muslim women's movements become apparent when comparing individual Muslim women. While Muslim women are frequently represented as a homogeneous category in both western and Islamic discourses, they have a wide range of life experiences in which religious identity is only one factor. Class, nationality, ethnicity, urban and rural disparities, and political forces such as war and occupation are often more relevant factors in their lives than religion. Additionally, Muslim women perform the duties of their religious identity in a wide variety of ways, which gives rise to a heterogeneous range of Muslim women's movements. Muslim women's activism is not limited to secular or progressive movements, but encompasses Islamist movements that justify their highly patriarchal ideology in religious terms. While re-examination of religious texts and practices plays an important role in many Muslim women's movements, in others they play a marginal role, either because these women prioritize secularist approaches, or because they are committed to upholding patriarchal interpretations as the only legitimate form of Islam.

Feminist re-examinations of the Qur'an, Hadith, and Islamic jurisprudence are based on the premise that oppressive gender practices have arisen from male domination of Islamic discourse and male (mis)interpretations of the foundational Islamic texts. Muslim women who set out to challenge these masculinist interpretations see feminism, at the least, as compatible with Islam, and at the most, as representing the true and original intent of the Qur'an. For some women, choosing to use an Islamic frame of reference to resist misogyny arises naturally from their religious commitment. For others, it may be at least partly instrumentalist, arising from the recognition that de-legitimizing oppressive gender relations requires women to refute patriarchal interpretations of Islam from a standpoint that is explicitly Muslim.

In Indonesia, Fatayat, the young women's wing of the major Islamic movement Nadhlatul Ulama, runs a wide range of initiatives aimed at gender empowerment including education, healthcare, crisis support, and family planning. They also tackle the issue of religious endorsement of domestic violence. The NU network of pesantren (Muslim schools) uses classical texts, the *Kitab Kuning* (Yellow Books) as the basis of their teaching. These texts have been widely criticized (including by many NU women) for their patriarchal concept of gender relations, including such assertions as that Muslim men have the right to hit their wives for disobedience and other alleged misconduct. Members of Fatayat participate in a project to publish critical analyses of the most popular texts, with commentaries disputing those passages that endow men with power over women.[27]

In contrast, theological debates have been of very limited relevance for the Revolutionary Association of the Women of Afghanistan (RAWA), whose stand on religious issues has been to assert that their political opponents distort Islam for their own purposes and that RAWA's broadly leftist ideology is not incompatible with "true" Islam. RAWA is highly secular in its political outlook, proclaiming that "only a government with secular orientation can thwart the nefarious designs of these reactionaries from the Dark Ages. It is only a secular government that can prevent the religion of Islam from being used as a retrogressive tool in the hands of fanatics. The people of Afghanistan have been Muslims for the past several centuries and will not allow gangs of rapists, murderers, and traitors to teach them their faith with a stick once again."[28] While theoretically such a worldview is not wholly incompatible with Fatayat's commitment to bringing about reform from within a religious discourse, in practice RAWA members focus on a secular and leftist critique that targets both violent patriarchal forces within Afghanistan, and the role of United States foreign policy in empowering such forces since its involvement in the anti-Soviet counterinsurgency.

Members of the women's wing of the Pakistani Islamist political party, the Jamaat-i-Islami, oppose both feminist readings of Islam and secularism. They claim that the "real" danger to Pakistani women comes not from discriminatory laws and religiously sanctioned social practices, but from the insidious creep of western sexual norms that threaten the integrity of family life. On this basis, they have staunchly defended legislation such as the Hudood Ordinances, under which thousands of Pakistani women have been imprisoned for alleged adultery. The Hudood Ordinances, they maintain, are God's laws, not man's laws, and are therefore beyond debate. They vehemently opposed even the limited reforms that were finally passed by the Pakistani parliament in 2006, that they claimed (with some plausibility) were intended to assuage President Musharraf's allies in the United States. They view the Ordinances as women's safeguard against western-style sexual exploitation, and claim that any injustices arise out of problems with implementation like police corruption, long delays in bringing cases to trial, and so on.

The inadequacy of imposing singular interpretations on social practices common across such a diverse range of women becomes apparent when we examine various women's deployment of Islamic dress codes. Muslim women's participation in the public sphere transgresses the view held by most conservative Muslims that the proper sphere for a woman is the home—although historically, seclusion of women has been a symbol of privilege and the preserve of the rich rather than a universal Muslim practice. The modern veil (in its various forms), far from being a symbol of seclusion, more often represents women's intention to participate in public life. Women may cover as a symbol of piety, as a signifier of urban modernity (because earlier generations of rural village women did not wear it), as a form of "patriarchal bargaining"[29] in which women trade donning conservative dress for physical mobility, or simply as a fashion statement. However, regardless of motivation, veiling is a highly public gesture, which is necessary only for women who make themselves visible to strangers, not for those who remain in the home.

Because of the high degree of exposure involved, Muslim women engaged in politics are particularly likely to wear some form of veil. However, since the ideological content of their politics is highly varied, their reasons for veiling also vary. My encounters with three groups of women illustrate this point: a group of young Indonesian women who teamed their hijabs with toothpaste smeared under the eyes (to alleviate the effects of teargas) and clipboards so as to document military and police misconduct during the student demonstrations that marked the final stages of military rule in Indonesia in 1999; the RAWA members who donned chadors or burqas while campaigning against the Taliban; and the members of the women's wing of the Jamaat-i-Islami in Pakistan who hold regular street demonstrations on a range of issues like human rights abuses in Kashmir, headscarf bans in France, blasphemous Danish cartoons, and most especially attempts to reform the notorious Hudood Ordinances. All these women wore some form of Islamic dress, but their reasons for doing so were very different.

For the young Indonesian students and human rights activists, their hijab is not an exclusionary symbol. They work with non-hijabis and indeed, with non-Muslims; their political engagement takes the form of a commitment to resisting militarism and achieving social justice rather than Islamizing Indonesia's political system. Their values are upheld by their religious faith, but not exclusive to it. However, they take pride in their identity as Muslims and express indignation and even hatred toward those who hold Islam up to ridicule. This is manifested in strong anti-American sentiments, although again, their anti-Americanism is only partially governed by religious identity; it is also informed by many years of United States support for the Suharto dictatorship. Furthermore, their anti-Americanism is not all encompassing—the words "This [Islamophobic books and movies] is why I hate America" were expressed during a dinner at McDonalds, the speakers dressed in hijabs teamed with American-style jeans and long-sleeved T-shirts. The hijabs, however, signal that they are Muslim rather than western, and they describe their headscarves primarily in terms of pride in their identity rather than modesty (and in fact, their jeans were too tight fitting to count as modest by the standards of many Muslims). Hijab in this instance provides a means of carrying Muslim identity into participation in the global (and often westernized) culture.

While these Indonesian students wear hijab as a symbol of ethno-religious pride, the members of the leftist RAWA use the *burqa* and the *chador* (both of which are used to cover the face as well as the hair) as instruments of subterfuge during their grassroots work in Afghanistan and Pakistan. Some of their detractors[30] add that their dress also serves as props in a form of attention-seeking theatre during their media appearances. During the rule of the Taliban, RAWA members engaged in highly transgressive and often dangerous activities, such as distributing their magazines and leaflets in the refugee camps and bazaars of Pakistan, or gathering evidence about Taliban abuses within Afghanistan itself. The *burqa*, which is common in Northern Pakistan and was famously made compulsory by the Taliban in Afghanistan, enabled RAWA activists to go undercover, quite literally. It rendered them anonymous as they went about their work in Pakistan, and it enabled them secretly to film Taliban atrocities with video cameras hidden beneath the enveloping fabric. A RAWA member filmed the execution of an Afghan woman in the Kabul soccer stadium; this footage provided the centerpiece for a high-profile documentary, *Behind the Veil*, which played on televisions around the world. RAWA does not advocate veiling out of religious sentiment. The organization describes the *chador* as an acceptable symbol of Afghan culture rather than Islam, and rejects the *burqa* altogether. Their Web site claims that members use it only instrumentally, to provide camouflage, and otherwise reject it: "we will NOT wear the veil as far as security and social discretion allow us, for we regard rejection of the veil as a symbolic form of resistance and defiance of the fundamentalists."[31] (The *burqa* is not RAWA's only form of protection, however. A couple of their activists showed me the switchblades that they carried for self-defense.) RAWA members use veiling as a form of camouflage, which helps them to blend in to communities where most women cover. As a form of security, it obscures their identities both when engaging in transgressive activities within Afghanistan and neighboring regions, and when performing on the global stage. In comparison with electronic forms of disguise, such as pixilation, veiling the face enables RAWA members to control their own degree of public exposure. However, it also draws power from established discourses about oppressed, veiled women. Azarbaijai-Moghaddam accuses RAWA of "fuel[ing] Orientalist notions of veiled Afghan women living in seraglios, jealously guarded by bearded Mussalmans wielding scimitars" as part of its campaign of "relentless self-promotion."[32]

Members of the women's wing of the Pakistani Islamist party, the Jamaat-i-Islami, also cover during their frequent street demonstrations. However, their political ideology concerning veiling is very different from that of the RAWA activists. The JI women regard veiling the hair as a religious obligation (some also cover their faces but regard this as praiseworthy rather than compulsory), and many of them believe that women who do not voluntarily veil should be forced to do so by law. They eschew western-style dress such as jeans, but their attire is not entirely Pakistani. Many wear the modern-style hijab, popular in the Middle East and Southeast Asia but uncommon in Pakistan, teamed with a niqab (face cover). The fact that they are covered during their street protests (and in all nonfamilial, mixed-gender public gatherings) offsets the transgressive potential of this incursion into public space. Party press releases announcing such actions always describe them as "a demonstration of veiled women." These veiled women signify "real" Pakistani women, who are happy for the state to enforce strict public morals, unlike westernized, elitist women who protest against the jailing of women, including rape victims, for adultery.

On closer examination, then, the categories 'Muslim woman' and 'veiled woman' entirely disintegrate. Veiling not only takes different physical forms, but also assumes different meanings, among women of varying religious and political worldviews. Muslim women seek legitimacy by drawing upon local discourses even while they participate in global trends and alliances. While religious discourse is deployed (by women as well as men) to justify extreme forms of misogyny, it is also appropriated by women to authenticate feminist agendas. While female activism is not necessarily feminist, religiously based activism may have feminist outcomes. However, religion is not the only source of identity among Muslim women, nor is religious authority the only source of their oppression. Therefore, Muslim women are best served by participating in multiple forms of activism, including transnational feminist alliances.

Conclusion

My intention in traversing a broad range of women's perspectives is to question claims of authenticity made on behalf of feminism or of Islam. The struggle for Muslim women's rights is both global and local, requiring responses at both levels. Transnational activism allows women to highlight the extent to which their lives are blighted by processes centered far from home, whether in the form of opportunistic foreign policy alliances or the imposition of neoliberal economic agendas. However, it is also necessary to contest 'local' demands that women conform to a narrowly defined model of supposed Islamic propriety. Developing alternative theologies and historiographies is one important strategy yet activism is most effective when it deploys multiple strategies to forge a link between local and transnational struggles.

Notes

1. See, for example, Sherifa Zuhur, *Revealing Reveiling* (New York: SUNY Press, 1992); Saba Mahmood, *The Politics of Piety: The Islamic Revival and the Feminist Subject* (Princeton: Princeton University Press, 2005).
2. See, for example, Anne McNevin, "Two Weeks in Peshawar" in this volume.
3. Christina Ho, "Cronulla, Conflict, and Culture: How Can Muslim Women Be Heard in Australia?" *UTSpeaks Public Lecture*, September 5, 2006, http://www.hss.uts.edu.au/social_inquiry/research/utspeaks_cronulla_conflict_culture.pdf (accessed March 19, 2008).
4. See, for example, Laura Bush, "Radio Address by Mrs. Bush," November 17, 2001, http://www.whitehouse.gov/news/releases/2001/11/20011117.html (accessed March 19, 2008).
5. Kay S. Hymowitz, "Why Feminism is AWOL on Islam," *City Journal* 13, no. 1 (2003), 293–305; Christina Hoff Sommers, "The Subjection of Islamic Women and the Fecklessness of American Feminism," *The Weekly Standard* 12 (2007); Phyllis Chesler, *The Death of Feminism: What's Next in the Struggle for Women's Freedom*? (New York, Palgrave Macmillan, 2005).
6. See Shakira Hussein, "The War on Terror and the Rescue of Muslim Women," in *Islam in World Politics*, ed. Nelly Lahoud and Anthony Johns (London: Routledge, 2005), 93–103.
7. Chandra Talpade Mohanty, "Under Western Eyes, Feminist Scholarship and Colonial Discourses," *Boundary2: An International Journal of Literature and Culture* 13, no. 1 (1984): 333–58.
8. Ibid., 337.
9. Ibid.; Marnia Lazreg, "Feminism and Difference—the Perils of Writing as a Woman on Women in Algeria," *Feminist Studies* 14, no. 1 (1988): 81–107.
10. Chandra Talpade Mohanty, "'Under Western Eyes' Revisited: Feminist Solidarity through Anticapitalist Struggles," *Signs* 28, no. 2 (2003): 502.
11. Ibid., 509.
12. Vron Ware, "Info-War and the Politics of Feminist Curiosity," *Cultural Studies* 20, no. 6 (2006): 534.

13. Lila Abu-Lughod, "Do Muslim Women Really Need Saving? Anthropological Reflections on Cultural Relativism and its Others," *American Anthropologist* 104, no. 3 (2002): 788.
14. See Ann Russo, "The Feminist Majority Foundation's Campaign to Stop Gender Apartheid: The Intersection of Feminism and Imperialism in the United States," *International Feminist Journal of Politics* 8, no. 4 (2006): 557–80.
15. Valentine M. Moghadam, *Globalizing Women: Transnational Feminist Networks* (Baltimore: Johns Hopkins University Press. 2005), 6.
16. Loretta Kensinger, "Plugged in Praxis: Critical Reflections on U.S. Feminism, Internet Activism, and Solidarity with Women in Afghanistan," *Journal of International Women's Studies* 5, no. 1 (2003), 1–28.
17. Moghadam, *Globalizing Women*, 2005.
18. Margot Badran and Miriam Cooke, ed., *Opening the Gates: A Century of Arab Feminist Writing* (London: Vigaro, 1990), xx.
19. "Sisters in Islam," http://www.sistersinislam.org.my/ (accessed March 19, 2008).
20. Ibid.
21. Miriam Cooke, "Multiple Critique: Islamic Feminist Rhetorical Strategies," *Nepantla: Views from the South* 1, no.1 (2000): 95.
22. Omaima Abou-Bakr, "Islamic Feminism? What's in a Name? Preliminary Reflections," *Middle Eastern Women's Studies Review* xv, no. 4 (2001), http://www.amews.org/review/reviewarticles/islamicfeminism.htm (accessed March 19, 2008).
23. Margot Badran, "Islamic Feminism Revisited," Countercurrents.org, February 10, 2006, http://www.countercurrents.org/gen-badran100206.htm (accessed March 19, 2008).
24. Valentine M. Moghadam, "Islamic Feminism and its Discontents: Toward a Resolution of the Debate," *Signs* 27, no. 4 (2002): 1142.
25. According to Moghadam's definition, this statement would not hold true for some of the women named as Islamic feminists by writers such as Miriam Cooke, who use a broader definition of the term.
26. Moghadam, "Islamic Feminism," 1158.
27. Interview with Fatayat member, 1999; see also Eka Srimulyani, "Muslim Women and Education in Indonesia: The Pondok Pesantren Experience," *Asia Pacific Journal of Education* 27, no. 1 (2007): 85–89.
28. RAWA, "RAWA's Standpoints," 2008, http://www.rawa.org/points.html (accessed March 12, 2008).
29. Deniz Kandiyoti, "Bargaining with Patriarchy," *Gender and Society* 2, no. 3 (1988): 274–90.
30. See Sippi Azarbaijani-Moghaddam, "Afghan Women on the Margins of the Twenty-First Century" in *Nation-building Unraveled? Aid, Peace and Justice in Afghanistan, ed.* Antonio Donini, Norah Niland, and Karin Wermester (Bloomfield, Conn.: Kumarian Press, 2004), 95–116.
31. RAWA, "RAWA Standpoints."
32. Azarbaijani-Moghaddam, "Afghan Women," 4.

PART IV

Linking Local with Global

Feminist Activism in the Pacific

CHAPTER 10

Gender Mainstreaming in a Post–conflict State

Toward Democratic Peace in Timor-Leste?

Nina Hall and Jacqui True

Gender equality is widely believed by international organizations and mainstream commentators to contribute to the consolidation of democratic norms and domestic and international peace.[1] The United Nations (UN) has promoted strategies for achieving gender equality as a central part of its peacebuilding and reconstruction programs. In Bosnia, Kosovo, and East Timor, UN missions have incorporated gender mainstreaming and gender-balanced decision-making policies and programs to foster civil society as means to ensure long-term peace and development. To what extent, though, are these institutional initiatives able to transform the deep-seated gendered social hierarchies in these new states? Feminist scholars argue that such hierarchies are at the root of violence against women, women's lack of voice, and political representation. They hold that any meaningful democratic strategy must eliminate these hierarchies to bring about political freedom and equality. In Timor these feminist perspectives on gender justice and equality are an emerging part of the public debate about the processes of democratization in state and civil society. They can be seen in speeches, communications, and reports of local women's organizations, donor agencies, NGOs, and the UN, however, this political activity has yet to be theoretically analyzed by feminist or nonfeminist scholars. Here we seek to highlight some of the gendered practices of democratization and assess the struggles within East Timorese civil society to forge a gender-equal democracy.

In this chapter we show how East Timorese women activists and gender entrepreneurs in the UN, donor governments, and international NGOs have collaborated but also disagreed in their struggle to promote gender equality. Three overlapping gender equality strategies were negotiated and implemented:

first, gender mainstreaming in policymaking, second, gender quotas in political representation, and third, the mobilization of women's voice in civil society. What is striking about the democratization process in Timor-Leste is that these three gender equality strategies have been advanced whereas in past nation-building projects, the goal of gender equality has been marginalized or at least traded-off as societies have sought to achieve other ostensibly more important goals.[2] The chapter reveals how the implementation of gender equality strategies was a contingent collaboration among particular gender entrepreneurs and activists from Timor and elsewhere with far-reaching implications for the construction of equal democracy.

Gender Perspectives on Peacebuilding and Democratization

Neoliberal institutionalist international relations (IR) scholars see democracy as contributing to enduring domestic and international peace. United Nations peacebuilding missions since the 1990s have sought to institutionalize democracy as an integral part of their postconflict operations. Like mainstream IR scholars, powerful states, and international organizations assume that nation-building efforts leading to democracy will promote the security and human rights of both men and women. But this assumption treats men and women's experiences of conflict and postconflict as the same and fails to take into account the gendered dimensions of democracy and security.[3] Feminist scholars of international relations argue that international peacekeeping and peacebuilding missions may not advance women's rights or improve their lives. They challenge the very concept of postconflict, which tends to mask the ongoing political violence and especially violence against women. Feminists focus on how military interventions even for peacebuilding purposes can contribute to the *insecurity* of individuals, particularly of marginalized and disempowered populations.[4]

For feminist IR scholars the increased incidence of sexual and domestic violence, forced prostitution, gang rape, honor killings, and sex trafficking during and after conflict is evidence that the so-called democratic peace does not diffuse democratic norms in private as well as public life. Too much stress on the use of force in peacekeeping and peacebuilding can have the effect of legitimating and consolidating a militarized social order. Such militarization over-valorizes masculine aggression and fuels gendered violence. Feminists do not see women as more peaceful or as better peacekeepers than men contrary to what some scholars and commentators claim.[5] Rather, IR feminists see peace and security in broad, multidimensional terms that include the elimination of all social hierarchies that lead to political and economic injustice.[6] Similarly, feminist scholars challenge mainstream approaches to democratization that focus nearly exclusively on free and fair elections and creating a multiparty system. Such an approach neglects the importance of political equality and does nothing to ensure women's as well as men's participation in democratic institutions.

By contrast, a feminist approach to democratization highlights the importance of informal democratic practices in schools, families, workplaces, and civil society as well as in formal political institutions.

Without institutional mechanisms to address gender inequalities feminists argue that democratization and peacebuilding may not bring about the same benefits for men and women. However, there are major opportunities to address gender inequalities in new states that are designing their democratic institutions for the first time. But these opportunities must be leveraged and advanced by local civil society and gender entrepreneurs with the support of political elites, international donors, and organizations.

There are two parts to this chapter. In the first part, we explore *why* gender equality strategies were introduced in Timor-Leste. In the second part, we investigate *how* gender equality strategies were implemented in a difficult, often violent and fragile, nation-building environment. We consider both the global and the local impetus for the promotion of gender mainstreaming in public policy, gender electoral quotas, and women's civic voice. Moreover, we analyze the close collaboration among advocates of gender equality in Timor civil society and international organizations that have shaped the respective gender equality initiatives.

The Impetus for Equal Democracy

The establishment of an independent, democratic East Timorese state took place in a broader global environment. By the 1990s gender equality had evolved as an international norm and was increasingly diffused by transnational advocacy networks and international organizations such as the United Nations.[7] Most countries had ratified the CEDAW Convention that legally required them to promote women's economic, social, and political rights and report on their progress in so doing. Women's activism had increased exponentially as western and nonwestern women's movements pooled their energies and linked a myriad of locally-specific campaigns for women's human rights and gender justice. Their activism reached a high point at the 1995 United Nations Beijing Fourth World Conference on Women.

At Beijing governments agreed to implement through national and international policymaking a wide-ranging Platform for Action (PFA) that was largely the result of women's lobbying efforts all around the world. Gender mainstreaming was a crosscutting theme in the Beijing PFA and seen as the best institutional mechanism for the advancement of women. Gender-balanced decision-making was also a major focus of international organizations in the late 1990s as women's movements turned their attention to the lack of women decision-makers in political institutions. At the global level, policymakers increasingly realized the crucial importance of gender parity in any meaningful democracy. The United Nations Security Council, which had never before formally discussed gender equality produced a resolution (UNSC 1325) mandating the equal participation of women in peacekeeping and peacebuilding processes. Furthermore, experiences in UN Peacekeeping Missions in Bosnia and Kosovo revealed how collaboration between gender entrepreneurs and local women's organizations could make a difference to peacebuilding and democratization.[8] The UN's role in Timor's nation building thus came at a time when it was a major advocate on the global stage for gender equality.

The local conditions supporting the creation of an equal democracy were also strong, particularly the existence of women's organizations within the East Timorese independence movement. Women have engaged in struggles to advance their rights at least since the 1970s. However, Timor-Leste has a very strong patriarchal culture, which has inhibited awareness of gender injustices in East Timorese society. Traditionally, girls married at a young age, often at thirteen or fourteen, and still do in some of the more isolated rural areas. The tradition of *barlake*, or bride price, meant that men purchased their wives and gained property rights over them.[9] Women did not traditionally hold any positions of power and their participation in village-level decision-making was limited. The arrival of the Portuguese in 1515 did not bring women many new opportunities to improve their status. The Portuguese instituted their own political system on top of the traditional governance system and women had no access to formal political power. The system allowed few chances to exercise full political, social or economic rights.

Decolonization, however, opened up the space for women to enter politics for the first time. In 1974, the Portuguese authorized the establishment of political parties in Timor. Female members of *Fretilin*, one of the new parties, established a women's wing, the Popular Women's Organization of Timor-Leste (OPMT). OPMT was the first overtly political women's group in Timor-Leste; it organized meetings to raise awareness amongst women of the independence struggle. The leader of OPMT saw Fretilin as "a people's organization which creates opportunities for women to participate in the revolution."[10] However, women's participation at the top was limited: for instance, there was only one woman, Rosa Bonaparte, in Fretilin's Central Committee.

The Indonesian occupation transformed women's lives in Timor-Leste. On December 12, 1975, Indonesia annexed Timor-Leste and executed leaders of Fretilin and OPMT, including Bonaparte. Timor became highly militarized and violence against women, particularly by members of the Indonesian Military and Police Force, was endemic.[11] Indonesian troops tortured, sexually harassed, raped, and often killed women they suspected were linked to the resistance movement. Yet at the same time, the Indonesian occupation gave some women new work opportunities: some entered the public service, others worked with NGOs and state-sponsored women's organizations. Many more women were involved in the resistance movement either as part of OPMT or in other clandestine networks. Some women also fought in Fretilin's military wing, *Falantil*.

Ironically, the Indonesian occupation and its violent abrogation of women's rights led women into the political realm to seek East Timorese independence. However, the primary focus was independence and there was little political space or support for seriously addressing gender equality issues.

This changed in the 1990s as East Timorese women campaigned widely on international and local levels explicitly for women's rights. East Timorese women in the diaspora networked with women's movements in Indonesia, Australia, and Portugal and attended international women's conferences. In the late 1990s, they used the peace process period to lobby for greater inclusion of women. Milena Pires, a leading East Timorese gender activist, for example, proposed the formation of a women's department in the National Council for East Timorese Resistance (CNRT). However, the East Timorese political elite tended to sideline women and did not often take seriously their suggestions.[12]

Independence, and the arrival of the UN and other international actors, created a new window of opportunity for women's political activism. In 1999, the UN organized an independence referendum in Timor. The East Timorese, including a large proportion of women, overwhelmingly voted for independence. The Indonesian forces violently withdrew massacring, raping, and burning much of Timor to the ground. UN peacekeeping troops were sent to Timor and the UN Transitional Authority in East Timor (UNTAET) was established. UNTAET had a unique mandate; it was responsible for organizing elections, maintaining security, establishing government institutions and infrastructure, as well as the day-to-day running of the state. It had the most powers of any UN mission ever.[13] UNTAET was the sovereign authority in Timor until 2002 and following Beijing PFA goals and the SC Resolution 1325, promoting gender equality was a mandate of the mission.

East Timorese women took the lead in campaigning for gender equality. The formation of a new state gave them political space to build their movement. In 2000, East Timorese women organized the first Women's Congress of Timor-Leste. Over five hundred women met to discuss and form their own platform for action inspired by the global Beijing PFA.[14] The congress was a pivotal turning point in the history of women in Timor. It included East Timorese expatriates who had left during the Indonesian occupation for Australia, Mozambique, and Portugal and returned home. It was the first time that so many women had been brought together from such a wide variety of backgrounds. It was at this congress that the women of Timor transitioned from "freedom fighters into . . . a women's movement."[15]

Implementing Equal Democracy

The women's movement was strongly unified in 2000 and this is one of the chief reasons for *why* gender equality strategies were adopted within Timor's democratization. But even in the late 1990s women's NGOs emerged in Timor and began to address sexual and gender based violence (SGBV). In this second part of the chapter we discuss *how*, through what processes and negotiations, the gender equality strategies of developing women's voice in civil society, integrating a gender perspective across government policymaking and ensuring women's presence in decision-making through electoral quotas were implemented.

Developing Women's Civic Voice and the Violence Against Women Campaign

Due to the all encompassing struggle for independence, it wasn't until the late 1990s that the first East Timorese women's NGOs emerged in Dili. In 1997 *Fokupers* was established followed in 1998 by both ETWAVE (East Timorese Movement Against Violence Towards Women and Children) and GFFTL (East Timor Young Women's Group). These NGOs marked a new phase of women's organizing in Timor; their primary priority was gender equality, rather than independence. As the former head of Fokupers, Manuela Pereira, explains, "One of the important things that we forgot to talk about [during the occupation] was that the women in East Timor, they suffer from gender inequality."[16] Fokupers, for example, set up shelters for victims of sexual and gender based violence (SGBV) committed by the Indonesian forces.

The 1999 independence referendum and violent Indonesian withdrawal was a critical moment for Timor's emerging women's movement. The UN arrived and international aid poured into the country to assist with the humanitarian crisis.[17] The UN established a vulnerable persons unit (VPU), aimed at working with victims of SGBV. This unit of UN police, experienced at working with SGBV, taught Fokupers new ways of supporting victims. A number of international NGOs, such as the International Rescue Committee (IRC), also worked on the issue. They looked for local organizations to assist and East Timorese women to employ thus fuelling the growth of the East Timorese NGO sector. As a result, the number of local NGOs working on gender increased dramatically in the early 2000s.

Through training and seminars, international NGOs introduced concepts of gender, domestic violence, human rights, and the CEDAW convention to a wide range of East Timorese women and men. Many of these participants were employed by international NGOs or started up their own local NGOs. Milena Vilanova, for example, who was employed by the IRC remembers when she first started working on SGBV in 2000, "I don't even know what gender is."[18] Other local NGOs emerged during this period such as the Alola Foundation, *Rede Feto*, and *Pradet* yet the movement was still driven by relatively urban, middle class activists based in Dili. The growth of this sector, and the increased awareness of SGBV, was in large part due to the international humanitarian aid that was given to strengthen East Timorese civil society. This was a critical transition period where civil society "came from a stage of thinking [where] there was no special attention for women's issues . . . to another era where we saw women's issues as a priority."[19]

After independence, East Timorese women were able to talk about *domestic* violence rather than just the violence against women perpetrated by the Indonesian military. Prior to the arrival of the international organizations, former *Fokupers* director, Pereira, had thought domestic violence was "normal" since it was "happening to everyone."[20] In 2000, the National Women's Congress identified domestic violence as a critical problem that needed to be addressed. The congress provided the impetus for a national campaign for a law against domestic violence.[21] By 2002, there was a strong coalition of local and international organizations campaigning for such a law in Timor. UNIFEM, a UN agency dedicated to gender equality, played a significant role in the formation of the East Timorese national campaign against domestic violence.[22]

Strikingly, in the space of a few years Timor developed a strong, vocal civil society with both men's and women's groups advocating for legal and policy change to address domestic violence. This coalescing of East Timorese civil society against domestic violence was a dynamic, organic process. Facilitated but not directed from above by international donors, the campaign against domestic violence both involved and was made possible by a series of ongoing negotiations between East Timorese and international gender advocates and entrepreneurs.

Engendering Policy: The Establishment of the GAU, OPE, and SEPI

The adoption of gender mainstreaming in the UN Transitional Administration in East Timor owes much to the advocacy of gender policy entrepreneurs, who pioneered and progressed ideas about gender equality and the institutional mechanisms to advance it in Timor. Milena Pires, a member of the National Council of East Timorese Resistance (CNRT) introduced the concept of gender mainstreaming in 1999.[23] She lobbied for a gender unit within the transitional government in the negotiations between the UN and the CNRT. On the UN side, Sherrill Whittington, a senior gender expert, also pushed for the inclusion of a gender affairs unit.[24] Although the UN "in the interests of economy" did not establish the unit, Whittington, went to Timor and worked with the one inexperienced UN gender advisor to establish a mandate and seek funding and staff for a unit.[25] It was due to Pires' initiative and Whittington's persistence that Timor was the first UN peacekeeping operation to set up a gender affairs unit.

The Gender Affairs Unit (GAU) developed a mutually supportive relationship with the East Timorese women's movement. From the outset, Whittington sought the input of women leaders, such as Maria Diaz, Micato Domingas, and Milena Pires.[26] After the Women's Congress in 2000, she worked with the leaders to turn their platform of action (PFA) into a policy document. Whittington and the congress leaders wrote to Sergio Vieira de Mello, special representative of the secretary general (SRSG) and demanded that UNTAET work with them on implementing their policy. The GAU adopted the platform as their mandate and it became a mechanism for the women's movement to realize their goals. By mid-2000, Timor had a unified women's movement and national institutional machinery that could collaborate on a common agenda for advancing women's rights.

International analysts initially staffed the GAU although its aims were to introduce both international and national staff to gender mainstreaming and to facilitate the development of policies with a gender perspective. It worked closely with the women's movement, meeting regularly with *Rede Feto*, the women's umbrella network. In 2002, the UNTAET mission withdrew and all its associated offices, including the GAU, were expected to be disbanded. Whittington took measures to ensure the long-term survival of the GAU. UN agencies had a longer mandate in Timor beyond the UNTAET operation so she embedded a United Nations Population Fund (UNFPA) project on SGBV in the GAU to keep it active and well funded.[27] In 2001, the GAU hired and trained local staff to take over its operations. The women's movement selected an experienced East Timorese woman leader, Maria Domingas Alves, "Micato," to head the Gender Affairs Unit. In less than two years, the first gender mainstreaming office in a UN Peacekeeping Operation had been established with UN and local political support.

The critical question was would the GAU survive the transition from UN rule to full independence in 2002? And if so, what form would the office take within the new East Timorese government? The GAU had the support of the SRSG, Sergio Vieira de Mello, who consulted Whittington and Micato on where the office should be positioned in the new government. One proposal from the women's movement was to form a Women's Ministry. However, Whittington argued a smaller policy unit in the office of the prime minister would be more conducive to gender mainstreaming. She feared that a ministry "was too big for a country of that size" and might be turned into a ministry for women, children, and welfare and its efforts to mainstream gender perspectives across and at all levels of policymaking would be lost.[28] SRSG, De Mello, and Prime Minister Mari Alikatiri endorsed her proposal for a smaller policy unit. Timor-Leste now had an Office for the Promotion of Equality (OPE) responsible for gender mainstreaming within government. It owed its creation to the collaboration between GAU staff and the women's movement. The GAU provided the institutional structure and rational for integrating gender perspectives in Timor-Leste's government.

The OPE inherited the GAU's policies, projects, and most importantly its understanding of gender mainstreaming as an across government policy strategy. Their main program, campaigning against SGVB and developing services to provide support for women survivors, was largely run by UNFPA's advisor to OPE. OPE had very little funding from the East Timorese government but was constantly being approached by donors.[29] For institutional support and administrative funding, OPE partnered with Irish Aid.[30] Irish Aid had a strong interest in supporting the women's movement and saw OPE as a crucial mechanism for promoting gender equality. They paid for an international gender advisor and in 2006, an international organizational advisor. These partnerships with UNFPA and Irish Aid offered OPE long-term financial support, gender expertise, and capacity building for organizational and professional development.

Micato brought to OPE her strong relationship with the women's movement. As the advisor to the prime minister on the promotion of equality, she was able to raise the profile of women in Timor and promote a gender perspective on policy. However, she faced many obstacles; she had no access to the Council of Ministers meetings and could only give advice indirectly to them through the prime minister. The OPE lacked skilled staff and thus did not have the capacity to review legislation or monitor government programs. Furthermore, the institution had a "very precarious" organizational structure; it was more program-based than a policy advisory unit.[31] These factors constrained the OPE's ability to ensure that potentially differential gender impacts on women and men were taken into account in the development of new government law and policies.

The 2006 East Timorese political crisis effectively put a stop to the OPE's work.[32] Micato resigned in protest at the way the Fretilin government handled the crisis. A new head, Aurora Ximenes, was soon nominated by the women's movement and appointed. However, she had little experience with gender analysis of policies.[33] All of the OPE's programs were put on hold and it was not until the new government was elected in 2007 that the OPE resumed its policy work. Under the new government the OPE became Secretary of State for Promotion of Equality (SEPI) and its new head was given power to make policy recommendations and to speak at the Council of Ministers. Despite this institutional strengthening SEPI has come under criticism from civil society organizations because it has not formally consulted with them, as did previous mainstreaming units. The leader of one important women's group claimed she had not yet met with SEPI and has no idea what their plans or programs are for 2008. A member of another NGO also expressed concern over whether the creation of SEPI was an effort to sideline gender mainstreaming and place all the responsibility for mainstreaming with SEPI rather than with all of government.[34] This was precisely what Whittington had warned against and sought to prevent when OPE was first created.

That gender mainstreaming has been successfully implemented in Timor–to the extent that there are institutional mechanisms to pursue it—is in large part due to the cooperation and pioneering work of gender advocates in the East Timorese women's movement, the UN and international donor agencies. By supporting local women's organizing, the GAU was able to foster a strong women's movement that also gave it local as well as international legitimacy. The women's movement then used the GAU as a mechanism to lobby the SRSG and the transitional government, and adapted the institution to suit their own goals.

Despite the high level of international support, however, OPE did not successfully implement gender analysis and impact assessments of government policies. It remains to be seen how SEPI will operate. If it is to be successful in mainstreaming a gender perspective in policymaking it will need to become expert not only in advising government but in engaging with local women's organizations that are the chief rationale for its existence and the most important promoters and diffusers of its work.

Campaigning for Gender Quotas

As well as gender mainstreaming and strengthening women's organizing in civil society, greater representation of women in politics was a central demand of the first East Timorese Women's Congress in June 2000. The Women's Congress PFA set a goal of at least 30 percent women in all decision-making bodies. A quota was seen as the most effective way to ensure women's representation. Rede Feto, the women's umbrella organization, made the campaign for gender quotas its first priority for the constitutional assembly elections in 2001. In this quota campaign, Milena Pires, was invaluable as an interlocutor lobbying the UN and publicizing the Timor campaign internationally.[35]

Pires and Rede Feto took the campaign for quotas to CNRT and UNTAET in 2000. The CNRT Congress unanimously passed a resolution to pressure UNTAET to adopt a policy of 30 percent female representation in decision-making bodies.[36] Rede Feto then lobbied UNTAET to endorse quotas for the upcoming elections. However, the UN was internally divided over quotas. While there was some support for quotas within UNIFEM and UNDP, senior UN officials in the Electoral Affairs Division (EAD) charged with administering Timor's national elections considered quotas problematic. The head of the EAD, Carina Perelli, was strongly against quotas. According to Whittington, she argued that quotas would set a "precedent for all sorts of other groups, and then we'll be having quotas for everyone's uncles and cousins in every election run by the UN."[37] Her position was supported by the head of the Department of Political Affairs (UN DPA) in Timor,[38] Peter Galbraith, who apparently saw quotas as "only happening in socialist countries."[39] Thus, the two key UN officials in charge of the Timor election opposed quotas.

The quota debate became "very fiery" and international in scope.[40] The campaign pitted the East Timorese women's movement, backed by international NGOs and some UN agencies against the UN DPA. The Catholic Institute for International Relations began a petition to support Rede Feto and lobby the UN. Publicized in newspapers and on Web sites such as East Timor Action Network's, the quota campaign was discussed by top officials at UN headquarters in New York. Angela King, the special advisor to the secretary-general was supportive of the East Timorese women's campaign and met with Kieran Prendergast the head of the DPA in New York.[41] UN officials in New York were puzzled why UNTAET was not supporting gender quotas.

At the same time as quotas were being debated in New York, DPA was putting pressure on the East Timorese National Council. They lobbied council members to vote against quotas.[42] As a result, many who had previously supported quotas, including some women who had acquired their seats through quotas, changed their mind. The DPA ruled against quotas, claiming, "electoral quotas for women (or any other group) do not constitute international best practice for elections."[43] Rede Feto, disappointed with the decision, petitioned outside the UN offices in Dili. They argued the DPA's decision undermined the CEDAW convention and UN Security Council Resolution 1325, and went against the collective organizing of East Timorese women. The decision to oppose quotas illustrates the complexity of the UN bureaucracy: while some UN agencies namely UNIFEM were strongly supporting the women's quota campaign, other agencies namely the DPA were directly opposing it.

The campaign to increase women's political participation was not completely lost, however. Although quotas could not be used, other affirmative action strategies were not ruled out. East Timorese women convinced senior UN officials that some sort of affirmative action was necessary. Sergio Vieira de Mello (SRSG in Timor) met with Peter Galbraith (head of DPA) and Whittington to discuss alternative strategies. De Mello suggested training forty women to stand as candidates in the election. Whittington was "so angry" at the meager effort that she replied, "we'll train a hundred to run for office."[44] It was also decided that political parties would receive extra airtime on radio and television if they included at least 30 percent women on their party list. De Mello and Xanana Gusmao made it a personal priority in their speeches leading up to the election to lobby for women's inclusion in party lists. Ironically, the refusal by the DPA to support quotas led the women's movement and UN gender entrepreneurs to work even harder to promote women's political representation. Rather than relying on a quota system, they collaborated, drawing on strategies developed by women's movements in other countries, to raise the profile of women and increase the skills, competency, and confidence of those wanting to stand.[45]

The result was extraordinary: women won twenty-three out of eighty-seven seats in parliament (26 percent). This ranked Timor thirty-third in the world and one of the highest in its region for the percentage of women in parliament.[46] A woman, Ana Pessoa, took the second most influential role in parliament, as minister for state administration. Because of the candidate training a new NGO was formed, the Women's Political Caucus, which became part of Rede Feto and is now the main organization supporting women's political representation. In 1999, Timor had no quotas, no precedent of affirmative action for women in politics, and no women's movement. By the end of 2001 a strong, unified women's movement had formed, and campaigned successfully for affirmative action strategies to ensure the inclusion of a sizable proportion of women in Timor's parliament.

In 2006, the quota debate returned. Timor-Leste was drafting its electoral law for the upcoming 2007 parliamentary elections. A coalition of NGOs including Caucus and Rede Feto worked with UNIFEM to campaign again for a 30 percent quota for women on party lists. This time the UN DPA had no power over the decision. In late 2006, a compromise between a coalition of NGOs and parliamentarians endorsed a candidate gender quota of 25 percent. The resulting electoral law stipulated, "lists of effective and alternate candidates must include at least one woman per every group of four candidates."[47] In 2007, the election result again was outstanding: 27 percent of parliamentary representatives were women; a two percent increase on the previous election in 2001. However, there was frustration among gender advocates over the way women were included in the party list. Most parties placed women as the last candidate in each group of four. Furthermore, women were not given as many executive positions as in the previous government.

Supported by international NGOs, Rede Feto initiated a campaign to ensure a large number of women entered the national East Timorese parliament. They leveraged international norms of gender equality and adapted women's caucusing strategies used around the world. Although the UN was divided, and blocked quotas, it did eventually support other affirmative action strategies, which led to women being trained in election campaigning and included on party lists. East Timorese women were successful in gaining greater representation in parliament because of their strong transnational networking. Moreover, after the departure of UNTAET gender advocates were able to reintroduce the quota debate and pass a gender electoral quota law.[48] Without the development of a strong East Timorese civil society voice for women and a supportive gender-mainstreaming unit within UNTAET, these quotas would have never been finally implemented in Timor.

Conclusion

What lessons can other states and international organizations learn from Timor-Leste's experience of building democracy? Which institutional strategies for gender equality work best? The Timor case illustrates the unique opportunity that new states and their international partners have to promote gender equality and women's participation in democratization processes. In Timor the three gender equality strategies evolved together and organically as their key advocates collaborated closely and were well connected to senior UN officials and Timor leaders. The women's movement both supported and was supported by the succession of gender mainstreaming institutions. The gender quota campaign, although initially unsuccessful, led to a flourishing of women's political voice and interest in politics. The Gender Affairs Unit in UNTAET was the major facilitator of the affirmative action efforts that brought a large number of women candidates into the Timor Parliament. However, while important institutional changes that have the potential to significantly change the status of women have been introduced in Timor, they have yet to seriously transform the unequal gendered structures of East Timorese state and society. For instance, the gender mainstreaming framework has been instituted but routine gender impact assessment is not being carried out. Thus, no public policy has been altered as a result of taking into account gender differences and inequalities. Similarly, more women in parliament and in cabinet positions have not translated in the short term into feminist platforms and policies. At the same time, the women's movement in Timor has become a strong and recognized force in national and international civil society with a diverse feminist political agenda that addresses both practical and strategic gender interests.

A feminist perspective on democratization and peacebuilding forces us to look at democratic institutions in terms of who is represented, who is present and absent, and in whose interest power is executed. Such a perspective reveals a democratic deficit when men dominate political institutions and women are absent or a minority voice in these institutions. Feminists argue that democracy requires all citizens, women and men, to be involved in the design of new institutions. They see democracy not merely in terms of a public sphere or set of political institutions but in terms of the underlying practices within a private sphere that includes the economy, civil society, and the family. Thus, democratizing a state and society requires collaboration between groups in public and private spheres and between institutional and noninstitutional actors. Consistent with this, a feminist perspective highlights the central role of civil society and women's organizing within civil society in building the collaborative relationships that establish democracy in everyday practice as well as in institutional design. In this regard, Timor-Leste has the potential to create a truly equal democracy having begun its nation-building process with institutionalized gender equality initiatives and women's voice at the heart of this process in civil society, and with the benefit of international learning, political and practical support.

Notes

1. Isabel Coleman, "The Payoff for Women's Rights," *Foreign Affairs* 83, no. 3 (2004): 80–95.
2. Maxine Molyneux, "Mobilization Without Emancipation? Women's Interests, State and Revolution," in *Transition and Development: Problems of Third World Socialism*, ed. Richard R. Fagen, et al. (New York: Monthly Review Press, 1985), 280–320.
3. Elizabeth Rehn and Ellen Johnson-Sirleaf, "Women, War, Peace: The Independent Experts," in *Assessment on the Impact of Armed Conflict on Women and Women's Role in Peace-building* (New York: UNIFEM, 2002); Pamela Paxton, "Women's Suffrage in the Measurement of Democracy: Problems of Operationalization," *Studies in Comparative International Development* 35, no. 3 (2000): 92–111; J. Ann Tickner, *Gender in International Relations: Feminist Perspectives on Achieving Global Security*

(New York: Columbia University Press, 1992); Sherrill Whittington, "Gender and Peacekeeping: The United Nations Transitional Administration in East Timor," *Signs* 28, no. 4 (2003):1283–88.

4. Cynthia Enloe, *Bananas, Beaches and Bases: Making Feminist Sense of International Politics* (London: Pandora, 1989).
5. See, for example, Francis Fukuyama, "Women and the Evolution of World Politics," *Foreign Affairs* 77, no. 5 (September/October 1998).
6. See Tickner, *Gender in International Relations*, 22–23, 54–55.
7. Jacqui True, "Gender Specialists and Global Governance Organizations: New Forms of Women's Movement Mobilization," in *Women's Movements: In Abeyance or Flourishing in New Ways?*, ed. Marian Sawer and Sandra Grey (New York: Routledge, 2008), chapter seven.
8. Lesley Abdela, "Kosovo: Missed Opportunities, Lessons for the Future," in *Development, Women, and War: Feminist Perspectives*, ed. Haileh Afshar and David Eade (Oxford: Oxfam, 2004), 87–99.
9. Sofi Ospina, "Participation of Women in Politics and Decision-Making in Timor-Leste: A Recent History," *Unpublished Report (*Dili: UNIFEM, 2006), 12.
10. Ibid., 16.
11. Ibid., 18–22; Gender Affairs Unit and Cliondah O'Keeffe, *Situational Analysis of Gender in Post-Conflict East Timor* (Dili, East Timor, 2002), 10–11.
12. Irena Cristalis and Catherine Scott, *Independent Women, The Story of Women's Activism in East Timor* (London: Catholic Institute for International Relations, 2005), 54–56.
13. Sue Downie, "UNTAET: State-building and Peace-building in East Timor," in *East Timor Beyond Independence*, ed. Damien Kingsbury and Michael Leach (Melbourne: Monash University Press, 2007), 29.
14. The Congress produced a new women's umbrella organization, *Rede Feto*, which literally means "women's network." It coordinated 16 women's organizations to strategically campaign on the East Timorese Platform of Action.
15. Sherrill Whittington (former director, UNTAET Gender Affairs Unit), in discussion with Nina Hall, November 8, 2007.
16. Manuela Pereira (former director, Fokupers), in discussion with Nina Hall, Dili, December 3, 2007.
17. Cecilia Brunnstrom, "Another Invasion: Lessons from International Support to East Timorese NGOs," *Development in Practice* 14, no. 4 (2003): 310–21.
18. Milena Vilanova (former trainer, IRC), in discussion with Nina Hall, Dili, November 23, 2007.
19. Interview, Pereira, 2007.
20. Ibid.
21. First Congress of Women of Timor Loro Sa'e, *Plan of Action*, June 2000.
22. In 2007 the prime minister, Xanana Gusmao and the president, José Ramos Horta, even spoke out against domestic violence and featured it on the campaign posters: "Hapara Violensia Kontra Feto" (Stop Violence Against Women Poster), Dili: *UNIFEM*, 2007.

23. Catherine Scott, "Are Women Included or Excluded in Post-Conflict Reconstruction?: A Case Study from East Timor, CIIR, June 30, 2003, http://www.peacewomen.org/resources/Timor-Leste/CIIRWomensPart03.html (accessed 13 June 2007).
24. Whittington is an Australian with experience working at the most senior levels on gender mainstreaming. For example, she was on the secretariat of the UN Fourth World Conference on Women at Beijing as a senior advisor in 1995. Following the conference, she worked in the gender section of UNICEF developing gender-mainstreaming guidelines.
25. Sergio Vieira de Mello quoted in Cristalis and Scott, *Independent Women*, 78.
26. Interview, Whittington, November 8, 2007; Maria Diaz (director, Rede Feto) in discussion with Nina Hall, Dili, December 1, 2007.
27. Interview, Whittington, November 8, 2007.
28. Ibid.
29. Sara Negrao (former international advisor, OPE), in discussion with Nina Hall, October 16, 2007.
30. Anna Trembath and Damian Grenfell, *Mapping the Pursuit of Gender Equality, Non-Government and International Agency Activity in Timor-Leste* (Melbourne, Australia: The Globalism Institute, RMIT University, 2007).
31. Interview, Negrao, 2007.
32. The 2006 political crisis in Timor involved 600 petitioners deserting the army and resulted in widespread civic violence, and thousands of internally displaced persons. However, there was no constitutional breakdown and the government stayed in power throughout the crisis.
33. Interview, Negrao, 2007.
34. Teresa Verdial de Araujo (advocacy manager, Aola Foundation) Dili, November 30, 2007.
35. Milena Pires, "Enhancing Women's Participation in Electoral Processes in Post-Conflict Countries: Experiences from East Timor," (paper presented to Expert Group Meeting on Enhancing Women's Participation in Electoral Processes in Post-Conflict Countries, Glen Cove, United States, January 19–22, 2004).
36. Pires, "Enhancing Women's Participation."
37. Interview, Whittington, November 8, 2007.
38. The Electoral Affairs Division is part of the Department of Political Affairs.
39. This is the view related by Sherrill Whittington, November 8, 2007.
40. Ibid.
41. Ibid.
42. Pires, "Enhancing Women's Participation."
43. Milena Pires, "East Timor and the Debate on Quotas." International IDEA, *Regional Workshop on the Implementation of Quotas: Asian Experiences* (Jakarta: September 2002), 38.
44. Interview, Whittington, November 8, 2007.
45. See Martha Alter Chen, "Engendering World Conferences: The International Women's Movements and the United Nations," in *NGOs, the UN and Global Governance*, ed. Thomas G. Weiss and Leon Gordenker (Boulder, CO: Lynne Rienner, 1996), 139–55. The Gender Affairs Unit (GAU), UNIFEM, and *Rede Feto* worked together to organise six weeks of back-to back training, 140 women were trained.

46. International Parliamentary Union Web site, *Women in National Parliaments*, http://www.ipu.org/wmn-e/classif.htm, January 31, 2007 (accessed September 6, 2007).
47. Article 12.3 of the Democratic Republic of Timor-Leste, *Law on the Election of the National Parliament*, Law No.6/2006, December 28, 2006.
48. In addition, in 2004 after the disbanding of UNTAET, three seats were reserved on every *Suco* (village) council for women. For the first time ever several women were elected as *Xefe de Suco*, head of the village.

CHAPTER 11

Shifting Terrains of Transnational Engagement

Women's Organizing in Fiji

Nicole George

The women's movement in Fiji has been described as one of the most vibrant, influential, and active in the Pacific.[1] Representatives from this country's women's groups have been energetic participants on the local, regional, and international stage since the 1960s. Their efforts have been integral to raising the local and global profile of issues such as violence against women, women's legal rights, women's role in the media, and women's political participation. Yet although these developments indicate 'progress' for women, historical comparisons of organizational activity on local questions related to reproductive health, and global questions of economic justice or rights to political self-determination, demonstrate important shifts in the way activists in this setting have understood the possibility of promoting feminist futures through transnational engagement.

In this chapter, I draw upon interview material gathered from women who have been active on the international stage from the 1960s onward. My aim, however, is not simply to document this activity, but also to demonstrate how the interplay of local and global factors influences transnational political behavior and hence, organizational abilities to promote alternate political agendas to the masculinist, state-oriented mainstream. I demonstrate how shifting geopolitical, sociocultural, religious, and economic imperatives on the local and global stage influence gender activists' understandings of the viability of transnational activity at particular historical junctures. This approach allows me to demonstrate how the spaces for women's transnational activity have been shaped by prevailing norms of gender subordination[2] and other power relations evident within Fiji and international politics.

This chapter has three sections. The first briefly explains what is meant by transnationalism, transnational feminism, and its relevance to discussions of women's political agency in Fiji. The second, longer section, examines the shifting terrain of women's transnational political engagement in this setting. The concluding section outlines some of the recent, dramatic events occurring in Fiji at the end of 2006, with a view to illustrating how new contingencies are set to impact upon the transnational work conducted by women's groups in this setting.

Transnationalism and Feminism

Interest in women's transnational political engagement is particularly evident within feminist scholarship.[3] In these works, the concept of transnationalism is loosely defined to signify "any actor, organization, or issue that could be either international or global in orientation."[4] This means that even where the focus upon women's organizations is essentially localized, attention is frequently drawn to the local and transnational "frequency" of organizational activity.[5] Hence, many studies describe how women's groups use transnational networks to make local questions of gender subordination resonate at the international level.[6] Reversing this lens, others focus upon the "significance of transnational advocacy and activist networks" at the local level, describing the various strategies employed by women's groups to promote international discourses contesting women's subordination.[7]

The concept of transnationalism is especially pertinent to any consideration of women's organizing in Fiji. In addition to their local activities, Fiji's women activists are energetic participants on the international stage. On one hand, they have demonstrated to regional and international audiences the specifically local factors contributing to women's subordination in Fiji. On the other hand, they have drawn upon internationally endorsed advocacy frameworks to protest phenomena that subordinate women in the local setting. However, as this chapter will make clear, the history of women's transnational political engagement in Fiji has also altered over time, reflecting shifting contingencies within the prevailing local and global political environment.

These considerations are particularly relevant when examining how women activists from the region respond to shifts in transnational feminism. Despite the fact that there is a strong feminist orientation to the advocacy undertaken by the organizations described in the following pages, the relationship between women's organizing and feminism in this setting has not been straightforward. Many of the religious and culturally aligned women's groups operating in this region have often avoided the term "feminism," which they view as posing a threat to the integrity of the family, highly valued in Pacific cultures, and promoting an agenda that is "anti-men."[8] For other women activists, the appeal of second-wave feminist thinking was strong but counter-acted by a perceived western bias in the transnational feminist debate of the 1960s and 1970s; a factor that made local identification with transnational feminist ideals problematic.[9] At later points, women activists in Fiji found it counter-productive to make explicit reference to transnational feminist ideals within a domestic political climate defined by a powerful strain of indigenous ethno-nationalism. Rather than incite the opposition of parochial, political actors who have rallied behind gendered interpretations of custom, culture, and religion in order to bolster their political authority, women activists in this setting have chosen to downplay the feminist aspects of their activity by framing their demands in a softer, locally acceptable language that has emphasized rights and equality. While there is therefore a conscious effort to soften the tone and substance of advocacy, women activists also express some frustration that their political activity requires these types of conciliatory tactics.

While these points will be considered in detail in the following discussion, they demonstrate the need for a close understanding of the way global and local shifts in political circumstance influence the articulation of transnational feminist ideals. As will be made clear, the interplay of global and local contingencies has a significant impact upon the ways in which feminist futures are conceptualized and promoted by women activists in this setting, at times enabling, at other times constraining, certain forms of feminist advocacy. Ultimately, this is an issue that has a broader significance for international relations (IR) scholarship concerned with the emergence of a global civil society. Many celebrate the current intensification of transnational civil society activity as likely to bring about a more just, participatory, and transparent system of global governance overall.[10] Yet within these accounts, there is little sustained consideration given to the interplaying global and local factors that shape the political agency of civil society actors at specific moments. This chapter therefore demonstrates the benefits in understanding that accrue when a more nuanced analysis of these processes is developed.

The 1960s and 1970s

Political life in Fiji displays strong communalist tendencies. This is a legacy of British colonialism, which brought a large population of Indian indentured laborers to these shores and encouraged a culture of division to emerge between the indigenous and Indian communities.[11] In the postcolonial setting these divisions continued and were strongly reflected within civil society, where membership in cultural and religious organizations, unions, and sporting bodies has often been defined on the basis of ethnicity. The make-up of many women's organizations in Fiji—faith-based welfare or development-focused—tended to reflect this broader communal orientation. Yet the segregation of women's organizing in Fiji was transformed in the early 1960s with the formation of Fiji's first branch of the Young Women's Christian Association (YWCA), an entity, which, despite its religious origins, promoted a multicultural and ecumenical ethos.[12] Within a few short years, members of the YWCA were to challenge longstanding aspects of political life in Fiji. This tendency was particularly evident in the advocacy program promoted by YWCA members, which was both local and transnational in orientation and took women's organizing in Fiji into the previously male-dominated terrain of national political debate for the first time.

These actions were not without controversy. In the lead-up to Fiji's 1970 independence, YWCA members made a strong submission to a public meeting on constitutional design. Here they made a radical stand, condemning the colonially instituted political structures that protected indigenous paramountcy in Fiji and calling for the abolition of Fiji's highest site of indigenous political authority, the Great Council of Chiefs.[13] In later years, the organization waged a sustained campaign for legalized abortion in Fiji, which brought the organization into direct contradiction with the teachings of Fiji's highly influential Catholic and Methodist Churches.[14]

The YWCA also took up issues that were international in scope. Members of the organization were closely involved in an important publication that was highly critical of Fiji's economic relations with Australia, branded as a form of neocolonialism.[15] From 1970 onward, the YWCA, along with other associations that included the University of the South Pacific's Student Association, the Fiji Council of Churches, and the newly-formed ATOM (Against Testing on Muroroa), also played a key role in campaigns against French nuclear testing programs conducted in the Pacific Island region. This coalition encouraged Fiji's political leaders to promote this issue aggressively on the international stage. Furthermore, the organization sought to raise local women's consciousness of the anti-nuclear cause by demonstrating how the environmental impact of continued testing had direct relevance to their health and daily lives.[16] Figures within the YWCA's leadership also played a key role in the organization of a regional conference held in 1974 to deliberate on nuclear issues and colonization in the Pacific.[17]

In 1975, Fiji's YWCA members appeared on the international stage, voicing a strong message of opposition to geopolitical trends in the Pacific region at the NGO Tribune staged in parallel to the first United Nations World Conference for Women held in Mexico City. Struggling to be heard within the relatively unstructured Tribune environment (described as functioning on the "creative edge of chaos"[18]) Fiji women, alongside other representatives from the Pacific, made noteworthy presentations, drawing attention to regional struggles waged by Pacific peoples for political sovereignty and a nuclear-free future.[19] At later regional and international meetings, an NGO-organized regional women's gathering held in Suva in 1975 and the UN Mid-Decade conference for women held in Copenhagen in 1980, these themes continued to predominate.[20]

Of course, not all regional delegates to these meetings subscribed to these points of view.[21] Nonetheless, an internationally focused advocacy agenda that emphasized the disempowering impacts of global structures upon Pacific Islands' populations, and particularly Pacific women, emerged as a signature of women's advocacy in this period, both in Fiji and across the region more generally. This trend was perhaps nowhere more apparent than at the regional conference for women convened by the United Nations Economic and Social Council for Asia Pacific and held in Suva in November 1980. The final declaration issued by delegates to this conference included strongly worded sections critical of many aspects of international engagement in the region including nuclear testing, aid distribution, and the impact of poorly regulated foreign investment.[22]

It is important to appreciate how prevailing political trends, local and global, encouraged formulation of a feminist agenda that linked local questions of gender disadvantage with broader questions related to global structural inequity. For example, YWCA members who were prominent on the local and transnational stage during this period were conscious of the fact that they were part of a significant moment of political transition. They likened the Independence era in Fiji to standing on a "new frontier," a time when long accepted protocols relating to indigenous political privilege could be challenged by new or provocative political agendas brought into the public domain. One key actor of the period, Amelia Rokotuivuna described the enabling nature of the prevailing political environment when she stated,

> at Independence there is a marriage of these ideas with the political agenda of the nation. You are in a climate that is like a new frontier. You feel that you are founding a nation and you have a pioneer attitude.[23]

Moreover, they had the impression that their activities were also legitimated, to a degree, by the fact that influential church groups and Fiji's political leaders were lending active support to their activities, particularly opposition to nuclear testing.[24]

At the same time, trends in international politics opened the way for advocacy that linked the predicament of women with global structural imbalances contributing to dependency in the developing world. In a period of heightened "Third Worldism," with the likes of Julius Nyere, Kwame Nkrumah, and Sekou Touré issuing demands for a global redistribution of political and economic power, and the G77 emerging as a powerful voting bloc within the UN, international attention was drawn to questions of structural imbalance within the global political economy. In this environment, postcolonial leaders saw their call for the creation of a New International Economic Order (NIEO) gain unanimous endorsement within the UN General Assembly and become mainstream items on the international policy-making agenda. These developments enabled a range of civil society actors to take up similar refrains within the transnational realm. And this lent currency to the efforts of women's groups who engaged in transnational advocacy that examined the global phenomena contributing to women's subordination in localized settings.

Yet Pacific women also recognized that internationally there was hesitation amongst certain groups of feminists with regard to transnational advocacy framed in these terms.[25] They often complained that their concerns were dismissed as a distraction, which diverted attention from a more centralized focus upon women's issues. For these reasons, Fiji's women activists often claimed they felt marginalized at international forums, perceived to be "not quite as feminist as Western feminists," and generally reluctant to use the term.[26]

Of course, in the domestic context these same women did not want to act in ways that suggested that a political discourse designed to advance the rights of women was inauthentic to the Pacific context. There were already many within the region's male dominated political classes, who were willing to use this line of argument to dismiss aspects of their activism in a blanket fashion.[27] Hence, there was a certain strategic value in advocacy that linked the subordination of Pacific women to broader arguments about the way that global structures disadvantaged Pacific Island communities as a whole. As the following discussion demonstrates, however, local feminist debate construed in these terms was less audible in later periods as a more localized, rights-focused basis for women's advocacy came to the fore.

Beyond the 'New Frontier': The 1980s and 1990s

The 1980s and 1990s saw new issue-focused women's groups form in Fiji whose members were politically active on the local, regional, and international stage. The first of these was the Fiji Women's Crisis Centre (FWCC) which was established in 1983. This organization sought to challenge the general culture of acceptance surrounding issues related to gender violence in Fiji. Early activities included counseling for victims of rape and violence, programs to increase community awareness of the phenomenon, and training sessions to address this issue in schools and within other women's groups. In later years the FWCC secured important financial and political support through transnational feminist networks, and in particular with organizations such as the Melbourne-based International Women's Development Agency and the Centre for Women's Global Leadership (CWGL), headed by Charlotte Bunch at Rutgers University, where long-time FWCC Coordinator, Shamima Ali, was trained.[28]

The other significant women's rights organization established in these years, the Fiji Women's Rights Movement (FWRM), was more directly focused on the legal and political structures that compounded women's subordination in Fiji. Early campaigns called for reform of Fiji's rape laws and better wage protection for women employed in the growth industries of the period, particularly garment manufacturing. In the 1990s, the FWRM advocated for Fiji to become a signatory to the United Nations Convention on the Elimination of Discrimination

Against Women (CEDAW). Fiji's accession to CEDAW in 1995 was subsequently used to leverage support for the drafting of a new Family Law Bill to replace the inherited, colonial statutes in this area, which were deemed outdated and discriminatory. The FWRM also created programs to promote women's representation in parliament in Fiji and throughout the region.

The emergence of these groups signified a new trend in gender politics in Fiji. These organizations took a far more issue-specific approach to the question of women's subordination than was apparent in the strategies pursued by the Fiji YWCA in earlier years. At the same time, gender advocacy became much more of a localized discussion, focused upon state obligations to protect women's human rights and correct the juridical aspects of women's subordination.[29] The broad structurally inclined critique of geopolitical influence in the region, and its impact upon local Pacific Island communities, and particularly Pacific Island women, was far more difficult to locate in this period. In its place, the FWCC and the FWRM were more inclined to address localized issues of concern and advocate for state recognition of women's human rights.

This is not to say that these organizations' advocacy was less provocative than that of earlier periods simply that it was provocative in different ways.[30] Certainly, many of the women involved in these organizations felt more easily able to identify with transnational feminist ideals at this time.[31] In part, this reflects the fact that the parameters of transnational feminist debate had altered to address a more inclusive politics covering "those norms and processes of gender construction and oppression that differentially advantage some women and men relative to others."[32] This broadening debate enabled Fiji-based activists to articulate a feminist vision on the international stage that could accommodate regional concerns and regional identifications. In contrast, within the domestic political context, a powerful strain of indigenous ethno-nationalism became increasingly apparent in the wake of two military coups perpetrated in 1987. These developments had an important impact upon the way women's organizations locally articulated this feminist vision in the years that followed.

The gendered impact of these events soon became clear. Levels of violence against women rose dramatically in the wake of the 1987 coups with the FWCC reporting a six-fold increase in incidents of this type. The post–coup regime embarked on a program of harsh economic restructuring, which had a particularly serious impact on low-income women.[33] Additionally, comments made by members of the post–coup regime appeared to legitimate the diffusion of chauvinistic attitudes in the broader social context. The widely reported jest made by coup leader, Sitiveni Rabuka, that Fijian men use idle hours on Sunday, the "Christian Sabbath," to kick "either a football or one's wife around,"[34] clearly exemplified this.

Members of this new regime rallied behind gendered interpretations of custom and culture as a means by which to legitimate their claims to political authority, cast doubt upon the political ambitions of Fiji's large Indian population, and quiet the opposition of pro-democracy activists through appeals to the vocabulary of indigenous rights. Consequently, the political space available to women's groups to articulate an explicitly feminist political agenda was severely constrained. This explains why the FWRM and FWCC were encouraged to align their feminist goals with the human rights framework. Unlike the YWCA, both organizations clearly judged it prudent to avoid critical discussion of the local impact of prevailing global economic imperatives at this point. These groups were well aware that the post–coup program of economic restructuring was having a detrimental impact upon large numbers of women and they sought to provide practical means of community support from their limited resources.[35] Nonetheless, in an environment where indigenous political figures used the national parliament to promote the view that women activists demanding "social, economic, and political equality for women" deserved to be raped,[36] a cautious public profile was mandatory. Demands for gender equality framed in human rights terms were clearly a prudent form of political engagement, as long as this message was further mediated in ways that referenced key sociocultural markers of identity.

Hence, women's organizations frequently sought to emphasize the consonance between human rights values and custom. They referenced traditional ideas about the complementary nature of gender roles within customary practices; ideas that have been downplayed across the Pacific Islands in contemporary times as a result of colonial and later global capitalist influences.[37] Similarly, they engaged in advocacy that rhetorically aligned human rights values with aspects of Christian, Hindu, and Moslem teaching, which promote respect and equality for women.[38] Although such strategies can be read as "creative" uses of local culture,[39] those involved in this type of activity also expressed some frustration that their ability to articulate a feminist agenda should be circumscribed or constrained in this way. On the one hand, they feared being "boxed in" by the communalism amplified within Fiji's political culture in the wake of the 1987 coups,[40] and that such strategies conceded too much territory to local parochialists. On the other hand, they recognized that feminist messages delivered in this manner referenced cultural protocols and belief systems that, in many instances, contributed to women's ongoing subordination.[41]

Of course, the local application of human rights frameworks was encouraged by developments occurring within the international political arena. From the early 1990s onward, human rights became a new transnational language for gender advocacy, thanks, in part, to the sustained campaigns waged by CWGL.[42] This transnational network sought to widen what feminists had often viewed as the "gender myopia" evident in human rights law that failed to recognize "oppressive practices against women as human rights violations."[43] At the 1993 United Nations Human Rights Conference convened in Vienna, networks of women activists successfully campaigned for violence against women to be recognized as a human rights issue, upon which states should have an international obligation to act.[44] The UN

General Assembly unanimously endorsed the decision later in 1993. Further international endorsement of human rights perspectives on gender disadvantage occurred during the UN's Fourth World Conference for Women, staged in Beijing in 1995, when this focus on gender violence was expanded to include issues related to women's health, sexuality, and reproduction.[45] Despite some level of opposition,[46] the final achievement of inter-governmental consensus on the Beijing Global Plan of Action (GPA) was hailed as a momentous achievement for women that "significantly expanded the horizons of previous [UN] conferences."[47]

Nonetheless, the GPA's incorporation of a human rights framework was seen to "obscure" the connections between "human rights abuses" and "current economic structures,"[48] a criticism particularly relevant to those sections of the GPA that appeared to promote the benefits of economic structural adjustment and trade liberalization.[49] Faith in the power of markets to provide women with opportunities that lead to their empowerment permeated aspects of this document, while scant attention was paid to the exploitative aspects of women's market participation, particularly in developing economies.[50]

This indicates a vastly different environment for transnational advocacy than was apparent in the 1960s and 1970s where the space for critical appraisal of the disempowering impacts of global political and economic structures was more expansive. This is not to suggest that women's economic disempowerment was not a key concern within the transnational advocacy environment in these later decades. Certainly, the issue of women living in poverty was a critical site of debate at the Beijing NGO Forum.[51] Moreover, at the Pacific Island regional level, a network of local scholars who had continually examined the gendered dimensions of social and economic disadvantage from this perspective forged important transnational connections with the critical Third World feminist organization DAWN (Development Alternatives for Women in a New Era).[52] Nonetheless, as the transnational appeal of human rights-focused feminist activity increased, less attention was given to questions that asked how Pacific women's local subordination was compounded by structural inequities prevailing within the global political economy. In combination with the domestic factors previously discussed, this shift encouraged women activists in Fiji to focus on demonstrating the localized causes of women's disadvantage and the need for improved juridical mechanisms that would enable women to redeem their rights.

2000 and Beyond

In the late 1990s a period of political reform took place in Fiji as the country moved toward a revised system of constitutional democracy and Rabuka began to soften his hardline nationalist agenda.[53] In a seemingly more liberal environment, Fiji's women's groups looked to the future with a greater sense of anticipation as they began to enjoy a more cooperative relationship with government than had been prevalent for most of the preceding decade. In 1999 elections, Rabuka's government was unexpectedly toppled from power. A coalition of parties headed by the Fiji Labour Party, and led by an Indo-Fijian, Mahendra Chaudhry, assumed political office. This development seemed, outwardly at least, to indicate a more positive era of multicultural political representation in Fiji, along with a more progressive environment in which to promote feminist politics.

However, almost immediately the legitimacy of the new government was questioned by indigenous nationalists who interpreted Chaudhry's political ascendancy as an affront to the principle of indigenous paramountcy. Within a year, nationalist political agitation became increasingly serious. As political volatility mounted, a group of civilian rebel insurgents invaded the parliamentary complex in Suva in May 2000 and attempted to overthrow the elected government.[54] For nearly two months, Fiji's Great Council of Chiefs and the military attempted to broker a deal with the rebels, while pro-coup supporters engaged in sporadic incidents of mob violence around the country, targeting Indo-Fijian businesses and property, state infrastructure, and policy and military outposts. The situation was finally brought to a resolution that saw the incumbent government dismissed, the chief coup-perpetrators arrested, and an interim government appointed, headed by Laisenia Qarase, a Lauan businessman with close ties to the indigenous establishment.[55]

This new regime rapidly sought to establish its ethno-nationalist credentials and quell potential sources of opposition. Within weeks, a policy of indigenous affirmative action was drafted, which outlined plans to protect Fijian rights to economic and political self-determination. At the same time, the regime sought to undermine the local political authority of pro-democracy, civil society groups. Prominent regime figures mounted public slur campaigns against organizations deemed too critical, and deregistered one particularly vocal organization, the Citizens' Constitutional Forum (CCF), depriving it of its charitable status. Yet such actions did not dissuade women's groups from becoming involved in political action opposed to the regime. From the beginning of the crisis, women's groups drawn from a variety of religious and cultural communities established an ecumenical peace vigil that met weekly at Suva's Anglican Cathedral. The Fiji Women's Rights Movement, adopting the line that "democracy is a precondition for the attainment of women's rights," provided crucial legal support for a High Court case mounted by the CCF that challenged the legality of the interim government.[56] The Fiji Women's Crisis Centre documented the gendered fallout from the coup, particularly the rise in violence perpetrated against women, and where possible provided direct assistance to vulnerable communities.[57]

When fresh elections were held in Fiji, a new indigenous nationalist party was swept into office under the leadership of the interim Prime Minister, Laisenia Qarase. This government continued its retaliatory posture toward those civil society groups deemed overly critical or capable of inciting widespread opposition. In these circumstances, women's groups in Fiji, were once again, inclined to follow a cautious path of political advocacy. In comparison to earlier periods, they described their feminist politics as a "gentler form" of political engagement that avoided the risk of hostile reprisal from state authorities.[58]

What this meant in practical terms became evident in the advocacy strategies utilized by prominent women's organizations to tackle issues such as economic disadvantage. The economic fallout of the 2000 coup contributed to a national economic downturn, which had a particularly harsh impact upon low-income women. Job losses in sectors such as garment manufacturing (because of international trade sanctions) and tourism were significant and foreign investment fell by one-third.[59] Echoing the policies put in place by the 1987 post coup military regime, the government engaged in policies of fiscal restraint. Reductions in public sector and welfare spending meant that even where applicants were considered sufficiently 'destitute' to receive government assistance, average weekly allowance payments went nowhere near the estimated weekly minimum amount needed to meet basic household needs.[60]

Women's groups such as the FWRM and the FWCC were certainly aware of what one activist described as the "bread and butter" challenges being faced by low-income women as well as within women-headed households.[61] However, in their advocacy, they tended to focus on poverty as a human rights issue, arguing that material forms of poverty should be understood as stemming from poverty of opportunity. This logic was clearly indicated in a 2002 publication released by the Regional Rights Resource Team, a Fiji-based organization aiming to promote human rights around the Pacific Islands, which had close ties to the FWRM. Here the RRRT argued,

> you need to think about what causes poverty in the first place. First you need to understand that poverty is not just financial. A person can also be poor in terms of how much or little access he or she has to resources like education and information due to a lack of opportunity. Therefore having human rights provides a basis through which people gain access to the resources they have been denied as a result of social, political and legal inequalities. Until every person has access to human rights, the cycle of poverty will not be broken.[62]

From this perspective, the predicament of those living in poverty was understood to be effectively addressed only when state mechanisms were put in place that enabled women to realize their economic rights and thus contest their economic subordination. Applying this framework to discussions of poverty put the emphasis on individual capacity for resistance and the individual's capacity to redeem her rights through juridical process. At the same time, almost no critical attention was paid to the government's economic policy-making agenda, which seemed only to reflect the broader aim of winning international economic credibility and, ultimately, foreign investment. Yet women's organizations were also working within a political environment where their activities were subject to intense state scrutiny and they were regularly accused of failing to respect cultural norms of consensus and "quiet diplomacy."[63] As such, this direction in advocacy is understandable given the prevailing circumstances, which worked against activists taking a more confrontational stand against the government on the issue of women's economic subordination.

At the same time representatives of women's groups also described the need to "dovetail' their agendas with those of their external donor partners whose emphasis upon establishing good governance in the region provided both opportunities and constraints for local civil society actors.[64] In Fiji, NGOs that incorporated aspects of the good governance agenda into their funding proposals were often the recipients of substantial external financial support. Yet these developments meant there was little inclination for local women's organizations to be critical of neoliberal trends shaping international aid-providers' policy and, particularly, the idea that economic opportunity was linked to empowerment. In Fiji, as in many other parts of the developing world, these initiatives have emphasized women's market participation as a more progressive and effective means of poverty alleviation and empowerment than other more literal forms of "social provisioning."[65] Ultimately, this means that that civil society groups aiming to contest the global and regional dominance of neoliberal approaches to development currently operate in a highly constrained local and global political space, a scenario that Claire Slatter likens to "treading water in rapids."[66]

Concluding Reflections

On December 5, 2006, Fiji suffered its fourth coup in a twenty year period as the military again assumed political control in the country, seeking to halt the endemic corruption and ethno-nationalist partisanship that it alleged to be hallmarks of the previous regime.[67] Members of the local women's movement, as well as other representatives of civil society groups, ignored the military warnings that opposition would not be tolerated and issued public calls for constitutional rule to be upheld. Some received pointed threats of physical violence if their criticism of the military was not halted.[68] Within a fortnight six pro-democracy activists, one, the coordinator of the Fiji Women's Rights Movement, were taken into Suva's military barracks, allegedly beaten and forced to walk ten kilometers through the rainy streets of Suva early on the morning of Christmas Day.[69] In the year since, reports of the military's alleged human rights abuses of former members of parliament, civil servants, media representatives, industry leaders, and civil society spokespersons have continued and number into the hundreds.[70]

Not all women's groups uphold this strong pro-democracy stand and some women activists describe the military take-over as a much needed intervention, which is mandated by a broader social justice agenda.[71] Nonetheless, there is broad opposition to the continuing human rights abuses and amongst all women's groups, there is a strong appreciation of the need to assume a guarded political profile in what is, once again, an authoritarian political climate. [72]

These events serve only to heighten the importance of developing frameworks of analysis that enable the relationship between transnationalism and civil society agency to be understood in relation to political context. This has not always been the case in international relations scholarship on this subject, nor within feminist scholarship that examines the transnational activity of women's organizations. While not all would agree that women's efforts to forge "multilayered"[73] networks of transnational "political understanding" have resulted in the women's movement becoming the most "global" of all the social movements,[74] there is no doubt that for many feminist scholars, women's transnational activity is understood to have enhanced women's political agency in both global and local contexts.[75]

Missing from these accounts is a close consideration of the way varying contextual factors—global and local—shape women's transnational political agency across time. As this chapter illustrates, terrains of transnational activity are influenced at particular historical junctures, by interplaying global and local contingencies that impact upon women activists' understandings of the viability of political activity at particular points in time. Analysis that aims to foreground the contingent aspect of political agency ultimately enables a closer appreciation of how feminist politics can be shaped, re-shaped, enabled, and constrained by political imperatives. This lesson has a significance for the burgeoning field of scholarship on transnational political activity in all its many and varied guises.

Notes

1. Margaret Jolly, "Beyond the Horizon? Nationalisms, Feminisms and Globalization in the Pacific," *Ethnohistory*, 52 (2005): 153.
2. Jude Howell, "Introduction," in *Gender and Civil Society: Transcending Boundaries*, ed. Jude Howell and Diane Mulligan (Abingdon, Routledge, 2005), 4.
3. Jindy Pettman, *Worlding Women: A Feminist International Politics* (Sydney: Allen and Unwin, 1996); Nancy Naples and Manisha Desai, ed., *Women's Activism and Globalization: Linking Local Struggles and Transnational Politics* (New York: Routledge, 2002); Peggy Antrobus, *The Global Women's Movement: Origins, Issues and Strategies* (London: Zed Books, 2004); Myra Marx Ferree and Aili Mari Tripp, ed., *Global Feminism: Transnational Women's Activism, Organizing, and Human Rights* (New York: New York University Press, 2006); Marianne Braig and Sonja Wolte, ed., *Common Ground or Mutual Exclusion? Women's Movements and International Relations* (London: Zed Books, 2002); Jude Howell and Diane Mulligan ed., *Gender and Civil Society.*
4. Karen M. Booth, "National Mother, Global Whore, and Transnational Femocrats: The Politics of AIDS and the Construction of Women at the World Health Organization," *Feminist Studies* 24 (1998): 120.

5. Nadjes S. Al-Ali, "Gender and Civil Society in the Middle East," *International Journal of Feminist Politics* 5 (2003): 224; Sonja Alvarez, "Advocating Feminism: The Latin American Feminist NGO 'Boom,'" *International Feminist Journal of Politics* 1 (1999): 181–209.
6. Jutta Joachim, "Framing Issues, Seizing Opportunities: The UN, NGOs and Women's Rights," *International Studies Quarterly* 47 (2003): 247–74; Jutta Joachim, "Shaping the Human Rights Agenda: The Case of Violence Against Women," in *Gender Politics in Global Governance*, ed. Mary K Meyer and Elizabeth Prügl (Lanham, MD: Rowman & Littlefield Publishers, 1999), 142–60; Karen Brown Thompson, "Women's Rights are Human Rights," in *Transnational Social Movements, Networks and Norms*, ed. Sanjeev Khagram et al. (Minneapolis, University of Minnesota Press), 96–122; Jacqui True and Michael Mintrom, "Transnational Networks and Policy Diffusion: The Case of Gender Mainstreaming," *International Studies Quarterly* 45 (2001): 27–57.
7. Naples and Desai, *Women's Activism and Globalization*, 34, 34–41; see also Jennifer Bickham Mendez, "Creating Alternatives from a Gender Perspective: Transnational Organizing for Maquila Workers' Rights in Central America," in *Women's Activism and Globalization*, ed. Naples and Desai, 121–41; Brooke Ackerly, "Women's Human Rights Activists as Cross-Cultural Theorists," *International Journal of Feminist Politics* 3, no. 3 (2001): 311–46; Elizabeth Friedman, "The Effects of 'Transnationalism Reversed' in Venezuela: Assessing the Impact of UN Global Conferences on the Women's Movement," *International Journal of Feminist Politics* 1 (1999): 357–81.
8. Shamima Ali in discussion with the author, Suva, March 2002; see also Jaqueline Leckie, "The Complexities of Women's Agency in Fiji," in *Gender Politics in the Asia-Pacific Region*, ed. Brenda Yeoh et al. (London: Routledge 2002), 156–79; Margaret Jolly, "Beyond the Horizon," 138–66.
9. Vanessa Griffen, *Women, Development and Empowerment: A Pacific Feminist Perspective, Report of a Pacific Women's Workshop, Naboutini, Fiji, March 23, 1986* (Kuala Lumpur: Asian and Pacific Development Centre, 1987), 6.
10. Richard Falk, "Global Civil Society: Perspectives, Initiatives, Movements," *Oxford Development Studies* 26 (1998): 99–111; Richard Falk, *On Humane Governance: Toward a New Global Politics* (Cambridge: Polity, 1995); Mary Kaldor, *Global Civil Society: An Answer to War* (Cambridge: Polity, 2003); John Keane, "Global Civil Society?" in *Global Civil Society 2001*, ed. Helmut Anheier, et al. (Oxford: Oxford University Press, 2002), 23–47; John Keane *Global Civil Society?* (Cambridge, Cambridge University Press, 2003); David Held, *Democracy and the Global Order: From the Modern State to Cosmopolitan Governance* (Stanford: Stanford University Press, 1995); David Held, "Democracy and Globalization," in *Re-imagining Political Community: Studies in Cosmopolitan Democracy*, ed. Daniele et al. (Stanford: Stanford University Press, 1998), 11–27; Daniele Archibugi, "Principles of Cosmopolitan Democracy," in *Re-imagining Political Community: Studies in Cosmopolitan Democracy*, ed. Daniele Archibugi et al. (Stanford: Stanford University Press, 1998), 198–232.
11. Donald Denoon, "New Economic Orders: Land, Labour and Dependency," in *The Cambridge History of the Pacific Islanders*, ed. Donald Denoon et al. (Cambridge:

Cambridge University Press, 1997), 218–52; Stewart Firth, "Colonial Administration and the Invention of the Native," in *Cambridge History*, ed. Denoon et al., 253–88; William Sutherland, *Beyond the Politics of Race: An Alternative History of Fiji to 1992*, Political and Social Change Monograph No. 15 (Canberra: RSPAS, ANU, 1992); Robbie T. Robertson and William Sutherland, *Government By The Gun: The Unfinished Business of Fiji's 2000 Coup* (Melbourne: Pluto, 2001); John Kelly and Martha Kaplan, *Represented Communities: Fiji and World Decolonization* (Chicago: University of Chicago Press, 2001).

12. Some might expect that as part of a worldwide, faith-based organization underpinned by Christian ideals, the YWCA could be unproblematically viewed as a conservative actor within the realm of women's organizing, no different from the various other faith-based women's groups operating in Fiji at this time. However, even though Christian tenets are a significant facet of YWCA activities around the globe, an increasingly ecumenical attitude began to develop within the World YWCA during this period as the organization demonstrated its commitment to women of other faiths or indeed of no faith. Similarly, examination of the resolutions passed by the YWCA World Council since that body's establishment in 1894, indicate that as the international scope of the organization expanded beyond its European origins, there was increased willingness to consider how issues related to social justice, peace, disarmament, development, and discrimination were experienced in different ways by women around the globe. Indeed, during the 1960s and 1970s, undoubtedly informed by its expanding global membership, the World YWCA began to adopt a more politically engaged and internationally focused perspective on women's needs than had been evident in previous decades (see World YWCA, *World YWCA Statements of Policy: 100 Years of Forward with Vision* (Geneva: YWCA, 1995).
13. *Fiji Times*, April 29, 1965.
14. Fiji YWCA, *Public Affairs Committee Record Book*, 1973.
15. Amelia Rokotuivuna et al., ed., *Fiji: A Developing Australian Colony* (North Fitzroy: IDA, 1973).
16. Claire Slatter, *Women Together: Report of the 3rd National Convention of the YWCA of Fiji September 10–13, 1976*, Suva (Suva: YWCA, 1976).
17. This conference inspired the foundation of the Nuclear Free and Independent Pacific Movement, which continues as an active organization to this day.
18. United Nations International Women's Year Secretariat, *Meeting in Mexico: World Conference of the International Women's Year* (New York: Center for Economic and Social Information/OPI, 1975), 37.
19. Kate Moore, *Report: United Nations International Women's Year Conference and Tribune: June–July 1975, Mexico City* (Canberra: ACFOA, 1975) 14.
20. Vanessa Griffen, *Women Speak Out! A Report of the Pacific Women's Conference. October 27–November 2* (Suva: Pacific Women's Conference, 1975); Bengt Danielsson, "Pacific Women Speak Out in Copenhagen," *Pacific Islands Monthly* 1973 (October), 21–22.
21. Vanessa Griffen, *Women Speak Out!*, 11.

22. UNESCAP, *Draft Report of the Subregional Follow-up Meeting for Pacific Women on the World Conference of the United Nations Decade for Women, Suva, Fiji October 29 to November 3, 1980* (Suva: 1980).
23. Amelia Rokotuivuna in discussion with the author, Suva, March 2002.
24. Yoko S. Ogashiwa, *Microstates and Nuclear Issues: Regional Cooperation in the Pacific* (Suva: Institute of Pacific Studies of the University of the South Pacific, 1991).
25. When voiced at the international women's conferences, these demands caused great disquiet amongst delegates from industrialized nations. In 1975, Ambassador Barbara White branded these types of protest attempts to divert attention away from women's issues and an "unnecessary politicization" of conference debate (United Nations International Women's Year Secretariat, *Meeting in Mexico*, 27). At the 1980 conference, efforts to define a global perspective of women's status again broke down as the same tensions emerged and intergovernmental deliberations were bogged down by debate on the establishment of the NIEO, the continuing policy of apartheid in South Africa, and the status of Palestine in the Middle East.
26. Vanessa Griffen, *Women, Development and Empowerment*, 6.
27. Ibid.
28. Shamima Ali in discussion with the author, Suva, April 2002.
29. Ibid.; Fiji Women's Rights Movement, *Herstory: A Profile of the Fiji Women's Rights Movement* (Suva: FWRM, 2000).
30. Shamima Ali, "The Women's Crisis Centre in Suva, Fiji," in *Women, Development and Empowerment*, ed. Vanessa Griffen, 37–44.
31. Shamima Ali, "The Women's Crisis Centre in Suva, Fiji"; see also Vanessa Griffen, "The Pacific Islands: All It Requires is Ourselves," in *Sisterhood is Global: The International Women's Movement Anthology*, ed. Robin Morgan (New York: Anchor Books, 1984), 517–24.
32. Myra Marx Ferree, "Globalization and Feminism: Opportunities and Obstacles for Activism in the Global Arena," in *Global Feminism: Transnational Women's Activism, Organizing, and Human Rights*, ed. Myra Marx Ferree and Aili Mari Tripp (New York: New York University Press, 2006), 7.
33. Public sector and welfare budgets were slashed, a new value-added tax was introduced, Fiji's currency was devalued twice in twenty-four months, and there were moves to deregulate wages and weaken labor organization in export industries such as garment manufacturing, a significant employer of women.
34. *Pacific Islands Monthly*, May 1994: 32.
35. 'Atu Emberson-Bain, "Women Poverty and Post-Coup Pressure," in *Tu Galala: Social Change in the Pacific*, ed. David Robie (New Zealand: Bridget Williams Books, 1992), 145–62; Zohl Dé Ishtar, *Daughters of the Pacific* (North Melbourne: Spinifex, 1994).
36. Ratu Telemo Ratakele, *Fiji Times*, May 2, 1995.
37. Margaret Jolly and Martha Macintyre, ed., *Family and Gender in the Pacific: Domestic Contradictions and the Colonial Impact* (Cambridge: Cambridge University Press, 1989); Mervyn J. Meggitt, "Women in Contemporary Central Enga Society, Papua New Guinea" in *Family and Gender in the Pacific*, ed. Jolly and Macintyre, 135–55; Joanna Schmidt, "Paradise Lost? Social Change and *Fa'afafine* in Samoa," *Current Sociology* 51 (2003): 417–32.

38. Margaret Jolly, "Beyond the Horizon?"
39. Ibid.; see also Brooke Ackerly, "Women's Human Rights Activists as Cross-Cultural Theorists."
40. Interview with Gina Houng Lee, Suva, April 2002.
41. Maila Stivens, "Introduction: Gender Politics and the Reimagining of Human Rights in the Asia Pacific," in Anne-Marie Hilsdon et al., ed., *Human Rights and Gender Politics: Asia-Pacific Perspectives* (London and New York, Routledge, 2000), 22; Margaret Jolly, "Women-Nation-State in Vanuatu: Women as Signs and Subjects in the Discourses of Kastom, Modernity and Christianity," in *Narratives of Nation in the South Pacific*, ed. Ton Otto and Nicholas Thomas (Amsterdam: Harwood Academic Publishers, 1997), 133–62; Vivien Cretton, "Cakobau's Sisters: Status, Gender and Politics in Fiji," *Working Paper No. 11, Gender Relations Centre* (Canberra: RSPAS, Australian National University, 2004); Eta Varani-Norton, "The Church Versus Women's Push for Change: The Case of Fiji," *Fijian Studies* 3 (2005): 223–47.
42. Kathryn Keck and Margaret Sikkink, *Activists Beyond Borders* (Ithaca: Cornell University Press, 1998).
43. Ursula O'Hare, "Realizing Human Rights for Women," *Human Rights Quarterly* 21 (1999): 364–402.
44. Keck and Sikkink, *Activists Beyond Borders*; Joachim, "Shaping the Human Rights Agenda"; Joachim, "Framing Issues, Seizing Opportunities."
45. Lois West, "The United Nations Women's Conferences and Feminist Politics," in *Gender Politics in Global Governance*, ed. Mary K. Meyer and Elizabeth Prügl (Lanham, MD: Rowman & Littlefield Publishers, 1999), 177–93.
46. As West notes, representatives from the Vatican, countries with a majority Catholic population, states headed by Muslim fundamentalist governments, and conservative Christian lobbies within the United States objected to the language used in many sections of the Platform for Action and in the preparatory conferences leading up to the 1995 Beijing Conference. See West, *op cit*, 189; see also Chilla Bulbeck, *Reorienting Western Feminisms: Women's Diversity in a Post-Colonial World* (Cambridge, Cambridge University Press, 1989), 189.
47. Gertrude Mongella cited Hilkka Pietilä, and Jeanne Vickers, ed., *Making Women Matter: The Role of the United Nations* (London: Zed Books, 1999), vii.
48. Krysti Justine Guest, "Activist," in *Back to Basics from Beijing: An Australian Guide to the International Platform for Action*, ed. Suzette Mitchell and Rima Das Pradhan (Deakin: ACFOA, 1997), 112.
49. United Nations Commission on the Status of Women, 1995, Fourth World Conference on Women: Platform for Action, http://www.un.org/womenwatch/daw/bejing/plat1.htm, paragraphs 16 and 18 (accessed February 6, 2008).
50. Bulbeck, *Reorienting Western Feminisms*, 176–79; Guest, "Activist."
51. Bina Agarwal, "From Mexico 1975 to Beijing 1995," *Indian Journal of Gender Studies* 3 (1996): 21–35; Bulbeck, *Reorienting Western Feminisms*, 171; Guest, "Activist," 110.
52. 'Atu Emberson Bain, ed., *Sustainable Development or Malignant Growth* (Suva: Marama Publications, 1994); Claire Slatter, "Banking on the Growth Model? The

World Bank and Market Policies in the Pacific," in Emberson-Bain, ed., *Sustainable Development*, 17–36.

53. A two-year period of consultation begun in the mid-1990s saw a new constitution formulated for the country, which created more equitable electoral structures, and for the first time established a Bill of Rights for Fiji's citizens.
54. Aside from asserting their defense of indigenous paramountcy, the coup plotters claimed they were attempting to reassert the authority of their regional chiefly confederacy with its traditional center located on the island of Bau. They argued that the traditional authority invested in the Bauan chiefs had been undermined by the ascendancy of another regional grouping, which had benefited from its close ties with Fiji's imperial governors, and continued to "stand at the helm of Fiji's politics" in the postcolonial era. See Jon Fraenkel, "The Coming Anarchy in Oceania? A Critique of the 'Africanization of the South Pacific Thesis," *Commonwealth and Comparative Politics* (2004): 301, http://apseg.anu.edu.au/exec/LAFIA_Pacific/08%20 PEB/fraenkel_africanisation_AUSPAC.pdf (accessed February 18, 2008).
55. Robertson and Sutherland, *Government by the Gun.*
56. FWRM, *FWRM 1986–2001.*
57. FWCC, *Pacific Women Against Violence* 5 (September 2000): 6; (April 2001): 6; (June/July 2001).
58. Imrana Jalal, unpublished interview with fem'Link Suva, October 2002; see also Regional Rights Resource Team, *Report on the Presentation of the First PIC Country Report to UN CEDAW (Government of Fiji Is.)* (Suva: UK-DFID-Pacific RRRT, 2002).
59. New Zealand Institute of Economic Research cited the "Latest Coup to Take Familiar Toll on Fiji Economy," *Fijilive*, February 2, 2007, *Pacific Island Report*, http://archives.pireport.org/archive/2007/february/02%2D02%2Dfj02.htm (accessed February 18, 2008).
60. Christy Harrington, "'Marriage' to Capital: the Fallback Positions of Fiji's Women Garment Workers," *Development in Practice* 14 (2004): 495–507.
61. Ibid.
62. Regional Rights Resource Team, *Right Hia: A Regional Rights Resource Team Newsletter* 1, January–March 2002.
63. Laisenia Qarase, cited in *Fiji Times*, November 2, 2002.
64. Claire Slatter in discussion with the author, Suva, April 2002.
65. Verónica Schild, "New Social Citizenship in Chile: NGOs and Social Provisioning under Neo-Liberalism," in *Gender Justice, Development and Rights*, ed. Maxine Molyneux and Shahra Razavi (Oxford: Oxford University Press, 2002), 172, 170–203.
66. Claire Slatter, "Treading Water in Rapids? Non-Governmental Organizations and Resistance to Neoliberalism in Pacific Islands States," in *Globalization and Governance in the Pacific Islands*, ed. Stewart Firth (Canberra: ANU E Press, 2006): 23, http://epress.anu.edu.au/globalgov_citation.html (accessed February 18, 2008).
67. VoreqeBainimarama,StatementofFijiCommanderBainimarama,December5,2006, *Pacific Islands Report*, http://archives,pireport.org/archive/2006/december/12%D 12%2Dst1.htm (accessed April 11, 2007); see also Ratu Joni Madraiwiwi, "Mythic Constitutionalism: Wither Fiji's Course in July 2007," *Workshop Paper* (Canberra:

State Society and Governance in Melanesia and the Pacific Centre, ANU College of Asia and the Pacific, ANU, 2007), http://rspas.anu.edu.au/papers/melanesia/conference_papers/0706_FijiCoup_Madraiwiwi.pdf (accessed February 23, 2008).

68. Imrana Jalal cited in *Daily Post*, December 14, 2006; the electronic copy of Imrana Jalal's statement outlining threats made to her via the telephone can be found at "Pacific People Building Peace Fiji Update 9," http://www.ecsiep.org/index.php?option=com_content&task=view&id=690&Itemid=43 (accessed February, 26, 2008).
69. *Fiji Times*, January 3, 2007.
70. These include two alleged deaths in military custody, deportations of foreign nationals working in Fiji's media, and temporary international travel bans placed upon local NGO representatives. For early documentation of this situation see "Monitoring Human Rights Abuses Fiji Coup 2006," http://www.defendingwomen-defendingrights.org/pdf2007/Updated260107Monitoring_FijiCoup2006 Shortversion.pdf (accessed February 25, 2008); see also SBS, "Fiji: After the Coup," *Dateline*, August 8, 2007, http://news.sbs.com.au/dateline/fiji_after_the_coup_130818 (accessed August 13, 2007); *Fiji Times*, December 14, 2006; February 26, 2006; March 8, 2007; *Fijilive*, July 17, 2007, Madraiwiwi, "Mythic Constitutionalism."
71. Personal communication with Women's Activist, Suva, February 2007. These differing responses to the coup reflect a broader split within civil society in Fiji with some organizations perceiving the military's actions as an assault on democratic values and other groups viewing the intervention as aiming to correct long-standing social inequities in Fiji. For a more extended examination of this situation, see Madraiwiwi, "Mythic Constitutionalism."
72. Virisila Buadromo cited "Fiji After the Coup," *SBS Dateline*. This view was reiterated personally to the author in the early months of 2007 by a number of women activists working in Suva with one women commenting that it would be plainly "naïve" to antagonize the military in the current context.
73. Pettman, *Worlding Women*, 212.
74. Uta Ruppert cited Peggy Antrobus, *The Global Women's Movement: Origins, Issues and Strategies* (London: Zed Books, 2004).
75. For accounts of the negative impact of transnationalism upon women's organizing, see Elizabeth Friedman, "Transnationalism Reversed"; see also Annelise Riles, *The Network Inside Out* (Anne Arbor, MI: University of Michigan Press, 2001).

CHAPTER 12

Reclaiming Pacific Island Regionalism

Does Neoliberalism Have to Reign?

Claire Slatter and Yvonne Underhill-Sem

Regionalism has always been a part of Pacific Island political solidarity.[1] The regionalism of intergovernmental organizations has been about more than simply "the creation of regional capacity."[2] One of its hallmarks has been its effectiveness in politically organizing Pacific Island states to collectively resist powerful outside interests that pose threats to Pacific Island interests. Nor has regionalism been the exclusive preserve of governments or states. Regional solidarity among peoples' movements has as long a history in the Pacific as intergovernmental regionalism. This solidarity has included movements for political independence or sovereignty, together with workers' and women's rights movements, environmental movements, and mobilization by Pacific churches, trade unions, and NGOs in support of peoples' struggles for freedom and justice. Regional solidarity has also been a key element in movements against nuclear testing, nuclear bases, and the transhipment and/or dumping of nuclear wastes. Over the last three to four decades, NGOs and social movements in the region have not only exerted pressure on independent Pacific Island governments to support their various struggles in defense of Pacific interests, they have also often challenged governments and political elites arrogating to themselves the exclusive right to speak for the region.[3] In sum, Pacific regionalism has reflected political solidarity both among Pacific Islands states, and among peoples of the Pacific organized in social movements, and has often seen a convergence in their respective agendas, especially in matters involving external political interests detrimental to Pacific Island ones.

In recent years, however, regionalism has taken a new turn, driven by neoliberal rationalities that are deeply embedded in the promotion and planning of regional economic markets that primarily serve external interests. The reconceptualization and re-creation of regionalism in a neoliberal frame has significant long-term implications for the livelihood options, development prospects, quality of life, and general well-being of Pacific Island people, especially women.

Drafted mostly by non-Pacific Islander men, "New Pacific Regionalism" is aimed at "deepen[ing] cooperation and integration among Pacific Island countries."[4] It is designed by the donors to facilitate the primary objective of opening up consumer, resource, investment, and labor markets in the Pacific to foreign suppliers of goods and services, under the banner of economic reform and good governance. Like the trade agreements with which they are linked, they are being negotiated and agreed to by Pacific Island states at the regional level without prior public debate or reference to elected representatives of people in national parliaments. In addition, despite the development rhetoric in which these new agreements are couched, and assertions about treasuring the diversity of the Pacific and honoring its cultures, traditions, and beliefs, the agreements being forged will in fact serve to undermine both traditional social and economic systems and values from which all Pacific people benefit. It will also be to the detriment of prospects for equitable and sustainable development in the region, from which Pacific women are being increasingly distanced.

This chapter reflects, from a gendered perspective, on the substitution of political regionalism by the new regionalism of market integration in the Pacific. It considers some of the implications of the new regionalism, and recent endeavors by people's organizations and movements to reclaim political regionalism in defense of Pacific Island peoples' long-term livelihood and cultural interests. It also reflects on the prospects offered by new regionalism for improving human rights and especially women's human rights or gender justice. In particular, it finds that gender inequality remains prevalent in the Pacific Islands. This is despite the ratification of CEDAW by a majority of Pacific Island states,[5] and repeated commitments by governments to the Pacific Platform for Action for the Advancement of Women (1994), the adoption of gender policies by CROP (Council of Regional Organizations in the Pacific) agencies, and the growing effectiveness of regional gender units in the two leading regional intergovernmental institutions, the Pacific Islands Forum Secretariat (PIFS) and the South Pacific Community (SPC). The inclusion of gender equality as one of fifteen strategic objectives of new regionalism's blueprint, the Pacific Plan, suggests that women have a stake in its implementation and Pacific feminists may engage with the Pacific Plan from this standpoint. Yet beyond perhaps broadening labor market access for trained nurses, and even this benefit has significant costs for labor-exporting countries, the new regionalism of market integration offers few prospects for improving the lives and standard of living of the majority of Pacific women.

The Pacific Plan and New Pacific Regionalism: A Neoliberal Framework for Regional Market Integration

In April 2004, Pacific Island Forum leaders gathered in Auckland for a special meeting to discuss the report of a review of the Forum by an Eminent Persons Group (EPG). Here, "a new vision" for the region was agreed upon–one that, in the words of Samoan Prime Minster Hon Tuilaepa Aiono Sailele Malielegaoi, emphasized "guaranteeing for our people free and worthwhile lives."[6] To give effect to their vision they called for the development of a "Pacific Plan for Strengthening Pacific Cooperation *and Integration*." This plan would aim to promote economic growth, sustainable development, good governance, and security—the four priority areas agreed to by the Forum Island leaders. According to the Samoan Prime Minister, the plan that was subsequently developed was intended to

> deepen cooperation and integration among Pacific Island countries and to establish where our people might gain the most through the pooling of resources of governance and the aligning of our policies. This endeavour might take us well beyond current levels of regional cooperation *and into a new phase of regional integration–a Pacific union of as yet unknown dimensions.* We want practical benefits for our people, and we want to retain the best of our traditions and cultures. But we also want initiatives which will transform our Pacific into a dynamic and progressive region capable of meeting the challenges of modernity and globalisation.[7]

In 2005, a joint Asian Development Bank (ADB) and Commonwealth Secretariat (CS) project on developing and implementing the Pacific Plan was tasked with providing a cost-benefit analysis of a new ("deeper") Pacific regionalism. The resulting report, entitled *Toward a New Pacific Regionalism*,[8] provides Pacific Island states with a roadmap for moving beyond the existing regionalism (of intergovernment meetings and regional endeavors in the provision of services) toward meeting what are stated as the region's "fundamental challenges," namely, "easing capacity constraints for governments *through increased provision of services*" and "creating economic opportunity for Pacific citizens *through increased market integration*."[9] Some of the services identified as needed but hampered by capacity constraints are clearly ones that are required for better implementation of reform commitments. Regional market integration was promoted, through a broadened PACER (Pacific Agreement on Closer Economic Relations), with investment, services, and labor mobility (something that the Forum Island countries, FICs, are most interested in) added to free trade in goods. This envisions bringing tangible, quantifiable, economic benefits to the region's citizens. The report also proposes a binding legal instrument involving trade, aid, and governance commitments for the FICs, citing ECOWAS (Economic Community of West African States) and MERCOSUR (Southern Common Market) as examples of successful binding regional cooperation models.

We discuss the ADB/CS report in some detail as it provides insights into the political and economic thinking behind the new Pacific regionalism. Club Theory, which is drawn from economics and applied to military alliances, international organizations, and cross border infrastructure and services, is curiously drawn upon in the ADB/CS report to reconceptualize sovereign states as "clubs." Since clubs are supposed to satisfy two "essential conditions" (to be "self-sustaining" and "provide a large enough pool of net benefits for each of its members")[10] and it could be argued that several of the Forum Island states are not independently self-sustaining in economic terms, it is suggested that micro-states do not qualify for sovereignty. Helen Hughes has made similar arguments at length.[11] While club theory may be useful for analyzing regional endeavors, the summary analyses of existing regional initiatives in the report do not appear to draw on the framework, and the lessons apparently learned from club theory appear to be only marginally related to the facts of the cases cited.

The language used in the report gives away the report's subtle neoliberal bias. The notion of *"essential sovereign functions"*[12] resonates with the delineated first functions of states theorized in World Bank governance literature, but narrows state functions to just two: "formulating and enforcing appropriate national policies" and "providing essential services such as health, education and policing."[13] The "erosion of *effective sovereignty*" (defined as the ability to carry out policies governments have "chosen for themselves") makes Forum Island states only "nominally sovereign," according to the report.[14] Hence, the effectiveness and validity of states is judged by how well they are able to implement the (reform) policies they have 'chosen' to put in place.[15] The reference to Pacific Island states as sovereign clubs ("created with the support, recognition and aid of the international community" even though they were "frequently subeconomic in size")[16] is ahistorical, taking no account of Pacific Island states' colonial history and/or the independence struggles from which they emerged.

Fourteen regional initiatives are proposed in the report. These are considered likely to yield high benefits (with costs and benefits for each estimated in dollar value) under the four Pacific Plan challenge areas. They include: a regional economic and statistical technical assistance facility to strengthen and supplement the PFTAC (Pacific Financial Technical Assistance Centre); regional capacity to assist customs officials collect revenue; a regional ombudsman; a regional panel of auditors; increased (temporary) labor market access to Australia and NZ; a regional aviation safety office, a joint purchasing facility for petroleum products, enhanced transparency/harmonization of fisheries access arrangements; liberalization of telecommunications markets; a regional nurse training facility; a regional sports institute; a regional statistical office; a regional body to protect intellectual property; and a regional training facility to provide civilian police training for international peacekeeping as well as for national service. Agreement on these regional initiatives is expected to have to overcome "considerable opposition" as, even though the benefits from both the governance initiatives and labor mobility will be shared by many, the "few losers" are often "well-organized, vocal, and in a position to effectively oppose reforms."[17]

All the report's proposed regional initiatives are reflective of the managerial audit culture associated with the reconfiguration of state and regional authority as the contradictions of neoliberalism at the national level become apparent at the regional level. Most involve the technical tracking of money (customs duties and taxes), communications, transport, and energy (aviation safety, petroleum, and telecommunications), mobile natural resources (fish), and trained people (workers, nurses, and sportspersons). Clearly missing are initiatives aimed at developing sustainable livelihoods. More importantly, these initiatives seem to ignore existing asymmetries among and within Pacific Island states—Pacific people do not all enjoy high levels of education, women as a group are still subordinated to men as a group, and life in urban centers is vastly different to village life where the majority of Pacific Islanders still live.

The report proposed that a legally binding agreement be negotiated among all Forum countries, establishing mutual obligations. That the negotiation will be between donor states within the Pacific Islands Forum (specifically Australia and New Zealand) and Pacific Island member states is quite clear from the proposal that all Forum *Island* governments make a commitment or binding agreement to good governance, in return for a renewable five to ten year aid and trade agreement. Three dimensions are highlighted to underscore the mutuality of obligations, which is what Australia and NZ will have to provide, to ensure a win-win outcome.

- *Aid commitments*: The report puts the case for continued aid to the Forum Island Countries. It says stability, continuity, and predictability are more important than the volume of aid *per se* but that additional resources for Pacific Plan initiatives, which should be met on an equal sharing basis by Australia and New Zealand, should supplement significant and guaranteed bilateral aid flows. It proposes that Australian and New Zealand aid to the region should reach 0.08 percent of their GDP, and that 25 percent of their total development budget should be allocated to Forum Island Countries.[18]
- *Trade commitments*: The report argues that trade should centre on a package of opportunities for "gainful employment for trained FIC nationals" through training and temporary movement arrangements through the region. This contrasts with the present situation of restricted movement of untrained Forum Island Country labor, and permanent and unrestricted movement of skilled labor to Australia and New Zealand, which works to the distinct advantage of the latter. In short, a managed trade and development approach to migration, with added resources for training facilities is proposed. Specifically, this means opening up labor markets in Australia and New Zealand and thereby employment opportunities for Pacific Island citizens, and establishing largely export-oriented regional training facilities for nursing, sports

and policing services to supply those markets. The proposed regional training facilities are to be aid rather than private sector funded, as in the Philippines, which is intended to ensure that the costs of educating and training this mobile labor will not only be borne by the supplying country.
- *Governance commitments*: To ensure that governance standards become a vital part of domestic economic life, the report proposes that clear means of financing obligations and bound commitments be made by FICs when negotiating with development partners.

A simultaneous, two-track negotiating process is recommended, with a range of concrete interventions such as implementation of the "highest yielding initiatives."[19] This first step is seen as a way to "build confidence in the process and . . . emerging partnership."[20] The second track is essentially the commencement of a process for negotiating a Pacific Plan or extended PACER agreement. In other words, the report is calling for the merger of a Pacific Plan with expanded PACER negotiations, which are seen as having if not very similar objectives then certainly very similar intentions and sharing an ideological position on regional integration.

The report argues that without a multifaceted trade and development agreement, the PACER negotiations (on a goods only agreement) are at risk of being unsuccessful in that a goods only agreement would primarily benefit Australia and NZ, with FICs bearing adjustment costs. While this is true, the early push to open negotiations on an expanded PACER, and to include investment and services as well as labor mobility (the part that Forum Island governments are most interested in) into the discussion in the belief that this will bring them some early gains, is problematic. In particular, it focuses on anticipated benefits from gaining market access in Australia and NZ (especially increased labor market access) without assessing or even noting the likely risks or costs of opening up Forum Island states' goods, investment and services markets under rules of reciprocity. The claim is indeed made that the Forum Island countries' greatest benefit from trade liberalization will not come from liberalized agriculture or industry, but from "the liberalized movement of people and the liberalization of services."[21] The report proposes that Japan be included in a Pacific free trade agreement since after the EPA (Economic Partnership Agreement) and PACER come into force, Japan will be the only major donor whose exports to the region will be subject to residual tariffs.

The report also calls for more resources to be given to the Pacific Islands Forum Secretariat to allow it to complete feasibility studies on the proposed regional initiatives, and the negotiations in track two. It is expected that the process of negotiating a substantial treaty arrangement could encourage a "perception" of regional bodies as "open to capture" by "donor interests" or the "international bureaucracy that manages them."[22] It is proposed that all Forum Island states have a representative based in Suva to have a voice in the decision-making and oversight body based at the Forum Secretariat.[23] This is seen as being a first step toward the eventual establishment of a 'Regional Senate.'

The report's arguments and proposals for regional initiatives are couched in a perspective sympathetic to Forum Island country interests. However, its single-minded focus on gains to be secured through strategic negotiation by Forum Island states with Australia and NZ under the rubric of the Pacific Plan and an expanded PACER is worrying. This is primarily because it does not examine the broader and longer term implications of region-wide market integration, specifically the implications of access to Forum Island country markets (for goods, services, and investment). It reflects a strategic approach of trying to secure some gains from a situation where everything is stacked against Forum Island states. Consequently, it is tantamount to taking a huge gamble with major risks. Further, the disembodied nature of discussions is hugely problematic in raising the visibility of particular groups of people, and in a distinctly gendered way.

There is no doubt that the fleshed-out Plan adopted by the Pacific Islands Forum Meeting in Port Moresby in October 2005 is essentially a road map for further trade liberalization in the region, under PICTA (Pacific Islands Countries Trade Agreement), PACER and the proposed EPA with the European Union. "Initiated, funded, promoted and broadly sculptured by the governments of NZ, Australia and Europe in particular"[24] this New Pacific Regionalism represents what Fry has referred to as "hegemonic regionalism."[25] What it overlooks and underestimates are tendencies toward what we might term "counter-hegemonic regionalism," indications of which include the recent democratic disruptions seen in Fiji, Solomon Islands, Tonga, and Vanuatu. These serve to lift the mat further on widespread practices of social violence that pervade the region. Most often directed toward women, social violence is the powder keg that cannot continue to be ignored if sustainable, democratic development and gender justice are to be realized.

Implications of the New Regionalism

Pacific regionalism specialist Greg Fry, in an analysis of three competing models of a redefined regional political community, raised questions about their "moral and political legitimacy" and political acceptability.[26] He suggested that the starting point for judging or assessing legitimacy is to ask the question, Who is Oceania for? And, as subsidiary questions, What does the community stand for as a set of values, practices and ideas? Who should be regarded as belonging to the community, and on what basis? Who can speak for it and determine its practice? Fry concluded, prematurely in our view, that in contrast to the Australian government proposal, and the Australian Senate Committee's proposal, the Pacific Eminent Persons Group proposal for a "more effective regionalism" had the most potential to gain the support of Pacific states, not least because it promised an "equal place at the table" and a more "inclusive community."[27] He acknowledged that it could be hijacked by Australia and redesigned to fit with the latter's "special responsibility to manage the region in the war of terror,"[28] but not that it may be harnessed to fit with and serve the broader agenda of economic and trade liberalization.

Elise Huffer,[29] in a substantive critique of the Pacific Plan, its origins, content and goals, reminds us that the Plan emerged from a review initiated by New Zealand Prime Minister, Helen Clarke. Huffer argues that it is "intimately tied to the redefining of the Pacific Islands Forum," a body which represents only heads of governments and states, does not "create space for wider discussion of important regional matters by the citizens of Forum Island countries,"[30] and whose Secretariat is "distant from the peoples of the region, as well as hierarchical and technocratic."[31] Huffer also recognizes the political implications of the Pacific Plan in setting

> an agenda for new levels of regional integration whereby Pacific island countries will gradually relinquish sovereignty over certain areas of governance, economic policy and security. As such, it sets the framework for a new political and economic order, even though the latter may be introduced incrementally.[32]

New Pacific Regionalism departs substantially from the autonomous, self-determining regionalism of earlier decades and is indeed an ideological cloak for the ongoing programme of liberalization that has been underway in the region since 1995, under the direction of the Pacific Islands Forum Secretariat. While rallying the support of Pacific Island states behind the vision of a Pacific Plan, New Pacific Regionalism works in effect to politically disorganize Pacific Island states and to replace an autonomously determined regional agenda with an imposed one. It also serves to obscure the main agenda of economic and trade liberalization. Challenging this agenda requires a critical appraisal of regional policy developments from the vantage point of ordinary Pacific Island people. In particular it needs to include Pacific Island women, whose historical exclusion from regional decision-making has remained unchanged, despite the ratification of CEDAW by a majority of Forum Island countries and the adoption of gender policies by most CROP agencies in the last decade.

Jane Kelsey[33] has analyzed some of the impacts of economic restructuring and liberalization that are already being seen in the region. Increasing economic insecurity and new labor market openings have made hundreds of families in Fiji reliant on the export earnings (remittances) of skilled nurses and unemployed soldiers, who have been leaving Fiji in droves to take up better paying jobs abroad. Remittance earnings are now a major source of national income in Fiji, constituting in 2006 almost 6.2 percent of GDP, according to the World Bank.[34] The high risks involved in undertaking contract work as armed security workers in the Middle East are offset by an attractive insurance policy, which makes the families of soldiers who die in service beneficiaries of handsome compensation payouts in U.S. dollars. The links between high risk, 'niche' labor markets for Fijian soldiers in the oil rich but war-torn regions of the Middle East and global economic/military/industrial interests on the one hand, and openings for southern providers of care work and neoliberal public policies in the North are evident. The social costs and insecurity associated with supplying labor to external markets under such artificially created conditions are significant, although they may tend to be discounted in the eager embracing of market openings and job opportunities abroad.

From research recently undertaken by one of the authors of this paper in Tonga and Vanuatu it is evident that liberalization is having unforeseen negative effects. The theoretical benefits of reduced import tariffs and wider consumer choices in food imports, for instance, have not brought improved health and well-being in Tonga. In Vanuatu, the benefits of investment liberalization in tourism are reaped by noncitizens.[35] A major unforeseen effect of the successful marketing of beachfront land by multinational real estate companies to foreign investors is the effective dispossession of custom landowners.

The rear guard action position being adopted by the Pacific Islands Forum Secretariat seems to be primarily focused on adjustment costs. Rather than defending Pacific self-determination, the position being taken appears to be "if you compensate for adjustment costs, we will happily commit to policy changes." Social impacts such as job losses are accepted as "adjustment costs," the de-humanizing and disembodying language of economics providing a convenient euphemism. However, it is recognized that such adjustment costs carry "increased risk of further alienating public opinion and elite opinion against increased integration."[36]

The Challenge from Social Movements and NGOs

It was from regional NGOs that the strongest criticism of New Pacific Regionalism, and specifically the Pacific Plan, came. In a statement issued in 2005, and signed by leading regional NGOs, the Plan was attacked for its 'empty' pronouncements about "treasur[ing] the diversity of the Pacific and seek[ing] a future in which its cultures, traditions, and religious beliefs are valued, honoured, and developed."[37] The NGO statement stopped short of linking the Plan to the main agenda of structural adjustment and liberalization. In July 2006, however, a gathering of NGOs in Nadi, organized by Oxfam NZ, raised concerns about the proposed Economic Partnership Agreement between Pacific ACP (African Caribbean and Pacific) states and the EU, and considered the findings of research undertaken in the region on the social impacts of liberalization. Participants at the meeting demanded that social impact studies be carried out before commencing negotiations on an EPA and any other trade agreement, particularly PACER. Attended by several women's NGOs, and the Fiji Nurses Association, which has been monitoring impacts on Fiji's public health system of the hemorrhage of experienced nurses from Fiji through avenues created by

Australasian (labor) recruitment agencies, a communiqué issued at the end of the meeting sent a clear message to Pacific political leaders:

> As civil society groups meeting in Nadi, Fiji, we believe that trade agreements must have just and equitable development at their heart. Genuine sustainable development—including economic, social, cultural, gender and environmental dimensions—must be the central pillar of these agreements. We are concerned that the proposed EPA in its current form will not fulfil these development objectives. To address this, there must be a stronger partnership between government and civil society in the Pacific, to ensure that all aspects of the EPA and possible alternatives are explored, to achieve the best outcomes for the peoples of the Pacific, both at national and regional levels.[38]

The coming together of Pacific NGOs for the first time to directly discuss trade liberalization and trade agreements, and their commitment to continuing to keep up the pressure on their governments to ensure that certain non-negotiable areas are not traded away, namely, ownership and use of customary land, cultural heritage, key public services, food security, and farmers' livelihoods, reflected a long overdue reclaiming of political regionalism by Pacific NGOs.[39]

Mindful of the fact that the EU had signed three bilateral fisheries agreements (with Solomon Islands, Kiribati, and FSM), thereby undermining the region's only real leverage in the negotiations, the conference press statement highlighted the need for solidarity among Pacific Island states in conducting these negotiations. Furthermore, it flagged the dangers posed by particular provisions that could find their way into the agreement. Included in the statement was the claim that:

> The Pacific is being short-changed. The European Union has promised to support development in the Pacific, but so far, these promises have not been fulfilled. . . . Pacific governments need to have solidarity when they negotiate for the Economic Partnership Agreement (EPA) with the European Union. . . . Particular provisions in the negotiations which could cause dangers to Pacific societies include the local impacts of foreign fisheries, unregulated tourism, lack of control over foreign companies, lack of government's right to regulate in the public interest, threats to public services such as water supplies, and pressures for alienation and foreign control of land.[40]

The Conference press statement also expressed concern about Australia and New Zealand making unfair demands on Pacific countries seeking accession to the WTO during bilaterals.

Engendering the Pacific Plan

The NGO critique did not fall on deaf ears. The evolution of the Pacific Plan since 2005 (in keeping with its projection as a "living document") has seen its inclusion of fifteen strategic objectives, aimed at addressing a broad range of issues and concerns, among them gender inequality. Strategic objective eight aims to improve gender equality by

> mainstreaming . . . gender issues throughout the other initiatives where appropriate, . . . the ratification and implementation of rights-based international and regional conventions and agreements and associated support for meeting, reporting and other requirements. . . . including the drafting, harmonisation and promotion of awareness of rights-based domestic legislation within the Pacific covering CEDAW on gender [and other stipulated international conventions].[41]

A number of other specific initiatives to support gender equality are identified in the Plan for immediate implementation, among them a focus on domestic, gender, and sexual violence in the police training initiative; incorporating gender impacts in cost-benefit analyses of regional activities; and strengthening statistical information systems in relation to sex disaggregated data provision. Meanwhile another initiative, aimed at increasing women's representation in national parliaments, is under implementation. Research has been jointly commissioned by the Forum Secretariat and UNIFEM on barriers to women entering national parliaments and a regional workshop has been held on strategies to raise women's parliamentary representation in line with commitments made by Forum Island countries. Attention to this issue is long overdue. In March 2005, the international feminist advocacy group, Women's Environment and Development Organization (WEDO) named six Pacific countries among the twelve states it dubbed the Dirty Dozen for not having a single woman member of parliament. The election of Lepolo Taunisila to the Tongan parliament later that year reduced the number of Pacific states identified for that dubious distinction to five.[42]

The engendering of the Pacific Plan, which we have revealed as a framework for deepening neoliberal reform and trade liberalization in the region, begs explanation. As explained in a Pacific Plan document, the issue of gender equality "has been recognized by Pacific Island leaders at the highest level," and the EPG report is cited for concluding that "Pacific institutions and processes need to be more gender sensitive and better acknowledge and encourage the participation of women in decision-making at all levels, as well as work toward the reduction and elimination of domestic violence, and the improvement of women's literacy and health." [43] The commitment to gender equality in the region is more than rhetorical. Gender policies have been adopted by all CROP agencies demonstrating one of the benefits of regional policymaking and monitoring of policy implementation. It is evidently intended that the Pacific Plan will include supporting countries in meeting their international commitments, for example, under CEDAW and the Convention on the Rights of the Child.[44] For at least a decade, the Pacific Islands Forum Secretariat has had a full-time (albeit aid-funded) gender advisor on its staff.

The ready inclusion of gender equality within a broader regional economic agenda that, in our view, will adversely affect the interests of a majority of Pacific Island women is rather ironic. As much as we might acclaim regional organizations for their gender policies and welcome the advantage this gives us to secure advances for women, we should recognize its limitations. It represents a narrow political perspective and legal–technocratic approach to advancing gender equality, one that is unlikely to achieve what feminists have come to call "gender justice." Moreover, it proposes to deliver gender equality in the context of deepening economic inequality at global, regional, and national levels as a result of neoliberal economic policies and free market trade policies. This disjuncture between an avowed commitment to gender equality on the one hand, and on the other, a disregard for the reality of growing economic inequality reflects the difference between feminist and multilateral state agendas. Therefore, while international feminist organizations call for both economic justice and gender justice, states and multilateral institutions prefer to treat poverty and gender inequality as discrete problems that can be 'fixed' without reference to their structural causes.

A recent strategic response by human rights organizations to the Pacific Plan effectively encourages the narrow approach of regional organizations. A seventy-page paper entitled *Ratification of International Human Rights Treaties: Added Value for the Pacific Region*, produced in November 2006 by the Regional Rights Resource Team (RRRT)[45] as part of a collaborative effort between the Pacific Island Forum Secretariat and the Regional Office of the High Commissioner on Human Rights (OHCHR), seeks to give direction to Pacific Island leaders and the Pacific Island Forum Secretariat on how they could give effect to the Pacific Plan's stated wish to elevate human rights as a core concern. While commending the Pacific Plan's attention to "addressing democracy and human rights, rather than predominantly focusing on economic growth,"[46] the paper's own focus was somewhat narrow in its primary concern with advancing civil and political rights, and its relative inattention to economic rights, or economic security and rights.

Among the rights that go unmentioned are the rights to a livelihood, employment, access to land for cultivation, and fair and just wages. While it is not generally surprising that such economic rights were sidelined, as they remain contentious and are indeed often challenged by proponents of the free market, it would have been appropriate to discuss economic rights in the context of economic security, which is discussed. Instead, the paper defined economic security in a way that fits comfortably with the neoliberal framework and the present macroeconomic policy environment in the region, that is, economic security concerns "access to resources, finance, and markets necessary to sustain acceptable levels of welfare and State power."[47] No mention is made of a fairer or more equitable distribution of resources or national wealth and income, nor of the importance of social safety nets for vulnerable groups of people in society. The theoretically greater access to resources, finance, and markets that are the promise of market liberalization is unlikely to reduce liberalization's negative social impacts in terms of increased income disparities and economic insecurity.

While discussing issues covered by the International Convention on Economic, Social and Cultural Rights (ICESCR), implicit reference is made to the right to development. In particular, there is explicit mention of the rights to education, health, work, and adequate standard of living, including food, clothing, and housing, and references to the poverty affecting 25 percent of the region's population and the poor conditions of many Pacific Islanders (measured by the percentage of the population with access to safe drinking water, and access to quality education). An obscure statement on the "opportunity for external and internal speculation on policies, which is always important to have in any Government"[48] does not appear to reflect any concern with developing self-determination, which would have been meaningful to state.

Embracing the opportunity presented by the Pacific Plan for advancing Pacific Island states' human rights commitments, is a valid strategy for advocacy, nonetheless it legitimates the main agenda of the Pacific Plan. There is an urgent need to examine the Plan's main agenda in terms of its likely gender impacts, and especially to consider what the wider and longer-term implications of economic and trade liberalization may be for Pacific Island women.

Conclusion

The antecedents of regional solidarity in the Pacific provide a critical perspective from which to understand contemporary calls for regional solidarity. In the early postcolonial period, the shared concerns of the leaders of newly independent Pacific countries were expressed as resistance to colonial interventions. NGOs and churches engaged in resisting continued colonial interventions in the region also developed distinctive regional identities. In this early period, the successful negotiation of nonreciprocal trading arrangements with former colonial powers was considered just dues for decades of economic appropriation from the colonies, even though the terms of reference were ultimately fraught with the contradictions for the small independent countries, dependant as they are always likely to be on the political and economic good will of larger metropolitan states.

In macrolevel political negotiations, regional solidarity has always been vital to securing the interests of Pacific Island states. Inherent in this process, dominated by male negotiators, was the disembodied practice of homogenizing the Pacific, with the imagined beneficiary of Pacific regional solidarity being, implicitly, male. Thus far, challenges to new regionalism have ignored gender concerns, dovetailing well with the disembodied rationalities of neoliberalism. Women's NGOs and feminist organizations in the Pacific have not yet taken issue with New Pacific Regionalism by examining its promises from a critical gender perspective. One of the promises of independence, from which political regionalism (which Pacific Island women within NGOs helped forge) sprang, was political and economic self-determination, which is at serious risk of being lost because of creeping new regionalism. On the other hand, for Pacific women of the twenty-first century, the promise of commitments signed onto by Pacific Island governments in Beijing and Cairo, and of CEDAW ratification, is women's full enjoyment of citizenship and human rights. Fulfillment of this promise demands both transformation of the gendered micropolitics of power that operate throughout the Pacific, and retention of traditional systems and practices, which help sustain social cohesion, equity, and access. The challenge is to reclaim Pacific regionalism from the clutches of neoliberalism and to build societies in the Pacific that are both economically just and gender just.

Notes

1. An earlier version of this paper was presented to a panel on "Feminist Movements in the Pacific Region" at the IAFFE Conference, Sydney University, July 7–9, 2006.
2. Richard Herr, "Pacific Island Regionalism: How Firm the Foundation for Future Cooperation?" in *Pacific Futures*, ed. Michael Powles (Canberra: Pandanus Books, 2006), 184.
3. Greg Fry, "Whose Oceania? Contending Visions of Community in Pacific Region-Building," Working Paper 2004/3 (Canberra: ANU, 2004), 11.
4. Hon Tuilaepa Aiono Sailele Malielegaoi, "The Future of Regionalism in the Pacific," *Annual Pacific Lecture (2005) of the Pacific Cooperation Foundation by the Prime Minister of Samoa and the (then) Chair of the Pacific Islands Forum* (March 2005), 3.
5. By 2005, all but four Pacific Island Forum states (Kiribati, Nauru, Solomon Islands, and Tonga) had become signatories to, or had ratified CEDAW. Fourteen years earlier, several Pacific leaders at the 1991 South Pacific Forum, in discussions of the "Report of a Seminar on CEDAW" held in Rarotonga in May that year, decried the imposition of western values (following a similar charge made at the seminar itself), asserted biblical teachings on the position of women, and claimed that there was no discrimination against women in their countries. See Jean Zorn, "Women, Custom & International Law in the Pacific," Occasional Paper No. 5, City University of New York, http://www.vanuatu.usp.ac.fj/journal_splaw/pal-dcosta-12.docpublications/Publications/Occasional_Papers.htm, 1999 (accessed February 20, 2008).
6. Malielegaoi, "The Future of Regionalism in the Pacific," 3.
7. Ibid; emphasis mine.
8. Roman Grynberg, *Towards a New Pacific Regionalism* (Manilla: ADB, 2005), http://www.adb.org/Documents/Reports/Pacific-Regionalism/vol2/vol2.pdf (accessed February 20, 2008).
9. Ibid., xix; emphasis original.
10. Ibid., xv.

11. See her article, "The Pacific is Viable," *Issues Analysis* 53, Centre for Independent Studies (December 2004): 2.
12. Grynberg, *Towards a New Pacific Regionalism*, 33; emphasis added.
13. Ibid.
14. Ibid; emphasis added.
15. Wesley-Smith notes the vastly different international environment today compared with that which facilitated the emergence of sovereign Pacific Island states, and the linking of sovereignty, for the first time, to performance-based criteria. See Terence Wesley-Smith, "There Goes the Neighborhood: The Politics of Failed States and Regional Intervention in the Pacific," in *Redefining the Pacific? Regionalism, Past, Present and Future*, ed. Jenny Bryant-Tokalau and Ian Frazer (Aldershot: Ashgate Publishing Limited, 2006), 121.
16. Grynberg, *Towards a New Pacific Regionalism*, 42.
17. Ibid., 148.
18. Ibid., 152.
19. Ibid., xxiv.
20. Ibid.
21. Ibid., 153.
22. Ibid., xxvi.
23. Ibid., 164.
24. Ron Crocombe, "Regionalism Above and Below the Forum: The Geographical/Culture Region, Asia Pacific and Others" in *Pacific Futures*, ed. Michael Powles (Canberra: Pandanus Books, 2006), 195.
25. Fry, "Whose Oceania?" 11.
26. Ibid., 5.
27. Ibid., 18.
28. Ibid.
29. Elise Huffer, "The Pacific Plan: A Political and Cultural Critique," in *Redefining the Pacific?*, ed. Bryant-Tokalau and Frazer, 160. See also Aroha Mead, *The Broader Pacific Plan, Tidying-up the Region: Commentary Prepared on the South Pacific Forum's Pacific Plan* (Wellington, Civil society groups throughout the Pacific region, 2005), for another critique.
30. Ibid., 159.
31. Huffer also records the interesting fact that the EPG, whose membership included Sir Julius Chan (Chair, PNG), Dr. Langi Kavaliku (Tonga), Bob Cotton (Australia), Teburoro Tito (Kiribati), and Maiava Iulai Toma (Samoa) as part of the review team, a reflection group, assistants who were all senior civil servants from NZ, and a support group whose members all came from the NZ Ministry of Foreign Affairs (and Trade). See Huffer, "The Pacific Plan," 158.
32. Huffer, "The Pacific Plan," 158.
33. Jane Kelsey, "Taking Nurses and Soldiers to Market—Trade Liberalization and Gendered Neo-colonialism in the Pacific," (paper presented to the 15th Annual Conference on Feminist Economics, Sydney, July 7–9, 2006).
34. Manjula Luthria, et al., *At Home and Away: Expanding Job Opportunities for Pacific Islanders through Labour Mobility* (Washington, DC: World Bank, 2006).

35. Claire Slatter, *The Con/Dominion of Vanuatu? Paying the Price of Investment and Land Liberalisation: A Case Study of Vanuatu's Tourism Industry* (Auckland: Oxfam New Zealand, 2006).
36. Grynberg, *Towards a New Pacific Regionalism*, 74.
37. Its signatories were: Council of Pacific Education (COPE), Disabled Peoples International (DPI), Fiji Women's Crisis Centre (FWCC), Pacific Women's Network Against Violence Against Women, Foundation of the People's of the South Pacific International (FSPI), Greenpeace–Pacific, South Pacific Oceanic Council of Trade Unions (SPOCTU), Pacific Concerns Resource Centre (PCRC), Pacific Conference of Churches (PCC), Pacific Foundation for the Advancement of Women (PACFAW), Pacific Islands Broadcasting Association (PINA), Pacific Islands Association of Non-Government Organizations (PIANGO), World Council of Churches (WCC)–Pacific, and World Wide Fund for Nature (WWF). All except FWCC are regional NGOs.
38. "Communique: Pacific Civil Society Meeting on Trade Negotiations, Nadi, Fiji, June 13–16, 2006," http://www.pacificplan.org (accessed February 20, 2008).
39. See Claire Slatter, "Treading Water in Rapids? Non-Governmental Organisations and Resistance to Neoliberalism in Pacific Island States," in *Globalisation and Governance in the Pacific Islands*, Australian National University E-Press (Canberra, December 2006), http://epress.anu.edu.au/ssgm/global_gov/mobile_devices/ch02.html (accessed February 20, 2008), for a fuller discussion of Pacific NGOs and resistance to neoliberalism in the Pacific Islands.
40. Ibid.
41. Pacific Islands Forum Secretariat (PIFS), *The Pacific Plan for Strengthening Regional Cooperation and Integration*, October 18, 2006, http://www.pacificplan.org/tiki-page.php?pageName=Pacific+Plan+Documents (accessed February 20, 2008).
42. *Pacific Beat*, University of the South Pacific 6, no. 1, February 27, 2006.
43. AusAid, "Gender and the Pacific Plan," in *The Pacific Plan: The Way Forward*, http://www.pacificplan.org/tiki-download_file.php?fileld+158 (accessed February 20, 2008).
44. Ibid.
45. OHCHR, *Discussion paper—Ratification of International Human Rights Treaties: Added Value for the Pacific Region*, November 28, 2006, initial draft by P. Imrana Jalal, Human Rights Advisor, Pacific Regional Rights Resource Team (RRRT/UNDP) for the OHCHR Regional Office for the Pacific, Suva.
46. Ibid.
47. Ibid.
48. Ibid.

CHAPTER 13

A Feminist Politics of Region?

Reflecting and Revisioning IR from Asia and the Pacific

Jindy Pettman

This chapter[1] reflects on a life lived in and around international relations, a life lived in and out of place. It does so in the context of both the discipline of International Relations (IR), and the region called the Asia-Pacific.[2] It asks what significance biography and nationality play in shaping academic research and personal politics; in particular, what it means to do feminist IR as an Australian, in the context of Asia and the Pacific.[3] Identity thus figures centrally—identity of the discipline and of feminist IR, and of feminism in Australia, in the region, and the world. So, too, does the notion of a feminist politics of location,[4] as I ask what pursuing feminism as an engaged practice means in terms of a feminist politics of region, at a time when domination relations operate so relentlessly in anti-feminist, militaristic, and exploitative ways.

Backgrounding

I have earned my academic living under many disciplinary labels over forty years. But my working life has been bookended with IR in the early and later years, and my initial IR training and experiences have been formative in all my work. At the same time, my engagement with (the subject matter of) IR did not spring fully-formed from my first university studies. Rather, it stemmed from my fascination with and misgivings associated with war, identity, belonging, and difference, which I now see as significantly shaped by my childhood and family experiences. These experiences are representative of Australian and international power plays and gender relations, which, in turn, became central to my research and teaching in my adult years.

My mother's family was early settlers[5] in eastern Australia; they were from Ireland and Scotland with a tradition of marrying out in each generation. In their rural, sectarian community, the only common meeting place, for men, was the rural fire-fighting brigade. That association proved fatal; when Australia declared war in World War I, the entire fire-fighting brigade volunteered in the name of King and Empire. My grandfather fought at Gallipoli, the archetypal foundation of the nation in men's blood on foreign soil. This is a long tradition in Australia, from the Sudan and Boxer rebellion in the nineteenth century to Iraq and Afghanistan today.[6] My grandfather returned injured and died in 1921, when my mother was a toddler. His brother died in France in November 1917. The war stories I was told were not the usual heroic ones—the recent rediscovery of letters from both men and a diary that my great uncle kept writing until just before his death has given immediacy to the disasters and the grief that marked my mother's growing up.[7]

War marked my father's family too. My father's father was German, living in Australia in 1914, escaping internment but subject to considerable nationalist attack and abuse, despite his own anti-militarism. War name changing gave us an anglicized family name, and a refusal of those with any memory of my grandfather or the German connections to speak to me about them. Nevertheless, silence does not mean absence, and the silences drew me to try to fill them in my imagination.

I was a war baby. My father left for (then) Dutch New Guinea shortly after I was born, and did not return home until well after the war ended, being involved in the demobilization of troops. My mother's war-shaped story, through her fatherless childhood with her farming and breadwinning mother who insisted that she go to university—one of only two women studying economics in the late 1930s—continued through her rapid rise in government departments and boards that channeled women into munitions factories and other war labor. After my birth, my mother returned to this work, until my father finally reappeared and insisted on the re-establishment of proper gender rules and the conventional division of labor, which returned her to home and housewifery.

Australia has a remarkably militaristic history for a small, geographically secure country that has only been invaded once, ending indigenous sovereignty. War and soldiering shadowed my family and my emerging political consciousness. These shadows and a somewhat sentimental humanism in my early teens led me to declare myself a pacifist and a socialist. Meanwhile, many migrants came to Australia fleeing war, violence, and exclusion based on minority political or dissident family associations. International conflicts can be mapped through the source countries of migration and refugees to Australia over the postwar decades. International identity markers continue to color conflicts within Australia, including recently through competing youth cultures and recreational violence in the Cronulla race riots of late 2005 between 'Australians' and 'Lebanese,' and conflicts between Kosovar and Serbian Australians at the declaration of Kosovan independence in February 2008. War and migration, identity and difference play through endless media, and political and academic debates about who "we" are, who is welcome here, and who is inevitably other. This reproduction of the national borderlines has in its latest manifestation, since 9/11, made Muslims of previously nationally designated migrants, and of near neighbors formerly marked by their Asian-ness, in complicated and contradictory deployment of terms like race, culture, and ethnicity. Now Asian difference is likely to be associated with insecurity, with threat and danger in terms of violent attack, and with religion in its more directly politicized guises.

Getting into IR

At school, history and geography drew me to difference in a country and decade seeking sameness. When I tried to demonstrate that nothing has been gained and much lost through wars, my female kin responded, Are you saying that my husband or father died for nothing? What appeared politically and morally obvious to me caused deep distress in those for whom I cared. At university in the early 1960s, I found people and politics more compatible. History was the logical choice. The accident of my joining a combined history and politics department at the University of Adelaide meant that I embarked on both. Together they fed my fascination with culture and with the problem of war. IR caught me, although its inattention to culture seemed strange to me. War was central; however, proffered disciplinary explanations fell a long way short on why the war option and the prerogative state could command such extraordinary loyalty from men and women who would never practice or condone violence in their own lives or communities. My primary problem became why did (most) men fight? And (most) women (appear to) acquiesce? How could war be, or be made to be? One of my key teaching texts was Waltz's *Man, the State and War*. I took the "Man" of the title literally as Men; I saw women as capable of violence (and leadership), but more likely to be peaceful, assuming our socialization for and experiences of nurturing roles and responsibilities to be the primary reason for this. I was puzzled by the association of men with reason and women with emotion, seeing much of the world's and family troubles as due to (some) men's emotions—greed, anger, competition, and aggression among them.

Meanwhile in the mid-1960s war came closer through Australia's growing involvement in Vietnam. I cut my activist teeth in opposition to the Vietnam War through Australian involvement in the all-powerful U.S. and western alliance. I organized and argued with those who opposed all war, as I was still inclined to do, and those who opposed this particular war. My first lecturing position involved teaching IR and Australian foreign policy, and giving visiting lectures to the military, which did not necessarily conform to my stereotypes. My study was driven by the impulse to understand, so as to change, and my subject areas were chosen because of my personal and political investments in them. There was no chance of my adopting an 'objective' social science approach so (rhetorically) popular in the discipline at the time.

My IR studies came together with my activism in my initial choice of PhD topic (in IR, at the London School of Economics, in 1969). I proposed to study liberation movements in southern Africa, influenced by my growing links with anti-apartheid and anti-colonial solidarity movements. However, my thesis came to centre on Zambia, then recently independent, still surrounded by white-ruled states, and reluctant base to different liberation movements.[8] My focus shifted to ask why a recently decolonized African state should be expected to become a nation-state in the western tradition, and preferably developed in the liberal democratic capitalist form, when its own cultures and power relations, while clearly impacted by colonization and capital, were so different? The growing Marxist-influenced and international 'development of underdevelopment' writings came to my attention too late to seriously inform my thesis, but the writings of Fanon[9] and others pointed me toward deep, structured separation of colonized and colonizer, to the personal, psychic, and emotional investments in and manifestations of power and powerlessness, and the role of color and culture in border enforcement.

My thesis came to be about colonization, nation- and state-building, and the deep implication of history and the international in domestic politics. Taken less than seriously in IR, for reasons I saw as more to do with my subject than my gender and youth, I puzzled over why my colleagues thought that nationalism, development, race, and nation were not IR.[10] Meanwhile, my continued involvement in southern African solidarity movements further strained my pacifism. On the one hand, I was strongly drawn to the belief that no war is ever justified, and further that the use of violence in itself generates more violence. On the other hand, if there is no possibility of change through nonviolent means and the existing relations are themselves violent, are we not bound to act against injustice? Such struggling led me away from any apparently easy, taken-for-granted pacifism, to ask, When, if at all, is violence justified as a political option? This question continues to haunt me, even as its shape and texture have shifted over the years.

Leaving IR, Finding Feminism

Meanwhile, after returning to Australia, I shifted my attention to development studies and the South Pacific. I began pursuing research closer to home in Papua New Guinea and the British Solomon Islands, both edging toward and then quickly becoming independent in the mid-late 1970s. Here again the cultural call featured, as I tracked younger nationalists, almost all men, through constitutional hearings and inquiries into adapting education that took on spreading ideas of African socialism and critical development studies in, for example, articulating a Melanesian way. For me it was a special privilege and joy to see arguments about state formation, national identity, and development being played out on the ground. I have always found such engagements a reality-check, as good practice needs good theory and good theory needs be informed by, and indeed is, good practice. I was also delighted to be able to explore these issues with clear relevance to, and location in, the lives and experiences of 'ordinary' people; in arguments such as whether adapting education for those who would (it was hoped) stay in their villages would result in a bifurcated society and restrict access to western education, skills and resources to an urban based elite; or whether decentralization or socialism could work; and what kinds of community, economy, and polity were imaginable, and whether or how they related to culture and to local and community relationships.[11] What women had to say about these matters interested me, in the spirit of representation, and in recognition of the rather different investments they may have had on account of their (gendered) responsibilities. However, my professional and political associations remained overwhelmingly male-dominated, although my social and friendship circles were more mixed.

In the late 1970s, these experiences led to my administering the Canberra-based year of a PNG tertiary training program, which took me to mission-based primary teachers' colleges spread through PNG, and into villages with students doing teaching practice. I was struck by the similarities between Zambia and PNG in terms of colonial power relations and the anxieties and language around race. Later, accompanying my PNG students through outback Australia to visit Aboriginal education centers, I was struck with the knowledge that we too had colonization, service and extraction ports, impoverished hinterland communities, race lines, and raced sex. I had long been an advocate of Aboriginal rights, more in support of human rights, inclusive citizenship, and anti-racism than grappling with the ongoing trauma of colonization in Australia. This position was already unsettled by my involvement in teaching contemporary Aboriginal studies.[12] Lacking credentials in this area and taking advantage of team teaching, I gave lectures on colonization, race in international perspective, and (after a fight) on gender. Now I found myself in places where 'language' was still spoken and Aboriginal women took the time to educate me about their lives, including often as members of the stolen generations.[13] I felt keenly that my identity as Australian demanded recognition of and resolute solidarity with indigenous rights movements. I also recognized in these women, often older than I, something of the silences from my own past, of women left to hold communities and families together in the face of damage to or disappearance of their men. I was humbled by my realization that, for all I had lectured on the state, for example, these women had incisive and often painfully learnt knowledge of state power and its intricate workings on their bodies that I had only guessed at.

Another of my courses at this time was *Education and Developing Nations*, which focused both on development and on how to teach development in schools. The "how to" elements of working in education had its attractions, yet I returned from summer break in the late 1970s to discover the course had been retitled *Education in a Multicultural Society*, with an Australian (soft multicultural, teacher, and service provider orientated) intention. I had inadvertently become a culture expert who could teach about local and international culture and others, apparently (in the minds of the bosses) endlessly substitutable. Those others needed education, and we could learn nothing from them. In the Australian and near-regional context, we were to deliver policy options and training for the better management of them, or for getting them to manage themselves.

My branching out into these various designated studies areas was facilitated by their rapid growth in the 1970s. After many years of increasingly tired conservative rule, the Labor Party won federal government in 1972, with a broad platform in support of indigenous rights, migrant rights, women's rights, and social justice.[14] One outcome was the rapid growth in training courses in line with the new times.[15] As in Women in Development (WID) internationally, what began as critical politics often became social problems, and the response one of service delivery or social control. I tried to find ways to make my tasks more congenial to me, and less threatening or matronizing to my students. In addition, teaching or talking about "them" became even more complicated as they began to join the classroom, for example, as indigenous trainees in the then Department of Aboriginal Affairs, whose recruitment depended on their undertaking Aboriginal studies. In the process, I was learning a lot about working across cultures, about the ethics and politics of teaching about others, and the necessity to take responsibility for my own position and privileges.

In trying to hone my own craft, my own politics, I had many supports, increasingly in feminism. I had returned to Australia just in time to join the Women's Electoral Lobby (WEL) in its 1972 pre-election interventions, and had links with those women in earlier Vietnam and anti-racism movements who protested their marginalization and now embraced the renewed visibility of the women's movement.[16] New texts, often from the United States, circulated, and women's groups multiplied, with divisions between left feminists and those labeled radical feminists. Feminism began its push in the academy, especially in history, philosophy, and sociology, and in "women in politics," the latter debating the new phenomenon of femocrats and the pros and cons of working through existing power structures. Later, theory became another divide, underscoring difficult relations between feminist academics and the outside despite many feminist academics' links with the women's movement. At the same time, issues of race and culture simmered, although a number of 'race relations feminists' had close working relations with indigenous women[17] and others, with migrant women's struggles and organizations, while some women activists within these identity categories did call themselves feminist.

These labels and special hues reflected the political constituencies and bases of mobilization in Australia through the 1970s and 1980s. At the time, a close colleague and I wrote an article titled "Beyond Category Politics"[18] bewailing the tendency to find ourselves always a little out of place: bringing up race in women's groups, women in anti-racist and migration fora and, in Helen's case especially (though I was learning), disability in all of the above. Sexuality debates fuelled further divisions over lesbianism and gay rights. The emerging feminist literature on intersectionality strongly appealed to me. So too did writings and discussions around alliances and coalition politics, most readily available in Australia through 'women of color' collections, which came from the United States and Britain.[19]

For a while, in my teaching I had been adding women, in *the* lecture on Aboriginal women or migrant women, and giving examples of women's experiences of work or health or violence that were clearly different from men's. Finding feminist ways to work and write drew me into international feminist networks, and publications. They prompted me to grapple more critically with the idea of difference, and to articulate a feminist politics of location, which began by identifying myself as a white settler-state woman and feminist in Australia, in the context of the region and the West.[20]

Returning to IR

My personal/political journey had by then become a lengthy conversation and series of collaborations across different border lines. A consistent thread seems to be thinking and working around difference, the boundaries between 'us' and 'them,' and trying to think beyond particular sets of identity markers that confound attempts to act inclusively. These boundaries I came to see as lying at the deeper heart of the exclusions and grievances that go into making the outsider, against whom violence becomes thinkable, doable, and even heroic. It was this connection between identity: difference and large-scale political violence that led me back to war, and to IR.

In 1986, at the beginning of the International Year of Peace, I joined the new Peace Research Centre at the Australian National University (ANU). Its brief was not unlike IR, begun in 1919 to investigate the causes of war and conditions of peace, in the hope that there would not be another such war. The Centre's funding came because of political demands on the federal Labor government by the revived peace movement. That movement included a women's peace camp, undertaken in consultation with Aboriginal owners, outside the U.S. military base at Pine Gap. My affiliations with labor-inclined and grassroots women's and peace groups that were an influential constituency in establishing the Centre may have worked in my favor, along with the new political attention to women. My IR qualifications provided credentials in the presumed feeder discipline for peace studies. For me, it sounded the perfect mix of study-teaching-writing-practice applied directly to my own deep peace convictions and struggles. In reality, it was not so simple. The Centre was in a mainstream elitist research school, which disapproved of 'polemical' 'political' writing (apparently, my style). Its gender politics were depressing: I had only two other female academic colleagues in the entire research school, one, fortunately, a feminist.[21] I found myself subject to more scrutiny than in my previous academic workplaces, especially in the face of right wing political attacks on the Centre; for example, they accused us of being Soviet stooges working to destabilize the Pacific.

Yet under the Peace Research Centre brief, and while arguing constantly with my superiors about that brief, I did find the resources to support my academic and political peace work as a feminist. This included organizing the Women and Conflict in Asia and the Pacific conference in 1990, where Australian academic activists joined with activists from Pacific island states, including women from Bougainville, a province of Papua New Guinea then experiencing a bitter secessionist war. Opening speaker Cynthia Enloe had just published *Bananas, Beaches and Bases: Making Feminist Sense of International Politics*. Asking, Where are the women? Cynthia revealed that women are in international politics, often where we might not expect them, and women absent because they are women. She drew attention to the kinds of masculinity, and gender relations, necessary for international politics to function. She took seriously women's experiences of the international, confronting the question of whose experiences and interests the discipline admits, and whose it excludes. She demonstrated how the international affects women's lives everywhere, though differently for differently placed women. In so doing, she extended the feminist call that the personal is political to: the international is personal, too.[22]

In the process, Cynthia encouraged me to return to IR as a feminist, which I did in 1991. As a reward for my teaching the big first year IR course (529 students!) and teaching Australian Foreign Policy and International Relations to Department of Foreign Affairs and Trade (DFAT) in-service students, I was free to develop my own course. I quickly designed *Gender and International Politics*, which was the testing-ground for my later book *Worlding Women: a feminist international politics*, published in 1996.[23]

My return to IR was supported and energized by two rather different but not unrelated feminist communities. The first was the emergence of a transnational feminist movement, from the 1985 UN women's conference in Nairobi and especially through the process around international conferences on reproductive rights (Cairo 1992), human rights and violence against women (Vienna 1993), and the Beijing women's conference (1995).[24] With growing (though not united) visibility and voice, forging language, strategies and connections, this movement made women players in international politics, and gender (more ambiguously) a part of the international lexicon. The second was the huge mainstream International Studies Association's (ISA) recently formed Feminist Theory and Gender Studies (FTGS) section, a product of the (late) coming of feminism to IR.[25] Both these developments underline the crucial role that feminist networks, conversations, workshops, and conferences play in feminist knowledge making and in supporting feminist activist scholars working in less than supportive institutions.

FTGS also seeded and nurtured the creation of the *International Feminist Journal of Politics* (IFJP) and supported me and my co-editors Gillian Youngs and Kathy Jones. The journal cast grew to include other international feminists from a range of disciplines and working bases.[26] We had fascinating debates about what makes a journal feminist, and how to write and edit in feminist ways, and through FTGS and the journal I finally felt part of an intellectual community, making meanings that connected with struggles—in the academy and outside it—that mattered to me. In turn, the journal has nurtured and showcased the remarkable growth of feminist international studies and enabled transnational feminist connections and debates to flourish, even in the toxic post–9/11 landscape.[27]

Return to Region

For me, 1997 was a crucial year: I became *IFJP*'s first home base editor,[28] and I moved to Women's Studies at ANU as its director. For the first time, I had a congenial work base,[29] in a small feminist space shared with a significant contingent of graduate students. This move was also pivotal in a return to region, which had shimmered on the edges of my consciousness for years, but lost out between my Australian working base and my international and somewhat North American IR affiliations. That juxtapositioning had already led me to attempts at articulating what it meant to be doing IR as an Australian feminist; whether there was anything different about working from this region, which attending northern conferences and reading other IR feminists' writings suggested. This prompted new questions about my politics of identity, with whom I saw myself in conversation, and organizing. Increasingly, there seemed to be missing pieces alongside the local, national, North American, and global contexts.

I sought out feminist literature from the region, I went to more regional conferences on gender and migration, for example, and I built stronger links with feminists in the region. These links both concretized and complicated region for me. Moving around Hong Kong, Taipei, Kuala Lumpur, Singapore, and later Bangalore, Bangkok, and Seoul,[30] I was always aware of the generosity of those organizing and hosting us, and the enormous privilege of such travel, and of the dangers of academic tourism. Feminism was, and is, the interweaving thread of these engagements, the enabling connection. But feminism is never an innocent position or identity. It is never set and is always contingent on negotiations, remakings, and power relations among feminists, too. Difference is an easy (never easy) label for the kinds of travel, work, and meaning making for which my own research and politics call. It challenges us to constantly rethink what gender means in different places, to different feminists; what we have in common, what separates us, and how we can, if we can, work together. It tests the kinds of understandings I had found in international feminist networks and collaborations. I knew it was in region that I wanted to work, albeit with the overarching frame of the global increasingly pressing in on us all, and FTGS/IFJP, its counter-community.

It was within this context that I drew up my new research project. I had in mind a trilogy, beginning with *Living in the Margins* (1992), an Australian take in international context, then *Worlding Women* (1996), an international text written from Australia, and now to feminism in the region. I bravely entitled this project "A Feminist Perspective on 'Australia in Asia,'" seeking to participate in, as well as write, a feminist politics of region.[31]

I imagined the project as the year 2000 approached: the project sought to weave together the disparate though always already related dimensions of my previous work. "Australia" became a recurring puzzle—and responsibility. Its making was as much by international forces as local and national ones, including intensifying globalization processes.[32] Throughout the 1990s, as IR's center of gravity moved uneasily from war and state alliances to market and political economies, so had Australia's relations with region moved from battlefield to marketplace, approaching 'Asia' as competition or opportunity in a restructuring, neoliberal turn.

I began the project with questions related to Australia and the region: What do we make of region now that we are going global? What do we make of Australia's relations with region? Do economics now trump the political and strategic? And what about cultural difference? (Apart from providing all those cultural awareness training programs?). Whose Australia is seeking Asian engagement? On whose terms? Moreover, Who or what is Asia?

The primary question was, What difference does gender make? More precisely, What difference does feminist insight make? The main game of Australia in Asia was masculinist, even where there were voices that questioned statist security, naturalized market superiority, and alliance politics. Feminists, it seemed, were not authorities on Australian foreign policy, let alone defense or relations with Asia. Who, then, was left out of the dominant account?

Of course, it is not hard to find women here, including women politically and theoretically engaged in these debates. Moreover, feminists are players in Australian Asian relations, especially at the level of NGOs, in regional fora, and campaigns. Nor is it hard to find gender, although articulated as a variable or less often, as a category of analysis. Feminism, however, goes further, to reveal that all relations, all manifestations of power and identity, and borders and boundaries, are themselves gendered. All these rely for their own conceptualization and operation on certain gendered understandings and associations, and simultaneously reproduce gender difference.[33]

I was excited to be focusing on region. I hoped to go beyond the deconstruction and gendering of (conventionally drawn) region, to its re-visioning through feminist engagements with/in region. However, the project was no sooner articulated than it was disrupted. First, the characterization "from battlefield to marketplace" had to be re-written by adding "and back to battlefield again." East Timor, long a thorn in the very complicated relations between Australia and Indonesia and cause of strong Australian-based activism for East Timorese independence, erupted in 1999 in a courageous referendum and bloody aftermath. The violence forced Australian government reaction, for fear of instability and worse, to its near north. After decades of focus on home defense, and concern with Indonesian sensibilities, it led Interfet—the UN military intervention—to establish and maintain 'peace.' While under UN auspices and supposedly for humanitarian purposes, this intervention was represented in Australia in nationalist, masculinist, colonial, and, at times, racist ways, reviving old wounds and 'civilizational' divides. The familiar war story re-emerged, gendered as always—the heroic masculine hero, Australia; the stigmatized male villain, Indonesia; and the feminized, passive East Timor, awaiting rescue.[34]

Going Global: Making War/Making Gender

Still, East Timor appeared to be local, as did coups in Fiji and troubles in PNG. Together they were read as danger in 'our own back yard,' and as confirming the continued pertinence of our political geography and our ongoing colonial associations. Quite quickly, however, there was another, even more dramatic change in global politics, which swung the focus of Australian attention from the region back to global politics again.

The attacks of September 11, 2001 and the consequent so-called War on Terror shattered the existing local security priorities. Prime Minister Howard, a western, pro-American man to his boot heels (who was genuinely struck by the tragedy that occurred while he was visiting Washington, D.C.), affirmed allegiance to the United States and firmly lined up alongside Blair and Bush. Australia first went into Afghanistan, and then into Iraq as one of the so-called Coalition of the Willing. We were back again on the world stage, in military interventions far from home.[35] These moves reinforced Australia's primary identity as white and western, part of the American alliance, fighting for (neo-liberal) freedom. In an apparent trumping of the region, these commitments were made without consulting Asian allies and in language that threatened to further alienate them. Security, long in the service of the state and dominant interests, was further militarized, and re-racialized. Borders were hardened to defend against possible terrorists, and equally against refugees, asylum seekers, and suspect citizens at home. Patriotism was revitalized, becoming increasingly coercive, exclusivist, and masculinist. Boundaries were re-marked by religion, especially Islam. In the process, Australia was re-membered as Christian, capitalist, western; in danger at home and abroad, part of a coalition of the right (in all senses): beleaguered, brave, and ready for war.[36]

On September 11, 2001, I was in Halifax, Canada, at an exhilarating international workshop of feminist journal editors, where careful attention was paid to balancing northern and southern representation, issues of translation, and solidarity.[37] We stayed on, marooned, for a week within sight of an airport filled with planes diverted from landing in the United States, glued to the television. A month later, I was in Bangalore, India, at a conference on Asian feminisms. Most participants were Indian or other South Asian, with other Asian participants and very few nondiasporic feminists from "the West." At a session on 9/11 and its implications, speaker after speaker acknowledged the tragedy and pain of the attacks, but despaired at American exceptionalism, and its apparent refusal to acknowledge how many others in other countries were already dealing with large-scale violence and grief, including in situations in which U.S. arms, alliances, or interests were deeply involved. Fears of military retaliation and growing surveillance and discrimination against those identified as different (justified by later events) filled the room with deep foreboding and a sense of despair. The specter of Empire closing in on spaces, both national and international, that feminists and other progressives had struggled so long to open up, was palpable. Conversations throughout the conference reiterated the bodily impact of the international on us all, regardless of our different positioning in relation to global power plays and accompanying violences. They also underlined the necessity of western feminists to take responsibility for and act against what was being done in their (my) name.

Feminists neither doubted the gendered nature of the attacks and their consequences nor that our work as feminist scholars and activists would be made all the more difficult, as anti-terrorism became the order of the day. Yet the events of 9/11 seemed to disappear women from public view, apart from their role in the war story, to legitimize military intervention. It disappeared feminists too, who were presumed to have nothing useful to say. But feminist learnings about peace and war, interstate relations, and race making, were by then voluminous, and Internet networks especially sprang quickly into connection and critique.[38] They were followed by post–9/11 published collections, mostly strongly internationalist in focus and contribution. They brought together scholars, activists, and practitioners, and revealed many (not surprisingly) to be all of these at once. They analyzed the dichotomies that left either no room for negotiating or for most of us to find a place from which to speak. They refused both terrorism and the war option. They drew attention to other sites and kinds of violence. They scrutinized the war story and its dangerous consequences for women. They insisted on women's multiple roles and their agency for and against identity and state violence. They called on us all to be accountable for how we act, or fail to act, and for the consequences of those actions.[39] They also insisted that we not be used as reasons why others must fight, or to justify state violence. "Not in our name" again became one way of resisting the appropriation of women's supposed security interests and vulnerabilities of militarization and its hard-core state. Meanwhile, the main game seemed like a reversion, kicking over decades of feminist anti-violence and anti-war work.

I had returned to Australia, to the government's commitment to the War on Terror, first in Afghanistan, and soon (in rather less international company), in Iraq. Public opinion initially opposed military intervention in Iraq, although once it took place, many Australians felt obliged to get behind the troops. The difficulties of maintaining opposition to that intervention while resisting the accusation of betraying the troops,[40] or even of treason, brought back memories of our early opposition to the war in Vietnam. It was shattering to be living in a country that was again at war far from home, for reasons mostly to do with the American alliance and our government's conviction that our security was directly tied to our identity as white, western, and militarized. Yet life went on much as normal, politically, until years passed and the mounting toll in Iraq finally led to a turn against the Australian government. This opposition was based mainly on the failure of the intervention, the growing feeling that it could not be won and might be harming our interests and our reputation. With the bombings in Bali, which killed Australians too, and other regional conflicts, more people came to believe that it was a mistake to invest so much so far away when there were real threats closer to home. What this demonstrates, I think, is that governments can lose wars at home, too; but that most people have not given up on war as a legitimate, if unfortunate, part of international politics and foreign policy. The problem of war, which had so troubled me when I was young, remains as intractable, as devastating, and as likely as ever.

Region/Feminisms

At a regional level, feminists kept on working, paying attention to the local and national impacts of these global politics and in solidarity with those whose lives were more directly impacted. But while 9/11 and its consequences now dominate IR, including in Australia, there were many war zones and identity conflicts in the region, preceding and continuing after 9/11. There have been recent coups in Thailand and Fiji, while military rule continues in Pakistan and Burma, and state militaries and militarized police play a significant role in many other Asian states. As anti-militarist feminists remind us, wars and organized political violence are among the greatest dangers to women, to development, environment, social relations, and health; but they do not simply 'break out.' They are sustained by, even as they sustain, wider processes of militarization, assaults on democracy and gender justice, and closure against others.

In the wake of 9/11 region has been reimagined. For many Australians, Asia remains an opportunity or necessity for prosperity, or competition, with careful attention to Japan, China, and sometimes to India. But often the region is again perceived as a threat, a region of conflict, of pre-political primitive passions, of religious mania that we have left far behind. Official, media and popular pronouncements, especially on the presumed predilection of Islam to violence and fanaticism, have set against Australians and others who might be Muslims. These representations recall the old war stories that separate them from us; they rely on and reproduce gender.[41] Their women are passive victims; our women are liberated; we support women's rights where they do not; their masculinity is a warped and dangerous kind, which may (again) require that we resort to force (in their countries) to save their women from their men. This, while imprisoning women and children who try to escape from those war-torn countries to the comparative safety of ours.[42] Australian feminists, too, face invidious pressure from those who profess women's rights for state purposes, and must refuse both the war option and the damage done to women in the name of culture.[43]

In the larger sense of region that I refer to here, as in prep coms, the media and the academy, 'Asia' is problematic: too large for most generalizations or prescriptions, too insular to recognize multiple connections to other sets of relations and power plays. Make that 'Asia-Pacific,' which includes Australia and New Zealand, and the differences and connections are complicated even further.[44] Pacific island feminists especially struggle in Asia-Pacific fora for notice and a voice for their mini-states, with severely limited resources for international advocacy.[45] In Australian terms, in activism, NGOs, governmental, and private enterprise, for example, the Pacific often turns out to mean the Southwest Pacific, especially Fiji, the Solomons, and Vanuatu (only sometimes New Caledonia). PNG occupies a special, and ambiguous, place in such groupings. These are the neighborhood, imagined differently for Australians[46] as holiday destinations (not PNG); aid recipients, or partners in particular women's projects or campaigns; resources and potential markets; and recently and ominously as the so-called arc of instability. In this latter construction, the Australian government commits money, expertise, and armed forces for our security and their stabilization. As Empire returned to central view globally, colonial, raced, and classed power returned in ever more blatant forms to our neighborhood, too.

The projection of Australian power in the Pacific became increasingly militarized, in the service of capital and the western alliance. As Australia built its market security state post– 9/11, it became heavily involved in military and police interventions, in Papua New Guinea and the Solomons in particular, that aim to restore order and 'good governance.' This constituted a commitment to build the neoliberal democratic state, from the outside if necessary. Such a state, should it be achieved, might be good for local elites, for foreign investment, and for Australia's (narrowly defined) security. However, it took little serious notice of local democratic forms or of the engagement of women and others already active as peace builders at local, community, national, and regional level. The new federal Labor government promises to shift the balance more in favor of humanitarian aid and cooperation, but it will be difficult to dismantle the statist and military security logic that has become dominant of late.

One of the most powerful impacts of 9/11 was that globalization and its regional inflections, long viewed mostly in cultural and/or economic terms in western analyses, are now so clearly implicated in militarization. The aftermath of 9/11 brought the prerogative state and the war option back into central place in the global, U.S. dominated system.[47] In the process, it brought together often-separate feminist critiques of globalization, economy, peace, war, and identity.[48] Shortly after 9/11, we convened at ANU an international workshop entitled "Gender and Globalization in Asia and the Pacific: Feminist Revisions of the International." At the opening plenary, southern feminist network DAWN's convener, Fijian Claire Slatter named this dangerous congruence as "globalized greed, militarism, and patriarchal fundamentalism, in all its diverse but related forms."[49] Transnational feminists were at that time arguing that globalization must figure centrally in feminist theorizing and struggles everywhere, including those that presented as local or nationally based.[50] What 9/11 underlined was that feminist struggles for gender justice today must oppose neoliberalism and militarization, as some transnational feminists had been arguing all along.

An International, Personal Postscript

Today, feminist praxis confronts powerful adversaries. Global power relations of domination and exploitation depend upon heavily militarized, nationalistic, and deeply gendered processes. The triad of contemporary global politics, capital, exclusivist identities, and militarism,[51] calls for a transnational feminist politics that is anti-capitalist, inclusive, and peaceable; that builds links across national and other border lines, while acknowledging local struggles and strategies; that practices solidarity while respecting difference, but never allowing difference to be used as a cultural alibi against women, or to divide feminists along national or regional lines. In Australia and the Pacific, within the ongoing legacy of colonization, plastic political representations of race, ethnicity, and nationality are an intrinsic part of feminist politics, too.

In this complex and dangerous mix, it is not always clear from the outside how to respond in crises like the 2006 Fiji coup,[52] when the attention of feminists in the country of crisis must be to the immediate. While international support may provide some cover and some comfort, misplaced contact might further endanger the very ones we want to sustain. The politics of location affect reception of such events everywhere, and local responses will probably differ. Being a feminist in this region—indeed, anywhere—means having strong international links and networks to know who to ask, how best to engage; to be able to listen, not to presume; but never to give up, either on solidarity or on feminism as a transnational connection of immense value and responsibility.

Whatever the question or the times, whatever the challenge on the ground or in scholarship, I am convinced that feminism must inform the answer and that feminist research, teaching, and writing is, by necessity, a form of critical, engaged practice. While the forces ranged against us are enormous, feminist theory, practice, and transnational linkages have a vibrant, energizing global effect of their own.

And not all the political news is bad. For Australians, more progressive social relations at home and internationalism abroad now appear possible. On February 12, 2008, the new Labor federal government opened its first parliamentary session with a local indigenous 'welcome to country.' The next day Prime Minister Rudd issued a groundbreaking and long overdue apology to indigenous people, especially to the Stolen Generations, their families and communities, and called for a more inclusive and socially just society; 69 percent of Australians supported the apology and February 13 has been declared national Sorry Day. Now, as the Prime Minister declared, the hard work begins—again.[53] However, feminism and its friends can find a little more space to move, and to claim.

Reflecting on my life in and around IR: war continues to haunt IR, and me. So does the identity/difference problematic and the political meanings given to the boundaries it makes. The bodily effects of violence, domination, and exploitation demonstrate the need for an embodied IR. In turn, insisting on seeing bodies, broken and bloodied, but also mobilized, and acting in concert, must make gender visible, and productive too. And all along there is another tension to dance along, between structure and agency, as we used to say; between acknowledging and tracking the huge processes and systematic sets of unequal relations, and the individuals and their built communities that make their way, though not in circumstances of their choosing.

I closed *Worlding Women*, more than a decade ago, calling for such an embodied IR, which is increasingly evident in recent feminist IR. Here I add a postscript. It relates to how I began the chapter, with reference to personal biography and a personal politics of location. IR, global and regional politics, and feminist politics, are all big calls. They can easily threaten to overwhelm us. Yet our feminist politics must be self-reflexive, in terms of our research agenda, our teaching practice, our activism, our relations with others—and in terms of our own biographies. How I have done IR as a feminist cannot be separated from my identity as an Australian woman living through the second half of the twentieth century and into the twenty-first century. As a postcolonial feminist, I must account for my privileges and my implication in the very power relations I study. In addition, as a feminist I pursue peace, which I believe lies at the heart of living together well at family,[54] community, national, and international levels. I am convinced at every turn that the international is personal, and the personal is international too.[55]

Notes

1. This chapter is an overview of a long career and draws on many conversations and many more publications. I cannot begin to name the many hundreds of feminists, and others, who contributed to my way. I include reference to a number of my

publications, which document and acknowledge some of those whose work and company were, and are, so important to me.

2. South Pacific feminists frequently object to this compression, fearing it appropriates and invisibilizes their Pacific; they prefer the designation "Asia and the Pacific," which I use here.
3. Some sections of this chapter are previewed, with rather different intent, in an overview of gender in IR, "Reflections on the Gendering of States, Sovereignty, and Security in the Study of International Relations," *Intersections*, special issue on Gendering Governance and Security in Australia, Asia and the Pacific 16 (2007). http://www.she.murdoch.edu.au/intersections (accessed March 24, 2008).
4. Adrienne Rich, *Blood, Bread and Poetry: Selected Prose, 1979–1985* (New York: Norton, 1986); for an earlier attempt to develop such a politics, see Jindy Pettman, "Towards a (Personal) Politics of Location," *Studies in Continuing Education* 13, no. 2 (1991): 153–66; Jindy Pettman, "Transcending National Identity: the Global Political Economy of Gender and Class," in *International Relations: Still an American Social Science?*, ed. Robert Crawford and Darryl Jarvis (New York: St. Martin's Press, 2001), 255–74.
5. This language speaks to painful contests around settlement, versus invasion. I use the expression settler state here to link Australia's experiences to colonial relations internationally. See Jindy Pettman, "Australia," in *Unsettling Settler Societies: Articulations of Gender, Race, Ethnicity and Class*, ed. Daiva Stasiulis and Nira Yuval-Davis (Sage, London, 1995): 65–94.
6. Overseas military adventures have long signaled Australia's drive for state security through foreign, imperial connections, first to Britain and then to the United States and the priority given to western allegiance and alliances. Contests around Australian identity are often presented as a conflict between history (white, western, capitalist, and democratic) and geography (in Asia and the Pacific). There have been moments of more internationalist bent, and longer times when attention to the region is generated by concerns strategic or economic, but always within a western alliance structure, that anchors identity and security. See Jindy Pettman, "A Feminist Perspective on Australia in Asia," in *Race, Colour and Identity in Australia and New Zealand*, ed. John Docker and Gerard Fischer (Sydney: UNSW Press, 2000), 143–57; Anthony Burke, *In Fear of Security: Australia's Invasion Anxiety* (Annandale: Pluto Press, 2001).
7. Including through my daughter, Tasha Seiken Sudan's, poetry: "fallen soldiers all of us knew / that never knew us."
8. The thesis was published as *Zambia, Security and Conflict* (New York: St. Martin's Press, 1974).
9. Octave Mannoni, *Prospero and Caliban: The Psychology of Colonization* (New York: Frederick A. Praeger, 1956); Albert Memmi, *The Colonizer and the Colonized* (Boston: Beacon Press, 1991, originally published 1957); Frantz Fanon, *Black Skin, White Masks*, trans. Charles Lam Markmann (New York: Grove, 1967).
10. Pettman, "Reflections on the Gendering States."
11. Jindy Pettman, "Adaptation in Education in Papua New Guinea," *The South Pacific Journal of Teacher Education* 9, no. 1 (1981): 55–60.

12. Until that time, Aboriginal studies were the preserve of anthropology and focused on traditional Aboriginal societies. See David Hollinsworth, *Race and Racism in Australia*, 2nd edition (Katoomba, NSW: Social Sciences, 1998).
13. Margaret Tucker, *If Everyone Cared: An Autobiography* (Melbourne: Grosvenor Press, 1987); Jackie Huggins and Rita Huggins, *Auntie Rita* (Aboriginal Studies Press: Canberra, 1994); HREOC, *Bringing Them Home: National Inquiry into the Separation of Aboriginal and Torres Strait Islander Children from Their Families* (Sydney: HREOC, 1997).
14. Sophie Watson, ed., *Playing the State: Australian Feminist Interventions* (Sydney: Allen and Unwin, 1990).
15. My in-service teaching at this time included workshops with ESL teachers who suddenly found themselves re-named multicultural advisers, a startling change for the assimilationists among them.
16. Ann Curthoys, *For and Against Feminism* (Sydney: Allen and Unwin, 1989).
17. A clear demonstration of feminist differences around indigenous issues emerged in furious Aboriginal women's response to a provocative intervention by Di Bell. See Jan Larbalestier, "The Politics of Representation: Aboriginal Women and Feminism," *Anthropolgoical Forum* 6, no. 2 (1990): 143–57; Jindy Pettman, "Gendered Knowledges: Aboriginal Women and the Politics of Feminism," *Journal of Australian Studies*, no. 35 (1992): 120–31.
18. Jindy Pettman and Helen Meekosha, "Beyond Category Politics," *Hecate*, 17, no. 2 (1991): 75–92.
19. Notably Gloria Hull, et al., ed., *All the Women are White, All the Blacks are Men, But Some of Us are Brave (*New York: Feminist Press, 1982); Cherrie Moraga and Gloria Anzadlua, ed., *This Bridge Called my Back: Writings by Radical Women of Colour* (New York: Kitchen Table 1983). See for an Australian example, Gillian Bottomley, Marie de Lepervanche and Jean Martin, ed., *Intersexions: Gender/Class/Culture/Ethnicity* (Sydney: Allen and Unwin, 1991). More recently, see Avtar Brah and Ann Phoenix, "Ain't I a Woman? Revisiting Intersectionality," *Journal of International Women's Studies* 5, no. 3 (2004): 75–86. For a retrospective on the impact of *This Bridge* in North American context, see M. Jacqui Alexander, *Pedagogies of Crossing: Mediations on Feminism, Sexual Politics, Memory, and the Sacred* (Durham: Duke University Press, 2005), 257–86.
20. Pettman, "Towards a (Personal) Politics of Location"; Jindy Pettman, *Living in the Margins: Racism, Sexism and Feminism in Australia* (Sydney: Allen and Unwin, 1992); Pettman, "Transcending National Identity."
21. Although in line with the usual gendered division of labor, there were many women employed as administrators and research assistants, and some women graduate students too.
22. Cynthia Enloe, *Bananas, Bases and Beaches: Making Feminist Sense of International Politics* (London: Pandora, 1990).
23. Jindy Pettman, *Worlding Women: a feminist international politics* (Sydney: Allen and Unwin; London: Routledge, 1996).
24. Peggy Antrobus, *The Global Women's Movement: Origins, Issues and Strategies* (London: Zed Books, 2004); Jindy Pettman, "Global Politics and Transnational Feminisms," in *Feminist Politics, Activism and Vision: Local and Global Challenges*,

ed. Luciana Ricciutelli, Angela Miles, and Margaret H. McFadden (London: Zed Books, 2005), 49–63.

25. FTGS Web site, http://www.femisa.org/ (accessed March 23, 2008).
26. IFJP Web site, http://www.tandf.co.uk/journals/titles/14616742.asp (accessed March 23, 2008).
27. Jane Parpart and Marysia Zalewski, ed., *Rethinking the 'Man' Question: Sex, Gender and Violence in International Relations* (London, Zed Books, 2008).
28. Crucial support and excellent company was provided by Judith Ion as the managing editor of the journal at ANU.
29. Though not necessarily easy, both in terms of the keenly contested meanings and different investments women's studies, and because women's studies at ANU was then under institutional fire, with restructuring and funding cuts that reactivated arguments about autonomy versus mainstreaming, and eventually led to re-casting women's studies as gender, sexuality, and culture.
30. Recent examples include the 2005 Association for Women's Rights in Development (AWID) conference on Feminists in Bangkok and the fifth Women's World conference in Seoul, both international but regionally infused because of their organization and location. AWID's Resource Net is an excellent source of information concerning feminist events, campaigns, and resources, see http://www.awid.org. Another source with substantial regional input is provided by the International Women's Development Agency (IWDA), which also engages in projects with sister NGOs in the Pacific and Asian states in particular, see http://www.iwda.org.au.
31. An early elaboration of this project appeared in Pettman, "A Feminist Perspective on Australia in Asia."
32. Marianne Marchand and Ann Sisson Runyan, ed., *Gender and Global Restructuring* (London: Routledge, 2000). I was tracing globalization through gendered migration for sex and service, focusing on flows from poorer south and southeast Asian states to richer Asian and Middle Eastern states, and on women's organizing and feminist responses to these women on the move. Jindy Pettman, "International Sex and Service," in *Globalization: Theory and Practice*, 2nd ed., ed. Eleonore Kofman and Gillian Youngs (Continuum, 2003), 158–72; and Jindy Pettman "Women on the Move: Globalization and Labour Migration from South and Southeast Asian states," *Global Society* 12, no. 3 (1998): 389–403.
33. There is a voluminous feminist IR literature elaborating this position. For an early example, see Carol Cohn, "Sex and Death in the Rational World of Defense Intellectuals," *Signs* 12, no. 41(1987): 687–718; and recently, Laura Sjoberg, "Gendered Realities of the Immunity Principle: Why Gender Analysis Needs Feminism," *International Studies Quarterly* 50, no. 4 (2006): 889–910.
34. As elsewhere in this chapter, the brief summary of a crisis and response gives little sense of the politics—including gender politics—involved; the gender politics of the intervention included a rhetorical and mostly marginalized policy attention to gender, Hilary Charlesworth and Mary Wood, "'Mainstreaming Gender' in International Peace and Security: East Timor," *Yale Journal of International Law*, 26 (2001): 313–17; see also Charlesworth, and Hall and True chapters in this collection; The Globalism Institute RMIT compilation of gender resources on Timor-Leste, http://www.timor-leste.org/gender.html (accessed March 22, 2008).

35. Currently Australia has nearly 3,000 military personnel serving overseas, including 1,400 in Iraq, 500 in Afghanistan, 800 in East Timor, and 140 in the Solomon Islands, *The Weekend Australian* (January 20–21, 2007): 8. *The Australian* announced, "the Australian Digger—the men and women of the Australian Defense Force who we are proud to collectively name recipients of the Weekend Australian's 2006 Australian of the Year." The supporting editorial noted that our diggers are "providing forward defense of our democracy against the threat of terror attack" (18). The new Labor government is planning to withdraw combat troops though not trainers and other support in Iraq, and taking up a more internationalist and less militarist stance overall.
36. Jindy Pettman, "Feminist International Relations Post 9/11," *Brown Journal of World Affairs* X, Issue. 2 (2004): 85–96; John Birmingham, "A Time for War: Australia as a Military Power," *Quarterly Essay*, no. 20 (2005); Anthony Burke, *Beyond Security, Ethics and Violence: War Against the Other* (Oxon: Routledge, 2007). Something of the shift is indicated when the Department of Immigration and Multicultural Affairs was renamed the Department of Immigration and Citizenship, and the further tightening of citizenship tests. The common experience of Anglo-American liberal democracies is clear, see for example Krista Hunt and Kim Rygiel, ed. *(En)Gendering the War on Terror* (Aldershot: Ashgate 2006).
37. The Feminist Knowledge Network (FNK-L). The Ricciutelli, Miles, and McFadden collection, *Feminist Politics, Activism and Vision: Local and Global Challenge* is the first publication of this network.
38. *International Feminist Journal of Politics*, "Forum: The Events of 11 September 2001 and Beyond," 4, no. 1 (2002): 95–115; "September 11 and its Aftermath: Movement Statements," in *Inter-Asian Cultural Studies* "September 11 and its Aftermath: Movement Statements," 3, no. 1 (2002): 121–33; Ammu Joseph and Kalpana Sharma, ed., *Terror, Counter Terror Women Speak Out* (London: Zed Books, 2003); "Roundtable: "Gender and September 11," in *Signs "Roundtable: Gender and September 11,"* 28, no. 1 (2002): 431–80; Pettman, "Feminist International Relations After 9/11." Much has followed; see, for example, Hunt and Rygiel, ed., *(En)Gendering the War on Terror*; the theme issue on "Feminist International Relations in the Age of the War on Terror: Ideologies, Religions and Conflict," in *International Feminist Journal of Politics* 8, no. 1 (2006); the special issue on "Gender Violence and Hegemonic Projects," in *International Feminist Journal of Politics* 8, no. 4 (2006).
39. Addressing U.S. feminist academics, but important to address here too, M. Jacqui Alexander stresses the importance of addressing colonization, class, and empire in women's studies and gender politics. "The question of just how not to do state work at a moment of empire is one of the most crucial questions we must confront" Alexander, *Pedagogies of Crossing*, 249.
40. Though I am reminded here of Virginia Woolf's assertion that women continue to collaborate in war making through every comfort given to fighting men. *A Room of One's Own and Three Guineas* (1938; repr. London: Penguin, 1993), 232–34.
41. Jean Bethke Elshtain, *Women and War* (New York: Basic Books, 1987); Krista Hunt and Kim Rygiel, "(En)Gendered War Stories and Camouflaged Politics," in Hunt and Rygiel, ed. *(En)Gendering the War on Terror*, 1–24.

42. Although the new federal Labor government promises some amelioration here.
43. Feminist collections post-9/11 stress the danger of the appropriation of women's rights by those whose militarized responses endanger women. Cynthia Enloe named these 'rights of convenience' in "Forum: the Events of 11 September 2001 and Beyond," *International Feminist Journal of Politics* 4, no. 1 (2002): 103.
44. Arif Dirlik, "The Asia-Pacific Idea: Reality and Representation in the Invention of a Regional Structure," *Journal of World History* 3, no. 1 (1992): 55–79; Claire Slatter and Yvonne Underhill in this collection.
45. An exception was the 2005 AWID Bangkok conference, where Pacific women were speakers at the opening and closing plenaries, and Pacific panels and the Pacific women poets readings were well attended, see Vanessa Griffen, "Local and Global Women's Rights in the Pacific," *Development* 49, no. 1 (2006): 108–12.
46. Greg Fry, "Framing the Islands: Knowledge and Power in Changing Australian Images of 'the South Pacific,'" *Contemporary Pacific* 9, no. 2 (1997): 305–44; see also E. Hau'ofa, "Our Sea of Islands," *The Contemporary Pacific* 6, no. 1 (1994): 148–61.
47. Pettman, "Feminist International Relations Post 9/11," 58.
48. Ibid.
49. Claire Slatter, "Tensions in Activism: Navigating the Global Spaces at the Intersections of State/Civil Society and Gender/Economic Justice," (paper presented to the Gender and Globalization in Asia and the Pacific: Feminist Revisions of the International workshop, Australian National University, Canberra, 2001). For a report on this conference, see Nicole George, "Women's Re-Visions of Globalization: Gender and Globalization in Asia and the Pacific: Feminist Revisions of the International Workshop," *International Feminist Journal of Politics* 4, no. 2 (2002): 268–77. Some of the most important feminist analysis and advocacy has long come from DAWN, a leading southern-based feminist network. From the mid-1980s, DAWN activists were amongst those who tracked intensifying neoliberalism and restructuring on the one hand and growing and deeply anti-feminist identity movements on the other, resisting feminist gains and claims. The DAWN 2001 video and accompanying material, "The Marketization of Governance," is an incisive and affecting critique of neoliberalism and its gendered effects.
50. Chandra Talpade Mohanty, "'Under Western Eyes' Revisited: Feminist Solidarity Through Anti-capitalist Struggles," *Signs* 28, no. 2 (2003): 499–537.
51. Pettman, "Feminist International Relations Post 9/11," 59.
52. FemLINKPACIFIC provides fascinating insight into the lead up to the December coup, including the mobilization of women's rights, human rights, and democracy NGOs in support of peacemaking, while stressing women's deep interest in and knowledge of security and government issues too. See femTALK eNews Bulletins through 2006, femlinkpac@connect.com.fj.
53. *Sydney Morning Herald*, February 13, 2008.
54. While I have covered much in this chapter, I have set aside the family of my adult life. No account of my life (which this chapter attempts in the specific context of IR, and the region) begins to make sense without the company of Dominic, Tasha, and Mike.
55. Again, with thanks to Cynthia Enloe for *Bananas, Bases and Beaches*.

Afterword

J. Ann Tickner

> Often what is best and most closely shared is not primarily with co-nationals, though some may be: but rather with those who share political alliances and theoretical passions, whatever their particular national or cultural background. Leaving home can unsettle or threaten us, but more often, in my experience, it builds learnings and relations that are liberating and immensely enjoyable—even though it is still good to return home, for a rest.[1]

Jindy Pettman's remarkable career as a scholar, teacher, and activist, to which this book pays tribute, is reflected in these words with which she concluded her groundbreaking article, "Gendering International Relations," published in the *Australian Journal of International Affairs* in 1993. In this article, Pettman asks how we might take women's experiences seriously and treat women as players in their own right on the stage of international politics. Asking, Where *are* the women? she was one of the first feminist scholars to bring their invisibility, and the resistance to gender analysis in the discipline of international relations (IR), to our attention. Pettman dedicated her scholarship to overcoming these disciplinary shortcomings. In her chapter in this volume, she tells us that she sees IR as the bookends of her career—beginning with a Ph.D. in International Relations in 1971, and returning to a more systematic engagement with the discipline in the 1990s. Yet all Jindy Pettman's work is engaged with global and local issues that *should* be included within the boundaries of IR.

Few of the authors who contributed to this volume may not identify themselves as IR scholars, yet the issues about which they write should be part of this discipline. Like Pettman, these scholars and activists have a passionate commitment to building learning and international relations that will liberate the many voices of those who 'live in the margins,' and whose lives both impact and are impacted by global politics. This volume's focus on the Asia-Pacific region is a fitting tribute to Pettman's return home, home being scholarship on feminist perspectives on Australia's relations with Asia.

Pettman's article in the *Australian Journal of International Affair* was published in 1993, one year after *Living in the Margins: Racism, Sexism and Feminism in Australia. Living in the Margins* made visible the lives of Aboriginal women in Australia. The article analyzes the politics of boundary-making where race, ethnicity, class, and gender act to render minority women invisible. It explores the foundations of the patriarchal state- and nation-building as a colonial project, and the meaning of militarized citizenship—issues that should be crucial to an emancipatory international relations. *Living in the Margins* counsels us to be sensitive to difference; it shifts the initial feminist IR question, Where are the women? to question the concept of women as a unitary category of analysis. It reminds us to be aware of the intersections of gendered identities with those of race, class, and cultural difference.[2]

In all her writings, Jindy Pettman is sensitive to her own privilege as a white woman in a settler society. *Living in the Margins* reminds us of the researcher's responsibility to recognize her own speaking position as well as the ethics of 'doing research' on those who can become objectified by our research, often with little tangible benefit to themselves. Yet Pettman advises us that sensitivity to difference, while crucial for recognizing racism and sexism, should not paralyze us. While being mindful of unequal power relations, and conflicting interests, and being careful not to appropriate others' struggles, we must recognize connections among women and work toward what she calls a politics of affinity.[3] All the authors in this book provide tangible evidence of a politics of affinity in their analyses of feminist transnational activism, from rural India to Vietnam to remote sites in the Pacific Islands.

Exploring hidden boundaries and the tensions between the politics of difference and affinity continue to be central themes in Pettman's more explicitly IR book, *Worlding Women: A Feminist International Politics*. In the introduction to *Worlding Women*, Pettman asks whether IR is, or can be, a place from which to do feminist work, given the traditional constitution of the field and its politics.[4] She asserts that answering this question in the negative concedes IR to those who currently determine its boundaries. *Worlding Women* is an important contribution to building a more inclusive, more genuinely international discipline. It investigates a wide variety of traditional IR subjects from war and peace to the global economy, but it does so with sensitivity to the lives of those whom IR has rendered invisible. Echoing the themes of Pettman's earlier work, *Worlding Women* focuses our attention on issues of colonialism, racism, sex trafficking, and migration, topics about which IR has been largely silent. Following Pettman's example, this volume offers us rich insights on many of these same issues.

For Pettman, "worlding women means recognising that women are in the world and in world politics, which, in turn, are profoundly gendered."[5] The chapters in this book offer strong support for this claim. Just as Pettman has traveled through the world looking for, and conversing with, the invisible ones in international relations, these authors take us on similar journeys. We learn about living in the margins of countries of the Asia-Pacific region—about their gendered economies and about the suffering caused by neoliberal restructuring. Appropriately for a feminist perspective on IR, these authors draw upon a variety of disciplines; they are engaged in policy and activist work and their experiences are varied, yet all cohere around the themes Pettman has addressed during her life 'lived in and out of place' as a scholar and activist. Echoing Pettman's feminist sensitivity to difference and her concern with agency, we learn about the many ways in which Muslim women enact political agency and about their troubled relationship with the hegemonic tendencies of western feminist scholarship. Many of the authors pose a question that has been central to Pettman's work, How can we improve the lives of the oppressed while maximizing their agency and ensuring the preservation of their core values? These writers' research and active engagement in transnational feminism offer us insight into making this goal possible.

Jindy Pettman reminds us that feminist politics is engaged politics—whether we are in the classroom or out in the wider world. No tribute to her would be complete without recognizing her roles of activist, scholar, teacher, and educator. Pettman has devoted a significant amount of time, not only to teaching and mentoring her students, but also to writing about how to teach gender, multiculturalism, and anti-racism. She has consulted, both at home and abroad, on racism, sexism, community relations in Australia, and on effective peacebuilding for UNESCO. All these activities demonstrate her commitment to what it means to be a responsible scholar.

On a personal note, I had the privilege of working with Jindy during my visit to the Australian National University in 1996. As always, she was engaged in a multiplicity of projects—supervising an unusually large number of Ph.D. dissertations, teaching feminist international politics in the political science department, and preparing to take on the role of Director of the Centre for Women's Studies. During my stay, she was asked to become the founding editor of a new journal, the *International Feminist Journal of Politics.* Given her multiple responsibilities, I counseled against taking on this huge project, but true to her passion for furthering the nascent field of feminist international relations, Jindy took on the task. The *IFJP* has become a premier journal in the field. Breaking down IR's traditional boundaries, the *IFJP* offers a rich array of scholarship about feminist global politics. Its commitment to interdisciplinarity, to highlighting research on topics normally not considered IR, and its inclusion of conversations and reflections from scholars and activists, is tribute to Jindy's re-visioning of IR in ways that take women seriously.

Jindy Pettman begins her chapter in this volume by describing her life as one lived in and out of place. She speaks of countless conversations and of the importance of listening to and learning from others. She tells us how her scholarship was formed by her own childhood experiences of war, which led her to a continual search for a deeper empathy with others, whether they are others marginalized by Australian society or those labeled dangerous others in the post–9/11 world.[6] Peace, Pettman claims, lies at the heart of living well together as families, communities, and members of a global society. Surely, this is a goal to which we IR feminists should aspire as we leave the comfortable intellectual spaces of our disciplines and strive to build international relations that are truly global and respectful of others. This volume is an important step toward the realization of this goal.

Notes

1. Jan Pettman, "Gendering International Relations," *Australian Journal of International Affairs* 47 (1993): 57.
2. Jan Pettman, *Living in the Margins: Racism, Sexism and Feminism in Australia* (St. Leonards, NSW: Allen and Unwin, 1992), 156.
3. Pettman, *Living in the Margins*, 157–58.
4. Jan Jindy Pettman, *Worlding Women: A Feminist International Politics* (Sydney: Allen and Unwin, 1996), viii.
5. Ibid., 213.
6. See Jan Jindy Pettman, "Feminist International Relations After 9/11," *Brown Journal of World Affairs* 10, no. 2 (2004): 85–96.

Bibliography

Abbott, Kenneth W. "International Relations Theory, International Law and the Regime Governing Atrocities in Internal Conflicts." In *The Methods of International Law*, American Society of International Law Studies in Transnational Legal Policy, no. 36, edited by Steven R. Ratner and Anne-Marie Slaughter. Washington, DC: ASIL, 2004.

Abdela, Lesley. "Kosovo: Missed Opportunities, Lessons for the Future." In *Development, Women, and War: Feminist Perspectives*, edited by Haileh Afshar and David Eade, 87–99. Oxford: Oxfam, 2004.

Abou-Bakr, Omaima. "Islamic Feminism? What's in a Name? Preliminary Reflections." *Middle Eastern Women's Studies Review* xv, no. 4 (2001). http://www.amews.org/review/reviewarticles/islamicfeminism.htm (accessed March 19, 2008).

Abu-Lughod, Lila. "Do Muslim Women Really Need Saving? Anthropological Reflections on Cultural Relativism and Its Others." *American Anthropologist* 104, no. 3 (2002): 783–90.

Ackerly, Brooke A., Maria Stern, and Jacqui True. "Feminist Methodologies for International Relations." In *Feminist Methodologies for International Relations*, edited by Brooke A. Ackerly, Maria Stern, and Jacqui True, 1–15. Cambridge: Cambridge University Press, 2006.

Ackerly, Brooke. "Women's Human Rights Activists as Cross-Cultural Theorists." *International Journal of Feminist Politics* 3, no. 3 (2001): 311–46.

Afshar, Haleh, ed. *Women and Politics in the Third World*. London: Routledge, 1996.

Agathangelou, Anna M., and L. H. M. Ling. *Transforming World Politics: From Empire to Multiple Worlds*. London: Routledge, forthcoming.

Agarwal, Bina. "Editorial: Re-sounding the Alert—Gender, Resources and Community Action." *World Development* 25 (1997): 1373–80.

Aiken, Linda H., James Buchan, Julie Sochalski, Barbara Nichols, and Mary Powell. "Trends in International Nurse Migration." *Health Affairs* 23, no. 3 (2004): 69–77.

Alagappa, Muthiah, ed. *Asian Security Practice: Material and Ideational Influences*. Stanford: Stanford University Press, 1998.

Alexander, M. Jacqui. *Pedagogies of Crossing: Mediations on Feminism, Sexual Politics, Memory, and the Sacred*. Durham: Duke University Press, 2005.

Ali, Shamima. "The Women's Crisis Centre in Suva, Fiji." In *Women, Development and Empowerment: A Pacific Feminist Perspective, Report of a Pacific Women's Workshop,*

Naboutini, Fiji, March 23, 1986, edited by Vanessa Griffen, 37–44. Kuala Lumpur: Asian and Pacific Development Centre, 1987.

Al-Ali, Nadjes S. "Gender and Civil Society in the Middle East." *International Journal of Feminist Politics* 5 (2003): 216–32.

Alvarez, Sonia. "Advocating Feminism: The Latin American Feminist NGO 'Boom.'" *International Feminist Journal of Politics* 1 (1999): 181–209.

———. *Engendering Democracy in Brazil: Women's Movements in Transition Politics*. Princeton: Princeton University Press, 1990.

Amer, Ramses. "The United Nations' Peacekeeping Operation in Cambodia: Overview and Assessment." *Contemporary Southeast Asia* 15, no. 2 (September 1993): 211–31.

Anderson, Bridget. *Doing the Dirty Work? The Global Politics of Domestic Labour*. London: Zed Books, 2000.

Andreas, Peter. "Illicit International Political Economy: The Clandestine Side of Globalization." *Review of International Political Economy* 11, no. 3 (2004): 631–52.

Antrobus, Peggy. *The Global Women's Movement: Origins, Issues and Strategies*. London: Zed Books, 2004.

Archibugi, Daniele. "Principles of Cosmopolitan Democracy." In *Re-imagining Political Community: Studies in Cosmopoliian Democracy*, edited by Daniele Archibugi, David Held, and Michael Köhler, 198–232. Stanford: Stanford University Press, 1998.

Askin, Kelly D., and Dorean M. Koenig, ed. *Women and International Human Rights Law: Introduction to Women's Human Rights Issues*. Ardsley, NY: Transnational Publishers, 1999.

Azarbaijani-Moghaddam, Sippi. "Afghan Women on the Margins of the Twenty-First Century." In *Nation-building Unraveled? Aid, Peace and Justice in Afghanistan*, edited by Antonio Donini, Norah Niland, and Karin Wermester, 95–116. Bloomfield, CT: Kumarian, 2004.

Baden, Sally, and Anne Marie Goetz. "Who Needs [Sex] When You Can Have [Gender]?" *Feminist Review* 56 (1997): 3–25.

Badran, Margot and Miriam Cooke. *Opening the Gates: A Century of Arab Feminist Writing*. Bloomington, IN: Indiana University Press, 1990.

Barker, Drucilla K. "Beyond Women and Economics: Rereading 'Women's Work.'" *Signs* 30, no. 4 (2005): 2189–209.

Barker, Drucilla K., and Susan F. Feiner. *Liberating Economics: Feminist Perspectives on Families, Work, and Globalization*. Ann Arbor: University of Michigan Press, 2004.

Barker, Drucilla K., and Edith Kuiper, ed. *Toward a Feminist Philosophy of Economics*. London and New York: Routledge, 2003.

Basu, Amrita, ed. *The Challenge of Local Feminisms: Women's Movements in Global Perspective*. Boulder, CO: Westview, 1995.

Baxi, Upendra. "Global Justice and the Failure of Deliberative Democracy." In *Democracy Unrealized*, edited by Okwui Enweror, et al., 113–32. Kassel: Hatje Cantz Publishers, 2001.

———. "'Global Neighborhood' and the 'Universal Otherhood': Notes on the Report of the Commission on Global Governance." *Alternatives* 21 (1996): 525–49.

Beck, Robert J. "International Law and International Relations: The Prospects for Interdisciplinary Collaboration." In *International Rules: Approaches from International*

Law and International Relations, edited by Robert J. Beck, Anthony Clark Arend, and Robert D. Vander Lugt. New York: Oxford University Press, 1996.

Behera, Navnita Chadha. "Introduction." In *Gender, Conflict and Migration*, edited by Navnita Chadha Behera, 21–71. New Delhi: Sage, 2006.

Birmingham, John. "A Time for War: Australia as a Military Power." *Quarterly Essay* 20 (2005).

Bleiker, Roland. *Divided Korea: Toward A Culture of Reconciliation*. Minneapolis: University of Minnesota Press, 2008.

Block, Fred. *Postindustrial Possibilities, A Critique of Economic Discourse*. Berkeley: University of California Press, 1990.

Boot, Max. *The Savage Wars of Peace: Small Wars and the Rise of American Power*. New York: Basic Books, 2002.

Booth, Karen M. "National Mother, Global Whore, and Transnational Femocrats: The Politics of AIDS and the Construction of Women at the World Health Organization." *Feminist Studies* 24 (1998): 115–39.

Booth, Ken, and Russell Trood, ed. *Strategic Cultures in the Asia-Pacific Region*. London: Palgrave McMillan, 1999.

Bottomley, Gillian, Marie de Lepervanche, and Jean Martin, ed. *Intersexions: Gender/Class/Culture/Ethnicity*. Sydney: Allen and Unwin, 1991.

Boutros-Ghali, Boutros, "Introduction." In *The United Nations and Cambodia 1991–1995*, the UN Blue Book Series, vol. 2. New York: UN Department of Public Information, 1995.

Braig, Marianne, and Sonja Wolte, ed. *Common Ground or Mutual Exclusion? Women's Movements and International Relations*. London: Zed Books, 2002.

Brah, Avtar, and Ann Phoenix. "Ain't I a Woman? Revisiting Intersectionality." *Journal of International Women's Studies* 5, no. 3 (2004): 75–86.

Brown, Richard, and John Connell. "Occupation-Specific Analysis of Migration and Remittance Behaviour: Pacific Island Nurses in Australia and New Zealand." *Asia Pacific Viewpoint* 47, no. 1 (2006): 135–50.

Brunnstrom, Cecilia. "Another Invasion: Lessons from International Support to East Timorese NGOs." *Development in Practice* 14, no. 4 (2003): 310–21.

Bulbeck, Chilla. *Reorienting Western Feminisms: Women's Diversity in a Post-Colonial World*. Cambridge, Cambridge University Press, 1989.

Bunch, Charlotte, and Niamh Reilly. *Demanding Accountability: The Global Campaign and Vienna Tribunal for Women's Human Rights*. New Brunswick, NJ: Center for Women's Global Leadership and New York: UN Development Fund for Women, UNIFEM, 1994.

Burke, Anthony. *Beyond Security, Ethics and Violence: War Against the Other*. Oxon: Routledge, 2007.

———. *In Fear of Security: Australia's Invasion Anxiety*. Annandale: Pluto, 2001.

Burke, Anthony, and Matt McDonald, ed. *Critical Security in the Asia-Pacific*. Manchester: Manchester University Press, 2007.

Burnham, Peter. "The Politics of Economic Management in the 1990s." *New Political Economy* 4, no.1 (1999): 37–54.

Butalia, Urvashi. *Other Side of Silence*. Delhi: Kali for Women, 1998.

Butler, Judith P. *Gender Trouble: Feminism and the Subversion of Identity*. New York: Routledge, 1990.

Camp, Stephanie M. H. *Closer to Freedom: Enslaved Women and Everyday Resistance in the Plantation South*. Chapel Hill: University of North Carolina Press, 2004.

Campbell, David. "Cultural Governance and Pictorial Resistance: Reflections on the Imaging of War." *Review of International Studies* 29 (2003): 57–73.

Chadya, Joyce M. "Mother Politics: Anti-Colonial Nationalism and the Woman Question in Africa." *Journal of Women's History* 15, no. 3 (2003): 153–57.

Chan, Stephen, Peter G Mandaville, and Roland Bleiker, ed. *The Zen of International Relations: IR Theory from East to West*. New York: Palgrave Macmillan, 2001.

Chandler, David P. *The Tragedy of Cambodian History: Politics, War and Revolution Since 1945*. New Haven: Yale University Press, 1991.

Charlesworth, Hilary. "Not Waving but Drowning: Gender Mainstreaming and Human Rights." *Harvard Human Rights Journal* 18 (2005): 1–18.

Charlesworth, Hilary, and Christine Chinkin. "Regulatory Frameworks in International Law." In *Regulating Law*, edited by Christine Parker, Colin Scott, Nicola Lacey, and John Braithwaite, 246–68. Melbourne: Oxford University Press, 2004.

———. "Sex, Gender and September 11," American *Journal of International Law* 96 (2002): 600–605.

———. *The Boundaries of International Law: A Feminist Analysis*. Manchester: Manchester University Press, 2000.

Charlesworth, Hilary, and Mary Wood. "'Mainstreaming Gender' in International Peace and Scurity: East Timor." *Yale Journal of International Law* 26 (2001): 313–17.

———. "Women and Human Rights in the Rebuilding of East Timor." *Nordic Journal of International Law* 71 (2002): 325–48.

Chen, Martha Alter. "Engendering World Conferences: The International Women's Movements and the United Nations." In *NGOs, the UN and Global Governance*, edited by Thomas G. Weiss and Leon Gordenker, 139–55. Boulder, CO: Lynne Rienner, 1996.

Chesler, Phyllis. *The Death of Feminism: What's Next in the Struggle for Women's Freedom*? New York: Palgrave Macmillan, 2005.

Chin, Christine B. *In Service and Servitude: Foreign Female Domestic Workers and the Malaysian "Modernity" Project*. New York: Columbia University Press, 1998.

Chinkin, Christine, and Hilary Charlesworth, "Building Women into Peace: The International Legal Framework." *Third World Quarterly* 27, no. 5 (2006): 937–57.

Chinkin, Christine, Shelley Wright, and Hilary Charlesworth. "Feminist Approaches to International Law: Reflections from Another Century." In *International Law: Modern Feminist Approaches*, edited by Doris Buss and Ambreena Manji. Portland: Hart Publishing, 2006.

Chopra, Jarat. "United Nations Authority in Cambodia." Occasional Paper No. 15. Providence: Thomas J. Watson, Jr. Institute for International Studies, 1994.

Chowdhury, Geeta, and Sheila Nair, ed. *Power in a Postcolonial World: Race, Gender and Class in International Relations*. New York: Routledge, 2002.

Churchill, Ward. *A Little Matter of Genocide: Holocaust and Denial in the Americas from 1492 to the Present*. San Francisco: City Lights Books, 1998.

Cohn, Carol. "War, Wimps, and Women: Talking Gender and Thinking War." In *Gendering War Talk*, edited by Miriam Cooke and Angela Woollacott, 227–46. Princeton: Princeton University Press, 1993.

———. "Sex and Death in the Rational World of Defense Intellectuals." *Signs* 12, no. 41 (1987): 687–718.

Cole, Catherine M., Takyiwaa Manuh, and Stephan F. Miescher. *Africa After Gender?* Bloomington: Indiana University Press, 2007.

Coleman, Isabel. "The Payoff for Women's Rights." *Foreign Affairs* 83, no. 3 (2004): 80–95.

Cook, Rebecca, ed. *Human Rights of Women: National and International Perspectives*. Philadelphia: University of Pennsylvania Press, 1994.

Cooke, Miriam. "Multiple Critique: Islamic Feminist Rhetorical Strategies." *Nepantla: Views from the South* 1, no.1 (2000): 91–110.

Cox, Robert, and Timothy J. Sinclair. *Approaches to World Order*. Cambridge: Cambridge University Press, 1996.

Crenshaw, Kimberle. "Mapping the Margins: Intersectionality, Identity Politics, and Violence Against Women of Color." *Stanford Law Review* 43 (1991): 1241–99.

Cretton, Vivien. "Cakobau's Sisters: Status, Gender and Politics in Fiji." Working Paper 11. Canberra: Gender Relations Centre, Australian National University, 2004.

Cristalis, Irena, and Catherine Scott. *Independent Women, The Story of Women's Activism in East Timor*. London: Catholic Institute for International Relations, 2005.

Crocombe, Ron. "Regionalism Above and Below the Forum: The Geographical/Culture Region, Asia Pacific and Others." In *Pacific Futures*, edited by Michael Powles. Canberra: Pandanus Books, 2006.

Curthoys, Ann. *For and Against Feminism*. Sydney: Allen and Unwin, 1989.

Curtis, Grant. *Cambodia: A Country Profile*. Stockholm: The Swedish International Development Agency, 1980.

Das, Veena. *Critical Events: An Anthropological Perspective on Contemporary India*. Delhi: Oxford India, 1996.

Davies, Margaret. "Taking the Inside Out: Sex and Gender in the Legal Subject." In *Sexing the Subject of Law*, edited by Ngaire Naffine and Rosemary Owens. Sydney: Law Book Company, 1997.

D'Costa, Bina. "Marginalized Identity: New Frontiers of Research for IR?" in *Feminist Methodologies for International Relations*, edited by Brooke A Ackerly, Maria Stern, and Jacqui True, 129–52. Cambridge: Cambridge University Press, 2006.

———. "Coming to Terms with the Past: Forming Feminist Alliance Across Borders." In *Women, Power and Justice: Global Feminist Perspectives. Volume I: Politics and Activism: Ensuring the Protection of Women's Fundamental Human Rights*, edited by Luciana Ricciutelli, Angela Miles, and Margaret McFadden, 227–47. London: Zed Books, 2005.

Debord, Guy. *Comments on the Society of the Spectacle*. London: Verso, 1998.

———. *The Society of the Spectacle*. Translated by Donald Nicholson-Smith. New York: Zone Books, 1995.

de Certeau, Michel. Translated by Steven Rendall. *The Practice of Everyday Life*. Berkeley: University of California Press, 1984.

De Goede, Marieke. "Beyond Economism in International Political Economy." *Review of International Studies* 29, no. 1 (2003): 79–97.

Dé Ishtar, Zohl. *Daughters of the Pacific*. North Melbourne: Spinifex, 1994.

Denoon, Donald. "New Economic Orders: Land, Labour and Dependency." In *The Cambridge History of the Pacific Islanders*, edited by Donald Denoon, Stewart Firth, Jocelyn Linnekin, Malama Meleisea, and Karen Nero, 218–52. Cambridge: Cambridge University Press, 1997.

Diehl, Paul F. *International Peacekeeping*. Baltimore: The Johns Hopkins University Press, 1994.

Dienstag, Joshua Foa. "Serving God and Mammon: The Lockean Sympathy in Early American Political Thought." *American Political Science Review* 90, no. 3 (1996): 497–511.

Dirlik, Arif. "The Asia-Pacific Idea: Reality and Representation in the Invention of a Regional Structure." *Journal of World History* 3, no. 1 (1992): 55–79.

Doty, Roxanne L. *Imperial Encounters: The Politics of Representation in North–South Relations*. Minneapolis: University of Minnesota Press, 1996.

Downie, Sue. "UNTAET: State-building and Peace-building in East Timor." In *East Timor Beyond Independence*, edited by Damien Kingsbury and Michael Leach. Melbourne: Monash University Press, 2007.

Doyle, Michael W. *UN Peacekeeping in Cambodia: UNTAC's Civil Mandate*. Boulder: Lynne Rienner, 1995.

Doyle, Michael W., and Nishkala Suntharalignam, "The UN in Cambodia: Lessons for Complex Peacekeeping," *International Peacekeeping* 1, no. 2 (Summer 1994): 117–47.

Dworkin, Ronald. *A Matter of Principle*. Cambridge: Harvard University Press, 1985.

Earth, Barbara. "Globalization and Human Rights as Gendered Ideologies: A Case Study from Northeast Thailand." *Gender, Technology and Development* 9, no.1 (2005): 104–22.

Ebihara, May M., Carol A. Mortland, and Judy Ledgerwood. "Introduction." In *Cambodian Culture since 1975: Homeland and Exile*, 1–26. Ithaca: Cornell University Press, 1994.

Ehrenreich, Barbara, and Arlie R. Hochschild. "Introduction." In *Global Woman: Nannies, Maids, and Sex Workers in the New Economy*, edited by Barbara Ehrenreich and Arlie R. Hochschild, 1–14. New York: Henry Holt, 2002.

Eisenstein, Zillah. *Against Empire: Feminisms, Race and the West*. New York: Palgrave Macmillan, 2004.

———. *The Color of Gender: Reimaging Democracy*. Berkeley: The University of California Press, 1994.

Elshtain, Jean Bethke. *Women and War*. Basic Books: New York, 1987.

Emberson-Bain, 'Atu. "Women, Poverty, and Post-Coup Pressure." In *Tu Galala: Social Change in the Pacific*, edited by David Robie, 145–62. New Zealand: Bridget Williams Books, 1992.

———, ed. *Sustainable Development or Malignant Growth: Perspectives of Pacific Islands Women*. Suva: Marama Publications, 1994.

Engle, Karen. "'Calling in the Troops': The Uneasy Relationship Among Women's Rights, Human Rights, and Humanitarian Intervention." *Harvard Human Rights Journal* 20 (2007): 189–226.

———. "Liberal Internationalism, Feminism, and the Suppression of Critique: Contemporary Approaches to Global Order in the United States," *Harvard International Law Journal* 46, no. 2 (2005): 427–40.

Enloe, Cynthia. *Maneuvers: The International Politics of Militarizing Women's Lives*. Berkeley: University of California Press, 2000.

———. *The Morning After: Sexual Politics at the End of the Cold War*. Berkeley: University of California Press, 1993.

———. *Bananas, Beaches and Bases: Making Feminist Sense of International Politics*. Berkeley: University of California Press, 1989.

Falk, Richard. "Global Civil Society: Perspectives, Initiatives, Movements." *Oxford Development Studies* 26 (1998): 99–111.

———. *On Humane Governance: Toward a New Global Politics*. Cambridge: Polity, 1995.

Fanon, Frantz. *Black Skin, White Masks*. Translated by Charles Lam Markmann. New York: Grove, 1967.

Feldman, Noah. *What We Owe Iraq: War and the Ethics of Nation Building*. Princeton: Princeton University Press, 2004.

———. *After Jihad: American and the Struggle for Islamic Democracy*. New York: Farrar, Straus and Giroux, 2003.

Ferree, Myra Marx, and Aili Mari Tripp, ed. *Global Feminism: Transnational Women's Activism, Organizing, and Human Rights*. New York: New York University Press, 2006.

Fetherston, Betts. "UN Peacekeepers and Cultures of Violence." *Cultural Survival Quarterly* 19, no. 1 (1995): 19–23.

Fiji Women's Rights Movement. *Herstory: A Profile of the Fiji Women's Rights Movement*. Suva: FWRM, 2000.

Firth, Stewart. "Colonial Administration and the Invention of the Native." In *The Cambridge History of the Pacific Islanders*, edited by Donald Denoon, Stewart Firth, Jocelyn Linnekin, Malama Meleisea, and Karen Nero, 253–88. Cambridge: Cambridge University Press, 1997.

Fitzsimmons, Tracy. "Engendering Justice and Security After War." In *Constructing Justice and Security After War*, edited by Charles T. Call, 351–74. Washington, DC: United States Institute of Peace, 2007.

Foucault, Michel. *Discipline and Punish: the Birth of the Prison*. Translated by Alan Sheridan. London: Penguin, 1991.

Friedman, Elizabeth. "The Effects of 'Transnationalism Reversed' in Venezuela: Assessing the impact of UN Global Conferences on the Women's Movement." *International Journal of Feminist Politics* 1 (1999): 357–81.

Friman, Richard, and Peter Andreas, ed. *The Illicit Global Economy and State Power*. Lanham, MD: Rowman & Littlefield, 1999.

Frum, David. *The Right Man: The Surprise Presidency of George W. Bush*. New York: Random House, 2003.

Fry, Greg. "Whose Oceania? Contending Visions of Community in Pacific Region-building." Working Paper 2004/3. Canberra: Department of International Relations, RSPAS, Australian National University, 2004.

———. "Framing the Islands: Knowledge and Power in Changing Australian Images of 'the South Pacific.'" *Contemporary Pacific* 9, no. 2 (1997): 305–44.

Fukuyama, Francis. "Women and the Evolution of World Politics." *Foreign Affairs* 77, no. 5 (September/October 1998).

———. "The End of History?" *The National Interest*, Summer (1989): 3–18.

Gartzke, Erik. "The Capitalist Peace." *American Journal of Political Science* 51, no. 1 (2007): 166–91.

Gender Affairs Unit, and Cliondah O'Keeffe, *Situational Analysis of Gender in Post-Conflict East Timor*. Dili: Gender Affairs Unit, 2002.

George, Nicole. "Women's Re-Visions of Globalization: Gender and Globalization in Asia and the Pacific: Feminist Revisions of the International Workshop." *International Feminist Journal of Politics* 4, no. 2 (2002): 268–77.

Ghosh, Amitav. "The Global Reservation: Notes Toward an Ethnography of International Peacekeeping." *Cultural Anthropology* 9, no. 3 (1994): 412–22.

Gibson-Graham, J. K. *The End of Capitalism (as we knew it): A Feminist Critique of Political Economy*. Cambridge: Blackwell, 1996.

Gill, Stephen. "Globalisation, Market Civilisation, and Disciplinary Neoliberalism." *Millennium* 23, no.3 (1995): 399–423.

Gilpin Robert. *The Challenge of Global Capitalism. The World Economy in the 21st Century*, Princeton: Princeton University Press, 2002.

Gills, Dong-Sook S., and Nicola Piper, ed. *Women and Work in Globalising Asia*. London: Routledge, 2002.

Goetz, Anne-Marie. *Women Development Workers: Implementing Rural Credit Programmes in Bangladesh*. New Delhi: Sage, 2001.

Grant, Rebecca, and Kathleen Newland. *Gender and International Relations*. Buckingham: Open University Press, 1991.

Griffen, Vanessa. "Local and Global Women's Rights in the Pacific." *Development* 49, no. 1 (2006): 108–12.

———. "The Pacific Islands: All It Requires is Ourselves." In *Sisterhood is Global: The International Women's Movement Anthology*, edited by Robin Morgan, 517–24. New York: Anchor Books, 1984.

Grynberg, Roman. *Toward a New Pacific Regionalism*. Pacific Studies Series, Asian Development Bank—Commonwealth Secretariat Joint Report to the Pacific Islands Forum Secretariat. Manila: Asian Development Bank, 2005.

Gutmann, Matthew. "Rituals of Resistance: a Critique of the Theory of Everyday Forms of Resistance." *Latin American Perspectives* 20:2 (Spring 1993).

Hakena, Helen. "Strengthening Communities for Peace in Bougainville." In *Conflict and Peacemaking in the Pacific: Social and Gender Perspectives, Development Bulletin*, special issue, no. 53: 17–19.

Halley, Janet. *Split Decisions: How and Why to Take a Break from Feminism*. Princeton: Princeton University Press, 2006.

Handrahan, Lori. "Rhetoric and Reality: Post-Conflict Recovery and Development—the UN and Gender Reform." In *The UN, Human Rights and Post-Conflict Situations*, edited by Nigel D. White and Dirk Klaasen. Huntington, NY: Juris Publishing, 2005.

Hanochi, Seiko. "Japan and the Global Sex Industry." In *Gender, Globalization, & Democratization*, edited by Rita Mae Kelly, Jane H. Bayes, Mary E. Hawkesworth, and Brigitte Young, 137–48. Lanham, MD: Rowman & Littlefield, 2001.

Harding, Sandra. "Introduction: Is There a Feminist Method?" In *Feminism and Methodology*, edited by Sandra Harding, 1–14. Bloomington: Indiana University Press, 1987.

Harding, Sandra, and Kathryn Norberg. "New Feminist Approaches to Social Science Methodologies: An Introduction." *Signs* 30, no. 4 (2005): 2009–15.

Harrington, Christy. "'Marriage' to Capital: The Fallback Positions of Fiji's Women Garment Workers." *Development in Practice* 14 (2004): 495–507.

Harris Rimmer, Susan. "East Timorese Women and Transitional Justice." In *Global Issues: Women and Justice*, edited by Sharon Pickering and Caroline Lambert. Sydney: Institute of Criminology, 2004.

Harriss-White, Barbara. "Female and Male Grain Marketing Systems, Analytical and Policy Issues for West Africa and India." In *Feminist Visions of Development*, edited by Cecile Jackson and Ruth Pearson, 189–213. London: Routledge, 1998.

Hau'ofa, Epeli. "Our Sea of Islands." *The Contemporary Pacific* 6, no. 1 (1994): 148–61.

Hawkesworth, Mary E. *Globalization and Feminist Activism*. Lanham, MD: Rowman & Littlefield, 2006.

Heininger Janet E. *Peacekeeping in Transition: The United Nations in Cambodia*. New York: The Twentieth Century Fund, Inc., 1994.

Held, David. "Democracy and Globalization." In *Re-imagining Political Community: Studies in Cosmopolitan Democracy*, edited by Daniele Archibugi, David Held, and Michael Köhler, 11–27. Stanford: Stanford University Press, 1998.

———. *Democracy and the Global Order: From the Modern State to Cosmopolitan Governance*. Stanford: Stanford University Press, 1995.

Hellum, Anne. "Human Rights and Gender Relations in Postcolonial Africa: Options and Limits for the Subjects of Legal Pluralism." *Law and Social Inquiry* 25 (2000): 635–56.

Herr, Richard. "Pacific Island Regionalism: How Firm the Foundation for Future Cooperation?" In *Pacific Futures*, edited by Michael Powles, 91–110. Canberra: Pandanus Books, Australian National University, 2006.

Hewitson, Gillian J. *Feminist Economics: Interrogating the Masculinity of Rational Economic Man*. Cheltenham: Edward Elgar, 1999.

Hevia, James L. *Cherishing Men from Afar: Qing Guest Ritual and the Macartney Embassy of 1793*. Durham: Duke University Press, 1995.

Ho, Ping-ti. *Youguan sunzi laozi de sanpian kaocheng* (Three Studies on Sun Tzu and Lao Tzu). Taipei: Institute of Modern History, Academica Sinica, 2002.

Hochschild, Arlie R. "Love and Gold." In *Global Woman: Nannies, Maids, and Sex Workers in the New Economy*, edited by Barbara Ehrenreich and Arlie R. Hochschild, 15–30. New York: Henry Holt, 2002.

Hollinsworth, David. *Race and Racism in Australia*. 2nd ed. Katoomba, NSW: Social Sciences, 1998.

hooks, bell. *Ain't I A Woman: Black Women and Feminism*. Boston: South End, 1981.

Hooper, Charolotte. *Manly States: Masculinities, International Relations, and Gender Politics*. New York: Columbia University Press, 2001.

Hoskyns, Catherine, and Shirin M. Rai. *Gendering International Political Economy*. CSGR Working Paper 170/05 (May 2005).

Howell, Jude, and Diane Mulligan. *Gender and Civil Society: Transcending Boundaries*. Abingdon: Routledge, 2005.

Huffer, Elise. "The Pacific Plan: A Political and Cultural Critique." In *Redefining the Pacific? Regionalism Past, Present and Future*, edited by Jenny Bryant-Tokalau and Ian Frazer, 157–74. Hampshire: Ashgate Publishing, 2006.

Huggins, Jackie, and Rita Huggins. *Auntie Rita*. Aboriginal Studies: Canberra, 1994.

Hull, Gloria, Patricia Scott, and Barbara Smith, ed. *All the Women are White, All the Blacks are Men, But Some of Us are Brave*. New York: Feminist, 1982.

Human Rights and Equal Opportunity Commission. *Bringing Them Home: National Inquiry into the Separation of Aboriginal and Torres Strait Islander Children from Their Families*. Sydney: HREOC, 1997.

Hunt, Krista, and Kim Rygiel, ed. *(En)Gendering the War on Terror*. Aldershot: Ashgate 2006.

Hunt, Michael. *Ideology and US Foreign Policy*. New Haven: Yale University Press, 1987.

Hunt, Swanee, and Cristina Posa. "Iraq's Excluded Women." *Foreign Policy* 143 (July/August 2004): 40–45.

Hussein, Shakira. "The War on Terror and the Rescue of Muslim Women." In *Islam in World Politics*, edited by Nelly Lahoud and Anthony Johns, 93–103. London: Routledge, 2005.

Huynh, Kim. *Where the Sea Takes Us: A Vietnamese-Australian Story*. Sydney: HarperCollins, 2007.

———. "Modernity and My Mum: A Literary Exploration into the (Extra)ordinary Sacrifices and Everyday Resistance of a Vietnamese Woman." *Frontiers: A Journal of Women Studies* 25, no. 2 (2004): 1–25.

Hymowitz, Kay S. "Why Feminism is AWOL on Islam." *City Journal* 13, no. 1 (2003). http://www.city-journal.org/html/13_1_why_feminism.html (accessed March 23, 2008).

Inter-Asian Cultural Studies. "September 11 and its Aftermath: Movement Statements." 3, no. 1 (2002): 121–33.

International Feminist Journal of Politics. Theme Issue on "Feminist International Relations in the Age of the War on Terror: Ideologies, Religions and Conflict." 8, no. 1 (2006).

———. Special Issue on "Gender Violence and Hegemonic Projects." 8, no. 4 (2006).

———. "Forum: The Events of 11 September 2001 and Beyond." 4, no. 1 (2002): 95–115.

Jaggar, Alison. "Love and Knowledge: Emotion in Feminist Epistemology." In *Feminisms*, edited by Sandra Kemp and Judith Squires, 188–93. Oxford: Oxford University Press, 1997.

James, Alan. "Peacekeeping in the Post-Cold War Era." *International Journal*, L2 (Spring 1995): 241–65.

Jayawardena, Kumari, and Malathi de Alwis, ed. *Embodied Violence: Communalising Women's Sexuality in South Asia*. Delhi: Kali for Women, 1996.

Joachim, Jutta. *Agenda Setting, the UN, and NGOs: Gender Violence and Reproductive Rights*. Washington, DC: Georgetown University Press, 2007.

———. "Framing Issues, Seizing Opportunities: The UN, NGOs and Women's Rights," *International Studies Quarterly* 47 (2003): 247–74.

———. "Shaping the Human Rights Agenda: The Case of Violence Against Women." In *Gender Politics in Global Governance*, edited by Mary K. Meyer and Elizabeth Prügl, 142–60. Lanham, MD: Rowman & Littlefield Publishers, 1999.

Jolly, Margaret. "Beyond the Horizon? Nationalisms, Feminisms and Globalization in the Pacific." *Ethnohistory* 52 (2005): 138–66.

———. "Women-Nation-State in Vanuatu: Women as Signs and Subjects in the Discourses of Kastom, Modernity and Christianity." In *Narratives of Nation in the South Pacific*, edited by Ton Otto and Nicholas Thomas, 133–62. Amsterdam: Harwood Academic Publishers, 1997.

Jolly, Margaret, and Martha Macintyre, ed. *Family and Gender in the Pacific: Domestic Contradictions and the Colonial Impact*. Cambridge: Cambridge University Press, 1989.

Joseph, Ammu, and Kalpana Sharma, ed. *Terror, Counter Terror Women Speak Out*. London: Zed Books, 2003.

Jung, Hwa Yol. "Confucianism and Existentialism: Intersubjectivity as the Way of Man." *Philosophy and the Phenomenological Research* 30, no. 2 (December 1969): 186–202.

Justine Guest, Krysti. "Activist." In *Back to Basics from Beijing: An Australian Guide to the International Platform for Action*, edited by Suzette Mitchell and Rima Das Pradhan. Deakin: ACFOA, 1997.

Kabeer, Naila. *Mainstreaming Gender in Social Protection for the Informal Economy*. Gender Mainstreaming in Development Series. London: Commonwealth Secretariat, 2008.

———. "Resources, Agency, Achievements: Reflections on the Measurement of Women's Empowerment." In *Gendered Poverty and Well-Being*, edited by Shahra Razavi, 27–56. Oxford: Blackwell, 2000.

Kaldor, Mary. *Global Civil Society: An Answer to War*. Cambridge: Polity, 2003.

Kamonpetch, Aungkana. "The Progress of Preliminary Phase of Khmer Repatriation." *Occasional Paper Series No. 6*. Bangkok: Indochinese Refugee Information Center, Institute of Asian Studies, Chulalongkorn University, May 1993.

Kandiyoti, Deniz, ed. *Women, Islam and the State*. Basingstoke: Macmillan, 1991.

———. "Bargaining with Patriarchy," *Gender and Society* 2, no. 3 (1988): 274–90.

Keane, John. *Global Civil Society*? Cambridge: Cambridge University Press, 2003.

———. "Global Civil Society?" In *Global Civil Society 2001*, edited by Helmut Anheier, Mary H Kaldor, and Marlies Glasius, 23–47. Oxford: Oxford University Press, Oxford, 2002.

Keck, Kathryn, and Margaret Sikkink. *Activists Beyond Borders*. Ithaca: Cornell University Press, 1998.

Kelly, John, and Martha Kaplan. *Represented Communities: Fiji and World Decolonization*. Chicago: University of Chicago Press, 2001.

Kempadoo, Kamala, and Jo Doezema, ed. *Global Sex Workers*. New York: Routledge, 1998.

Kennedy-Pipe, Caroline. "Whose Security? State-Building and the 'Emancipation' of Women in Central Asia." *International Relations* 18, no. 1 (2004): 91–107.

Kensinger, Loretta. "Plugged in Praxis: Critical Reflections on U.S. Feminism, Internet Activism, and Solidarity with Women in Afghanistan." *Journal of International Women's Studies* 5, no. 1 (2003), 1–28.

Khan, Shahnaz. "Reconfiguring the Native Informant: Positionality in the Global Age," *Signs* 30, no. 4 (2005): 2017–35.

Kirsch, Gesa E. "Friendship, Friendliness, and Feminist Fieldwork." *Signs* 30, no. 4 (2005): 2163–72.

Kirshenbaum, Gayle. "Who's Watching the Peacekeepers?" *Ms*. (May/June, 1994).

Koskenniemi, Martti. "Book Review: 'Dorinda Dallmeyer, ed. Reconceiving Reality: Women and International Law'." *American Journal of International Law* 89 (1995): 227–30.

Kooiman, Jan. *Governing as Governance*. London: Sage, 2003.

Krasner, Stephen. "International Law and International Relations: Together, Apart, Together." *Chicago Journal of International Law* 1 (2000): 93–100.

Lacey, Nicola. "Feminist Legal Theory and the Rights of Women." In *Gender and Human Rights*, edited by Karen Knop, 13–56. Oxford: Oxford University Press, 2004.

Lal, Jayati. "Situating Locations: The Politics of Self, Identity, And 'Other' In Living and Writing the Text." In *Feminst Dilemmas in Fieldwork*, edited by Diane L. Wolf, 185–214. Boulder: Westview, 1996.

Larbalestier, Jan. "The Politics of Representation: Aboriginal Women and Feminism." *Anthropolgoical Forum* 6, no. 2 (1990): 143–57.

Lazreg, Marnia. "Feminism and Difference—the Perils of Writing as a Woman on Women in Algeria." *Feminist Studies* 14, no. 1 (1988): 81–107.

Leckie, Jaqueline. "The Complexities of Women's Agency in Fiji." In *Gender Politics in the Asia-Pacific Region*, edited by Brenda S. A.Yeoh, Peggy Teo, and Shirlena Huang, 156–79. London: Routledge, 2002.

Ledgerwood, Judy. "UN Peacekeeping Missions: The Lessons from Cambodia." *Analysis from the East-West Center* 11. Honolulu: East–West Center, March 1994.

———. *Analysis of the Situation of Women in Cambodia*. Phnom Penh: UNICEF, February/ June, 1992.

Lee-Koo, Katrina. "Feminism." In *An Introduction to International Relations: Australian Perspectives*, edited by Richard Devetak, Anthony Burke, and Jim George, 75–77. Cambridge: Cambridge University Press, 2008.

———. "Security as Enslavement/ Security as Emancipation: Gendered Legacies and Feminist Futures in the Asia-Pacific." In *Critical Security in the Asia-Pacific*, edited by Anthony Burke and Matt McDonald, 231–46. Manchester: Manchester University Press, 2007.

Lepani, Katherine. "Everything Has Come up to the Open Space: Talking about Sex in an Epidemic." Working Paper 15. Canberra: Gender Relations Center, ANU, 2005.

Li, Dongpuo. "Sunzi zhanzhengguan xinlun" (A New Approach to Sun Tzu's View of War). *Zhexue Baijia*, no. 6 (2007): 190–92.

Li, Wai-Yee. "The Idea of Authority in the Shih Chi (Records of the Historian)." *Harvard Journal of Asiatic Studies* 54, no. 2, December (1994): 345–405.

Lim, Lin Lean, ed. *The Sex Sector: The Economic and Social Bases of Prostitution in Southeast Asia*. Geneva: International Labor Office, 1998.

Lindio-McGovern, Ligaya. "Alienation and Labor Export in the Context of Globalization: Filipino Migrant Domestic Workers in Taiwan and Hong Kong." *Critical Asian Studies* 36, no. 2 (2004): 217–38.

Ling, L. H. M. "Borders of Our Minds: Territories, Boundaries, and Power in the Confucian Tradition." In *States, Nations, and Borders: The Ethics of Making Boundaries*, edited by Margaret Moore and Allen Buchanan, 86–100. Cambridge: Cambridge University Press, 2003.

———. "Borderlands: A Postcolonial–Feminist Alternative to Neoliberal Self/Other Relations." In *Mehrheit am Rand? Geschlechterverhaeltnisse, globale Ungleichheit und transnationale Loesungsansaetze*, edited by Susanne Zwingel, Heike Brandt, and Bettina Bross. Berlin: VS Verlag, forthcoming.

———. *Postcolonial International Relations: Conquest and Desire between Asia and the West*. London: Palgrave Macmillan, 2002.

———. "Rationalizations for State Violence in Chinese Politics: The Hegemony of Parental Governance." *Journal of Peace Research* 31, no. 4, November (1994): 393–405.

Lloyd, Genevieve. *Man of Reason*. Minneapolis: University of Minnesota Press, 1993.

Lo, De-shun, ed. *Sun tzu Bing fa*. Taipei: Li-ming Wen Hua Publishing House, 1991.

Lorentzen, Lois, and Jennifer Turpin, ed. *The Women and War Reader*. New York: New York University Press, 1998.

Luthria, Manjula, Ron Duncan, Richard Brown, Peter Mares, and Nic MacLellan. *At Home and Away: Expanding Job Opportunities for Pacific Islanders through Labour Mobility*. Washington, DC: World Bank, 2006.

Lycklama à Nijeholt, Geertje. "Women in International Migration." In *A Commitment to the World's Women*, edited by Noleen Heyzer. New York: UNIFEM, 1995.

MacKinnon, Catharine. *Are Women Human? And Other International Dialogues*. Cambridge: Harvard University Press, 2006.

Mahmood, Saba. *The Politics of Piety: The Islamic Revival and the Feminist Subject*. Princeton: Princeton Unversity Press, 2005.

Maimbo, Samuel M., Richard H. Adams, Jr., Reena Aggarwal, and Nikos Passas, ed. *Migrant Labour Remittances in South Asia*. Washington, DC: World Bank, 2005.

Manchanda, Rita, ed. *Women, War and Peace in South Asia: Beyond Victimhood to Agency*. New Delhi: Sage Publishers, 2001.

Manne, Robert, and David Corlett. "Sending Them Home: Refugees and the New Politics of Indifference," *Quarterly Essay*, no. 13 (2004).

Mannoni, Octave. *Prospero and Caliban: The Psychology of Colonization*. New York: Frederick A. Praeger, 1956.

Marchand, Marianne, and Ann Sisson Runyan, ed. *Gender and Global Restructuring*. London: Routledge, 2000.

McMichael, Philip. *Development and Social Change: A Global Perspective*. 2nd ed. Thousand Oaks, CA: Pine Force, 2000.

Mead, Aroha Te Pareake. *The Broader Pacific Plan, Tidying-up the Region: Commentary Prepared on the South Pacific Forum's Pacific Plan*. Wellington: Civil Society Groups Throughout the Pacific Region, 2005.

Mecready, Douglas M. "Learning from Sun Tzu." *Military Review* (May/June 2003): 85–88.

Meggitt, Mervyn J. "Women in Contemporary Central Enga Society, Papua New Guinea." In *Family and Gender in the Pacific: Domestic Contradictions and the Colonial Impact*, edited by Margaret Jolly and Martha Macintyre, 135–55. Cambridge: Cambridge University Press, 1989.

Mehta, Uday S. "Liberal Strategies of Exclusion." In *Tensions of Empire: Colonial Cultures in a Bourgeois World*, edited by Frederick Cooper and Ann Laura Stoler, 59–86. Berkeley: University of California Press, 1997.

Memmi, Albert. *The Colonizer and the Colonized*. Boston: Beacon, 1991 (1957).

Mendez, Jennifer Bickham. "Creating Alternatives from a Gender Perspective: Transnational Organizing for Maquila Workers' Rights in Central America." In *Women's Activism and Globalization: Linking Local Struggles and Transnational Politics*, edited by Nancy Naples and Manisha Desai, 121–41. London: Routledge, 2001.

Menon, Ritu, and Kamla Bhasin. *Borders and Boundaries: Women in India's Partition*. Delhi: Kali for Women, 1998.

Mesquita, Bruce Bueno de, James D. Morrow, Randolph M. Siverson, and Alastair Smith. "Testing Novel Implications from the Selectorate Theory of War." *World Politics*, no. 56 (2004): 363–88.

Meyer, Mary K., and Elisabeth Prügl. *Gender Politics in Global Governance*. Lanham, MD: Rowman & Littlefield, 1999.

Miller, Mark Crispin. *The Bush Dyslexicon: Observations on a National Disorder*. New York: Norton, 2003.

Min, Gap. "Korean 'Comfort Women': The Intersection of Colonial Power, Gender and Class." *Gender and Society* 17, no. 6 (December 2003): 938–57.

Moghadam, Valentine M. *Globalizing Women: Transnational Feminist Networks*. Baltimore: Johns Hopkins University Press, 2005.

———. "Islamic Feminism and its Discontents: Toward a Resolution of the Debate." *Signs* 27, no. 4 (2002): 1135–71.

Mohanty, Chandra Talpade. *Feminism Without Borders: Decolonizing Theory, Practicing Solidarity*. Durham: Duke University Press, 2003.

———. "'Under Western Eyes' Revisited: Feminist Solidarity through Anticapitalist Struggles." *Signs* 28, no. 2 (2003): 499–537.

———. "Under Western Eyes, Feminist Scholarship and Colonial Discourses." *Boundary 2: An International Journal of Literature and Culture* 13, no. 1 (1984): 333–58.

Molyneux, Maxine. "Mobilization Without Emancipation? Women's Interests, State and Revolution." In *Transition and Development: Problems of Third World Socialism*, edited by Richard Fagen, Carmen D. Deere, Jose L. Coraggio, 280–320. New York: Monthly Review, 1985.

Moraga, Cherrie, and Gloria Anzadlua, ed. *This Bridge Called My Back: Writings by Radical Women of Colour*. New York: Kitchen Table, 1983.

Moser, Caroline, and Fiona Clark, ed. *Victims, Perpetrators or Actors: Gender, Armed Conflict and Political Violence*. London: Zed Books, 2001.

Morrow, Jonathan, and Rachel White. "The United Nations in Transitional East Timor: International Standards and the Reality of Governance." *Australian Yearbook of International Law* 22 (2002): 1–46.

Moser-Puangsuwan, Yeshua. "U.N. Peacekeeping in Cambodia: Whose Needs Were Met?" *Pacifica Review* 7, no. 2 (1995): 103–27.

Mushakoji, Kinhide. "Engendering the Japanese 'Double Standard' Patriarchal Democracy." In *Gender, Globalization, and Democratization,* edited by Rita Mae Kelly, Jane H. Bayes, Mary E. Hawkesworth, and Brigitte Young, 205–22. Lanham, MD: Rowman & Littlefield, 2001.

Mysliwiec, Eva. *Punishing the Poor: The International Isolation of Kampuchea.* Oxford: Oxfam, 1988.

Nakaya, Sumie. "Women and Gender Equality in Peacebuilding: Somalia and Mozambique." In *Building Sustainable Peace*, edited by Tom Keating and W. Andy Knight, 143–66. Tokyo: UNUP, 2004.

Naples, Nancy, and Manisha Desai, ed. *Women's Activism and Globalization: Linking Local Struggles and Transnational Politics.* London: Routledge, 2002.

Naylor, R. T. *Wages of Crime: Black Markets, Illegal Finance, and the Underground Economy.* Ithaca: Cornell University Press, 2002.

Nesiah, Vasuki. "From Berlin to Bonn to Baghdad: A Space for Infinite Justice." *Harvard Human Rights Journal* 17 (2004): 75–98.

Niou, Emerson M., and Peter C. Ordershook. "A Game-theoretic Interpretation of Sun Tzu's The Art of War." *Journal of Peace Research* 31, no. 2 (1994): 161–74.

Niu, Xian Zhong. *Sun tzu san lun: cong gu bing fa dao xin zhan lue.* Taipei: Mai Tian Publishing House, 1996.

Nyers, Peter. *Rethinking Refugees: Beyond States of Emergency.* New York: Routledge, 2006.

O'Brien, Patty. *The Pacific Muse: Exotic Femininity and the Colonial Pacific.* Seattle: University of Washington Press, 2006.

O'Brien, Robert, Anne Marie Goetz, Jan Aart Scholte, and Marc Williams, ed. *Contesting Global Governance: Multilateral Economic Institutions and Global Social Movements.* Cambridge: Cambridge University Press, 2000.

Ogashiwa, Yoko S. *Microstates and Nuclear Issues: Regional Cooperation in the Pacific.* Suva: Institute of Pacific Studies of the University of the South Pacific, 1991.

O'Hare, Ursula. "Realizing Human Rights for Women." *Human Rights Quarterly* 21 (1999): 364–402.

Ong, Aihwa. "Mother's Milk in War and Diaspora." *Cultural Survival Quarterly* (Spring 1995): 61–64.

Orford, Anne. *Reading Humanitarian Intervention: Human Rights and the Use of Force in International Law.* Cambridge: Cambridge University Press, 2003.

Parreñas, Rhacel Salazar. "The International Division of Reproductive Labor: Paid Domestic Work and Globalization." In *Critical Globalization Studies,* edited by Richard P. Appelbaum and William I. Robinson, 237–47. New York: Routledge, 2005.

Parpart, Jane, and Marysia Zalewski, ed. *Rethinking the 'Man' Question: Sex, Gender and Violence in International Relations.* London: Zed Books, 2008.

Parpart, Jane, Shirin M. Rai, and Kathleen Staudt, ed. *Rethinking Empowerment: Gender and Development in a Global/Local World.* London: Routledge, 2002.

Pateman, Carole. *The Sexual Contract*. Cambridge: Polity, 1988.

Paxton, Pamela. "Women's Suffrage in the Measurement of Democracy: Problems of Operationalization." *Studies in Comparative International Development* 35, no. 3 (2000): 92–111.

Pearson, Ruth. "The Social is Political: Towards the Reconceptualization of Feminist Analysis of the Global Economy." *International Feminist Journal of Politics* 6, no. 4 (2004): 603–22.

Peterson, V. Spike. "Getting Real: The Necessity of Poststructuralism in Global Political Economy." In *International Political Economy and Poststructural Politics*, edited by Marieke de Goede, 119–38. London: Palgrave International Political Economy Series, 2006.

———. "How (the Meaning of) Gender Matters in Political Economy." *New Political Economy* 10, no. 4 (2005): 499–521.

———. "Feminist Theories Within, Invisible to, and Beyond IR." *Brown Journal of World Affairs* X, no. 2 (Winter/ Spring 2004): 35–46.

———. *A Critical Rewriting of Global Political Economy: Integrating Reproductive, Productive, and Virtual Economies*. London: Routledge, 2003.

———. *Gendered States: Feminist (Re)Visions of International Relations Theory*. Boulder, CO: Lynne Reinner, 1992.

Peterson, V. Spike, and Anne Sisson Runyan, ed. *Global Gender Issues*. Boulder: Westview, 1993.

Pettman, Jindy. "Reflections on the Gendering of States, Sovereignty and Security in the Study of International Relations." *Intersections: Gender, History and Culture in the Asian Context* 15 (May 2007). http://wwwsshe.murdoch.edu.au/intersections/issue15/pettman.htm (accessed March 23, 2008).

———. "Questions of Identity: Australia and Asia." In *Critical Security Studies and World Politics*, edited by Ken Booth, 159–77. Boulder, CO: Lynne Rienner, 2005.

———. "Global Politics and Transnational Feminisms." In *Feminist Politics, Activism and Vision: Local and Global Challenges*, edited by Luciana Ricciutelli, Angela Miles, and Margaret H. McFadden, 49–63. London: Zed Books, 2005.

———. "Feminist International Relations After 9/11." *Brown Journal of World Affairs*, 10:2 (2004): 85–96.

———. "International Sex and Service." In *Globalization: Theory and Practice*, 2nd edition, edited by Eleonore Kofman and Gillian Youngs, 158–72. Continuum, 2003.

———. "Transcending National Identity: the Global Political Economy of Gender and Class." In *International Relations: Still an American Social Science?*, edited by Robert Crawford and Darryl Jarvis, 255–74. New York: St. Martin's, 2001.

———. "A Feminist Perspective on Australia in Asia." In *Race, Colour and Identity in Australia and New Zealand*, edited by John Docker and Gerard Fischer, 143–57. Sydney: UNSW Press, 2000.

———. "Women on the Move: Globalization and Labour Migration from South and Southeast Asian States." *Global Society* 12, no. 3 (1998): 389–403.

———. "Body Politics: International Sex Tourism." *Third World Quarterly* 18, no.1 (1997): 93–108.

———. *Worlding Women: A Feminist International Politics*. Sydney: Allen & Unwin, 1996.

———. "Australia." In *Unsettling Settler Societies: Articulations of Gender, Race, Ethnicity and Class*, edited by Daiva Stasiulis and Nira Yuval-Davis, 65–94. London: Sage, 1995.

———. "Gendering International Relations." *Australian Journal of International Affairs* 47 (1993): 47–62.

———. *Living in the Margins: Racism, Sexism and Feminism in* Australia. St. Leonards, NSW: Allen and Unwin, 1992.

———. "Gendered Knowledges: Aboriginal Women and the Politics of Feminism." *Journal of Australian Studies* 35 (1992): 120–31.

———. "Towards a (Personal) Politics of Location." *Studies in Continuing Education* 13, no. 2 (1991): 153–66.

———. "Adaptation in Education in Papua New Guinea." *The South Pacific Journal of Teacher Education* 9, no. 1 (1981): 55–60.

———. *Zambia, Security and Conflict*. New York: St. Martin's, 1974.

Pettman, Jindy, and Helen Meekosha, "Beyond Category Politics." *Hecate* 17, no. 2 (1991): 75–92.

Pietilä, Hilkka, and Jeanne Vickers, ed. *Making Women Matter: The Role of the United Nations*. London: Zed Books, 1999.

Piper, Nicola. "Gendering the Politics of Migration." *International Migration Review* 40, no. 1 (2006): 133–64.

———. "Feminization of Labor Migration as Violence Against Women: International, Regional, and Local Nongovernmental Organization Responses in Asia." *Violence Against Women* 9, no. 6 (2003): 723–45.

Pollack, Mark, and Emilie Hafner-Burton. "Mainstreaming Gender in Global Governance." *European Journal of International Relations* 8 (2002): 339–73.

Rai, Shirin M. "Gendering Global Governance." *International Feminist Journal of Politics* 6, no.4 (2004): 579–601.

———. *Gender and the Political Economy of Development: From Nationalism to Globalization*. Cambridge: Polity, 2002.

Randall, Stephen J. "Peacekeeping in the Post-Cold War Era: The United Nations and the 1993 Cambodian Elections." *Behind the Headlines* (Spring 1994): 1–16.

Rao, Arati. "The Politics of Gender and Culture in International Human Rights Discourse." In *Women's Rights Human Rights: International Feminist Perspectives*, edited by Julie Peters and Andrea Wolper, 167–75. New York: Routledge, 1995.

Reid, Elizabeth. "Transformational Development and the Wellbeing of Women." *Development Bulletin* 64 (2004): 16–20.

Rehn, Elizabeth, and Ellen Johnson-Sirleaf. "Women, War, Peace: The Independent Experts." In *Assessment on the Impact of Armed Conflict on Women and Women's Role in Peace-building*. New York: UNIFEM, 2002.

Resurrecion, Bernadette. "Women's Politics in Asia—Conference Report." *Gender, Technology and Development* 7, no. 3 (2003): 441–42.

Rich, Adrienne. *Blood, Bread and Poetry:Selected Prose, 1979–1985*. New York: Norton, 1986.

Robertson, Robbie T., and William Sutherland. *Government By The Gun: The Unfinished Business of Fiji's 2000 Coup*. Melbourne: Pluto, 2001.

Robinson, Court. "Rupture and Return: Repatriation, Displacement and Reintegration in Battambang Province Cambodia," *Occasional Paper Series No. 7*. Indochinese Refugee Information Center, Institute of Asian Studies, Chulllongkorn University, November 1994.

Rokotuivuna, Amelia, et al., ed. *Fiji: A Developing Australian Colony*. North Fitzroy: IDA, 1973.

Rosen, Stephen Peter. "Military Effectiveness: Why Society Matters." *International Security* 19, no. 4 (1995): 5–31.

Rosenau, James. "Towards an Ontology for Global Governance." In *Governance Without Government: Order and Change in World Politics*, edited by Martin Hewson and Timothy Sinclair, 287–301. Cambridge: Cambridge University Press, 1999.

Runyan, Anne Sisson, and V. Spike Peterson. "The Radical Future of Realism: Feminist Subversions of IR Theory." *Alternatives* 16 (1991): 67–106.

Russo, Ann. "The Feminist Majority Foundation's Campaign to Stop Gender Apartheid: The Intersection of Feminism and Imperialism in the United States." *International Feminist Journal of Politics* 8, no. 4 (2006): 557–80.

Sassen, Saskia. *Cities in a World Economy*. 2nd ed. Thousand Oaks, CA: Pine Forge, 2000.

———. *Globalization and Its Discontents: Essays on the New Mobility of People and Money*. New York: The New Press, 1998.

Schild, Verónica. "New Social Citizenship in Chile: NGOs and Social Provisioning under Neo-Liberalism." In *Gender Justice, Development and Rights*, edited by Maxine Molyneux and Shahra Razavi, 170–203. Oxford: Oxford University Press, 2002.

Schmidt, Joanna. "Paradise Lost? Social Change and Fa'afafine in Samoa." *Current Sociology* 51 (2003): 417–32.

Scott, James C. *Domination and the Arts of Resistance: Hidden Transcripts*. New Haven: Yale University Press, 1990.

———. *Weapons of the Weak: Everyday Forms of Peasant Resistance*. New Haven: Yale University Press, 1985.

Scott, James C., and Benedict J. Tria Kerkvliet. *Everyday Forms of Peasant Resistance in South-East Asia*. London: Frank Cass, 1986.

Secretariat of State for Women's Affairs, Kingdom of Cambodia. *Cambodia's Country Report: Women in Development*. Phnom Penh, July 1994.

Segal, Gerald. "The PLA and Chinese Foreign Policy Decision-Making." *International Affairs* 57, no. 3 (1981): 449–66.

Sharp, Rhonda, and Ray Broomhill. "Budgeting for Equality: The Australian Experience." *Feminist Economics* 8, no.1 (2002): 25–47.

Shawcross, William. *Deliver Us From Evil: Peacekeepers, Warlords and a World of Endless Conflict*. New York: Simon and Schuster, 2000.

Signs 28. "Roundtable: Gender and September 11." No. 1 (2002): 431–80.

Sjoberg, Laura. "Gendered Realities of the Immunity Principle: Why Gender Analysis Needs Feminism." *International Studies Quarterly* 50, no. 4 (2006): 889–910.

Slatter, Claire. *The Con/Dominion of Vanuatu? Paying the Price of Investment and Land Liberalisation: A case study of Vanuatu's Tourism Industry*. Auckland: Oxfam, 2006.

———. "Treading Water in Rapids? Non-Governmental Organizations and Resistance to Neoliberalism." In *Pacific Islands States in Globalization and Governance in the*

Pacific Islands, edited by Stewart Firth. Canberra: ANU E-Press, 2006. http://epress.anu.edu.au/globalgov_citation.html (accessed February 18, 2008).

———. "Banking on the Growth Model? The World Bank and Market Policies in the Pacific." In *Sustainable Development or Malignant Growth: Perspectives of Pacific Islands Women*, edited by 'Atu Emberson-Bain, 17–36. Suva: Marama Publications, 1994.

Smith, Tammy. "Post-War Bosnia and Herzegovina: The Erosion of Women's Rights under International Governance." *Critical Half* 3, no.2 (Fall 2005): 38–42.

Soguk, Nevzat. *States and Strangers: Refugees and Displacements of Statecraft*. Minneapolis: University of Minnesota Press, 1999.

Srimulyani, Eka. "Muslim Women and Education in Indonesia: The Pondok Pesantren Experience." *Asia Pacific Journal of Education* 27, no. 1 (2007): 85–89.

Stallabrass, Julian. "Spectacle and Terror." *New Left Review* 37 (2006): 87–106.

Steans, Jill. *Gender and International Relations*. 2nd edition. London: Polity, 2006.

———. "Engaging from the Margins: Feminist Encounters with the 'Mainstream' of International Relations." *The British Journal of Politics and International Relations* 5, no. 3 (August 2003): 428–54.

Stivens, Maila. "Introduction: Gender Politics and the Reimagining of Human Rights in the Asia Pacific." In *Human Rights and Gender Politics: Asia-Pacific Perspectives*, edited by Anne-Marie Hilsdon, Martha Macintyre, Vera Mackie, and Maila Stivens, 1–36. London: Routledge, 2000.

———. "Theorizing Gender, Power, and Modernity in Affluent Asia." In *Gender and Power in Affluent Asia*, edited by Krishna Sen and Maila Stivens, 1–34. London: Routledge, 1998.

Sunder, Madhavi. "Enlightened Constitutionalism." *Connecticut Law Review* 37, no. 4 (2005): 891–906.

Sutherland, William. *Beyond the Politics of Race: An Alternative History of Fiji to 1992*. Political and Social Change Monograph 15. Canberra: Research School of Pacific and Asian Studies, Australian National University, 1992.

Sylvester, Christine. *Feminist International Relations: An Unfinished Journey*. Cambridge: Cambridge University Press, 2002.

———.*Feminist Theory and International Relations in a Postmodern Era*. Cambridge: Cambridge University Press, 1994.

Tabet, Gihane. "Women in Personal Status Laws: Iraq, Jordan, Lebanon, Palestine, Syria." *SHS Papers in Women's Studies/ Gender Research* 4. Paris: UNESCO, July 2005.

Teaiwa, Teresia K. "Globalizing and Gendered Forces: The Contemporary Militarization of Pacific/Oceania." In *Gender and Globalization in Asia and the Pacific*, edited by Kathy E. Ferguson and Monique Mironescu. Honolulu: University of Hawaii Press, forthcoming.

Tetreault, Mary Ann, and Ronnie D. Lipschutz. *Global Politics as if People Mattered*. Boulder, CO: Rowman & Littlefield, 2005.

Thompson, Karen Brown. "Women's Rights are Human Rights." In *Transnational Social Movements, Networks and Norms*, edited by Sanjeev Khagram, James V. Riker, and Kathryn Sikkink, 96–122. Minneapolis: University of Minnesota Press, 2002.

Thompson, Mark R. "Female Leadership of Democratic Transitions in Asia." *Pacific Affairs* 75, no. 4 (Winter 2002/2003): 535–55.

Tickner, J. Ann. "Feminism Meets International Relations: Some Methodological Issues." In *Feminist Methodologies for International Relations*, edited by Brooke A. Ackerly, Maria Stern, and Jacqui True, 19–41. Cambridge: Cambridge University Press, 2006.

———. "What Is Your Research Program? Some Feminist Answers to International Relations Methodological Questions." *International Studies Quarterly* 49, no. 1 (2005): 1–21.

———. *Gendering World Politics: Issues and Approaches in the Post-Cold War Era*. New York: Columbia University Press, 2001.

———. "You Just Don't Understand: Troubled Engagements Between Feminists and IR Theorists." *International Studies Quarterly* 41, no. 4 (December 1997): 611–32.

———. *Gender in International Relations: Feminist Perspectives on Achieving Global Security*. New York: Columbia University Press, 1992.

Tow, William T. *Asia-Pacific Strategic Relations: Seeking Convergent Security*. Cambridge: Cambridge University Press, 2001.

Tow, William T., Ramesh Thakur, and In-Taek Hyun, ed. *Asia's Emerging Regional Order: Reconciling Traditional and Human Security*. New York: United Nations University Press, 2000.

Trembath, Anna, and Damian Grenfall. *Mapping the Pursuit of Gender Equality, Non-Government and International Agency Activity in Timor-Leste*. Melbourne: The Globalism Institute, RMIT University, 2007.

True, Jacqui. "Gender Specialists and Global Governance Organizations: New Forms of Women's Movement Mobilization." In *Women's Movements: In Abeyance or Flourishing in New Ways?*, edited by Marian Sawer and Sandra Grey, 91–104. New York: Routledge, 2008.

———. "Mainstreaming Gender in Global Public Policy." *International Feminist Journal of Politics* 5, no. 3 (2003): 368–96.

True, Jacqui, and Michael Mintrom. "Transnational Networks and Policy Diffusion: The Case of Gender Mainstreaming." *International Studies Quarterly* 45 (2001): 27–57.

Truong, Thanh-Dam. *Sex, Money and Morality: Prostitution and Tourism in Southeast Asia*. London: Zed Books, 1990.

Tucker, Margaret. *If Everyone Cared: An Autobiography*. Melbourne: Grosvenor, 1987.

Ullman, Harlan, and James P. Wade. *Shock and Awe: Achieving Rapid Dominance*. http://www.gutenberg.org/etext/7259 (accessed March 11, 2008).

United Nations. *Report of the Secretary-General on Women, Peace and Security*. UN Doc. S/2006/770 27, September 2006.

———. *Women and Peace and Security: Report of the Secretary-General*. UN Doc. S/2004/814, October 13, 2004.

United Nations Commission on the Status of Women. "Fourth World Conference on Women: Platform for Action." 1995. http://www.un.org/womenwatch/daw/bejing/plat1.htm (accessed February 6, 2008).

United Nations Development Program. *Arab Human Development Report: Creating Opportunities for future Generations*. New York: United Nations Publications, 2002.

———. *Human Development Report 2002*. New York: Oxford University Press, 2002.

United Nations Department of Peacekeeping Operations and the Joint United Nations Program on HIV/AIDS. "Protect Yourself and Those You Care About Against HIV/AIDS." New York: United Nations, April 1998.

United Nations Division for the Advancement of Women. "Women 2000: The Role of Women in United Nations Peacekeeping." No. 1, December 1995.

———. *World Survey on the Role of Women in Development*. New York: United Nations, 1999.

———. "Report from the National Women's Summit." Phnom Penh: UNIFEM, March 5–8, 1993, n.p.

Utting, Peter, ed. *Between Hope and Insecurity: The Social Consequences of the Cambodian Peace Process*. Geneva: United Nations Research Institute for Social Development, 1994.

van Bich, Pham. *The Vietnamese Family in Change: The Case of the Red River Delta*. Surrey: Curzon, 1999.

Van Staveren, Irene. "Global Finance and Gender." In *Civil Society and Global Finance*, edited by Jan Aart Scholte and Albrecht Schnabel, 228–46. London: Routledge, 2002.

Varani-Norton, Eta. "The Church Versus Women's Push for Change: The Case of Fiji." *Fijian Studies* 3 (2005): 223–47.

Wade, Robert H. "Is GlobalizationRreducing Poverty and Inequality?" *World Development* 32, no. 4 (2004): 567–89.

Wallace, Heather. "Gender and the Reform Process in Vanuatu and Solomon Islands." *Development Bulletin* 51 (March 2000): 23–25.

Waller, Marguerite R., and Jennifer Rycenga, ed. *Frontline Feminisms: Women, War, and Resistance*. New York: Routledge, 2001.

Ware, Vron. "Info-War and the Politics of Feminist Curiosity: Exploring New Frameworks for Feminist Intercultural Studies." *Cultural Studies* 20, no. 6 (2006): 526–51.

Watson, Sophie, ed. *Playing the State: Australian Feminist Interventions*. Sydney: Allen and Unwin, 1990.

Waylen, Georgina. "You Still Don't Understand: Why Troubled Engagements Continue between Feminists and (Critical) IPE." *Review of International Studies* 32 (2006): 145–64.

———. *Gender in Third World Politics*. Boulder: Lynne Rienner, 1996.

Wei, Zhanwu, and Zhongxiang Jing. "Lun 'Sunzi bingfa' zhong de zhexue tixi yu zheli tedian (On the Philosophical System and Philosophical Distinguishing Characteristics of Sun-tzu's *Art of War*)." *Journal of Jilin National University*. Humanities and Social Science Edition, no. 1 (February2007): 9–12.

Wesley-Smith, Terence. "There Goes the Neighborhood: The Politics of Failed States and Regional Intervention in the Pacific." In *Redefining the Pacific? Regionalism, Past, Present and Future*, edited by Jenny Bryant-Tokalau and Ian Frazer. Aldershot: Ashgate Publishing, 2006.

West, Lois. "The United Nations Women's Conferences and Feminist Politics." In *Gender Politics in Global Governance*, edited by Mary K Meyer and Elizabeth Prügl, 177–93. Lanham, MD: Rowman & Littlefield Publishers, 1999.

Whittaker, Andrea, ed. *Women's Health in Mainland Southeast Asia*. Binghamton, NY: Haworth, 2002.

Whittington, Sherrill. "Gender and Peacekeeping: The United Nations Transitional Administration in East Timor." *Signs: Journal of Women in Culture and Society* 28, no. 4 (2003): 1283–88.

Whitworth, Sandra. *Men, Masculinities and UN Peacekeeping: A Gendered Analysis*. Boulder, CO: Lynne Rienner, 2004.

Willman, Navarro Alys. "Making it at the Margins: The Criminalization of Nicaraguan Women's Labor under Structural Reform." *International Feminist Journal of Politics* 8, no. 2 (2006): 243–66.

Wilson, Lynn. *Speaking to Power: Gender and Politics in the Western Pacific*. New York: Routledge, 1995.

Wolf, Diane L. "Preface." In *Feminist Dilemmas in Fieldwork*, edited by Diane L. Wolf, ix–xii. Boulder: Westview, 1996.

———. "Situating Feminist Dilemmas in Fieldwork." In *Feminist Dilemmas in Fieldwork*, edited by Diane L. Wolf, 1–55. Boulder: Westview, 1996.

Woodward, Alison. "Gender Mainstreaming in European policy: Innovation or Deception?" Wissenschaftzentrum Berlin fur Sozialforschung Discussion Paper FS I, 2001.

Woolf, Virginia. *A Room of One's Own and Three Guineas*. London: Penguin, 1993 (1938).

World Bank. *Global Economic Prospects: Economic Implications of Remittances and Migration*. Washington, DC: World Bank, 2006.

———. *World Development Report 2002: Building Institutions for Markets*. Washington, DC: Oxford University Press, 2002.

Yang, Liou. "Guanzi de guojia guanxi sixiang ganwei" (A Brief Probe into Guanzi's Inter-State Theory). *Guanzi xuekan* 4 (2006): 9–11.

Yang, Shan-ch'un. *Sun Tzu*. Taipei: Zhishufang Publishers, 1999.

Yeoh, Brenda S. A., and Katie Willis, ed. *State/Nation/Transnation: Perspectives on Transnationalism in the Asia-Pacific*. London: Routledge, 2004.

Yeoh, Brenda S. A., Peggy Teo, and Shirlena Huang. "Introduction." In *Gender Politics in the Asia-Pacific Region*, edited by Brenda S. A. Yeoh, Peggy Teo, and Shirlena Huang, 1–16. London: Routledge, 2002.

Young, Brigitte. "Globalization and Gender: A European Perspective." In *Gender, Globalization, and Democratization*, edited by Rita Mae Kelly, Jane H. Bayes, Mary E. Hawkesworth, and Brigitte Young, 27–47. Lanham, MD: Rowman & Littlefield Publishers, 2001.

Young, Iris Marion. *Justice and the Politics of Difference*. Princeton: Princeton University Press, 1990.

Yuval-Davis, Nira. *Gender and Nation*. London: Sage, 1997.

Yuval-Davis, Nira, and Floia Anthias, ed. *Woman, Nation, State*. Hampshire: MacMillan, 1989.

Zalewski, Marysia. "Do We Understand each Other Yet? Troubling Feminist Encounters With(in) International Relations." *British Journal of Politics and International Relations* 9, no. 2 (2007): 302–12.

———. "Well, What is the Feminist Perspective on Bosnia?" *International Affairs* 71, no. 2 (1995): 339–56.

Zalewski, Marysia, and Jane Parpart, ed. *The "Man" Question in International Relations*. Boulder, CO: Westview, 1998.

Zhao, Tingyang. "Rethinking Empire from a Chinese Concept 'All-under-Heaven' (*Tian-xia*)." *Social Identities* 12, no. 1 (January 2006): 29–41.

Zimmerman, Cathy, Sar Samen, and Men Savorn. "Plates in a Basket Will Rattle: Domestic Violence in Cambodia." Phnom Penh: Asia Foundation, 1994.

Zuhur, Sherifa. *Revealing Reveiling*. New York: State University of New York Press, 1992.

Index

9/11,18, 59, 146, 213, 219, 222, 223, 224, 225, 235, 252

aboriginal rights, 215
activism: and advocacy, 13, 180; and comfort women's tribunal, 13; and feminism, 7; and feminist; scholarship, 108; and governance, 109; and IR 4, 10, 214, 226; and political agency, 143, 150, 154, 163; in East Timor, 163, 221; in Fiji, 7; in the Pacific, 7, 9, 224; local and transnational, 155, 161; of everyday resistance, 6
advocacy, 5, 10, 13, 161, 165, 176–83, 185, 186, 205, 207, 224, 231
Afghanistan xvii, 7, 12, 22, 35, 59, 64, 66, 117, 119, 124–26, 144, 151, 153, 154, 212, 221, 223, 238, 248
agency,xi, 6, 7, 13, 108, 123, 125, 130, 143, 144, 147, 165, 176, 177, 187, 222, 226, 235
Akashi, Yasushi, 87
Angkor Revolution,79
anti-racism, 215, 216, 235
anti-terrorism, 222
Art of War, the, 6, 59, 60, 61, 63, 67, 71, 72, 251, 257
ASEAN, 79, 80
Association for Women's Rights in Development (AWID), 229, 231
Australia, ix, x, xii, xiv, 22, 44, 47, 55, 117, 119, 155, 163, 178, 198, 199, 200–204, 211–17, 220–25, 233, 235, 239, 245, 252, 253

Bangladesh, 45, 49, 88, 244
Barlake, 162
Behind the Veil, 153
Beijing Platform for Action (PFA), 161, 163, 165, 168
bin Laden, Osama, 59, 66
Blair, Tony, 221
blue helmet, 78
bombings, 66, 77, 223
Bosnia-Herzegovina, 28
Bretton Woods institutions, 25, 103
Bush, George W., 5, 22, 25, 59, 60, 63, 144, 155, 221, 243, 250
Butler, Judith, 106, 107, 240

Cambodia, 6, 77–89, 238, 239, 240–42, 245, 248, 251, 254, 259
Cambodian People's Party (CPP), 79
capitalism, 39, 41, 42, 63, 64, 82, 101, 102, 105, 107, 109, 146
China, 5, 12, 47, 69, 70, 72, 79, 80, 223
citizenship, 254
class, xiii, 5, 20, 40, 43, 45, 46, 48, 55, 96, 97, 101, 105, 106, 108, 109, 115, 119, 123, 125, 126, 145, 164, 234
classical liberalism, 63, 70
Coalition Provisional Authority (CPA), 25, 27, 28
cold war, the, x, xiv, 64, 66, 78, 80, 89, 104, 135, 138, 243, 246, 253, 256
colonialism, 63, 130, 138, 141, 177, 234
comfort women, 13, 250
Commonwealth Secretariat (CS), 197, 244, 247

Convention on the Elimination of All Forms of Discrimination against Women (CEDAW), 143, 150, 161, 164, 169, 181, 196, 202, 205, 208
critical inquiry, 116
critical scholars, 40
critical security, xii, 239, 248, 252
critical theory, 8, 39, 129

Debord, Guy, 106, 107, 241
de Certeau, Michel, 131, 141, 241
decolonization, 29
de Mello, Sergio Vieira, 23, 165, 166, 169, 173
democracy, xii, 36, 161, 163, 171, 238, 242, 243, 245, 251, 252
development, xi, xii, xiii, xiv, 6, 8, 10, 44, 49, 50, 95, 97, 102, 104, 105, 125, 159, 166, 167, 170, 177, 184, 186, 196, 197, 199–201, 204, 207, 214, 215, 223
Development Alternatives for Women in a New Era (DAWN), xiv, 183, 225, 231
diplomacy, 63, 67, 68, 186

East Timor, 22–25, 27, 34, 44, 159, 163–65, 168, 221, 240–42, 244, 251, 258. *See also* Timor-Leste
Economic and Social Council, the (ECOSOC), 30, 31, 36
electoral quotas, 161, 164, 169
emancipation, 4, 6, 12, 129, 130, 141
emancipatory, 7, 9, 11, 12, 32, 131, 136, 145, 234
empowerment, 6, 12, 21, 28, 29, 95, 97, 104, 109, 124, 129, 150, 151, 183, 186
entrepreneurs, 159, 160–62, 165, 169
epistemological, 60, 105
epistemology, 8, 71
ethnicity, xiii, 5, 40, 43, 45, 48, 105, 146, 150, 177, 213, 225, 234
everyday resistance,129, 130, 131, 133, 135, 137, 139, 141, 240, 246
extremism, 4
extremist, 147

Falantil, 162
femininity, 9, 21,107
feminism, xiii, xiv, 4, 7, 11, 19, 52, 127, 144, 147, 148, 155, 176, 187, 214, 216, 219, 220, 233, 237, 238, 240, 241, 243–46, 248, 250, 253, 254, 256
feminist ethic, 5, 6, 7, 9, 129
feminist methodology, 126
feminist research, x, 5, 6, 7, 115, 116, 127, 225
Feminist Theory and Gender Studies (FTGS), 218–20, 229
feminization, 10, 40, 41, 50, 105, 253
Fiji, ix, xiv, 7, 13, 49, 175–86, 201–04, 221, 223–25, 237, 238, 241–48, 254–57
financialization, 40, 41, 48
Foucault, Michel, 106, 243
French war, 134
fundamentalism, 41, 146, 225

Gender Affairs Unit, Timor-Leste's (GAU), 23, 165–67, 173
gender analysis, 167, 168, 233
gender equality, 7, 12, 27, 30, 143, 149, 159–67, 170, 171, 182, 196, 205, 206
gender justice, 159, 161, 196, 201, 206, 223, 225
gender mainstreaming, 7, 29, 30, 31, 109, 159–61, 165–68, 170–73
gender politics, 10, 55, 103, 181, 217, 230
Ghazali, Zaynab al, 149
globalization, xi, xiii, xiv, 13, 51, 53, 55, 187, 225, 238, 242, 244, 245, 247, 249–55, 258
Global Plan of Action, Beijing (GPA), 183
Global Political Economy (GPE), 40. *See also* International Political Economy (IPE)

global politics, 3, 5, 6, 8, 10, 11, 146, 221, 223, 225, 233, 235. *See also* International Relations
governance, xi, xiii, xiv, 6, 10, 36, 63, 71, 95–111, 126, 162, 177, 186, 196–200, 202, 224, 238, 240, 243, 245, 247–57
Gusmao, Xanana, 24, 169, 172

hegemonic, 71, 99, 100, 104, 131, 201, 235
Hobbes, Thomas, 63, 71
Ho Chi Minh, 135
Howard, John, 144, 221
huairou yuanren, 70
Huda Shar'awi, 147
human rights, xi, 5, 10, 12, 13, 20–32, 62, 84, 100, 124, 152, 153, 160, 161, 164, 181–87, 196, 206–8, 215, 218, 231
Hun Sen, 78, 79
hypermasculinity, hypermasculine, 5, 71, 59, 65

identity (politics of,), xi, xii, 10, 13, 29, 43, 44,53, 89, 119, 126–28, 143, 146–54, 182, 211, 212, 214–28, 240, 241, 248, 252
ideology, 12, 45, 99, 104, 106, 107, 130, 138, 150, 151, 154
India, 6, 47, 49, 64, 88, 95, 103, 119, 222, 223, 234, 241, 245, 250
Indonesia, x, 7, 22, 43, 45, 80, 151, 152, 153, 162, 163, 221, 255
informalization, 39, 40, 41, 42, 48, 50, 51, 56
injustice, 160, 214
insecurity, 4, 10, 84, 160, 202, 203, 207, 213
institutions, 100, 102, 251, 258
International Convention on Economic, Social and Cultural Rights (ICESCR), 207
International Court of Justice, 20, 30
International Criminal Court, 21, 30, 37
International Feminist Journal of Politics (IFJP), 219, 220, 235
International Feminist's Union Congress, 147
International Force East Timor (INTERFET), 22
international law, 5, 10, 19, 20, 21, 23–25, 27–37, 208, 237, 238, 240, 243, 248, 251
International Law Commission (ILC), 20, 30
International Monetary Fund (IMF), 12, 102
International Political Economy (IPE), 15, 51,101, 257. *See also* Global Political Economy (GPE),
International Relations (IR) (as a discipline), 3–13, 20, 51, 115–18, 123, 126, 127, 131, 132, 140, 141, 160, 177, 211, 213, 214, 217–20, 223, 226, 233–35, 240, 241, 252, 254, 256. *See also* global politics
International Studies Association (ISA), 218
Iran, 117
Iraq, x, 5, 22, 25–28, 35, 56, 59, 60, 62, 64–66, 71, 117, 144, 212, 221, 223, 243, 246, 255
Islam, xii, 7, 26, 119, 143, 145–52, 153, 155, 221, 224, 246, 247
Islamic feminism, 144, 147–50
Islamic jurisprudence, 151
Islamist, 107, 143, 148–50, 152, 154

Jamaat-i-Islami, 152
justice, 20, 32, 34, 98, 118, 148, 149, 153, 175, 186, 192, 195, 206, 216, 238, 241, 243, 245, 251, 254, 258

Khmer People's National Liberation Front, the (KPNLF), 79
Khmer Rouge, 77, 79–82, 85
Kiribati, 204, 208, 209
Kosovo, 28, 159, 162, 237
Kurdish Alliance, 26

legitimacy, 28, 63, 65, 97, 100, 143, 150, 154, 167, 184, 201
liberalism, 63, 101, 108
liberalization, 41, 43, 183, 198, 200–205, 207
Lon Nol, General, 79

Malaysia, 45, 88
Marcos, Imelda, 129
markets, 30, 41, 43, 44, 46, 51, 99, 100–102, 104, 105, 107–9, 119, 134, 138, 183, 195, 196, 198–201, 203, 206, 207, 224
Marxism, 141
masculinity, 9, 21,107, 218, 224
migration, 10,16, 39, 40, 42–47, 49, 50, 54, 116, 117, 127, 199, 212, 217, 219, 234, 237, 239, 249, 252, 253, 258
militarization, 16, 160, 222, 223, 225, 255
modernist/positivist, 40
modernity, 53, 240, 246, 247, 255
modernization, 60
Muslim Brotherhood, 149

Nadhlatul Ulama, 151
nation building, 66, 162
National Council of East Timorese Resistance (CNRT), 163, 165, 168
nationalism, xiii, 10, 27, 45, 147, 177, 181, 214, 258
National United Front for an Independent, Neutral, Peaceful and Co-operative Cambodia (FUNCINPEC), 79
Nawal es-Sadaawi, 149
neoliberalism, xiii, 7, 39–42, 45, 50, 63, 64, 71, 72, 101, 102, 104, 108, 109, 147, 148, 155, 160, 186, 195–206, 220, 221, 224, 234, 249, 254
neo-Marxists, 103
networks, 7, 11, 13, 27, 42–44, 50, 99, 100, 102, 104, 143, 144, 146, 147, 161, 162, 176, 180, 182, 187, 217, 218, 220, 222, 225
New International Economic Order (NIEO), 179, 190
New Zealand, xii, xiv, 44, 47, 199, 202, 204, 224, 239, 242, 252
Ngo Dinh Nhu, Madame, 129

Okinawa, 66
ontology, 8, 69, 71
orientalism, 145
Other, the, 28, 30, 55, 63, 64, 71, 88, 98, 144, 145, 164, 239, 248, 249, 258

Pacific Islands Forum Secretariat (PIFS), 196, 210
Pacific Plan, 7, 196, 197, 198, 199, 200, 201, 202, 203–7, 246, 250
Pakistan, 6, 7, 49, 116–20, 124–26, 152–54, 223
Papua New Guinea, x, xiv, 214, 218, 224, 250, 253
Paris Peace Agreements, 80, 82
partnership, 200, 204
patriarchy, 107, 129, 141, 143–45, 148, 247
peacebuilding, 22, 91, 159–62, 171, 235, 251
peacekeeping, 6, 22, 24, 77–89, 125, 126, 160, 162, 163, 165, 166, 198, 238, 242, 244–58
Pettman, Jindy v, ix, x, xiii, xv, 3, 5, 7, 9, 12, 13, 19, 20, 32, 43, 46, 55, 129, 141, 187, 211, 212, 214, 216, 218, 220, 222, 224, 226, 233–5, 252, 253
Philippines, the, x, 43, 45, 49, 64, 65, 66, 129, 200
Popular Women's Organization of Timor-Leste (OPMT), 162
postcolonial, xi, xii, 5, 8, 10,39, 40, 88, 145, 177, 179, 207, 226, 240, 245, 249
poststructuralism, 8
pracheta, 95

Productive Economy (PrE), 42, 44, 45. *See also* Reproductive Economy (RE)

queer theory, 8

race, xiii, 5, 20, 39, 40, 43, 45, 48, 53, 60, 99, 146, 212–16, 222, 225 233, 234, 240, 242, 245, 252, 253, 255
racism, 44, 98, 233–5, 245, 253
realism, 127, 254
realist, 60, 139
Rede, 164, 166, 168–70, 173
refugee studies,116, 117
regionalism, xii, 7, 195, 196, 197, 198, 201, 202, 204, 207, 208
ren, 68–71. *See also* tianxia
Reproductive Economy (RE), 44, 47, 48. *See also* Productive Economy (PrE)
Reproductive, Productive, and Virtual (RPV), 5, 39, 40, 41, 42, 50
Revolutionary Association of the Women of Afghanistan (RAWA), 151–54
Robinson, Mary, 23

Saddam Hussein, 27, 59, 60
sathin, 95, 96, 97, 104
Saudi Arabia, 13, 45, 46
secular, 7, 26, 28, 95, 143, 149, 150, 151
secularism, 152
Self/Other, 63, 249
Sexual and Gender-Based Violence (SGBV), 164, 166
Sharia, 26, 35
Shiite party, 26
Sihanouk, Price Norodom, 79, 80, 90
Singapore, 45, 219
Sisters in Islam, 148
socialism, 138, 171, 214, 215, 250
social movements, 83, 97, 147, 187, 195
solidarity, 7, 98, 146, 147, 195, 204, 207, 214, 215, 222, 223, 225
Solomons, 214, 224
South Korea, 47, 66
South Pacific Community (SPC) 196
sovereignty, 19, 20, 106, 117, 125, 178, 195, 198, 202, 212, 252
Soviet Union, 64, 79, 80, 104, 106
spectacle, 100, 106, 107, 124, 241, 255
Sri Lanka, 43, 45, 49, 88
SS Lotus, 20
State-building, 5, 6, 22, 23, 25–29, 32, 44, 65, 214
stolen generations, 215
Structural Adjustment Policies (SAP), 43
Sun Tzu, 5, 6, 59–63, 67–72, 245, 248, 250, 258
Supreme National Council (SNC), 80

Taliban, 12, 66, 124, 125, 143, 147, 152, 153
terrorism, 4, 50, 72, 222
Thailand, 79, 223, 242
Thucydides, 60
tianxia, 69–71. *See also* ren
Timor-Leste, 5, 7, 35, 159, 160–62, 166, 170, 171, 256. *See also* East Timor
Trade-Related Aspects of Intellectual Property Rights (TRIPS), 106
tribunal, 23, 13, 239

United Nations Advance Mission in Cambodia (UNAMIC), 80
United Nations Beijing Fourth World Conference on Women, 161
United Nations Children's Fund (UNICEF), 95, 97, 104, 248
United Nations Development Fund for Women (UNIFEM), 22, 34, 83, 87, 165, 168, 169, 170, 171, 205, 239, 249, 253, 257
United Nations Development Program (UNDP), 168, 210
United Nations Economic and Social Commission for Asia and the Pacific (UNESCAP), 12, 190
United Nations Educational Scientific and Cultural Organization (UNESCO), 235, 255
United Nations High Commissioner for Refugees, Office of the (UNHCR), 80, 84, 126

United Nations Security Council (UNSC) Resolution 1325, 162
United Nations Transitional Authority in Cambodia (UNTAC), 6, 77–89, 242
United Nations Transitional Authority in East Timor (UNTAET), 22–24, 27, 163, 165, 166, 168, 170, 242
United Nations, the (UN), xiv, 7, 21–24, 28, 30, 31, 34, 36, 77–89, 103, 104, 124, 150, 159, 162–70, 178, 179, 182, 183, 218, 221, 239, 240, 242–44, 247, 248, 256, 258
universalism, 148

Viet Minh, 132–35
Vietnam xii, 6, 59, 79, 80, 129, 135, 137–39, 213, 216, 223, 234
Virtual Economy (VE), 44, 48, 51

Waltz, Kenneth, 213
war on terror xii, 12, 117, 119, 144, 155, 221, 223, 246
West, the xii, 5, 7, 12, 55, 61, 64, 72, 79, 119, 145, 146, 147, 197, 217, 222, 240, 242, 245, 248, 249, 252, 257
Women in Development (WID), 216
Women's Development Project, the (WDP), 95, 96, 97
Women's Electoral Lobby, the (WEL), 216
Women's Environment and Development Organization (WEDO), 205
women's movements, 7, 97, 144, 147, 148, 150, 161, 163, 169
women's rights, 5, 10, 12, 13, 22–28, 145, 146, 148, 155, 160, 163, 166, 180, 184, 195, 216, 224, 231
World Bank, the, 12, 49, 102, 198, 202, 249, 255, 258
World Health Organization, the (WHO), 21, 85, 187, 239
World Trade Organization, the (WTO), 102, 106, 204

Xianghua, 70, 71

YWCA 177–79, 181, 182, 189

Zambia, 214, 215, 253